Language Use and Language Learning in CLIL Classrooms

AILA Applied Linguistics Series (AALS)

The AILA Applied Linguistics Series (AALS) provides a forum for established scholars in any area of Applied Linguistics. The series aims at representing the field in its diversity. It covers different topics in applied linguistics from a multidisciplinary approach and it aims at including different theoretical and methodological perspectives. As an official publication of AILA the series will include contributors from different geographical and linguistic backgrounds. The volumes in the series should be of high quality; they should break new ground and stimulate further research in Applied Linguistics.

Editor

Susanne Niemeier
University of Koblenz-Landau

Volume 7

Language Use and Language Learning in CLIL Classrooms
Edited by Christiane Dalton-Puffer, Tarja Nikula and Ute Smit

Language Use
and Language Learning
in CLIL Classrooms

Edited by

Christiane Dalton-Puffer
University of Vienna

Tarja Nikula
University of Jyväskylä

Ute Smit
University of Vienna

John Benjamins Publishing Company
Amsterdam / Philadelphia

The paper used in this publication meets the minimum requirements of
American National Standard for Information Sciences – Permanence of
Paper for Printed Library Materials, ANSI z39.48-1984.

Library of Congress Cataloging-in-Publication Data

Language use and language learning in CLIL classrooms / edited by Christiane Dalton-
    Puffer, Tarja Nikula, Ute Smit.
    p.   cm. (AILA Applied Linguistics Series, ISSN 1875-1113 ; v. 7)
Includes bibliographical references and index.
1.   Language and languages--Study and teaching.   I. Dalton-Puffer, Christiane, 1961- II.
    Nikula, Tarja. III. Smit, Ute.
P51.L358   2010
418.0071--dc22   2010038019
ISBN 978 90 272 0523 0   (Hb ; alk. paper)
ISBN 978 90 272 8751 9   (Eb)

John Benjamins Publishing Co. · P.O. Box 36224 · 1020 ME Amsterdam · The Netherlands
John Benjamins North America · P.O. Box 27519 · Philadelphia PA 19118-0519 · USA

Table of contents

Acknowledgements · VII

Preface · IX

Introduction

Charting policies, premises and research
on content and language integrated learning · 1
   Christiane Dalton-Puffer, Tarja Nikula & Ute Smit

PART I. General and theoretical issues

On the natural emergence of language structures in CLIL:
Towards a theory of European educational bilingualism · · · · · · · · · · · · · · 23
   Francisco Lorenzo & Pat Moore

The pragmatics of L2 in CLIL · 39
   Didier Maillat

PART II. CLIL at the secondary level

A cross-sectional analysis of oral narratives
by children with CLIL and non-CLIL instruction · · · · · · · · · · · · · · · · · · · 61
   Julia Hüttner & Angelika Rieder-Bünemann

Using a genre-based approach to integrating content
and language in CLIL: The example of secondary history · · · · · · · · · · · · 81
   Tom Morton

Effects of CLIL on a teacher's classroom language use · · · · · · · · · · · · · · · 105
   Tarja Nikula

Writing and speaking in the history class: A comparative analysis
of CLIL and first language contexts · 125
   Ana Llinares & Rachel Whittaker

Language as a meaning making resource in learning
and teaching content: Analysing historical writing in content
and language integrated learning · 145
   Heini-Marja Järvinen

The CLIL differential: Comparing the writing of CLIL
and non-CLIL students in higher colleges of technology   169
   Silvia Jexenflicker & Christiane Dalton-Puffer

Written production and CLIL: An empiricial study   191
   Yolanda Ruiz de Zarobe

PART iii. CLIL at the tertiary level

Metadiscursive devices in university lectures: A contrastive analysis
of L1 and L2 teacher performance   213
   Emma Dafouz Milne and Begoña Núñez Perucha

Language Matters: Assessing lecture comprehension
in Norwegian English-medium higher education   233
   Glenn Ole Hellekjær

CLIL in an English as a lingua franca (ELF) classroom:
On explaining terms and expressions interactively   259
   Ute Smit

Conclusion

Language use and language learning in CLIL: Current findings
and contentious issues   279
   Christiane Dalton-Puffer, Tarja Nikula & Ute Smit

Subject index   293

Acknowledgements

As so typical of publication projects, this book – and we as its editors – have benefitted from an array of fortunate events and a range of supportive people, whose help we would like to acknowledge. Our most hearty thanks go to

- the numerous participants at the Symposium of the AILA Research Network on "CLIL and immersion classrooms: applied linguistic perspectives" during the AILA 2008 conference in Essen, Germany, whose interest and involvement sparked off the idea of publishing a CLIL volume;
- the editors Susanne Niemeier and Kees van Vaes for taking the idea of this volume on board and helping it through to fruition, not least with their speedy communication;
- the contributors for being so disciplined in their time-keeping and patience with us editors;
- Heidi Byrnes, Robert Wilkinson and Dieter Wolff, whose criticism was enriching in its diversity and helped crystallize and sharpen the contents in significant ways, especially of the introductory and final chapters;
- Christina Gefäll, Corinna Weiss and Pamela Zankl, whose editing abilities kept us on the straight and narrow with regard to questions of form.

Finally, our collaboration as a team can look back over a number of successfully completed projects and we'd like to take this opportunity to thank each other for being great colleagues, collaborating constructively despite the geographical distance. Skype and Google.docs made many things possible, but personal meetings turned out even more helpful, maybe because the laughs shared when face-to-face proved a highly important energizer to us and the volume.

Preface

This book is a product of the AILA (International Association of Applied Linguistics) Research Network *CLIL and Immersion Classrooms: Applied Linguistic Perspectives*, which brings together applied linguists interested in a broad set of questions relating to education in an additional language. The Research Network has been particularly active in exploring the European CLIL context, which is understandable given that CLIL has spread rapidly across the continent since the early 1990s. The increasing popularity of CLIL is partly due to the European-level political support that it receives for being a useful means with which to increase the degree of multilingualism in Europe, partly its motivating forces arise out of current processes of globalization and internationalization with their challenges for language education (e.g. Cameron & Block 2002; Luke, Luke & Graham 2007).

The reasons for establishing this research network derive from the fact that, despite a rapid upsurge of CLIL research during the 1990s, classroom discourse-focused research initially lagged behind as CLIL researchers' interests first centred around questions of implementation, good practice and learning outcomes (for an overview see Dalton-Puffer & Smit 2007b: 7–15). In 2005, a symposium held in Vienna gathered together applied linguists interested in classroom-based CLIL research. Apart from its immediate success as a forum for applied linguistic exchange on CLIL (cf. Dalton-Puffer & Smit 2007a), this meeting also led to the creation of a research network (ReN) within AILA in 2006. Since then the ReN *CLIL and Immersion Classrooms: Applied Linguistic Perspectives* (www.ichm.org/clil/) has been an active platform connecting applied linguists who focus their research interests on educational settings that make use of an additional language for teaching and learning in diverse content areas, thus engaging in content and language integrated learning. Based on annual meetings, e.g. the 2nd CLIL Symposium in Vienna in September 2007, the ReN Symposium at the AILA World Congress in Essen in August 2008, the CLIL Symposium in Miraflores, Spain, in September 2009 and the CLIL Symposium in Jyväskylä, Finland in June 2010, the research network has not only grown in size, but also in terms of research interests and output (cf. Dalton-Puffer & Nikula 2006; Dalton-Puffer & Smit 2007a; Smit & Dalton-Puffer 2007; Smit, Schiftner & Dalton-Puffer 2010). One can rightly expect that at its final event at the AILA World Congress in Beijing in August 2011, the current strong European focus will be complemented by research into CLIL and immersion activities in other parts of the world, especially Asia.

References

Cameron, D. & Block, D. (eds). 2002. *Globalization and Language Teaching.* London: Routledge.

Dalton-Puffer, C. & Nikula, T. (eds). 2006. Current research on CLIL. *VIEWS – Vienna English Working Papers* [Current Research on CLIL: Special issue] 15(3).

Dalton-Puffer, C. & Smit, U. (eds). 2007a. *Empirical Perspectives on CLIL Classroom Discourse.* Frankfurt: Peter Lang.

Dalton-Puffer, C. & Smit, U. 2007b. Introduction. In *Empirical Perspectives on CLIL Classroom Discourse,* C. Dalton-Puffer & U. Smit (eds), 7–23. Frankfurt am Main: Peter Lang.

Luke, A., Luke, C. & Graham, P. 2007. Globalization, corporatism, and critical language education. *International Multilingual Research Journal* 1(1): 1–13.

Smit, U., Schiftner, B. & Dalton-Puffer, C. (eds). 2010. Current research on CLIL 3. *VIEWS – Vienna English Working Papers* [Special issue] 19(3).

Charting policies, premises and research on content and language integrated learning

Christiane Dalton-Puffer, Tarja Nikula & Ute Smit
Universität Wien, Austria/Jyväskylän yliopisto, Finland/
Universität Wien, Austria

1. Defining CLIL

Content and language integrated learning (CLIL) can be described as an educational approach where subjects such as geography or biology are taught through the medium of a foreign language, typically to students participating in some form of mainstream education at primary, secondary but also tertiary level. This means that, as far as classroom practices are concerned, CLIL resembles other forms of bilingual education programmes such as content-based instruction and immersion education as these exist in North American contexts (Brinton, Snow & Wesche 2008 [1989]: 7f; Genesee 1987). The most influential source has probably been Canadian Immersion, designed to foster the acquisition of the second national language French by speakers of the other (dominant) national language English in the 1960s.

However, there are certain features of European CLIL that differentiate it from other forms of bilingual education. CLIL is about using a foreign language, not a second language. That is to say, the language of instruction is one that students will mainly encounter at school since it is not regularly used in the wider society they live in. It also means that the teachers imparting CLIL lessons will normally not be native speakers of the target language. Neither are they, in most cases, foreign-language experts but content-experts. Furthermore, CLIL is usually implemented once learners have already acquired literacy skills in their mother tongue, i.e. students rarely learn to read and write through a foreign language but can transfer already existing literacy skills *to* the foreign language. According to Wolff (2007: 15–16), CLIL differs from other content-based approaches in that "classroom content is not so much taken from everyday life or the general content of the target language culture but rather from content subjects, from academic/ scientific disciplines or from the professions". This means that CLIL lessons at school are usually scheduled as content-lessons (e.g. biology, music, geography) while the target language also continues as a subject in its own right in the shape of foreign language lessons taught by language specialists. Sometimes, though, it can also be construed as a foreign language teaching *method* (Richards & Rogers 2001), especially in primary education contexts. In essence, then, CLIL resembles non-language content teaching that entails a foreign language enrichment measure (cf. Torres-Guzman 2007: 50).

Recently however, CLIL proponents have tended to discursively stress the goal behind CLIL as "a dual-focused educational approach" that is neither exclusively language learning nor subject learning but rather a "fusion" of both (Coyle, Hood & Marsh 2010: 41–45). Taking this as a given, CLIL would always involve a combination of content and language aims (Maljers, Marsh & Wolff 2007: 8). This has led some proponents into calling for a specific CLIL-teaching methodology that would establish CLIL as a kind of self-contained meta-subject defined by its own didactics (cf. Hallet 1999; Otten & Wildhage 2003). If that can be formulated, and we confess a certain amount of skepticism on this account, it certainly is a thing of the future.

In the meantime what characterizes CLIL more than anything is the remarkable variety of practices that can be found under its umbrella. (For a particularly expansive understanding see Mehisto, Marsh & Frigols 2008: 13; see also Coyle; Hood & Marsh 2010). The fundamental variable in this range of realizations of CLIL seems to be a quantitative one, captured in the question 'how much foreign language exposure do students get?': CLIL programmes may be short-term or long-term, ranging from a sequence of lessons spanning a few weeks to entire school-years to entire school-careers. Within the time allotted, the intensity of foreign language deployment may vary considerably: low-intensity programmes where only selected aspects of the material covered (e.g. readings) may be done in the FL to high-intensity programmes, aiming for an exclusive use of the target language. This results in a wide range of organizational forms, such as short-term, high-intensity language showers, medium-term and medium-intensity cross-curricular modules, doing one or two subjects in the foreign language for several school years, forms of double immersion that are long-term and high-intensity and many other variants in between, including the deployment of more than one teacher.

One generalization that can be safely made for CLIL programmes in Europe is that the logic according to which they operate is that of the content subjects. It is the curriculum of the content-subject that is delivered in the foreign language while language goals may be high but remain implicit (cf. Dalton-Puffer & Smit 2007b: 12; Wolff 2007: 16). That is to say that on the continuum by which Stoller (e.g. 2004: 261) distinguishes between language-driven and content-driven programmes, European CLIL practices can clearly be found towards the content end.

The theoretical and practical implications entailed in this educational praxis will be discussed in more detail in the concluding chapter of this volume.

It is certainly justified to regard CLIL as a major educational innovation that took hold in many national education systems from the 1990s onwards, but, paradoxically, it is equally appropriate to point out that teaching and learning in a foreign language is an ancient practice that could be found in many civilizations of the past. To mention only one example, consider the role Latin enjoyed for centuries as a language of instruction and learning across Europe (cf. also Mehisto, Marsh & Frigols 2008: 9). In fact, being educated in a prestigious foreign language has been the prerogative of elite education at prestigious institutions for centuries. An essential difference of present-day CLIL, therefore, is the fact that it is rooted within mainstream education: all the contexts reported on in this book are part of publicly financed educational provision. It cannot be denied though that a lingering flavour of elitism has most likely contributed to the enthusiastic acceptance of CLIL by parents (and some students), in particular as regards being instructed through English, whose status is high given its prominence as the de facto international language of today.

A final note is in order on the term CLIL itself: the term was coined in the early 1990s (Mehisto et al. 2008: 9) in the context of a European expert initiative, most likely with the intention to create a neutral and generally accessible label to facilitate communication among international experts. The term CLIL thus functions as an umbrella not only for a wide array of educational practices but also for an even wider array of terms tied to specific lingua-cultural, national, educational and disciplinary traditions. It has found acceptance among language experts, researchers and teacher educators and is spreading also among practising teachers at varying speeds in different contexts (cf. Eurydice 2006). Given the dynamics of the area over the last 15 years, the term has acquired some characteristics of a brand-name, complete with the symbolic capital of positive ascriptions: innovative, modern, effective, efficient and forward-looking. It is the intention of volumes like the present one to sound out the basis of these ascriptions so that the teaching approach continues to thrive on theoretically and empirically sound foundations and the label 'CLIL' retains its open nature as an umbrella term for many realities of non-language content teaching through an additional language.

2.   CLIL in Europe: Policy and implementation

Traditionally, language policy has been conceived of as a matter of deliberate and rational decisions taken at central points in government agencies, ministries or government councils, in order to steer development in a certain direction (Ferguson 2006: 16f). More recent approaches, however, advocate a more comprehensive view on language policy (e.g. Ricento 2006). Spolsky's (2004) model, for instance, postulates language practices, beliefs and management as three levels of social action that in their interrelatedness allow for an "expanded view of language policy" (Shohamy 2006: 57). The spread of CLIL across Europe (and indeed elsewhere), the speed of which "has surprised even the most ardent of advocates" (Maljers, Marsh & Wolff 2007: 7) is a perfect case illustrating the appropriacy of such a change in perspective. From the very beginning, the fire of CLIL has been fuelled from various sides: high-level policy and grass-roots actions, motivated by widespread language beliefs. If one was to decide which of the two came first, we are inclined to think that it was actually the grass-roots beliefs and activities of parents and teachers which, practically simultaneously at countless locations, ignited the CLIL engine and keep it going. These were individuals reacting to what they rightly perceived as major shifts in the fabric of post-industrial society: an economy becoming increasingly internationally interwoven and requiring ever better educated employees, the presence of an international workforce in higher level jobs, the knowledge of certain languages being crucial on the job market (e.g. Ferguson 2006: 128f). In other words, CLIL seemed to promise their children/students an edge in the competition for employment. On the other end of the spectrum, high-level political agents, some of them supra-national, also began to awaken to these insights and to steer their language management activities accordingly. In our discussion we will in the following focus on Europe and the activities of two European institutions (the EU's European Commission and the Council of Europe) but analogous processes can be observed in other parts of the world (Li 2002; Tollefson & Tsui 2004; Tsui & Tollefson 2007).

A political union of some 490 million citizens, organized into 27 nation states, featuring 23 official languages (plus numerous regional and minority languages) has no choice but to be multilingual and language policy has a crucial role in implementing the EU's 'unity in diversity principle'. Official formulations of language policy clearly reflect this aim, usually in combination with the economic dimension.

> The European Union actively encourages its citizens to learn other European languages, both for reasons of professional and personal mobility within its single market, and as a force for cross-cultural contacts and mutual understanding. [...] The ability to understand and communicate in more than one language [...] is a desirable life-skill for all European citizens. Learning and speaking other languages [...] improves cognitive skills and strengthens learners' mother tongue skills; it enables us to take advantage of the freedom to work or study in another Member State.   (European Commission 2008: Chapter 14)

Since 1995 the principle that "[u]pon completing initial training every [European citizen] should be proficient in two Community foreign languages" in addition to their mother tongue has been repeatedly propagated and it was also suggested that "secondary school pupils should study certain subjects in the first foreign language learned" (European Commission 1995). The importance of learning at least two further languages in addition to the mother tongue was highlighted again in the 2002 Barcelona proposal from a meeting by heads of state and government, and in 2003 a communication from the European Commission explicitly stated that CLIL "has a major contribution to make to the Union's language learning goals" (European Commission Communication 2003: 8). In dialogue with these high-level policy declarations, a number of cross-national expert initiatives have strived to support implementation by disseminating conceptualizations, model materials and curricular guidelines (e.g www.clilcompendium.com; www.ccn-clil.eu; www.clilconsortium.jyu.fi/). Concurrently, CLIL also figures prominently among the activities of the Council of Europe's language policy unit, the European Centre for Modern Languages (http://www.ecml.at/activities/intro.asp).

Different countries have responded to calls for CLIL in different ways, but today some kind of CLIL implementation can be found in nearly all EU and Council of Europe member states (Eurydice 2006). What makes the European situation particularly intriguing, perhaps, is that, as regards language management, the juncture between policy declaration and policy implementation is rather diffuse: while general policy lines are formulated at EU-level, it is not 'Brussels' that decides on educational legislation and financing but the 27 national governments. CLIL has thus been characterized in many countries by a kind of 'void in the middle' situation, where practitioners were active in their local contexts, of necessity reinventing the wheel time and again, while national government agencies were benignly looking on these activities that were in welcome accordance with the EU policies they had subscribed to, but without committing to positive action in terms of providing guidelines, teacher education and additional funding (Eurydice 2006). Some countries, however, have made substantial investments in both CLIL implementation and research, a case in point being Spain where there are numerous ongoing CLIL related research and development projects (Eurydice 2006; Fernández Fontecha 2009; Lasagabaster & Ruiz de Zarobe 2010). Another example are The Netherlands where a national accreditation system for CLIL schools has established explicit quality parameters and a supply of teacher and school development measures (www.europeesplatform.nl/sf.mcgi?2681 and Anne Maljers personal communication).

A range of socioeconomic, political and socio-psychological forces are always at play when bilingual education programmes are established and this is no different for CLIL. Our discussion in this section has focused on Europe, not least because all the research contexts presented in this volume are located on this continent, but we are convinced that the major fault-lines will be recognizable to readers from other parts of the world. In the next section we will turn to examining the assumptions underlying these language policy activities.

3.   Underlying assumptions

While CLIL in Europe tends to be strongly content-driven, policy statements and stakeholder views (cf. Dalton-Puffer 2007) actually indicate expectations that are squarely centred on students improving significantly in their foreign language competence, rather backgrounding aspects of content learning. This is surprising insofar as general gains such as intercultural awareness or deeper cognitive processing on subject matter are an integral part in expert-designed CLIL concepts (cf. www.CLILCompendium.com; CLIL Matrix;[1] Coyle 1999). It seems, however that they have so far had little impact on general beliefs on the added value of CLIL (for further discussion see the concluding chapter).

Expectations associated with CLIL classes as efficient and effective language learning settings are fuelled by a widespread dissatisfaction with the outcomes of school-based foreign language learning and a somewhat stereotypical view of foreign language lessons as a series of mechanistic grammar drills. CLIL is thus constructed as a context that can deliver the goods more reliably and with less pain for the learners. It is worth asking the question what assumptions lie behind such expectations.

CLIL is regularly referred to as an educational environment where naturalistic language learning can take place, implying that the best kind of language learning proceeds without formal instruction. Language acquisition is thus seen to unfold in a self-propelled manner whereby meaningful language input of any kind triggers the ultimate development of a full L2 communicative competence regarding both, the rules of system and rules of use. The underlying learning theory is thus one that is reception-based. These implicit base-line assumptions show a good fit with Krashen and Terrell's *Natural Approach* (1983) and Krashen's Monitor Model (1985), which continues to be the most prominent reception-based theory of language acquisition outside academic research circles. As is well known, the basic idea of the model is that if the language learner is exposed to input which is comprehensible either because of the context in which it occurs or through intentional simplification, acquisition will occur, especially if the learning situation is

---

1.   See www.ecml.at/mtp2/CLILmatrix/index.htm.

characterised by positive emotions. The latter condition is widely thought to be fulfilled in CLIL by virtue of the fact that language mistakes are neither penalized nor corrected in CLIL classrooms. As pointed out above, in a model like Krashen's input is regarded as a trigger which sets into motion self-organized, innate mental mechanisms that run their course through subsequent linguistic stages. The language learner is thus regarded essentially as a self-contained language processor and grammar builder.

It should be noted that such a view of second language learning implies that the processes of foreign language acquisition are similar to those of first language learning.[2] No fundamental difference is assumed between monolingual first language acquisition in early childhood and plurilingual acquisition later in life. This presumption is endorsed by the widespread conviction that an early start must of necessity be advantageous to the ultimate outcome of second language learning resulting in the slogan 'the earlier the better'.

Needless to say that second language acquisition as a discipline has significantly developed and rethought these ideas in the last 25 years and we would like to mention only some cornerstones: the affirmation, in the Interaction Hypothesis (e.g. Long 1996), that attention to negative evidence gleaned from conversational interaction will propel learners' acquisition of vocabulary, morphology and syntax. The attention part of this was distilled into Schmidt's Noticing Hypothesis (1990). At roughly the same time, Swain (e.g. 1995) formulated her claim that only the self-regulated production of utterances which encode their intended meanings forces learners to actively process morphosyntactic aspects of the foreign language, an activity which will result in the expansion of their command of linguistic means and the deeper entrenchment of what they already know. Not unimportantly for the CLIL context, Swain's Output Hypothesis rests on empirical research done in Canadian immersion classrooms. The general drift of these ideas has also fed into the development of a position that stresses the importance of "focus on form" during the learning process, i.e. paying attention in specific contexts to formal, lexico-grammatical aspects of language as carriers of meaning. This position has helped to shape Lyster's (2007) formulation of a "counterbalanced approach" that accords equal weight to meaning focus and form focus in immersion education. Certainly with regard to Canadian Immersion education, which has been one of the prime conceptual reference points (in the beginnings) of European CLIL, we can detect a clear movement away from relying solely on the self-propelled, implicit language learner. An even more fundamental move away from the theorems underlying the Natural Approach is embodied in views of learning as fundamentally contextual

---

2.   Our interchangeable use of *learning* and *acquisition* is intentional.

and socially distributed as they are now widely accepted in education. Language is without doubt a cognitive phenomenon but it is just as much a social phenomenon. Consequently, its acquisition can be conceived of as a process which is socially construed (e.g. Lantolf 2002; Swain 2000). Under these premises human beings learn through interacting with other social beings, language being a particularly powerful semiotic means for participating and performing in the activities and encounters of the social world. As social encounters involve specific persons, in specific roles at specific times and places, the context of situation becomes instrumental rather than coincidental in the language acquisition process and learning in general. The interaction between 'experts and novices' as well as between 'peers' promotes the learner's "internalisation of knowledge co-constructed in shared activity" (Donato 1994: 41). Without denying the relevance of the views discussed above, we believe that sociocultural theory furnishes the base-line understandings in which learning in CLIL classrooms can best be understood and how it should consequently be viewed.

The contributors to this volume share the understanding that the language learning of students in CLIL is determined in fundamental ways by the institutional setting. CLIL happens in speech events called 'lessons' in well known institutions called 'school' or 'university'. This institutional environment underscores that CLIL classrooms are *classrooms* exhibiting the respective characteristics in terms of participant roles, goals, physical setting, temporal structure and the like. Consequently, CLIL classrooms share a great deal more with traditional language lessons than a somewhat constructed maximal contrast would make one believe. What a constructivist-contextual theory of language learning in CLIL certainly entails is the requirement that research focus very closely on the language behaviour of the participants, analysing the web of their interactions and relating the resulting interpretations to evidence about learning outcomes (or vice versa). The contributions to *Language Use and Language Learning in CLIL* thus set out to show in some detail how language learning in CLIL contexts is mediated by the contingencies of classroom talk as the central stage of institutional learning and the kinds of pedagogies that are routinely practiced in them.

4.   Overview of research on CLIL

As pointed out above, CLIL has spread in Europe since the early 1990s and this is also well reflected in the research landscape. CLIL initiatives and programmes have been analysed right from the start from various perspectives, such as language planning or didactics (e.g. Breidbach, Bach & Wolff 2002; Marsh 2002). During the first decade of CLIL research, the emphasis was largely on coming to terms with the phenomenon and providing macro-level information about CLIL to practitioners, politicians and researchers via surveys, guidelines for implementation and suggestions for good practice (see Dalton-Puffer & Smit 2007a). Given that CLIL as an educational model has a tendency to cut across and upset some traditional certainties in educational units, making it 'costly' if not in financial then in symbolic terms, it is understandable that accountability, especially in terms of finding out about the learning outcomes, has also been an issue from the start. Some of the earliest research publications on CLIL type programmes have been of this kind (Wode et al. 1996) and it is a theme of continuing interest. There are now three larger-scale studies on language learning outcomes from The Netherlands, Spain and Germany (Admiraal, Westhoff & de Bot 2006; Lasagabaster 2008; Zydatiß 2007) and numerous more specific ones, dealing with individual aspects of language competence like vocabulary, pronunciation and morphosyntax (e.g. Seregély 2009; Sylvén 2004; several contributions in Ruiz de Zarobe & Jimenez Catalán 2009). Complementing language learning, there is somewhat less extensive, but nonetheless important work on cognitive aspects of learning in CLIL (e.g. Gajo 2007; Jäppinen 2005; van de Craen et al. 2007).

With the increase in both CLIL activities and research, awareness has risen about the complexity of factors involved in CLIL, and about the need for further research to explore its possibilities and constraints and to provide insights to help further develop CLIL as an educational approach. This has led to a noticeable growth of research especially during the latter half of this decade, ranging from individual papers in international journals to special issues in research journals (Coyle & Baetens Beardsmore 2007), edited volumes on CLIL (e.g. Carrió-Pastor 2009; Dalton-Puffer & Smit 2007a; Marsh & Wolff 2007; Ruiz de Zarobe & Jimenez Catalan 2009; Wilkinson & Zegers 2007) and in-depth explorations about specific aspects of CLIL such as classroom discourse (Dalton-Puffer 2007; Smit 2010), vocabulary acquisition (Sylvén 2004), bilingual disciplinary knowledge (Airey 2009) and the effects of CLIL on mastering content knowledge in L1 (Lim Falk 2008).

In order to offer a general overview of published work on CLIL, Dalton-Puffer and Smit (2007b: 12–15) conceptualized it as a quadrant consisting of macro-micro and process-product dimensions. As they show, there is a great deal of variation depending on whether the main focus in publications lies on process or product dimensions of macro-level phenomena (e.g. reports of the implementation of CLIL programmes, descriptions of general guidelines on CLIL) or on process or product dimensions of micro-level phenomena (e.g. studies on CLIL classroom practices, outcome studies on language attainment and content knowledge). While the quadrant continues to be a useful heuristic for viewing the CLIL publication scene, it may be helpful to take into consideration a third dimension, that of language-content. In other words, there are studies that can be placed on either end of this continuum due to their focus on either language or content whereas those that systematically seek to combine language and content considerations would occupy the middle position. Figure 1 illustrates the ensuing three-dimensional model of the CLIL research space.

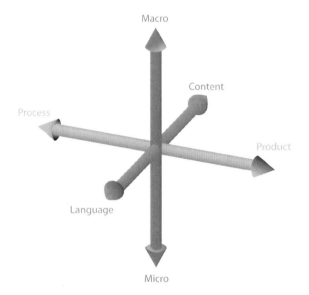

Figure 1. Three-dimensional CLIL research space

As regards more specific themes in CLIL research, a closer look at research on language learning in CLIL reveals that the prominence of speaking skills among the language goals of CLIL is also reflected in the preference given to the oral mode in CLIL research right from its inception (e.g. Dalton-Puffer 2007; Dalton-Puffer & Nikula 2006; Dalton-Puffer & Smit 2007a). Listening has received much less detailed attention so far, even though it is of course contained in general language competence survey studies (e.g. Lasagabaster 2008; Zydatiß 2007). Research on written performance of CLIL students has started to gain momentum only recently (but see Vollmer et al. 2006; Whittaker & Llinares 2009).

Another emergent theme is the construct of learning that seeks to integrate linguistic and conceptual concerns, often informed by Systemic Functional Linguistics (e.g. Coetzee 2009; Llinares & Whittaker 2007; Vollmer et al. 2006). These studies have pushed forward our understanding of literacy as a function of subject-specific competence both in its written and its oral variety. A recent study by Airey (2009) extends this interest to spoken bilingual scientific literacy at university level. Importantly, most of these studies take a process-oriented perspective, working with naturalistic discourse data, analysing language use as an observable correlate of classroom learning. This type of methodology is also present in many other studies, some of which foreground more specifically linguistic categories in their analysis (e.g. Dafouz 2007), while others work with typically discourse analytic categories (e.g. Mariotti 2006; Smit 2008), and yet others with concepts rooted in discourse pragmatics (e.g. Nikula 2005, 2007, 2008; Smit 2010). While the borders between different approaches are fluid, their common interest is to understand what characterizes CLIL classrooms as discourse practices and as learning environments, and to reveal commonalities and contrasts both with L1 classrooms and traditional foreign language teaching.

Another growing concern has been to capture the perceptions and attitudes of students, teachers and other stakeholders involved in CLIL programmes (cf. several of the contributions in the first two issues of *International CLIL Research Journal*). These studies aim to gauge the experiences of CLIL participants beyond the local and anecdotal level, often combining quantitative and qualitative methodologies (e.g. Casal & Moore 2009; Coonan 2007; Dalton-Puffer et al. 2008, 2009; Lasagabaster & Sierra 2009; Mehisto & Asser 2007).

Theoretical discussions on language learning theories underlying CLIL have so far tended to be integrated into empirical research studies (but see Casal 2007; Dalton-Puffer 2009). Finally, there is the question whether CLIL can and will play a noticeable role in the development of educational language policies across the continent (e.g. Lorenzo 2007; Lorenzo et al. 2009).

5.   On theoretical and methodological trends

In general terms, applied linguistics provides the most common theoretical and methodological backdrop for CLIL research. However, within this broad area it is also possible to define different theoretical orientations and methodological framings in CLIL research. Firstly, given the interest in language learning in CLIL, there is the large field of second language acquisition (SLA) research which has offered methodological frames and investigative techniques, especially when considering CLIL students' linguistic performance in testing situations. The SLA perspective, given its underlying view of language as a structured system and of learning as largely a psycholinguistic-cognitive phenomenon has brought along certain structural emphases. This means that CLIL students' language mastery has often been approached from the perspective of how well they (often in comparison to those receiving regular language instruction) master specific areas of language such as vocabulary (e.g. Jiménez Catalan et al. 2006), grammatical structures (e.g. Martínez Adrián & Gutierréz Mangado 2009), pronunciation (e.g. Gallardo del Puerto et al. 2009) and combinations of different skill areas (e.g. Ruiz de Zarobe 2008). On the whole, research outcomes have pointed towards beneficial effects of CLIL on various areas of language learning, i.e. it seems to have potential as a language learning environment. However, further research is needed to explore to what extent positive outcomes are due to more extensive exposure to the language, and to what extent the combined effect of content and language instruction is at play.

Another branch of CLIL research can be distinguished by its primary attention to language use rather than language learning in CLIL contexts, questions of language learning being brought in by implication rather than by direct focus. The theoretical underpinnings for such research often derive from discourse analysis and pragmatics rather than, or in combination with, SLA. However, also within this research orientation CLIL students' discourse performance has often been compared to that of students involved in regular language teaching. The results indicate that CLIL seems to result in language use that is qualitatively different from that in foreign language classrooms: CLIL students for example tend to be more active and competent interactionally (Gassner & Maillat 2006; Nikula 2005); CLIL contexts have also been shown to provide more opportunities for students to make use of discourse pragmatic strategies as they often use the foreign language for more diverse functions and for more complex meaning negotiations than their peers in language lessons (Nikula 2005, 2008). Thirdly, and as foregrounded in the label CLIL itself, a central concern in CLIL is the question of how content and language learning is integrated and how these integrated practices can be analysed. This question, as argued above, has most commonly been pursued from within the framework of Systemic Functional Linguistics and by researchers exploring how students master subject and genre specific ways of presenting knowledge (e.g. Coetzee 2009; Llinares & Whittaker 2007; Vollmer et al. 2006). This research has helped emphasize that, as regards language learning in CLIL, a focus on learning subject-specific registers, genres and discourses rather than on language learning as accumulation surface-level forms is of great benefit.

6.   Introducing the volume

This volume is divided into three parts. Part One focuses on *general and theoretical issues* relevant to CLIL as a popular teaching approach in Europe. The two papers in this section probe the popularity of CLIL and suggest two explanations for why this approach seems to offer previously unexploited language learning opportunities that complement traditional foreign language learning. Francisco Lorenzo and Pat Moore make a case for the strong communicative need experienced by learners when participating in content classes and the substantial positive impact this circumstance has had on their Spanish students' English language skills. These skills, it is argued, have partially developed incidentally and in close relation to the content-based literacy needs, thus also calling into question the still wide-spread practice of using native speakers' language competence as language learning target models. Didier Maillat's contribution expands on that point by exploring CLIL-based language use from a pragmatic perspective and by arguing for a cognitive model as a way of elucidating how far CLIL classes are especially beneficial settings for language learning.

Part Two is concerned with *CLIL in diverse European educational settings at the secondary level*. Depending on the respective national educational system, the age range of the learners concerned varies and can include ten- to nineteen-year olds. Reflecting this large and educationally crucial age bracket, more than half of all contributions to this volume belong in this section. Internally, the seven contributions are further subdivided according to language mode. The first three deal with spoken, the last three with written language production; the middle paper, by Llinares and Whittaker, considers both modes. At the same time, each of the seven contributions addresses a specific research interest. Tom Morton uses teacher and learner reconstructions of historical events as a basis for his argument in favour of language-focused curricula that should be informed by the Systemic Functional Linguistic understanding of 'genre'. Julia Hüttner and Angelika Rieder-Bünemann's contribution presents a detailed analysis of oral narratives, produced in L2 English as compared to the L1 German by CLIL vs. mainstream learners, and argues for the marked influence CLIL instruction has had on the production of more complex morpho-syntactic and narrative elements. The potential of comparing production in English vs. the L1 for gaining micro-level insights in CLIL processes is also exploited in the two following papers. Tarja Nikula presents a case study of one teacher's Biology teaching in his L1 Finnish and in English and exemplifies that, contrary to the teacher's self-assessment, his classroom discourse reveals language-specific interactional patterns. Ana Llinares and Rachel Whittaker's contribution offers a detailed systemic functional linguistic analysis of written and oral texts produced by Spanish CLIL vs. mainstream learners in their respective medium of instruction, English L2 or Spanish L1.

The theme of writing in different languages is also of central concern to Heini-Marja Järvinen's study: it, too, offers research support for the need for genre-based CLIL teaching. The final two contributions in this section compare CLIL learners' written English with that of EFL learners in their respective country, Austria and the Basque country, Spain. Both studies support previous research in that the detailed linguistic analyses show CLIL learners performing better on most dimensions of English text production. Silvia Jexenflicker and Christiane Dalton-Puffer's analysis, however, points to a general weakness amongst Austrian learners as regards the textual level of their literacy competence while Yolanda Ruiz de Zarobe's longitudinal study underlines the success inherent in sustained CLIL teaching and learning.

Part Th ree presents a Spanish, a Norwegian and an Austrian study, each focused on *integrating content and language at the tertiary level*. By analyzing lectures given in Spanish and English by the same lecturers, Emma Dafouz Milne and Begoña Núñez Perucha can identify language-dependent differences in organizational patterns and linguistic devices. Once more addressing lectures, Glenn Ole Hellekjær's questionnaire-based survey focuses on Norwegian students' levels of, and problems with, comprehending lectures given in English as compared to Norwegian. Finally, Ute Smit's study deals with the discourse function of explaining in truly international classroom interaction and thus approaches the issue of content and language integration from the so-far underexplored angle of English functioning as a learning community's lingua franca.

While the themes chosen for the three sections – theoretical concerns, secondary and tertiary education – allow for a revealing and, we hope, helpful categorization of the contributions, their brief descriptions have already indicated that this volume features additional themes across the papers, among them:

- participant focus (teacher, student, interaction)
- mode (oral or written)
- specific language use (genre, proficiency testing)
- research methodology (Systemic Functional Linguistics, Discourse Pragmatics)
- comparative focus (L1, EFL)

To aid readers interested in pursuing these themes in a concentrated fashion, Figure 2 offers a matrix representation of themes and chapters: chapter numbers are indicated across the top row, thematic foci appear in the left-most column.

Contributions Themes	1	2	3	4	5	6	7	8	9	10	11	12
Focus on Teacher			x		x					x		
Focus on Student	x	x	x	x		x	x	x	x		x	
Focus on Interaction			x	x		x						x
Oral Mode			x	x	x	x	x			x	x	x
Written Mode	x		x			x	x	x	x			
Genres	x		x	x		x	x			x	x	
Proficiency testing	x			x		x	x	x	x			
Systemic Functional Linguistics	x		x			x	x			x		
Discourse Pragmatics		x			x							x
Comparison with L1	x	x		x	x	x	x			x	x	
Comparison with EFL			x					x	x			

Figure 2. Themes and their treatment in volume chapters

In the concluding chapter, Christiane Dalton-Puffer, Tarja Nikula and Ute Smit offer a brief summary of the main issues dealt with in the contributions to the volume, taking this as a basis of a potentially contentious discussion of what they consider pressing issues in CLIL research: the problematic nature of comparative research, the tension between policy and reality, the predominance of English as CLIL language, and the ways in which 'content' and 'language' can and should be integrated.

References

Admiraal, W., Westhoff, G. & de Bot, K. 2006. Evaluation of bilingual secondary education in the Netherlands: Students' language proficiency in English. *Educational Research and Evaluation* 12(1): 75–93.

Airey, J. 2009. *Science, Language and Literacy: Case Studies of Learning in Swedish University Physics* [Uppsala Dissertations from the Faculty of Science and Technology]. Uppsala: University of Uppsala. <http://urn.kb.se/resolve?urn=urn:nbn:se:uu:diva-9547>.

Breidbach, S., Bach, G. & Wolff, D. 2002. *Bilingualer Sachfachunterricht: Didaktik, Lehrer-Lernerforschung und Bildungspolitik zwischen Theorie und Empirie.* Frankfurt: Peter Lang.

Brinton, D.M., Snow, M.A. & Wesche, M.B. 2008. *Content-based Second Language Instruction,* 2nd edn. Ann Arbor MI: The University of Michigan Press.

Carrió-Pastor, M.L. (ed.). 2009. *Content and Language Integrated Learning: Cultural Diversity.* Bern: Peter Lang.

Casal Madinabeitia, S. 2007. The integrated curriculum, CLIL and constructivism. *Revista española de linguística aplicada* 1: 55–65.

Casal, S. & Moore, P. 2009. The Andalusian bilingual sections scheme: Evaluation and consultancy. *International CLIL Research Journal* 1(2): 36–46.

Coetzee-Lachmann, D. 2009. Assessment of Subject-specific Task Performance of Bilingual Geography Learners: Analysing Aspects of Subject-specific Written Discourse. Ph.D. Dissertation, University of Osnabrück.

Coonan, C.M. 2007. How are students engaged in subject learning through the foreign language. Activites for learning in a CLIL environment. In *Diverse Contexts Converging Goals. CLIL in Europe,* D. Marsh & D. Wolff (eds), 153–169, Frankfurt: Peter Lang.

Coyle, D. & Baetens Beardsmore, H. (eds). 2007. Research on Content and Language Integrated Learning (CLIL Special issue). *Journal of Bilingual Education and Bilingualism* 10(5).

Coyle, D. 1999. Theory and planning for effective classrooms: Supporting students in Content and Language Integrated Learning contexts. Planning for effective classrooms. In *Learning through a Foreign Language: Models, Methods and Outcomes,* J. Masih (ed.), 46–62. London: CILT.

Coyle D., Hood, P. & Marsh, D. 2010. *CLIL: Content and Language Integrated Learning.* Cambridge: CUP.

Dafouz, E., Núñez, B., Sancho, C. 2007. Analysing stance in a CLIL university context: Non-native speaker use of personal pronouns and modal verbs. *The International Journal of Bilingual Education and Bilingualism* 10(5): 647–662.

Dalton-Puffer, C. & Nikula, T. (eds). 2006. Current research on CLIL. *VIEWS. Vienna English Working Papers* 15(3). (Special issue: *Current Research on CLIL*).

Dalton-Puffer, C. & Smit, U. (eds). 2007a. *Empirical Perspectives on CLIL Classroom Discourse*. Frankfurt: Peter Lang.

Dalton-Puffer, C. & Smit, U. 2007b. Introduction. In *Empirical Perspectives on CLIL Classroom Discourse*, C. Dalton-Puffer & U. Smit (eds), 7–23. Frankfurt: Peter Lang.

Dalton-Puffer, C. 2007. *Discourse in Content and Language Integrated Learning (CLIL) Classrooms* [Language Learning & Language Teaching 20]. Amsterdam: John Benjamins.

Dalton-Puffer, C. 2009. Communicative competence and the CLIL lesson. In *Content and Language Integrated Learning: Evidence from Research in Europe*, Y. Ruiz de Zarobe & R.M. Jiménez Catalán (eds), 197–214. Bristol: Multilingual Matters.

Dalton-Puffer, C., Hüttner, J., Jexenflicker, S., Schindelegger V. & Smit, U. 2008. *Content and Language Integrated Learning an Österreichs Höheren Technischen Lehranstalten: Forschungsbericht*. Wien: bm:ukk.

Dalton-Puffer, C., Hüttner, J., Schindelegger, V. & Smit, U. 2009. Technology geeks speak out: What students think about vocational CLIL. *International CLIL Research Journal* 1(2): 17–25.

Donato, R. 1994. Collective scaffolding in second language learning. In *Vygotskian Approaches to Second Language Research*, J.P. Lantolf & G. Appel (eds), 33–56. Norwood NJ: Ablex.

European Commission Communication. 2003. Promoting language learning and linguistic diversity: An action plan 2004–2006. <http://ec.europa.eu/education/doc/official/keydoc/actlang/act_lang_en.pdf>.

European Commission. 1995. White paper on education and learning: Teaching and learning. Towards the learning society. <http://europa.eu/documents/comm/white_papers/pdf/com95_590_en.pdf>.

European Commission. 2008. Languages and Europe: Language learning. <http://europa.eu/languages/en/chapter/14>.

Eurydice. 2006. Content and Language Integrated Learning (CLIL) at school in Europe. Directorate-General for Education and Culture of the European Commission. <http://eacea.ec.europa.eu/ressources/eurydice/pdf/0_integral/071EN.pdf>.

Ferguson, G. 2006. *Language Planning and Education*. Edinburgh: EUP.

Fernández Fontecha, A. 2009. Spanish CLIL: Research and official actions. In *Content and Language Integrated Learning: Evidence from Research in Europe*, Y. Ruiz de Zarobe & R.M. Jiménez Catalán (eds), 3–21. Bristol: Multilingual Matters.

Gajo, L. 2007. Linguistic knowledge and subject knowledge: How does bilingualism contribute to subject development? *The International Journal of Bilingual Education and Bilingualism* 10(5): 563–579.

Gallardo del Puerto, F., Goméz Lacabex, E. & García Lecumberri, M.L. 2009. Testing the effectiveness of content and language integrated learning in foreign language contexts: The assessment of English pronunciation. In *Content and Language Integrated Learning: Evidence from Research in Europe*, Y. Ruiz de Zarobe & R.M. Jiménez Catalán (eds), 63–80. Bristol: Multilingual Matters.

Gassner, D. & Maillat, D. 2006. Spoken competence in CLIL: A pragmatic take on recent Swiss data. *VIEWS. Vienna English Working Papers* 15(3): 15–22. (Special issue: *Current Research on CLIL*).

Genesee, F. 1987. *Learning through Two Languages: Studies of Immersion and Bilingual Education*. Rowley MA: Newbury House.

Hallet, W. 1999. Ein didaktisches Modell für den bilingualen Sachfachunterricht: The bilingual triangle. *Neusprachliche Mitteilungen* 1999(1): 23–27.

Jäppinen, A.-K. 2005. Cognitional development of mathematics and science in the Finnish mainstream education in Content and Language Integrated Learning (CLIL) – teaching through a foreign language. *Language and Education* 19(2): 148–169.

Jiménez Catalán, R.M., Ruiz de Zarobe, Y. & Cenoz, J. 2006. Vocabulary profiles of English foreign language learners in English as a subject and as a vehicular language. *VIEWS – Vienna English Working Papers* 15(3): 23–27. (Special Issue: *Current Research on CLIL*).

Krashen, S.D. & Terrell, T.D. 1983. *The Natural Approach: Language Acquisition in the Classroom.* Hayward CA: Alemany Press.

Krashen, S.D. 1985. *The Input Hypothesis.* London: Longman.

Lantolf, J.P. 2002. Sociocultural theory and second language acquisition. In *Oxford Handbook of Applied Linguistics*, R.B. Kaplan (ed.), 104–114. Oxford: OUP.

Lasabagaster, D. & Sierra, J.M. 2009. Language attitudes in CLIL and traditional EFL classes. *International CLIL Research Journal* 1(2): 4–17.

Lasagabaster, D. & Ruiz de Zarobe, Y. 2010. *CLIL in Spain: Implementation, Results and Teacher Training.* Newcastle upon Tyne: Cambridge Scholars Publishing.

Lasagabaster, D. 2008. Foreign language competence in Content and Language Integrated courses. *The Open Applied Linguistics Journal* 1: 31–42.

Li, D.C.S. 2002. Hong Kong parents' preference for English-medium education: Passive victims of imperialism or active agents of pragmatism? In *Englishes in Asia: Communication, Identity, Power & Education*, A. Kirkpatrick (ed.), 29–62. Melbourne: Language Australia.

Lim Falk, M. 2008. *Svenska i engelskspråkig skolmiljö: Ämnesrelaterat språkbruk i två Gymnasieklasser* ('Swedish in an English-language school environment: Subject-based language use in two upper secondary classes') [Stockholm Studies in Scandinavian Philology: New Series 46]. Stockholm: University of Stockholm.

Llinares, A. & Whittaker, R. 2007. Talking and writing in the social sciences in a foreign language: A linguistic analysis of secondary school learners of geography and history. *Revista española de linguistica aplicada* 1: 83–94.

Long, M.H. 1996. The role of the linguistic environment in second language acquisition. In *Handbook of Second Language Acquisition*, W. Ritchie & T.K. Bhatia (eds), 413–468. San Diego CA: Academic Press.

Lorenzo, F. 2007. An analytical framework of language integration in L2 content-based courses: The European dimension. *Language and Education* 21(6): 502–514.

Lorenzo, F., Casal, S. & Moore, P. 2009. The effects of content and language integrated learning in European education: Key findings from the Andalusian bilingual sections evaluation project. *Applied Linguistics Advance Access.* <http://applij.oxfordjournals.org/cgi/content/abstract/amp041v1>.

Lyster, R. 2007. *Learning and Teaching Languages through Content: A Counterbalanced Approach* [Language Learning & Language Teaching 18]. Amsterdam: John Benjamins.

Maljers, A., Marsh, D. & Wolff, D. 2007. Foreword. In *Windows on CLIL: Content and Language Integrated Learning in the European Spotlight*, A. Maljers, D. Marsh & D. Wolff (eds), 7–9. The Hague: European Platform for Dutch Education.

Mariotti, C. 2006. Negotiated interactions and repair. *VIEWS. Vienna English Working Papers* 15(3): 33–40. Special issue: *Current Research on CLIL*).

Marsh, D. & Wolff, D. (eds). 2007. *Diverse Contexts – Converging Goals. CLIL in Europe.* Frankfurt: Peter Lang.

Marsh, D. (ed.). 2002. CLIL/EMILE – the European dimension: Actions, trends and foresight potential. European Commission Report. Public Services Contract DG EAC 36 01 Lot 3.

Martínez Adrián, M. & Gutierrez Mangado, M.J. 2009. The acquisition of English syntax by CLIL learners. In *Content and Language Integrated Learning: Evidence from Research in Europe*, Y. Ruiz de Zarobe & R.M. Jiménez Catalán (eds), 176–196. Bristol: Multilingual Matters.

Mehisto, P. & Asser, H. 2007. Stakeholder perspectives: CLIL programme management in Estonia. *International Journal of Bilingual Education and Bilingualism* 10(5): 683–701.

Mehisto, P., Marsh, D. & Frigols, M.J. 2008. *Uncovering CLIL: Content and Language Integrated Learning in Bilingual and Multilingual Education*. Oxford: Macmillan Education.

Morton, T. 2009. Integrating language and content in secondary CLIL history: The potential of a genre-based approach. In *Content and Language Integrated Learning: Cultural Diversity*, M.L. Carrió-Pastor (ed.), 133–148. Bern: Peter Lang.

Nikula, T. 2005. English as an object and tool of study in classrooms: Interactional effects and pragmatic implications. *Linguistics and Education* 16(1): 27–58.

Nikula, T. 2007. The IRF pattern and space for interaction: Observations on EFL and CLIL classrooms. In *Empirical Perspectives on CLIL Classroom Discourse*, C. Dalton-Puffer & U. Smit (eds), 179–204. Frankfurt: Peter Lang.

Nikula, T. 2008. Learning pragmatics in content-based classrooms. In *Investigating Pragmatics in Foreign Language Learning, Teaching, and Testing*, E. Alcón & A. Martinez-Flor (eds), 94–113. Clevedon: Multilingual Matters.

Otten, E. & Wildhage, M. 2003. *Praxis des bilingualen Unterrichts*. Berlin: Cornelsen Scriptor.

Ricento, T. 2006. *An Introduction to Language Policy: Theory and Method*. Oxford: Blackwell.

Richards, J.C. & Rodgers, T.S. 2001. *Approaches and Methods in Language Teaching*. Cambridge: CUP.

Ruiz de Zarobe, Y. & Jiménez Catalán, R.M. (eds). 2009. *Content and Language Integrated Learning: Evidence from Research in Europe*. Bristol: Multilingual Matters.

Ruiz de Zarobe, Y. 2008. CLIL and foreign language learning: A longitudinal study in the Basque country. *International CLIL Research Journal* 1(1): 60–73.

Schmidt, R. 1990. The role of consciousness in second language learning. *Applied Linguistics* 11: 129–158.

Seregély, Eva. 2009. "I know this word. (I think) It means …" – Lexical competence and self-assessment in CLIL and traditional EFL classrooms. *VIEWS. Vienna English Working Papers* 18(2): 42–70.

Shohamy, E. 2006. *Language Policy: Hidden Agendas and New Approaches*. London: Routledge.

Smit, U. 2008. "What I think is important [is] to know how to explain it.": Explaining lexical items in English as a lingua franca in international higher education. In *Sprachen lernen – Menschen bilden: Dokumentation zum 22. Kongress für Fremdsprachendidaktik der Deutschen Gesellschaft für Fremdsprachenforschung (DGFF) Gießen, Oktober 2007* [BFF – Beiträge zur Fremdsprachenforschung, vol. 10], E. Burwitz-Melzer, W. Hallet, M.K. Legutke, F.-J. Meißner & J. Mukherjee (eds), 279–288. Hohengehren: Schneider Verlag.

Smit, U. 2010. *English as a Lingua Franca (ELF) in Higher Education: A Longitudinal Study of Classroom Discourse*. Berlin: Mouton de Gruyter.

Smit, U. & Dalton-Puffer, C. (eds). 2007. Current research on CLIL 2. *VIEWS. Vienna English Working Papers* 16(3). [Special issue: *Current Research on CLIL (2)*.

Spolsky, B. 2004. *Language Policy*. Cambridge: CUP.

Stoller, F.L. 2004. Content-based instruction: Perspectives on curriculum planning. *Annual Review of Applied Linguistics* 24: 261–283.

Swain, M. 1995. Three functions of output in second language learning. In *Principle and Practice in Applied Linguistics: Studies in Honour of H.G. Widdowson*, G. Cook & B. Seidlhofer (eds), 125–144. Oxford: OUP.

Swain, M. 2000. The output hypothesis and beyond: Mediating acquisition through collaborative dialogue. In *Sociocultural Theory and Second Language Learning*, J.P. Lantolf (ed.), 97–114. Oxford: OUP.

Sylvén, L.-K. 2004. Teaching in English or English Teaching? On the Effects of Content and Language Integrated Learning on Swedish Learners' Incidental Vocabulary Acquisition. Ph.D. dissertation, University of Gothenburg.

Tollefson, J.W. & Tsui, A.B.M. (eds). 2004. *Medium of Instruction Policies: Which Agenda? Whose Agenda?* Mahwah NJ: Lawrence Erlbaum Associates.

Torres-Guzman, M. 2007. Dual language programs: Key features and results. In *Bilingual Education: An Introductory Reader,* O. Garciá & C. Baker (eds), 50–63. Clevedon: Multilingual Matters.

Tsui, A.B.M. & Tollefson, J.W. (eds). 2007. *Language Policy, Culture and Identity in Asian Contexts.* Mahwah NJ: Lawrence Erlbaum Associates.

Van de Craen, P., Ceuleers, E. & Mondt K. 2007. Cognitive development and bilingualism in primary schools: Teaching maths in a CLIL environment. In *Diverse Contexts – Converging Goals: CLIL in Europe*, D. Marsh & D. Wolff (eds), 185–200. Frankfurt: Peter Lang.

Vollmer, H.J., Heine, L., Troschke, R., Coetzee, D. & Küttel, V. 2006. Subject-specific competence and language use of CLIL learners: The case of geography in grade 10 of secondary schools in Germany. Paper presented at the ESSE8 Conference in London, 29 August 2006.

Whittaker, R. & Llinares A. 2009. CLIL in social science classrooms: Analysis of spoken and written productions. In *Content and Language Integrated Learning: Evidence from Research in Europe*, Y. Ruiz de Zarobe & R.M. Jiménez Catalán (eds), 215–234. Bristol: Multilingual Matters.

Wilkinson, R. & Zegers, V. (eds). 2007. *Researching Content and Language Integration in Higher Education.* Maastricht: Maastricht University Language Centre.

Wode, H., Burmeister, P., Daniel, A., Kickler, K.-U. & Knust, M. 1996. Die Erprobung von deutschenglischen bilingualem Unterricht in Schleswig-Holstein: Ein erster Zwischenbericht. *Zeitschrift für Fremdsprachenforschung* 1996/7(1): 15–42.

Wolff, D. 2007. CLIL: Bridging the gap between school and working life. In *Diverse Contexts – Converging Goals: CLIL in Europe*, D. Marsh & D. Wolff (eds), 15–25. Frankfurt: Peter Lang.

Zydatiß, W. 2007. Bilingualer Fachunterricht in Deutschland: Eine Bilanz. *Fremdsprachen Lehren und Lernen* 36: 8–25.

Websites mentioned

www.ccn-clil.eu
www.clilcompendium.com
www.CLILCompendium.com
www.clilconsortium.jyu.fi/
http://clil.uni.lu/CLIL/
www.ecml.at/activities/intro.asp
www.ecml.at/mtp2/CLILmatrix/index.htm
www.europeesplatform.nl/sf.mcgi?2681
www.ichm.org/clil/

PART I

General and theoretical issues

On the natural emergence of language structures in CLIL

Towards a theory of European educational bilingualism

Francisco Lorenzo & Pat Moore
Universidad Pablo de Olavide, Sevilla, Spain

It is important to ensure that the implementation of modern European educational bilingualism be based on sound theoretical underpinnings. We discuss the development of L2 competence, as evidenced in sentence and text grammar, gauging the extent to which the incidental language learning favoured by a CLIL (Content and Language Integrated Learning) approach appears to satisfy the requirements of content learning. Secondary CLIL learners were given writing prompts designed to produce short passages of academic type language. The resulting texts are employed to discuss (a) the alignment of content and grammar and the primacy of semantic considerations; (b) transfer between L1 and L2 and the undeniable role of the L1, and (c) interlanguage levels and the need for realistic attainment models. They also serve to illustrate the importance of communicative need in CLIL-type approaches.

1. Introduction

CLIL [Content and Language Integrated Learning] is employed as an umbrella term to denote European models of bilingual education aimed at foreign, second, minority and/or heritage languages. As such it covers a vast scope of potential learning scenarios. European CLIL is strengthened by being a movement which has grown from grassroots at the same time as it has been the focus of top down linguistic and educational policy initiatives (Admiraal, Westhoff & de Bot 2006: 77; Dalton-Puffer & Nikula 2006: 4; Lorenzo 2007: 506; Marsh et al. 1997: 10). Nonetheless, researchers are beginning to voice concerns over the fact that CLIL implementation may be outpacing CLIL theory:

> CLIL is still far from being a consolidated and fully articulated educational model [...] a great deal more needs to be done, for instance, in order to consolidate the theoretical underpinnings of CLIL and create a conceptual

framework that is both coherent and applicable to different local conditions. (Dalton-Puffer 2008: 139; see also Van de Craen, Mondt, Allain & Gao 2007)

The research here presented was designed to contribute to precisely this task. We focus primarily on linguistic development within CLIL, particularly L2 development, although given the integrative nature of the approach we will also need to touch on questions relating to L1, cognition and subject knowledge.

This study was carried out with 2nd year secondary learners and in this scenario we feel that the principles of language immersion as set out in Wesche (2002: 358) provide a clear rationale for linguistic development:

a. Young humans are naturally equipped to acquire language knowledge incidentally.
b. To become fluent, children need very frequent and varied exposure to the second language for an extended period of time.
c. Language should not be taught as a system but should be made available to learners.

At the outset we should emphasise the fact that one of the key characteristics of linguistic development within bilingual learning relates to the fact that it implies vehicular use of language as a tool for the gathering and sharing of knowledge: Language as the means of study rather than the object of study. CLIL brings a new relevance to second language development – while traditional FL classrooms tend to treat learners as (deficient) *novices*, CLIL classrooms treat them as (efficient) *users* (Nikula 2005: 54, 2007; Dalton-Puffer 2007, 2008). In tandem, studying an established curricular subject through the L2 confers "immediate pertinence" to the task-in-hand (Baetens Beardsmore 2002); from a content perspective, research has found that CLIL students engage more with content texts than with traditional FL texts (Morgan 1999: 35; Wolff 2002: 48). These factors combine to imbue CLIL-type learning with real meaning and authenticity, both of which are integral to the development of communicative competence. In relation to this it is worth pointing out that both teachers and learners report heightened involvement and motivation when engaged in CLIL type learning (Allen & Davies 2009; Lasagabaster & Sierra 2009; Merisuo-Storm 2007; Seikkula-Leino 2007).

On the assumption that it is fundamental to communicative competence, inasmuch as it has a crucial role to play in the shaping of meaning, this chapter focuses on the acquisition/emergence of L2 morphosyntax within immersion-type bilingual programmes. Although CLIL and CLIL related research is a relative new-comer to the Applied Linguistics scene, the question of how L2 grammar should be dealt with in such scenarios has already generated significant interest. Key questions relate to whether explicit attention to form is desirable and/or necessary and if so, how it should be operationalised (Järvinen 2005; Lorenzo 2007, 2008; Lyster 1998; Mariotti 2006; Marsh 2008; Mohan & Beckett 2003; Pérez-Vidal 2007; Serra 2007).

Much of the above research has sought to identify corollaries between pedagogic practice and communicative outcomes by comparing data obtained through the recording and transcription of spoken exchanges during classroom observation with the results of subsequent (often finely tuned) linguistic evaluation. This article switches the focus and takes spontaneous written learner output as a starting point. Rather than progressing from observed teaching to evidence of learning we start with the latter and infer conclusions regarding the former.

We assume that the teaching of content via the L2 is not compatible with a traditionally conceived formal structural language syllabus. Nonetheless, language learning is occurring and we will attempt to identify emergent linguistic structures and rhetorical moves which can be linked with content. We use the term 'emergent' to imply that this is language which is evolving naturally through incidental learning.

2. Methodology

The informants for the current study consisted of secondary state school learners (n. 150), aged 12–13, from ten distinct schools distributed across the different provinces of Andalusia, at the beginning of their second year of bilingual instruction. These learners, in a formal classroom context, were given a series of content-focused writing prompts designed to produce short passages of academic type text and were asked to respond to half in their L2 (English) and half in their L1 (Spanish) although the ultimate choice of which language to use when was left to the learners.

The design of the prompts was predicated on a semantic framework of basic 'knowledge structures' (KSs) (Mohan 1986, 1989, 2007). Research within Systemic Functional Linguistics has suggested that six core KSs, in binary generic/specific pairings: Classification/Description; Principles/Sequence; Evaluation/Choice, serve to provide a heuristic tool which can bridge the common goals of content and language (see Mohan 2007: 310 for an overview). Not only do the KSs facilitate the conceptualisation of aims within individual content subjects, they can also be envisaged across the curriculum. Academic (and indeed socio-cultural) development is perceived as the ability to progress from the subjective concrete to the objective abstract and KSs incorporate this distinction. From an SFL perspective learning is seen as essentially a linguistic process (eg. Halliday 1975) and we are therefore interested in the language which the learners employ when dealing with these concepts. We are particularly interested in their manipulations of typical academic language functions such as defining, hypothesising, describing, opinion giving etc.; the rhetorical structures and linguistic forms which they employ in order to render them and the degree to which their output conflates with standard norms.

From a content perspective, the prompts focused on areas of the Social and Natural Sciences, subjects which are taught in the L2 within the CLIL programmes. In order to guarantee familiarity, some of the prompts were shaped around local historical and demographic questions (eg. *Who was Cristobal Colón* [Christopher Columbus] *and what did he do? Describe the capital city of your province*) while others were reinforced by their presence in the media at the time (eg. *What is climate change?*). They all covered areas which, in line with national curricula guidelines, had previously and recently been the focus of teaching. This approach ensured that the learners' cognitive schemata were already in place and that the main focus of the task would be the shaping and expression of said schemata in the L2.

It is important to note here, however, that the learners were not prepped in any way for this specific task. There was no explicit pre-teaching or rehearsal of key language and no scaffolding other than the prompts themselves. The intention was to let the learners decide how best to deal with each item; to see how they appeared to interpret the basic premise and how they formulated a response. Accordingly, there was also no *a priori* selection of specific morphosyntactic features or structures; the intention was to allow the resulting data to shape findings.

For the purposes of the current paper the discussion is organised around three core interlocking research questions. In the first place we want to explore the relationship between content and language in the learner output. In expert user academic language particular linguistic and rhetorical structures are congruent with particular functions (e.g., conditionals to hypothesise, modals to mark stance) but we also know that our respondents are not (yet) expert users. It will therefore be interesting to see how, and how successfully, the learners express academic functions and whether it is possible to identify patterns of use in the corpus of student texts.

The second question relates to transfer. One of the characteristics of European CLIL lies in the fact that learners will have had and continue to have the opportunity to develop their L1 in tandem with the L2. We assume that L1 academic knowledge will aid the learners in the elaboration of responses, indeed we would go so far as to say that it is crucial (Vollmer 2008) and we conceive of this knowledge as linguistically grounded. It follows that the student texts should contain examples of rhetorical structures which they have acquired in L1 content learning yet which they have also recognised in, and can apply to, L2 content learning.

The third question relates to the degree of L2 competence which the learners display. Having received no more than a little over one year of bilingual instruction, these learners are at a relatively early stage of L2 development and, as previously noted, we should not expect them to behave like expert users. The corpus of student texts should, nevertheless, provide insights relating to their stage of interlanguage development.

3. Results and discussion

This section will provide an illustrative selection of student samples and will attempt to establish connections between written output and the learning processes that the texts appear to demonstrate. The learner writing can be interpreted as a window on cognitive and language behaviour, suggesting which route is followed for language learning, use and consolidation. This ties in closely with research on production skills and second language acquisition (see Doughty & Long 2003 for a review).

3.1 Samples from the corpus

The learner samples below will serve to illustrate the discussion which follows. It is worth pointing out that each of these extracts comes from a different writer and that they can therefore be taken to represent a typical selection of learner texts. For each prompt there are three L2 responses (A–C) and two L1 responses (D–E) [with translation].

---

1. *Who was Cristobal Colón* [Christopher Columbus] *and what did he do?*

   A. *Cristobal Colón was an explorer. A Lot of people say he was Spanish. Other people he was Italian. He discovered America, one of the biggest continents on Earth. He started on Huelva. He sailed thinking he was going to India but he didn't.*

   B. *He was an adventurer who was looking for a new and quicker route to China but instead he dicovvered America.*

   C. *Cristobal Colón was the person that discovers America and he takes from there food like tomatoes, and potatoes and tobacco. He did it in 1492.*

   D. *Fue el hombre que descubrió América. En Córdoba le pidió permiso y Isabel la Católica para descubrir si la tierra era redonda dandole una vuelta al mundo con tres barcos. Murió sin saber que había descubierto América.*
      [He was the man who discovered America. In Cordoba he asked Isabel the Catholic for permission to find out if the world was round by sailing around it in three boats. He died without knowing that he had discovered America.]

   E. *Fue un hombre que intentó descubrir la India pero se equivocó de rumbo y en vez de la india descubrió América. Fue en tres barcos la Pinta, la Niña y la Carabela.*
      [He was a man who tried to discover India but he went the wrong way and instead of India he discovered America. He went in three boats: the Pinta, the Niña and the Carabela.]

2. *Describe the capital city of your province*

   A. *The capital city of my province is Cordoba. Its not really populated but it's not small populated either. It's a very modern city. There are a lot of shops and it's a clean city.*

   B. *It is no a very big city. It is very beautiful and you can see a lot of monuments. I think that they can live less than 1 million people, I don't know exactly. It's a small city with a lot of restaurants and shopping centers.*

   C. *Granada is a beautifall city. There are lots of different people, and most of the people are very nice. I've never experienced violence or robbery in granada. You can see the Alhambra (a beautiful palace) the Albayin (the old part of Granada), the cathedral, Museums. There are lots of things to do.*

   D. *La capital de mi provincia es Sevilla. Es importante porque hay monumentos, porque es grande y porque viven millones de persona. Pero para mi la mejor ciudad es Córdoba porque es más hermosa.*
   [The capital of my province is Sevilla. It's important because there are monuments, because it's big and because millions of people live there. But I think Cordoba is the best city because it's more beautiful.]

   E. *Malaga es una ciudad muy grande. Yo creo que vive al rededor de un millón de personas pero no lo sé. Es un ciudad grande con muchos edificios pero también hay muchas cosas viejos que puedes ver por ejemplo en un museo.*
   [Malaga is a very big city. I think about a million people live there but I'm not sure. It's a big city with lots of buildings but there are also lots of old things that you can see, for example in a museum.]

3. *What is climate change?*

   A. *It is when the world's climate changes because of pollution. It will make the world hotter, there won't be any glaciers and the water level will rise.*

   B. *It's the accumulation of CO^2 that the cars produce. We must use the bike or public transport!!*

   C. *The climate change is the most important problem in the world at the moment and we have to save our planet if we want to live here.*

   D. *El cambio climático es el conjunto de efectos que esta trayendo la contaminación sin control. Sus consecuencias van a ser: El conjunto de polos va a derretirse, por ello, aumentará el nivel del mar, habrá menos precipitaciones, contribuirá a la desertización, aumentará la temperatura varios grados, y los veranos serán mucho más calurosos.*
   [Climate change is the complex of effects resulting from uncontrolled contamination. The consequences are going to be: the poles are going to melt, which means the sea level will rise, there will be less precipitation, it will contribute to desertification, the temperature will rise several degrees, and the summers will be much hotter.]

   E. *El cambio climático es el cambio que esta sufriendo nuestro planeta que hace cambiar el relieve, que mata animales y sobre todo nos perjudica a nosotros y a nuestra tierra no la hagamos sufrir por favor.¡Cuidemos de ella!*
   [Climate change is the change which our planet is undergoing which will make the relief change, which kills animals and above all damages us and please let's not make our planet suffer. Let's look after it!]

4. *What is a rainbow?*

    A. *It's when it been raining and there a bit of vapour in the air and the sun shines trough there and shine out in different colours because it works like a prism.*

    B. *A rainbow is a light of seven colours: red, yellow, blue, green, purple, etc. It's produced when a light sun through some water in it is conbert in the seven colours of the rainbow.*

    C. *A rainbow is an arc of colors. Its made when the rain is finished, there's a lot of sun…well that's when a rainbow comes out.*

    D. *Un arco iris se produce cuando hay agua en el aire – por ejemplo la lluvia o una catarata, y el sol brilla en ella y esto produce un arco iris que es un arco con 7 colores.*

    [A rainbow is produced when there is water in the air – for example rain or a waterfall, and the sun shines in the water and this produces a rainbow which is an arch of 7 colours.]

    E. *Un arco iris es la descomposición de colores formada cuando los rayos de sola iluminan las gotas de lluvia y aparecen los 7 colores.*

    [A rainbow is the separation of colours formed when the sun's rays illuminate the raindrops and the seven colours appear.]

3.2   The alignment of grammar and content in CLIL learner discourse

We were looking for patterns of use and the results demonstrate that learners do tend to employ specific structures in accordance with specific task types, and that in general they are aware of and attempt to adhere to academic norms. This gives credence to Bygate's suggestion that learners develop a set of "linguistic muscles" which will automatically be flexed when circumstances dictate (1999: 39). To illustrate, in the L2 responses provided, *it*-subject sentences abound when students define concepts [3A, 4B] and *there*-subject sentences are frequent in descriptions of places [2A, 2C], conditionals appear when learners hypothesise [3C], passives are frequently employed to describe scientific processes [4B, 4C], adjectival strings are common in descriptions [4B] and contrastive subordinate clauses appear in historical narrative [1A, 1B]. This idea is not new to task-based literature and appears to hold for minority learners in multilingual situations (Dufficy 2004; Loschky & Bley-Vroman 1993) but to our knowledge this is the first time that it has been addressed within CLIL where non-minority language learners are involved. The results obtained suggest that, in planning for bilingual learning, it would be difficult to divorce language use from content goals as there appears to be a degree of natural symbiosis between them.

One further point related to correlations between task and language – which is after all of crucial import in content and language integration – deserves comment. From our research on CLIL implementation (e.g. cf. Lorenzo, Casal & Moore 2009), we have come to a tentative conclusion that content teachers tend to prioritise lexis as the key to integration, emphasising that learners require the terminology of the discipline in order to grasp the area content in an L2. Language teachers, on the other hand, are more likely to focus on sentential grammar items. To provide concrete examples, their concerns centre on how to cover WWII in history lessons if learners do not have a thorough understanding of the verb system, including compound past forms; or how to explain animal symbiosis in a science lesson without a prior coverage of reciprocal pronoun systems or last but no less challenging how to describe pulley systems if students lack a firm grasp of spatial relations as expressed in the L2 prepositional system.

These two stances logically reflect the traditional pedagogic priorities of each of the interested parties. It should be remembered that, within the Spanish educational system at least, content teachers tend to have little (if any) grounding in language development whereas many language teachers, themselves the product of form-biased instruction, have been trained to consider explicit grammar instruction crucial to L2 acquisition. If CLIL is to be truly integrative, however, it will require a third way – success in educational innovation cannot rely solely on teachers adopting new materials; they also need to reconstruct their pedagogical values (Markee 2001: 125). We have come to the conclusion that in CLIL, content teachers need to become more aware of the meta-lexical language demands of their subjects, and language teachers need to develop a more textual (and less sentential) appreciation of language.

The samples above demonstrate that learners possess significant abilities in manipulating academic content in CLIL with limited grammatical resources. Rather than lexis or grammar *per se* analysis of the corpus leads us to suggest that the key to integration may well lie in the *notion*. This is not a new concept, indeed the idea of a notional syllabus in language development first evolved in the seventies, alongside the shift towards more communicatively oriented pedagogies. The notional syllabus argues for the primacy of semantic need in the organisation of language teaching. While not denying the importance of grammar it does reject the need for ordered exposure to the grammar of the system and the idea of any one to one relation between form and meaning (Wilkins 1976: 19 and 55).

Rather than compound progressive verb tenses, reciprocal pronouns or spatial prepositions when covering WWII, symbiotic relations in the animal kingdom, or the pulley system in an L2, a notional approach would argue that what students need in order to cognitively grasp the area content are the notions of time in contrasting past actions, of cause and effect and their reciprocity and of spatial relations. One of the clear advantages of a notional approach in CLIL with younger and/or lower level learners is that notions can be represented in different language forms (with different degrees of success) at different competence levels.

In sample 1A the learner goes beyond concrete facts to acknowledge the debate around Colombus' origins. Speculation regarding the character's birthplace prompts the student to frame their message hypothetically, thereby employing one of the classic academic functions. Aware (perhaps) of their limited ability to produce sophisticated English structures, the learner has opted for a paratactic structure avoiding connectors: *A lot of people say he was Spanish. Other people he was Italian.* The writer has deconstructed the syntax of the sentence to bare minimalism, yet maintains the recognition of subjectivity.

In sample 4A the learner constructs a chain of reasoning in order to frame their response as contextually situated cause and effect. Once again this represents typical academic language. Employing a range of simple connectors the learner produces a clause string which opens with a temporal reference, is expanded with dependent clauses and closes with a causative: *It's when it been raining and there a bit of vapour in the air and the sun shines trough there and shine out in different colours because it works like a prism.* Harking back to the generic/specific distinction discussed in relation to knowledge structures, we can see the learner leaning towards more abstract ideas: they may not command conditional forms yet they have employed a time referent *when* which semantically functions in the same way as a generic (or zero) conditional.

Overall, while it is true that accuracy is still problematic and that the texts could be criticised as lacking in style, the learners display an impressive flexibility in responding to the communicative needs of the task. The academic functions have been realised competently and meaning is clear.

3.3 The transfer of L1 academic knowledge into an L2

Transfer has long been of interest in second language acquisition research (see Gass & Selinker 1983; Kellerman 1995; Odlin 1985, 2003) and has naturally received attention in bilingual education (Friesen & Jared 2007; Marian & Kaushanskaya 2007; Olivares 2002; Verhoeven 2007). The concept refers to the amount and type of L1 material that learners perceive of as being compatible with the L2.

The resulting texts demonstrate considerable learner competence in attempting to comply with academic stylistic norms. This observation holds for both languages. Each prompt resulted in a set of L1 texts and a set of L2 texts and the fact that peers who responded in L2 employed similar moves and devices to those who responded in the L1 demonstrate high degrees of positive transfer, particularly regarding rhetorical moves. The sample above is replete with chunks which demonstrate the transposition of academic type language which learners possessed in Spanish and did not hesitate to paste into the L2. Examples show attempts at tentative language typical of academic settings where authors employ hedges to mark stance (*I think that they can live less than; I don't know exactly* [2B] and see 2E) and to reformulate (*…well, that's when a rainbow comes out* [4C] and see 2D). Other typically academic rhetorical moves include elaborative paraphrase

(...*America, one of the biggest continents on Earth* [1A]; *the Alhambra (a beautiful palace)* [2C] and see 4D); expansion *(There are lots of different people, and most of the people are very nice.* [2C] and see 2E); exemplification (...*food like tomatoes, and potatoes* [1C] and see 4D); justification (*I've never experienced violence or robbery in granada* [2C] and see 2D) and enumerations as found in academic prose, a feature that students feel safe to import from their L1 without risks of major mistakes: *(it is when the world's climate changes because of pollution. It will make the world hotter, there won't be any glaciers, the water level will rise* [3A] and see 3D). Metaphorical grammar is also in evidence, with nominalisation (*the accumulation of* CO^2 [3B] and see 4E) and the transposition of negative particles from verb phrases to noun phrase (*It is a no very big city* [2B] and see 3D). Furthermore, although not explicitly instructed to do so, learners provide solutions to perceived problems (*We must use the bike or public transport!!* [3B] and see 3E).

These findings substantiate the idea that, at least when comparing Spanish and English – as in the current study – CALP is indeed a linguistically transferable macro-skill (Cummins 1979, 1981, 1984).

3.4   The growth of L2 interlanguage in CLIL

Many of the texts in the corpus feature highly sophisticated language – both from the perspective of sentence length and structural complexity – which one would not normally expect of L2 learners at the beginning of their second year of study. Dummy-subject sentences, for example, are often particularly problematic for non-expert Spanish speakers who are used to pro-drop; and *that* clauses frequently become **what* clauses due to the fact that the two are homonyms in Spanish. The past simple/present perfect distinction does not function the same way in Spanish as in English and yet in the sample there are signs that learners are picking up L2 norms – for example present perfect for personal experience as in 2C (*I've never experienced...*). Furthermore, no traditional structurally informed syllabus for beginners would ever have dared include the range of conditionals, of modals or of connectors represented in the corpus of learner texts.

As noted, there are still problems with accuracy. Related to this fact, we need to raise two further issues, in the form of deficit theories, which form-based instruction has traditionally taken as a rationale for the thesis that structural items necessitate implicit attention. The first argument relates to *fossilisation*, or, to put it simply, the idea that if errors are not corrected they will become entrenched. When initially proposed, this notion appeared extremely attractive (Seliger 1978; Selinker & Lamadella 1978; Vigil & Oller 1976) yet while it has been the subject of much discussion it has never really progressed beyond "a vague concept which lacks significant scientific underpinnings" (DeKeyser 2005: 12). Another pro-form argument, frequently linked to fossilisation, relates to what was initially termed *pidginisation* (Schumann 1978) which posits that without form-focused episodes learners might stabilise at a "plateau" (eg. Ellis 1990: 52; Pica 1984: 73), which, although it would render them communicatively efficient, would be hampered by restrictive simplification and result in a deficient repertoire, lacking more elaborated structures.

It may well be, however, that the integration of content helps to minimise the likelihood of these two scenarios. Selinker himself suggested that "catching learners at the beginning of (academic) discourse domains might lower the fossilisation curve" (1984, in 1992: 252). Longitudinal immersion research has provided evidence that bilingual students are continually reformulating their interlanguage as new and increasingly complicated academic tasks demand more precise responses, hence providing opportunities for natural spontaneous noticing and remedial evolution (Harley 1992; Serra 2007).

The corpus obtained in the present study contains frequent examples demonstrating clear emergent abilities with regard to more complex grammar such as subordination, conjunctions and modification (especially if we remember that these are learners who have only had one year of bilingual instruction). Consider 2A: *It is not really populated but it is not small populated either* or 1B: *He was an adventurer who was looking for a new and quicker route to China but instead he dicovvered America* or 3C: *The climate change is the most important problem in the world at the moment and we have to save our planet if we want to live here.* Of course, more longitudinal studies will be necessary to gauge the degree to which these abilities are refined.

One final point needs to be made in this section: When we talk of learner interlanguage we conceive of "some sort of in-between language or grammar" (Selinker 1992: 2), *en route* to, but falling short of, competence. Nonetheless, fuelled by the recognition of the quintessence of non-native speakerhood, the last few years have seen a re-conceptualisation of this idea. Emerging descriptions of English as an International Language (aka English as a Lingua Franca) (Jenkins 2004, 2006a, 2006b; McKay 2003; Seidlhofer 2001, 2003, 2004; Seidlhofer, Breiteneder & Pitzl 2006) are contributing towards an alternative, non-deficit view, of competence. A more realistic attitude to error, such as the *let-it-pass* principle (Seidhofer 2004), could help to reduce the anxiety which strict adherence to NS standards often entails. It would also conflate with the primacy of content in CLIL.

4. Conclusion

This chapter focuses on second language development within Content and Language Integrated Learning in an attempt to identify features which can contribute to the elaboration of CLIL theory. At the outset we noted that the vehicular use of the L2 in content learning makes it an approach which implies authentic, meaningful use of the language and as such conflates with communicative goals. The analysis of the corpus of texts underlines this idea: when presented with the prompts the respondents were not told where our interests lay and they appear to have interpreted them as genuine requests for content information (which of course they were). The resulting texts display considerable abilities in recognising and responding to communicative need while also clearly demonstrating the primacy of that need. This is seen in relation to three key terms in the psycholinguistics of second language: restructuring, transfer and interlanguage. From the evidence provided a number of implications follow for CLIL implementation.

The first concerns CLIL syllabus construction. The data and interpretation provided lead us to suggest that in expressing academic content learners turn to the language system as a whole and employ structures which could not be foreseen in a mainstream formal language syllabus consisting of sentential grammar items. It would appear that the primary compulsory language in CLIL might more fruitfully be represented by notions (equality, duration, possibility, dependence and so on and so forth). Above all, students need to activate semantic categories for content learning and as the grammatical expression of these categories is multifaceted any approach to grammar needs to be flexible. On reflection, it does make sense that a meaning-oriented approach such as CLIL would be predicated on semantic structure, much better represented by the whole concept of notion than grammar. If this hypothesis holds, the implications for CLIL syllabus construction are obvious.

The second point relates to the relationship between L1 and L2 knowledge. The learner corpus contained both L1 and L2 responses to each prompt and we were clearly able to identify frequent evidence of positive transfer. From this it follows that it is crucial that integration include and incorporate L1 development – after all, the goal is *bilingual* education. From this perspective CLIL can be seen as highly compatible with the idea of *Languages Across the Curriculum*, a pan-curricular approach to language development which recognises the essentially linguistic nature of learning and which, alongside CLIL, has recently been the focus of European language planning initiatives (see Grenfell 2002; Kolodziejska & Simpson 2002; Vollmer 2006).

Finally, the question of second language development is inextricably tied up with the eternal linguistic diametric between prescription and description. From this perspective the learner texts serve to demonstrate the dangers of extremism: if one adopts a traditional, accuracy-based prescriptive stance, the linguistic errors in the corpus could blind one to the evidence of content learning which they contain. Conversely, a purely descriptive approach would belittle the need for learners to be continually reflecting upon and reformulating both concepts and their linguistic expression.

References

Admiraal, W., Westhoff, G. & de Bot, K. 2006. Evaluation of bilingual secondary education in the Netherlands: Students' language proficiency in English. *Educational Research and Evaluation* 12(1): 75–93.

Allen, F. & Davies, B. 2009. Vocational options: The impact of a vocational context on teaching and learning modern foreign languages at Key Stage 4. *Language Learning Journal* 37(1): 51–70.

Baetens Beardsmore, H. 2002. The significance of CLIL/EMILE. In *CLIL/EMILE The European Dimension – Action, Trends and Foresight Potential,* D. Marsh (ed.), 20–26. Jyväskylä: University of Jyväskylä.

Bygate, M. 1999. Task as context for the framing, reframing and unframing of language. *System* 27: 33–48.

Cummins, J. 1979. Cognitive/academic language proficiency, linguistic interdependence, the optimum age question and some other matters. *Working Papers on Bilingualism* 19: 121–129.

Cummins, J. 1981. The role of primary language development in promoting educational success for language minority students. In *Schooling and Language Minority Students: A Theoretical Framework,* California State Board for Education (eds), 3–49. Los Angeles CA: California State University, Evaluation, Dissemination, and Assessment Center.

Cummins, J. 1984. Bilingualism *and Special Education: Issues in Assessment and Pedagogy.* Clevedon: Multilingual Matters.

Dalton-Puffer, C. 2008. Outcomes and processes in Content and Language Integrated Learning (CLIL): Current research from Europe. In *Future Perspectives for English Language Teaching,* W. Delanoy & L. Volkmann (eds), 139–157. Heidelberg: Carl Winter.

Dalton-Puffer, C. 2007. *Discourse in Content and Language Integrated Learning (CLIL) Classrooms* [Language Learning & Language Teaching 20]. Amsterdam: John Benjamins.

Dalton-Puffer, C. & Nikula, T. (eds). 2006. *VIEWS. Vienna English Working Papers* 15(3). (Special issue: *Current Research on CLIL*).

Dalton-Puffer, C. & Smit, U. 2007. *Empirical Perspectives on CLIL Classroom Discourse.* Frankfurt: Peter Lang.

DeKeyser, R. 2005. What makes learning second language grammar difficult? A review of issues. *Language Learning* 55(1): 1–25.

Doughty, C. & Long, M. (eds.). 2003. *The Handbook of Second Language Acquisition.* Malden MA: Blackwell.

Dufficy, P. 2004. Predisposition to choose: The language of an information gap task in a multilingual primary classroom. *Language Teaching Research* 8(3): 241–261.

Ellis, R. 1990. *Instructed Second Language Acquisition: Learning in the Classroom.* Oxford: Blackwell.

Friesen, D.C. & Jared, D. 2007. Cross-language message and word-level transfer effects in bilingual text processing. *Memory and Cognition* 35(7): 1542–1556.

Gass, S. & Selinker, L. (eds). 1983. *Language Transfer in Language Learning. Issues in Second Language Research.* Rowley MA: Newbury House.

Grenfell, M. (ed.). 2002. *Modern Languages across the Curriculum*. London: Routledge.

Halliday, M.A.K. 1975. *Learning how to Mean: Explorations in the Development of Language*. London: Edward Arnold.

Harley, B. 1992. Patterns of second language development in French immersion. *Journal of French Language Studies* 2: 159–183.

Järvinen, H–M. 2005. Language learning in Content-Based Instruction. In *Investigations in Instructed Second Language Acquisition,* A. Housen & M. Pierrard (eds), 433–456. Berlin: Walter de Gruyter.

Jenkins, J. 2004. ELF at the gate: The position of English as a Lingua Franca. In *IATEFL Liverpool Conference Selections,* A. Pulverness, (ed.), 33–42. Kent: IATEFL.

Jenkins, J. 2006a. Current perspectives on teaching World Englishes and English as a Lingua Franca. *TESOL Quarterly* 40(1): 157–181.

Jenkins, J. 2006b. Points of view and blind spots: ELF and SLA. *International Journal of Applied Linguistics* 16(2): 137–162.

Kellerman, E. 1995. Crosslinguistic influence: Transfer to nowhere? *Annual Review of Applied Linguistics* 15: 125–150.

Kolodziejska, E. & Simpson, S. 2002. *Language across the Curriculum: Network Processing and Material Production in an International Context.* Graz: European Centre for Modern Languages and Council of Europe.

Lasagabaster, D. & Sierra, J.M. 2009. Language attitudes in CLIL and traditional FL classes. *International Journal of CLIL Research* 1(2): 4–17.

Lorenzo, F. 2007. An analytical framework of language integration in L2-content based courses. *Language and Education* 22: 502–15.

Lorenzo, F. 2008. Instructional discourse in bilingual settings. An empirical study of linguistic adjustments in content and language integrated learning. *Language Learning Journal* 36: 21–33.

Lorenzo, F., Casal, S. & Moore, P. 2010. The effects of Content and Language Integrated Learning (CLIL) in European education: Key findings from the Andalusian bilingual sections evaluation project. *Applied Linguistics* 31(3): 418–442.

Loschky, L. & Bley-Vroman, R. 1993. Grammar and task-based methodology. In *Tasks and Language Learning: Integrating Theory and Practice,* G. Crookes & S. Gass (eds), 123–167. Clevedon: Multilingual Matters.

Lyster, R. 1998. Form in immersion classroom discourse: In or out of focus? *Canadian Journal of Applied Linguistics* 20: 53–82.

Markee, N. 2001. The diffusion of innovation. In *Innovation in English Language Teaching,* D. Hall & A. Hewings (eds), 118–126. London: Routledge, Macquarie University and the Open University.

Marian, V. & Kaushanskaya, M. 2007. Cross linguistic transfer and borrowing in bilinguals. *Applied Psycholinguistics* 28: 369–390.

Mariotti, C. 2006. Negotiated interactions and repair. *VIEWS. Vienna English Working Papers* 15(3): 33–39.

Marsh, D. 2008. Language awareness and CLIL. In *Encyclopedia of Language and Education,* 2nd edn, Vol. 6: *Knowledge about Language,* J. Cenoz & N.H. Hornberger (eds.), 233–246. Oxford: Elsevier.

Marsh, D., Nikula, T., Takala, S., Rohiola, U. & Koivisto, T. 1997. *Language Teacher Training and Bilingual Education in Finland.* <http://userpage.fu-berlin.de/~elc/tnp1/SP6NatRepFI.pdf>.

McKay, S. 2003. Towards an appropriate EIL methodology: Re-examining common ELT assumptions. *International Journal of Applied Linguistics* 13(1): 1–22.

Merisuo-Storm, T. 2007. Pupils' attitudes towards foreign-language learning and the development of literacy skills in bilingual education. *Teaching and Teacher Education* 23(2): 226–235.

Mohan, B. 1986. *Language and Content*. Reading MA: Addison-Wesley.

Mohan, B. 1989. Knowledge structures and academic discourse. *Word* 40(1–2): 89–105.

Mohan, B. 2007. Knowledge structures in social practice. In *International Handbook of English Language Teaching*, J. Cummins & C. Davison (eds), 303–316. Berlin: Springer.

Mohan, B. & Beckett, G. 2003. A functional approach to research on Content-Based Language Learning: Recasts in causal explanations. *The Modern Language Journal* 87(3): 421–432.

Morgan, C. 1999. Teaching history in a foreign language: What language? In *Learning through a Foreign Language: Materials, Methods and Outcomes*, J. Masih (ed.), 30–45. Lancaster: CILT (Centre for Information on Language Testing and Research).

Nikula, T. 2005. English as an object and tool of study in classrooms: Interactional effects and pragmatic implications. *Linguistics and Education* 16(1): 27–58.

Nikula, T. 2007. Speaking English in Finnish content-based classrooms. *World Englishes* 26(2): 206–223.

Odlin, T. 1985. *Language Transfer: Cross-linguistic Issues in Language Learning*. Cambridge: CUP.

Odlin, T. 2003. Cross-linguistic transfer. In *The Handbook of Second Language Acquisition*, C. Doughty & M. Long (eds), 436–486. Oxford: Blackwell.

Olivares, R.A. 2002. Communication, constructivism and transfer of knowledge. *International Journal of Bilingualism and Bilingual Education* 5(1): 4–19.

Pérez Vidal, C. 2007. The need for focus on form in content and language integrated approaches: An exploratory study. In *Models and Practice in CLIL*, F. Lorenzo, S. Casal, V. Alba-Quiñones & P. Moore (eds), 39–54. Rioja: Revista Española de Lingüística Aplicada (RESLA).

Pica, T. 1984. Questions from the language classroom: Research perspectives. *TESOL Quarterly* 28(1): 49–79.

Schumann, J. 1978. *The Pidginization Process: A Model for Second Language Acquisition*. Rowley MA: Newbury House.

Seidlhofer, B. 2001. Closing a conceptual gap: The case for a description of English as a Lingua Franca. *International Journal of Applied Linguistics* 11(2): 133–158.

Seidlhofer, B. 2003. *A Concept of International English and Related Issues: From 'Real English' to 'Realistic English'?* Strasbourg: Language Policy Division – Council of Europe.

Seidlhofer, B. 2004. Research perspectives on teaching English as a Lingua Franca. *Annual Review of Applied Linguistics* 24: 209–239.

Seidlhofer, B., Breiteneder, A. & Pitzl, M.L. 2006. English as a Lingua Franca in Europe: Challenges for applied linguistics. *Annual Review of Applied Linguistics* 26: 3–34.

Seikkula-Leino, J. 2007. CLIL learning: Achievement levels and affective factors. *Language and Education* 21(4): 328–341.

Seliger, H. 1978. Implications of multiple critical periods hypothesis for second language learning. In *Second Language Acquisition Research*, W. Ritchie (ed.), 11–19. New York NY: Academic Press.

Selinker, L. 1992. *Rediscovering Interlanguage*. London: Longman.

Selinker, L. & Lamendella, J. 1978. Two perspectives on fossilization in interlanguage learning. *Interlanguage Studies Bulletin* 3(2): 143–191.

Serra, C. 2007. Assessing CLIL in primary school: A longitudinal study. *The International Journal of Bilingual Education and Bilingualism* 10(5): 582–602.

Van de Craen, P., Mondt, K., Allain, L. & Gao, Y. 2007. Why and how CLIL works. An outline for a CLIL theory. *VIEWS. Vienna English Working Papers* 16(3): 70–79.

Verhoeven, L. 2007. Early bilingualism, language transfer and phonological awareness. *Applied Psycholinguistics* 28(3): 425–459.

Vigil, N. & Oller, J. 1976. Rule fossilization: A tentative model. *Language Learning* 26(2): 281–295.

Vollmer, H. 2008. Constructing tasks for Content and Language Integrated assessment. In *Research on Task-based Language Learning and Teaching. Theoretical, Methodological and Pedagogical Perspectives*, J. Eckerth & S. Siekmann (eds.), 227–290. Frankfurt: Peter Lang.

Vollmer, H. (ed.). 2006. *Language across the Curriculum*. Strasbourg: Language Policy Division.

Wesche, M. 2002. Early French immersion: How has the original Canadian model stood the test of time? In *An Integrated View of Language Development: Papers in Honour of Henning Wode*, P. Burmeister, T. Piske & A. Rohde (eds), 357–379. Berlin: Wissenschaftlicher Verlag Traer.

Wilkins, D. 1976. *Notional Syllabuses*. Oxford: OUP.

Wolff, D. 2002. On the importance of CLIL in the context of the debate on plurilingual education in the European Union. In *CLIL/EMILE the European Dimension – Action, Trends and Foresight Potential*, D. Marsh (ed.), 44–48. Jyväskylä: University of Jyväskylä.

The pragmatics of L2 in CLIL

Didier Maillat
Université de Fribourg, Switzerland

Results, drawn from naturally occurring classroom interactions in CLIL environments collected in Switzerland, are used to argue that a theoretical proposal can be made about the specific impact that CLIL has on second language learning. Based on the observation of a combination of qualitative and quantitative data, it will be claimed that CLIL offers a learning environment which favourably influences the conditions of L2 use and, therefore, its acquisition.

Specifically, the model suggested here argues for a pragmatic effect – the *mask effect* – which is taken to facilitate the spoken production of CLIL students. This effect is related to current research in the cognitive psychology of bilingualism as it links the *mask effect* with an ability to focus on the relevant aspects of the task at hand while inhibiting irrelevant ones.

1. Introduction

In this paper, I want to use insights drawn from the analysis of naturally occurring classroom interactions in CLIL environment in order to discuss the input of the pragmatic module in language acquisition processes. In particular, I will argue that the specific conditions of language use set by CLIL give rise to a pragmatic effect which favours acquisition by lowering the affective filter.

In the first part of the paper, an alternative interface between pragmatics and SLA is introduced which proposes that pragmatic principles are partly guiding the acquisitional processes as they have to compensate for a reduced proficiency in L2.

A series of observations is then used to determine a specific set of conditions in L2 use under which the spoken production of immersion students appears to be stimulated well beyond the minimal one-word or one-syntactic-constituent turns which are often regarded as being the pitfall of the spoken production of immersion students (see e.g. Cummins & Swain 1986; Genesee 2004).

I will then proceed to offer a pragmatic account of the relevant data and argue that there is a specific pragmatic response to the conditions of use determined by CLIL environments. This pragmatic effect is referred to as the *mask effect*. In the last part of the discussion, a quantitative survey will be used to track down the impact that the *mask effect* has in the longer term on the language competence of the students.

In the last section of the paper, an argument will be put forward which draws a parallel between the pragmatic and communicative phenomena observed and higher-order skills. In particular, I will argue that the *mask effect* constitutes a pragmatic component of a much wider-ranging cognitive skill induced in bilingual environments.[1]

2.   Which pragmatics of SLA?

At the interface where the two fields of Pragmatics and Language Acquisition meet, researchers have paid specific attention to the type of relationship which holds either between First Language Acquisition (FLA) and the competence required to use language in context (see Clark 2004 for a review), or between Second Language Acquisition and the kind of knowledge required to use that second language (L2) in context (see Alcón & Martinez-Flor 2008; Nikula 2008; Kasper 1989, 1996; Kasper & Rose 2002). In other words, the pragmatics of Language Acquisition is mostly interested in the acquisition of pragmatic skills and their appropriate application in either L1 or L2.

A good example of the first type of accounts is found below. In such an approach the child's acquisition processes as he gradually builds up his skills as a language user constitute the object of study. Clark (2004: 563) writes that she focuses on the development of pragmatic knowledge as a child acquires communicative skills. As a consequence, her contribution to the pragmatics of language acquisition looks at

> some aspects of pragmatic development and the evidence that children are attending to speaker intentions on the one hand, and to what the addressee already knows on the other. Attending to these factors in an exchange requires that children make use of common ground, updating it as needed; it also requires that they take note of speech acts, and learn which inferences to draw from what speakers do and don't say [...].

In other words, Clark is interested in the acquisition of pragmatic skills in L1.

At the interface between pragmatics and SLA on the other hand, Kasper, as well as Blum-Kulka (Blum-Kulka 1982; Blum-Kulka et al. 1989; Kasper 1989, 1996; Kasper & Blum-Kulka 1993a, 1993b) make a claim for studies which touch

---

1.   I wish to thank the editors and two anonymous reviewers for their careful reading of earlier versions of this paper. Their discussion and feedback have greatly contributed to the presentation of the ideas I argue for. The usual caveat remains.

upon the domain of interlanguage pragmatics. Kasper and her colleagues (see also Kasper & Rose 2002) define interlanguage pragmatics as a relatively new branch of linguistics that studies the acquisition of the competence to carry out linguistic actions in an L2.[2] That is to say the exact L2 equivalent of Clark's perspective. This particular focus is sometimes presented as trying to account for the acquisition of Hymes' communicative competence (see Hymes 1972) from a productive and receptive point of view. In this framework, pragmatics is regarded as one component of language competence that must be mastered by learners in order to reach full competence in L2 (see also Schauer 2006). A similar idea is entertained by e.g. Jarvis & Pavlenko (2008: 106–7; see also Bachman 1990), who write about a form of pragmatic competence which consists of both a sociolinguistic and an illocutionary component. This competence is inherently part of our communicative competence in L1, and it is taken to bear on the learner's competence in L2 as pragmatic transfers take place from L1.

The perspective adopted here differs from these approaches in that I want to investigate how pragmatic principles are used to overcome the limitations experienced by the learner in L2. This type of pragmatic analysis of acquisitional processes is cognate with the work carried out within the theoretical framework of optimality theory as discussed in e.g. Blutner & Zeevat (2003) where optimisation processes in L1 and L2 are re-analysed in terms of a bidirectional process. By bidirectionality it is understood that information generated through the interpretative processes can feed back into the structural knowledge of the language that the learner builds (see Blutner 2000; Jäger 2004). In other words this type of model assumes that interpretative processes can (re-)shape the language system of the learner. In this sense it contrasts sharply with a model of acquisition that regards pragmatics as a module which works independently of the core modules (morphology, syntax, phonology, semantics, lexicon) as a last meaning enrichment process. Jäger (2004), in particular, shows how pragmatic constraints on morpho-syntactic case markers can lead to their grammaticalisation. Thus, OT investigates how pragmatic constraints can affect the learning algorithm.

As a point of departure I would like to consider the very foundations of pragmatics. In his book on *Presumptive Meanings*, Levinson (2000) justifies the need for a pragmatic engine through the existence of what he calls a 'bottleneck' in human communication. He writes:

> The central background fact, an information-theoretic observation, is that human speech encoding is relatively very slow: the actual process of phonetic articulation is a bottleneck in a system that can otherwise run about four times faster […].

---

2. L2 stands for any language which is learned after L1. In this sense, it can be understood as standing for L2, L3, etc. In the remainder of this paper, I will gloss over this distinction.

> Now the solution to the encoding bottleneck [...] is just this: [...] find a way to piggyback meaning on top of the meaning.   (Levinson 2000: 6)

Levinson (2000) goes on to argue for the evolutionary inevitability of the pragmatic heuristics which allow human beings to overcome the limitation of the language encoding system through inferential processes. In the neo-Gricean model he develops, he proposes that there are three essential heuristics underlying human inferences:

1. Q-Principle 'What isn't said, isn't'.
2. I-Principle 'What is simply described is stereotypically exemplified'.
3. M-Principle 'What's said in an abnormal way, isn't normal'.

Thereby, re-defining the original principles governing language use that were first formulated by Grice (1957; see also Horn 1984, 2004). That neo-Griceans should do with 3 heuristics for what Grice sought to capture with one principle and 4 maxims is not what is at stake here. Instead, I wish to argue that the very basic explanation provided above by Levinson (2000) straightforwardly describes why pragmatics should occupy a very central position in the investigations of language acquisition, not so much as a particular sub-component of the language competence – be it in L1 or in L2 – but rather as a key cognitive system which governs production and comprehension during the intermediate acquisitional stages. This, I will claim, constitutes another form of pragmatic approach to SLA and it will constitute the line taken in this paper.

Let me clarify this point by quickly going back to Levinson's earlier metaphor. It could be said that during second language acquisition, additional constraints bear on the L2 language system. Typically, what characterises the language system of an L2 learner, for instance, is that it is under considerable pressure at a lexical, semantic, syntactic, morphological, and phonological level, to convey a particular thought through words. To pursue Levinson's image, the bottleneck in L2 learning contexts is much narrower than in normal – L1 – communication environments. It follows, by extension of Levinson's rationale, that the inferential engine of the human cognitive system will have to compensate for even greater limitations. That is to say, using Selinker's original terminology (1972), that interlanguage systems rely more heavily on pragmatic enrichment of meaning; or, to put it differently, that the coarser, the more rudimentary a learner's language is, the more she will depend on inferential processes to make up for the limitation of that same system.

In fact, that this should be the case follows quite inevitably from the object of study that pragmatics has set for itself. Pragmatics focuses on the principles governing the construction of meaning in context, or in use. In that respect, the acquisition phase sets very different conditions on language use and it can be legitimately expected that during acquisition the new – more limiting – conditions will bear on language use. As a consequence we expect specific pragmatic strategies to arise in order to calculate meaning in use, i.e. in order to either produce or comprehend the intended meaning. In addition we predict that the same general pragmatic principles which govern unmarked forms of language use will apply here and will yield the appropriate inferences that will compensate for the narrower bottleneck constituted by L2.

Assuming that this claim is on the right track, it ensues that the theoretical models and tools developed in pragmatics should provide the SLA researcher with the adequate descriptive apparatus required in order to understand the intensive and fundamental inferential work imposed on the learner by the limitation of his language system. For example, if we go back to the three neo-Gricean heuristics presented above, we can see how the strained interlanguage system of a learner will put each heuristic under higher pressure. This is particularly true with respect to production situations. Thus, lexical gaps may jeopardise the applicability of the Q-heuristic, while a necessarily simplified syntactic output may weaken the I-heuristic. For instance, when producing an utterance, a learner may omit some important pieces of information not because they do not exist, as would be inferred from the Q-heuristic, but because the adequate lexical entries fail him; or, when describing an abnormal – non-stereotypical – scene, a learner might use only the standard, simple form he knows, thereby breaking the I-heuristic.

As I already emphasised above, the actual pragmatic model within which the discussion is couched is irrelevant at this point. In Grice's original account, a limited language system can be regarded as increasing the stress on the maxim of quantity (e.g. the learner may not always be able to provide the right amount of information and might settle for a less informative utterance) or she might have to bypass some of the sub-components that make up the maxim of manner (e.g. when she fails to disambiguate her utterance due to lexical shortcomings).

Similarly, within the framework of Relevance theory (Carston 2002; Sperber & Wilson 1995), the Gricean model has been reduced to one overarching principle of optimal relevance which is assessed as an optimal balance between cognitive efforts required to process the utterance's meaning and the cognitive effects generated by the interpretation of that same utterance. The model could be said to combine two heuristics: (1) *Minimise cognitive effort*; (2) *Maximise cognitive effect*. Accordingly, the learner's language system will upset the search for optimal relevance as it will put more strain on the first heuristic, requiring more effort to process the utterance. As can be seen in the previous paragraphs, the legitimisation of a pragmatic effect on language learning is not the result of one's adopting a particular theoretical framework. On the contrary, it appears to capture a fundamental aspect of language learning. Incidentally, according to Sperber & Wilson (1995), the model they develop has an overall cognitive validity. That is to say that, in their view, pragmatic principles are regarded as reflecting more general cognitive processes which regulate the use of cognitive resources. The last section of this paper will draw on the underlying cognitive nature of pragmatic heuristics, as I will show how a cognitively grounded theory of pragmatics can use insights from cognitive psychology to explain some of the effects that influence language learning, more specifically Content and Language Integrated Learning.

Generally, the main consequence of this type of pragmatic approach to an SLA framework is that all Gricean and post-Gricean traditions expect that the typical limited command of L2 achieved by the learner will put extra stress on the system. Effectively, there will be an increased tension between the learner's communicative intention and the requirements of the heuristics. In other words, L2 will require that some specific strategies are used to satisfy the principles with fewer linguistic options. The second consequence of the application of these principles while processing utterances in an L2 is that it will give rise to new specific uses of the heuristics to overcome the communicative limitations in L2.

In this paper, I will explore the latter line of enquiry as I will consider the contribution that pragmatics can make to a better understanding of late second language acquisition within a CLIL educational environment. In other words, I will not look at the development of pragmatic competence as highlighted in the quotation from Clark (2004) but I propose to study some pragmatically-derived strategies within a CLIL environment instead. As the perspective outlined in the preceding paragraphs has attracted little attention to this date, I propose to show how a pragmatic theory of SLA can contribute to our understanding of language learning in the classroom by focussing on language learning as it takes place in a CLIL environment. Indeed, CLIL can be regarded as imposing a specific environment on L2 use thereby determining particular pragmatic processes. In the remainder of this paper, I wish to test the applicability of the theoretical framework briefly sketched above in order to understand some phenomena observed in CLIL settings. Thus, the goal pursued here will be to identify and analyse some of the specific constraints set on language use in CLIL environments and how they give rise to specific pragmatic strategies. More precisely, I wish to investigate the hypothesis that the specific learning environment of CLIL – i.e. conditions on L2 use – might have a positive impact on the contextual pressure which affects the learner's L2 system – i.e. the conditions of L2 learning. In other words, I will suggest that CLIL can have a facilitating effect on language learning by relieving some of the added – L2-induced – stress bearing on the language system.[3]

---

3.   In other words, it is argued that the CLIL bottleneck differs from other L2 bottlenecks, which produces a different pragmatic response.

3.   Pragmatic effects in CLIL

As pointed out in Johnson & Swain (1997: 3), any kind of immersion education (of which CLIL is regarded as a specific form) has to (ideally) achieve three distinct goals. The first goal concerns the medium of instruction (L2) in which the student is expected to acquire sufficient proficiency. The second goal is to ensure that the mastery of the subject matter taught through the medium of L2 is not negatively affected by the immersive environment. Third, it is important – especially to parents – that the student's competence in her L1 does not suffer from the educational environment. Following the discussion in Section 1, the focus of this paper will be primarily on the first component as we will consider CLIL as a set of conditions affecting language (i.e. L2) use. Specifically, the productive oral skills of students learning an L2 within a CLIL environment will be under scrutiny.

3.1   Data

For this purpose, I will be considering two sets of data. First, a qualitative analysis of naturally occurring classroom interactions (see Maillat & Gassner 2007; Maillat 2007; Maillat & Serra 2009) was used to identify two contrasting types of spoken production. This data is taken from a corpus of classroom interaction which was collected as part of a research project on "Integrated construction of linguistic and content-based knowledge through bilingual education at secondary and tertiary levels." The corpus (mostly) comprises data from upper-secondary late immersion programmes in Switzerland. The dominant language is either German or French, and the target languages are either German, French or English. The various participating institutions have adopted different types of CLIL programmes which are all, to varying degrees, late partial immersion programmes. The students are aged between 16 and 20.

The collection of this data systematically included a test group as well as a control group which followed a traditional (non-immersive) programme. This comparative design allowed us to identify a certain number of interaction types which did not seem to generate the same kind of production on the part of the students in the test group as those in the control group. The next subsection focuses on these discrepancies.

The second set of data corresponds to a quantitative survey based on a questionnaire handed out to a large sample (N = 235) of test and control subjects at two participating institutions which offered a CLIL programme in English with French as the dominant L1. The questionnaire elicits self-evaluative comments from the participants on various aspects of their attitude towards and proficiency in the target language (English in this instance).

The addition of a second quantitative design provides a second piece of empirical evidence which independently confirms the findings qualitatively derived in the first analysis thereby reinforcing the validity of the initial observations.

3.2   Spoken production or classroom activity?

According to scholars who have looked into these questions, immersive programmes, despite the more extensive exposure to L2, seem to have a moderate impact on the productive skills of the students (Genesee 2004: 552). This statement appears to apply even more strongly to spoken production (see Genesee 2004 for a review). Indeed, the close analysis of classroom interactions taking place in Swiss late secondary CLIL programmes with English as the medium of instruction, in a dominantly francophone environment (in Geneva), has shown (see Gassner & Maillat 2006; Maillat & Gassner 2007; Maillat & Serra 2009) that in some cases the spoken production of CLIL students can be described as sub-sentential, discursively poor or minimal, and relying mostly on bare noun phrases and nominal heads.[4]

However, the same corpus also demonstrates that other forms of interaction can yield a much more advanced spoken output, involving full sentences and, more importantly, exploiting complex discursive strategies. For instance, these exchanges illustrate the use of conversational techniques such as the management of overlaps, and topic management. Students also co-construct utterances and participate in other-initiated completion/repair turns.

In trying to account for the observed variation in spoken output, it would obviously be interesting to try and isolate some of the conditions which give rise to more complex uses of L2, as well as to find out what might explain minimal contributions (see also Nikula 2008). As for the latter type, the analysis shows on the one hand that the floor is overwhelmingly dominated by the teacher and that she frames the discourse so as to constrain the students' production to precisely the kind of turns that were identified earlier. For instance, the teacher uses *wh*-questions which target nominal phrases (e.g. *What else did they grow?* – *Wheat*), thereby conversationally limiting the production to sub-sentential elements. Another constraining frame consists in eliciting repair turns on the part of the students by providing incomplete turns (*Milk sure... milk... milk and some* [rising intonation]... – *Cheese*), which syntactically constrains the output to a bare nominal head. As can be seen from the

---

4.   The data discussed here is part of the corpus collected in a research project entitled "Integrated Construction of linguistic and content-based knowledge through bilingual education at secondary and tertiary levels" (FNS no 405640–108656) funded by the Swiss National Science Foundation which was presented in Section 3.1 above.

above examples, this type of classroom interaction strongly influences the spoken production of students.

The following excerpt illustrates the very phenomena we have just highlighted during a CLIL history class with English as the target language and French as the dominant language. This is a good example of a kind of interaction which formats and limits the students' spoken production (in bold below).

Excerpt 1. History class in CLIL taught in English to second-year students in a late immersion programme with French as the mainstream language (Ens=teacher; E=students; [=overlap).

1-	(…).	what's the modern times by the way/ (silence) Anastasia
2-E		our time/
3-Ens		not at all. very good mistake. modern times is not our time. ok/
4-E		[before the contemporary
5-E		[ah
6-E		just before
7-E		just before the contemporary
8-Ens		**ye:s (3 sec) before the contemporary period. exactly what did you want to say Tanja/**
9-E		XX middle ages
10-Ens		**exactly. do you remember we have the antiquity/. after the antiquity what do we have/**
11-E		middle age
12-Ens		**the middle ages. which finish when/**
13-E		[ah
14-E		[1492
15-E		[discovery
16-E		[ah
17-Ens		yes. exactly. 1492. discovery of America by Mister/
18-E		[Columbus

In this context, it would be interesting to study to what extent the double nature of CLIL favours constraining exchanges of the kind discussed here as the teacher simultaneously tries to introduce a new topic and to provide the students with the necessary lexical background. The qualitative analysis which was referred to above does not provide the relevant quantitative information to corroborate or contradict the hypothesis which posits that CLIL might have a limiting force on conversational exchanges by favouring constrained turns of the kind discussed here, but it constitutes an exciting area for future research on the effect of the interactional patterns used specifically in CLIL classrooms.

When it comes to identifying the kind of classroom interaction which seems to have a positive impact on the spoken production of CLIL students, there are a few observations which are particularly worth mentioning as they are relevant for our purposes.

First of all, the very same topic can give rise to diametrically different spoken productions depending on the kind of discursive framework used. Thus, whereas CLIL students contributed mere concepts – expressed as bare NPs – when asked to find arguments for and against colonisation during a history class, the same group of students engaged in an advanced, elaborate conversational joust when asked to express these arguments in a role-play involving colonisers and colonised. In the following excerpt we see how the teacher's contributions are in the background while the students produce much more elaborate turns.

Excerpt 2. History class in CLIL taught in English to second-year students in a late immersion programme with French as the mainstream language (Ens=teacher; E=students; [=overlap).

Ens	so Anastasia you wanted to say something
E	Tanja
Ens	Tanja [what did you write
E	[they want him to bring ah: comfort to the civilisation that didn't know it
Ens	mmh
E	that manufacture goods and so on
Ens	is it. was it a success/
E	yes they did
Ens	sure Irina
E	they really X
Ens	they did improve the style of life
Es	yes
Ens	and so on. yes (Xname Xname)
E1	XXX that ah (Xname) but it's a reality that they are uncivilised and we have to teach them ah: the our way of life and ah: how to be ah: like ah like us to be human and ah:

Laughter

E1	because these ah: they don't know how to read how to write they are always quarrelling they they live like 200 years ago
E	it's not because the are like this that we have to be racist with them
E1	no we are helping them

Second, the much richer type of interaction described earlier was triggered in a biology class (CLIL) during an activity in which pairs of students were asked to play the role of two CEOs promoting the genetically modified organisms produced by their firm in front of an audience of potential customers (played by the rest of the class and the teacher). This type of evidence converges with the previous observation on a possible link between role-play activities and spoken production in CLIL.

Finally, when the same biology teacher ran the very same role-play activity in the control – i.e. non-CLIL – class with French as the medium of instruction, the kind of output generated by the students was astonishingly much more limited even though they had to 'perform' in the dominant L1. In this second case, we see students adopting fairly complex conversational structures in the presentation proper (i.e. the part which they prepared at home), and limiting themselves to minimal turns in the (absence of topic management, absence of role re-assignment, absence of complex overlaps and other-initiated turn completions).

3.3   Through the bottleneck: The pragmatics of CLIL

Through these observations, we see that the spoken production of CLIL students seems to benefit greatly from role-play activities. Coming back to our earlier theoretical claims, it appears that the specific conditions that CLIL imposes on L2 use seem to combine advantageously with role-play in that it liberates, as it were, the spoken production of the students. I will argue that this is the result of a particular pragmatic effect which efficiently releases some of the constraints bearing on the learner (i.e. widens the bottleneck). That is to say, that the strong contrast noted in role-play activities in L2 CLIL environments is assumed to give us a rare insight into the *specific* pragmatic strategies applied by the CLIL learner to overcome the limitations in her L2. Furthermore, I claim that the observed facility in role-play is also indicative of a cognitive advantage in the learning process. Let us first look at the former argument.

As pointed out earlier, the positive effect of role-play on the spoken output appears to be greater in L2 than in L1. These results are to be analysed in connection with other observations made in the literature on SLA. Chaudron (2003: 781), in a review of techniques used in SLA research, notes for instance that "role plays allowed much more opportunity for the subjects to display their conversational competence, in topic management in particular" (as can be seen in excerpt 2). According to Tabensky (1997: 39), who has worked specifically on role plays in the context of SLA, the positive effect illustrated in the above examples is to be understood in the context of Krashen's (1976, 1981, 1985) notion of *affective filter*. For Tabensky, the combination of L2 and role play can enhance the spoken production of learners as the L2 can offer a kind of refuge from certain anxieties experienced in L1. As he points out, following Krashen, a weak affective filter favours acquisition, whereas a strong affective filter deters it. In view of the evidence quoted earlier, it is claimed that CLIL combines ideally with role play to lower the anxiety felt by the learners, thereby positively affecting their spoken production. In other words, the specificity of L2 use noted in role-play activities in CLIL settings supports the claim that L2 functions as a *mask* (see below) which, in turn, means that L2 functions as an affective filter that lowers anxiety and facilitates learning. This, I claim, explains how the conditions on L2 *use* determined by CLIL can have an impact on L2 *learning*.

The effect that anxiety levels can have on the spoken production in L2 is a well-established phenomenon (see Gardner & McIntyre 1993; Horwitz 2001; Horwitz et al. 1986; Norton 2000; Spolsky 1989). In their overview of factors bearing on language learning, Mitchell & Myles (1998: 24–25) consider the various components posited by Spolsky (1989). Anxiety is mentioned as one of the affective factors, alongside motivation and attitudes, and it is held to have a generally debilitating influence on SLA (see also MacIntyre & Gardner 1989, 1994a, 1994b). Anxiety is also identified in Norton (2000: 122) as affecting primarily spoken production. Interestingly, in her discussion of anxiety, Graham (1997: 93) distinguishes between anxiety as a personality trait and the kind of anxiety which is generated by L2, namely state anxiety, also called *language anxiety*. I argue that it is precisely this latter form of anxiety which is lowered in the contexts discussed previously. Crucially, echoing work done by Horwitz et al. (1986; see also Horwitz 2001), she argues further that language anxiety arises in part from the "frustration and apprehension of the learner who has well-developed thoughts and opinions but a limited second language vocabulary to express them" (Graham 1997: 94); in other words, one of the main sources of anxiety – which is known to hinder acquisition – is, crucially, the awareness that the learner has of the narrower bottleneck induced by L2.

Going back to the first claim made in the first paragraph of this section, it remains to be seen why CLIL would favour such a lowering effect on anxiety in spoken production tasks. As argued earlier, pragmatic heuristics essentially offer a means to compensate the bottleneck defined by Levinson (2000). We saw that by extension the same pragmatic system is assumed to take over in order to overcome an L2-induced bottleneck. Accordingly, it is argued that a pragmatic effect is triggered in an immersive environment like CLIL which releases some of the constraints affecting language use, thereby lowering anxiety as predicted by the definition of 'communication apprehension' suggested by Horwitz et al. (1986). This pragmatic effect is called the *mask effect* and it functions on three distinct pragmatic levels governing discourse contextualisation (see Gassner & Maillat 2006; Maillat 2007; Maillat & Gassner 2007;

Maillat & Serra 2009): the deictic level, the referential level, and the epistemic level. Let us look at these in turn.

On a deictic level, the contextual anchoring of discourse onto a given social hierarchy is withheld allowing personal and social deixis to be reset (Levinson 1983), together with the power relations which are determined within this hierarchy. As a result the constraints governing the use of e.g. politeness markers, terms of address, register, and formality are eased, which actively contributes to lessening the affective filter (i.e. anxiety) experienced by the learner when speaking in L2. A very good example of this phenomenon is found in excerpt 2 above when the student switches to *we/us* when discussing the colonisers' justification. From a discursive perspective, deictic disconnection also allows the learner to re-assign the conversational roles and to question the educational hierarchy between teacher and learner. This form of regained discursive freedom gives rise to the enhanced topic management skills noted in our data and referred to by Chaudron (2003). For example, during the biology class mentioned above where students were asked to play two CEOs, a student effectively gains control over the topic by interrupting the topic-assignment turn attempted by the teacher with 'No wait!', thereby clearly breaking the normal social hierarchy.

Pragmatic principles are also responsible for assigning referents, via a form of contextually determined meaning saturation known as explicature in Sperber & Wilson's framework (1995; Carston 2002). A similar form of contextual disconnection as the one observed on a deictic level releases the constraint on reference assignment. The relevance of this second form of pragmatic loosening is particularly salient in role play activities which crucially rely on the learner's ability to construct an alternative experiential environment (Tabensky 1997: 31). Reference is therefore assigned in an alternative environment in which the referents assigned in normal uses of the language are not affected. This explains the stronger impact that role play activities can have on spoken production as noticed in the contrasting output during two different tasks – only one of which involved playing in role – on the topic of colonisation (see above).

Finally, in the third form of contextual disconnection, the epistemic commitment of the speaker to the validity of her statements is also reduced, which allows a distinction between speaker and learner identities, hence the notion of *mask*. From a theoretical point of view this corresponds to a weakened application of the maxim of quality as defined by Grice (1957) since the learner's own personal beliefs are not affected. Again, even though it is claimed that it is not limited to them, the pertinence of such a pragmatic loosening is particularly strong in role play activities, which explains the observations made earlier.

As pointed out before, the availability of these three types of pragmatic releases on the constraint governing L2 use can be related with role play activities.

Nevertheless, it is claimed that role play activities only exploit the full potential of pragmatic strategies that are *licensed* by the CLIL environment.

Crucially, however, the very possibility of the *mask effect* depends on the status of L2 as the medium of instruction and not as the subject matter as is the case in CLIL. Thus, it is the status of L2 (as the medium and not as the subject) which determines the specific conditions of L2 use in CLIL and which licenses the application of the pragmatic strategies described above under the label *mask effect*. In traditional teaching environments (e.g. EFL) L2 is the subject matter which determines the achievement of the learner in the classroom. In other words, the fact that L2 can function as a 'refuge' to quote Tabensky (1997) and that L2 use relies on specific pragmatic strategies, follows from the fact that, in CLIL, L2 competence is always a non-focal learning target. In a traditional setting, though, L2 competence constitutes the learning goal and determines the learner's success/failure. In this respect, the *mask effect* is much more than a feature of classroom role plays as it is to be linked to more fundamental processes which contribute to a lower affective filter which ultimately facilitates acquisition. Crucially, it is argued that L2 cannot function as a mask in the classical language classroom as it is then associated with the very goal of learning which will increase the affective filter. As a result, the pragmatics of L2 use in the language classroom will not give rise to the *mask effect*. In the following section, I will present independent evidence for the kind of long-term impact that the *mask effect* is posited to have on the spoken production of CLIL students, outside role-play activities.

3.4   Further evidence for the *mask effect*

Evidence of the deep impact the *mask effect* has on L2 competence is found in quantitative data that was collected in the schools in which the classroom investigations reported above took place. A total of 235 students (123 CLIL students and 78 control students; 34 control students were categorised separately in the results because they would not have had the required grades to enter the CLIL programme (they are referred to as 'non-admissible' below) filled in a questionnaire which assessed various motivational and attitudinal factors about L2 (English in this instance; see Maillat & Kohli 2008).[5] This data concerns late partial immersion CLIL students in a 4 year upper-secondary programme with French as the mainstream L1. Students are between 16 and 20 years old.

---

5.   The CLIL and control groups have been normalised with respect to scholarly achievements in order to avoid any bias in favour of the immersion group.

In Table 1 below we see that students who followed the CLIL programme ('immersion') display a stronger desire to actively use their skills in speaking in L2 (92% vs. 71% when you combine the 'as often as possible' and 'sometimes' answers) than control students ('non-immersion'). The contrast is marked more clearly in the highest category (45% vs. 27% selected the 'as often as possible' option). Also, students on the traditional programme indicate that they are much more likely to avoid L2. Although these results describe self-evaluations that would have to be tested in order to check if they correspond to actual behaviours, they clearly demonstrate that CLIL education fosters a greater eagerness to communicate in L2, as a result, it is argued, of the *mask effect* which lowers the affective filter. Most importantly, this kind of evidence shows that the influence that a CLIL environment might have on the spoken production should also be assessed at a metalinguistic level. Thus, when assessing the payoff of a CLIL education in terms of spoken production, one should also consider the higher communicative confidence experienced by the students – which is a direct consequence of a lower anxiety.

Table 1. % of answers to the question 'How often do you try to speak English?' (N=235)

	% non-admissible	% non-immersion	% immersion
as often as possible	14.7	< 26.9	< 4.7
sometimes	50	43.6	47.2
when I have to	32.4	> 25.6	> 4.9
never	2.9	2.6	
		1.3	3.3

Another striking result is that if we separate students according to the year they are in, we clearly see two opposing temporal trends as more and more CLIL students indicate that they seek to speak English 'as often as possible' (up from 32% to 64%) while fewer and fewer students from the control group do so (down from 55% to 10%). I interpret this type of trend as showing the gradual reinforcement of the *mask effect*.

Figure 1 draws a similar picture. It is based on two questions which tried to assess the participants self-assessed willingness to use English in different communicative contexts, with either English as the mother tongue of the interlocutor or English as a lingua franca. Figure 1 illustrates the fact that CLIL students think of themselves as more willing to communicate with native speakers of L2 or to use L2 as a lingua franca. These two categories measure the development of a desire to apply one's multilingual competence in various communicative contexts.

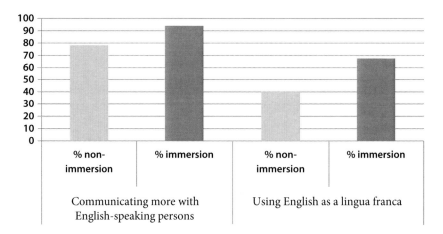

Figure 1. % of positive answers to the question 'Which of the following goals did you reach through your high-school education?' (N=201)

The latter result is particularly interesting (40% vs. 66%) as it shows that whereas a clear majority of CLIL students have developed a sense of multilingual communicative mode through L2, only a minority of students from the control group share that belief.

4.   Conclusion: Cognitive echo

This paper has investigated the specific conditions that CLIL imposes on L2 use. Furthermore, it has shown that these specific constraints give rise to a CLIL-related pragmatic strategy which has a facilitating impact on the spoken production of learners, and more generally on learning processes. Further evidence of the long-term effect of this *mask effect* has been found through an alternative empirical design. In the remaining paragraphs I would like to envisage the possible cognitive underpinnings of these findings.

As was pointed out in the opening section, pragmatics shares many of its most central assumptions with the wider field of cognitive science (see Levinson 2000 or Sperber & Wilson 1995). As a way of concluding on the relevance of pragmatic studies in research on SLA, I wish to pursue a line expressed by Kroll and Sunderman (2003) who argue that there is a continuum of cognitive processes which unites the phenomena that are typically regarded as characteristic of second language acquisition – as would be the case in a late partial immersion programme – and facts that pertain to the proficient mastery of two languages in bilinguals. Furthermore, they believe that the existence of such a continuum will inevitably lead to converging theoretical models which will treat intermediate SLA stages and bilingualism as degrees on a scale of cognitive processes.

Building up on Kroll and Sunderman (2003), it should follow that the pragmatic – and hence cognitive – strategies described above might be reflected in other cognitive processes which have been identified in bilinguals. Bialystok (1991, 2001, 2005) has concentrated most of her research on the cognitive specificity of the bilingual mind. According to her, in the very complex, experimentally grounded evidence available to us in the field of cognitive psychology, there is essentially one feature which distinguishes the cognitive performance of the bilingual child:

> Inhibition is the essential factor in distinguishing the performance of the bilingual children, so it may be that bilingualism exerts its effect primarily on the inhibition component of attention.   (Bialystok 2005: 425)

She goes on to explain that inhibition skills allow for a better allocation of cognitive resources to solve any kind of task at hand. To put it plainly, bilinguals develop an enhanced ability to inhibit irrelevant information and to only focus their attention on relevant elements.

If second language acquisition is a developmental stage on a continuum of cognitive processes which has proficient bilingualism as one pole, the above quotation can be extended to claim that inhibition is a feature associated with the more advanced stages on this continuum. In this view, the pragmatic strategies presented in the preceding sections would best be described as the pragmatic counterpart to the inhibition ability developed by the bilingual mind.[6] In other words, the *mask effect* is a pragmatic inhibitor that allows the L2 learner to concentrate all her cognitive resources on the communicative task at hand and to overcome the L2 bottleneck. Specifically, it consists of a deictic, a referential, and an epistemic inhibitor. That same pragmatic inhibition would also explain the lower anxiety level experienced by learners. As was claimed earlier, the *mask effect* is licensed by the specific conditions bearing on L2 use in CLIL environment – crucially the status of L2 as a medium of instruction – which would put CLIL students this much further on the SLA-bilingualism continuum.

---

6. The technical term 'inhibition' is slightly unfortunate in connection with a pragmatic effect which is said to 'lower anxiety' ! It should be clear, however, that the cognitive skill of 'inhibition' which applies to attention is completely unrelated to the non-theoretical notion of inhibition which corresponds to a form of emotional anxiety.

References

Alcón, E. & Martinez-Flor, A. 2008. Investigating *Pragmatics in Foreign Language Learning, Teaching, and Testing*. Clevedon: Multilingual Matters.

Bachman, L.F. 1990. Fundamental *Considerations in Language Testing*. Oxford: OUP.

Bialystok, E. 1991. *Language Processing in Bilingual Children*. Cambridge: CUP.

Bialystok, E. 2001. *Bilingualism in Development: Language, Literacy & Cognition*. Cambridge: CUP.

Bialystok, E. 2005. Consequences of bilingualism for cognitive development. In *Handbook of Bilingualism: Psycholinguistic Approaches*, J.F. Kroll & A.M.B. de Groot (eds), 417–32. Oxford: OUP.

Blum-Kulka, S. 1982. Learning how to say what you mean in a second language. *Applied Linguistics* 3: 29–59.

Blum-Kulka, S.E., House, J.E. & Kasper, G.E. 1989. *Cross-cultural Pragmatics: Requests and Apologies*. Norwood NJ: Ablex.

Blutner, R. 2000. Some aspects of optimality in natural language interpretation. *Journal of Semantics* 17: 189–216.

Blutner, R. & Zeevat, H. 2003. *Optimality Theory and Pragmatics*. Basingstoke: Palgrave Macmillan.

Carston, R. 2002. *Thoughts and Utterances*. Oxford: Blackwell.

Chaudron, C. 2003. Data collection in SLA research. In *Second Language Acquisition*, J. Doughty & M.H. Long, 762–828. Malden MA: Blackwell.

Clark, E.V. 2004. Pragmatics and language acquisition. In *The Handbook of Pragmatics*, L.R. Horn & G. Ward (eds), 562–577. Oxford: Blackwell.

Cummins, J. & Swain, M. 1986. *Bilingualism in Education*. London: Longman.

Gardner, R.C. & MacIntyre, P.D. 1993. A student's contributions to second-language learning. Part II: Affective variables. *Language Teaching* 26(1), 1–11.

Gassner, D. & Maillat, D. 2006. Spoken competence in CLIL: A pragmatic take on recent Swiss data. *VIEWS. Vienna English Working Papers* 15(3): 15–22.

Genesee, F. 2004. What do we know about bilingual education for majority-language students? In *The Handbook of Bilingualism*, T.K. Bathia & W.C. Ritchie. Oxford: Blackwell.

Graham, S. 1997. *Effective Language Learning: Positive Strategies for Advanced Level Language Learning*. Clevedon: Multilingual Matters.

Grice, H.P. 1957. Meaning. *The Philosophical Review* 66(3): 377–388.

Horn, L.R. 1984. Toward a new taxonomy for pragmatic inference: Q-based and R-based implicatures. In *Meaning, Form and Use in Context*, D. Schiffrin (ed.), 11–42. Washington DC: Georgetown University Press.

Horn, L.R. 2004. Implicature. In *The Handbook of Pragmatics*, L.R. Horn & G. Ward (eds), 3–28. Oxford: Blackwell.

Horn, L.R., & Ward, G.L. (eds). 2004. *The Handbook of Pragmatics*. Malden MA: Oxford: Blackwell.

Horwitz, E.K. 2001. Language anxiety and achievement. *Annual Review of Applied Linguistics* 21: 112–126.

Horwitz, E., Horwitz, M., & Cope, J. 1986. Foreign language classroom anxiety. *Modern Language Journal* 70: 125–32.

Hymes, D. 1972. On communicative competence. In *Sociolinguistics*, J.B. Bride & J. Holmes (eds), 269–293. Harmondsworth: Penguin.

Jäger, G. 2004. Learning constraint sub-hierarchies: The bi-directional gradual learning algorithm. In *Optimality Theory and Pragmatics*, R. Blutner & H. Zeevat (eds), 251–287. Basingstoke: Palgrave Macmillan.

Jarvis, S. & Pavlenko, A. 2008. *Crosslinguistic Influence in Language and Cognition*. London: Routledge.

Johnson, R.K. & Swain, M. 1997. *Immersion Education: International Perspectives*. Cambridge: CUP.

Kasper, G. 1989. Variation in interlanguage speech act realization. In *Variation in Second Language Acquisition: Discourse and Pragmatics*, S. Gass, C. Madden & L. Selinker (eds), 37–58. Clevedon: Multilingual Matters.

Kasper, G. (ed.). 1996. Development of pragmatic competence. *Studies in Second Language Acquisition* 18(2). (Special issue).

Kasper, G. & Blum-Kulka, S. 1993a. *Interlanguage Pragmatics*. Oxford: OUP.

Kasper, G. & Blum-Kulka, S. 1993b. Interlanguage pragmatics: An introduction. In *Interlanguage Pragmatics*, G. Kasper & S. Blum-Kulka (eds), 3–17. Oxford: OUP.

Kasper, G. & Rose, K.R. 2002. *Pragmatic Development in a Second Language*. Oxford: Blackwell.

Krashen, S. 1976. Formal and informal linguistic environments in language acquisition and language learning. *TESOL Quarterly* 10: 157–168.

Krashen, S. 1981. *Second Language Acquisition and Second Language Learning*. Oxford: Pergamon.

Krashen, S. 1985. *The Input Hypothesis: Issues and Implications*. London: Longman.

Kroll, J.F. & Sunderman, G. 2003. Cognitive processes in second language learners and bilinguals: The development of lexical and conceptual representations. In *The Handbook of Second Language Acquisition*, C. Doughty & M.H. Long (eds), 104–129. Malden MA, Oxford: Blackwell.

Levinson, S.C. 2000. *Presumptive Meanings: The Theory of Generalized Conversational Implicature*. Cambridge M: The MIT Press.

Levinson, S.C. 1983. *Pragmatics*. Cambridge: CUP.

MacIntyre, P. & Gardner, R.C. 1989. Anxiety and second language learning: Toward a theoretical clarification. *Language Learning* 39: 251–275.

MacIntyre, P. & Gardner, R.C. 1994a. The effects of induced anxiety on three stages of cognitive processing in computerised vocabulary learning. *Studies in Second Language Acquisition* 16(1): 1–17.

MacIntyre, P. & Gardner, R.C. 1994b. The subtle effects of language anxiety on cognitive processing in the second language. *Language Learning* 44: 283–305.

Maillat, D. 2007. Production, motivation and immersion education: Some recent Swiss data. In *Langues en contexte et en contact: Hommage à Cecilia Serra*, Gajo, L. (ed.). *Cahiers de L'ILSL* 23.

Maillat, D. & Kohli, S. 2008. Immersion tardive partielle en anglais : Motivation, attitudes, auto-évaluation et satisfaction. Presentation given at the *3ème rencontre intersite de l'enseignement bilingue*, Haute-Ecole Pédagogique, Lausanne.

Maillat, D. & Gassner, D. 2007. L2 identity: Language as a mask in immersion education. In *Interaction et pensée: Perspectives dialogiques*, M. Grossen (ed.), 19–25. (Special issue: *Actualités Psychologiques*).

Maillat, D. & Serra C. 2009. Immersive education and cognitive strategies: Can the obstacle be the advantage in a multilingual society? *International Journal of Multilingualism* 6(2): 186–206.

Mitchell, R. & Myles, F. 1998. *Second Language Learning Theories*. London: Arnold.

Nikula, T. 2008. Learning pragmatics in content-based classrooms. In *Investigating Pragmatics in Foreign Language Learning, Teaching, and Testing*, E. Alcón & A. Martinez-Flor (eds), 94–113. Clevedon: Multilingual Matters.

Norton, B. 2000. *Identity and Language Learning: Gender, Ethnicity and Educational Change.* Harlow: Longman.

Schauer, G. 2006. Pragmatic awareness in ESL and EFL contexts: Contrast and development. *Language Learning* 56(2): 269–318.

Selinker, L. 1972. Interlanguage. *International Review of Applied Linguistics in Language Teaching* 10(3): 209–231.

Sperber, D. & Wilson, D. 1995. *Relevance: Communication and Cognition.* London: Blackwell.

Spolsky, B. 1989. *Conditions for Second Language Learning: Introduction to a General Theory.* Oxford: OUP.

Tabensky, A. 1997. *Spontanéité et interaction: Le jeu de rôle dans l'enseignement des langues étrangères.* Paris: L'Harmattan.

PART II

CLIL at the secondary level

A cross-sectional analysis of oral narratives by children with CLIL and non-CLIL instruction

Julia Hüttner & Angelika Rieder-Bünemann
University of Southampton, UK/Universität Wien, Austria

The study presented investigates the English language learning outcomes of 44 German-speaking children in year 3 of secondary school, of whom 22 are in CLIL strands, while the other group follow standard curricula. This investigation focuses on the acquisition of oral narrative competence, using a picture story related by each pupil in German and English as data base. Aspects of language competence investigated include degrees of narrative competence (e.g. mentioning of plot elements, shifting perspectives), morphological/syntactic language regularities (e.g. tense forms) and the use of communicative strategies (i.e. coping with lexical gaps). The results point towards improved oral narrative abilities of CLIL pupils. There are, however, differences in the various competence aspects investigated, indicating that CLIL instruction most markedly affects more complex elements.

1. Introduction

Within Europe, school settings represent the mainstream environments for foreign language learning, with English being the predominantly taught language. Moreover, stakeholders in education are interested in increasing the efficiency of English as a foreign language (EFL) instruction at schools, which has led to the introduction of several new approaches to EFL teaching, including CLIL.

In line with this general European trend, Austrian schools have been introducing CLIL over the last 15 years in a variety of programmes and in diverse intensity. While the belief in the positive effects is strong on the part of the stakeholders involved, empirical research investigating this effect has been lagging behind, but has gained important impulses from, e.g. Dalton-Puffer (2007), Dalton-Puffer & Smit (2007) and Mewald & Spenger (2005). Importantly, the issue of precisely which differences can be observed in the performance of pupils attending CLIL strands of education and those attending regular strands needs further investigation. This should help establish whether the reported beneficial effects of CLIL (cf. e.g. Lasagabaster 2008;

Ruiz de Zarobe 2007b; Wolff 2007; Zydatiß 2007) are supported. More precisely, research needs to address whether for both the content subject and the foreign language curricular aims and objectives are met, whether there are any specific areas that are more affected by CLIL instruction than others, and finally, if there are particular pupils for whom CLIL works better than for others.

This paper addresses this gap by focusing on a comparison of the foreign language achievements of learners in CLIL and in regular secondary school programmes. The specific aspect of language competence we address is the ability to tell a picture story coherently and cohesively in the foreign language English, including the use of communicative strategies to overcome lexical gaps. The genre of oral narratives has been chosen since, as Georgakopoulou (1997: 1) states, the "narrative is viewed [...] as inescapably fundamental in human life" and it is precisely this fundamentality which makes narratives especially suitable for encouraging language production of children. The use of picture stories, in turn, encourages the production of similar stories, allowing for group comparisons with regard to the treatment of particular features of oral narratives.

2.   Theoretical background

2.1   Narratives

Oral narratives have received considerable interest from a variety of fields over the last 20 years. Specifically in the growing research area of genre analysis, the genre of (oral) narrative has been given due attention as a 'primary' genre both in the sense of being a genre underlying many other genres, as well as being central to the process of acquiring language (cf., e.g. Martin & Rose 2008: ch. 2 on stories in school-learning). The latter focus has also given rise to research on the developmental patterns in first and second language acquisition of this particular genre, which point to a complex interplay of various factors related to the genre itself, to the linguistic resources available to the story-tellers and to their cognitive development. (cf. Berman & Slobin 1994, Verhoeven & Strömqvist 2001; Dannerer 2004; Kang 2003 & 2006; Villareal Olaizola & García Mayo 2008).

While the ability to 'tell stories' is clearly not all that is involved in language proficiency, a focus on one genre that is familiar to children in both their L1 and their L2 is an efficient way of gaining rich, yet comparable, foreign language data from a group of learners (for an overview of narrative properties cf. Georgakopoulou 1997). Since the ability to produce narratives represents a skill that children start to acquire as early as 2 years of age (cf. McCabe & Peterson 1991), narratives constitute a particularly useful device for studying aspects of L2 learners' competences.

Moreover, research has shown that oral narrative competence is related to other language skills like reading comprehension, both in an L1 as well as an L2 context (cf. Bensoussan 1990; Cain & Oakhill 1996; Fitzgerald & Spiegel 1983; Kang 2003). Cain & Oakhill (1996), for example, demonstrated that children's ability to tell apt stories based on story structure knowledge may be a decisive factor for reading comprehension ability.

As far as the L1 is concerned, the development of narrative competence can be seen to consist of four stages (cf. Boueke & Schülein 1991; Boueke et al. 1995):

1. Individual narrative units are described as isolated events and so the story does not show either local or global connections.
2. The individual sequences are connected by creating linear and causal sequences. The most typical connector is 'and then'.
3. At the third level, narratives are structured locally and episodes are structured hierarchically (e.g. clause subordination).
4. Finally, stories are globally structured and features of thematic coherence are linked to causal structure.

Research on narrative development in an L2 is not unanimous in suggesting clear stages. Generally, studies in L2 language narratives tend to note differences between L2 and L1 narrative production; the variation between individual study results, in fact, seems to lie in diverse degrees of importance attached to overall foreign language proficiency as an indicator of narrative competence (cf. Myles 2003; Schmidlin 1999; Viberg 2001) versus more general issues of a maturational effect (cf. e.g. Kupersmitt & Berman 2001, and most other contributors in Verhoeven & Strömqvist 2001).

As far as research on narratives in the CLIL context is concerned, studies investigating oral narrative productions in this specific environment (usually comparing CLIL vs. non-CLIL strands of schools) are still relatively rare. While these studies focus on a variety of different language/genre aspects, they generally imply that CLIL students tend to outscore their non-CLIL counterparts with regard to various (L2) proficiency levels (cf. Hüttner & Rieder-Bünemann 2007; Ruiz de Zarobe 2007a,b; Villareal Olaizola & García Mayo 2008). When comparing narratives from pupils with bilingual schooling to L1 narratives from monolingual programmes, however, it was found that bilingual narratives tend to be underdeveloped in relation to monolingual stories with regard to several linguistic variables showing narrative competence (cf. Ordóñez 2004).

As regards the methods used to elicit oral narratives from children, picture stories have proved a reliable medium to encourage children to produce narratives in a context where they have experience with this medium, since this provides a common basis for comparing the children's narrative productions (cf. Berman & Slobin 1994: 41–42). While the sequence of events is predetermined in this setting, there is nevertheless not one 'objectively' correct version, since the narrator is free to choose the perspective of the narration. Yet, a story has to fulfil certain criteria in order to be considered generically well-formed: the action needs to be linguistically cohesive and thematically coherent, addressing both competences at the macro- and micro-level of language and genre proficiency (cf. Berman & Slobin 1994: 40).

As will be shown below, the picture stories used served as a basis for eliciting not only information on the children's competences in the genre of narratives, but also for eliciting information on children's grammatical competence and their abilities to apply strategies to cope with their limitations in the resource L2. As regards the latter, we focused on the use of communicative strategies in the two groups observed.

2.2   Communicative strategies

Communicative strategies are commonly defined as a means of learners to overcome inadequacies of their interlanguage resources, mainly of a lexical type. (Ellis 1994: 196) There are, however, two important further criteria that occur in many definitions of communicative strategies, namely problematicity and consciousness (Faerch & Kasper 1983: 31; Dörnyei & Scott 1997: 182; Kasper & Kellerman 1997: 2).

Problematicity refers to the speakers' identifying a problem in their attempted communication and developing a strategy to overcome this problem. Despite criticism raised against the inclusion of this criterion (cf. Bialystok 1990: 3–4), we argue for problematicity as a defining feature of communicative strategies. To us, the fact that native language production also includes language features that are or resemble communicative strategies is not a sufficient counter-argument and might only be seen as indication that strategic language use is a feature of both L1 and L2 language production. Indeed, simply because in native speaker conversations lexical problems are less likely to occur does not mean that they do not occur at all. Even competent speakers of their L1 might find that they lack certain technical vocabulary, or feel they need to adjust their use of more specific terminology according to the background of their interlocutors. The frequent occurrence of flagging devices, such as hesitations, or even explicit comments on the speaker's lack of knowledge of a certain term, also points towards learners perceiving a lexical gap as a problem.

The second frequently occurring criterion in defining communicative strategies is consciousness, sometimes related to intentionality. This is based on the assumption that a strategy is a conscious technique used to achieve a goal (Dörnyei & Scott 1997: 183, 185). Various problems surround the notion of consciousness as a defining feature, most of these connected to the difficulty of ever unambiguously defining a process (or a plan or a strategy) as conscious (cf. Bialystok 1990: 88–103; Faerch & Kasper 1983: 37). While this issue remains unsolved, the use of consciousness in the definition of another phenomenon appears difficult.

Therefore, we define communicative strategies as means used by speakers to overcome linguistic problems, typically lexical gaps. Speakers are aware of these gaps and view them as (potential) problems for communication. Thus, an element of problematicity is included in the definition, but we avoid the use of consciousness as a defining criterion. In this study, problematicity is operationalised as requiring the presence of flagging devices, such as hesitations, fillers, questions, re-formulations, surrounding a potential communicative strategy. Thus, non-target-like lexical items that were not marked by such flags were considered not to represent strategic language use on the part of the learners and therefore not included in the lists of communicative strategies.

As regards the precise classification of different communicative strategies and the related taxonomies, several models have been proposed (cf., e.g. Bialystok 1990; Dörnyei & Scott 1997; Poulisse 1990; Tarone 1977). For the purposes of this study, our focus lay on so-called compensatory strategies, i.e. those used by speakers to achieve their intended meaning, assuming that the criterion of problematicity has also been met (cf. Poulisse 1990: 21). We follow Poulisse (1990: 60–63, 109–113) in classifying compensatory communicative strategies into two groups, i.e. conceptual and linguistic strategies, divided further as follows:

- Conceptual:
    - Analytic (word coinage, circumlocution, description, paraphrase)
    - Holistic (approximation)
- Linguistic (or Code):
    - Transfer (language switch, literal translation, foreignising)
    - Morphological creativity (verbal, mime)

We included two further types of strategy accounted for in other studies, i.e. reduction strategies, including avoidance (message abandonment, message replacement) and interaction strategies (including appeals for assistance/help). (cf. Bialystok 1990: 129ff; Faerch & Kasper 1983: 38ff). A focus on communicative strategies seemed motivated for this study since it was hypothesised that there might be a difference between groups concerning children's ability to cope with lexical gaps without resorting to their L1.

In the present study, the aspects of language competence investigated include degrees of narrative competence, morphological/syntactic language regularities and the use of communicative strategies.

3.   Setting and participants

3.1   CLIL in Austria

In Austria, CLIL started its life under the label *EaA* (Englisch als Arbeitssprache – English as a working language) in the late 1980s/early 1990s, first in secondary and primary schools, and soon afterwards also in colleges of engineering, arts and crafts. A characteristic of Austrian CLIL programmes is that they are *grass roots* initiatives of (groups of) teachers, head teachers or parents at specific schools.

The CLIL programme under investigation here is the so-called Vienna Bilingual Schooling Programme (VBS), which was founded in 1994 and covers nursery, primary and secondary schools.[1] The VBS makes explicit reference to the targets formulated by the European Commission with regard to fostering foreign language competence in European citizens, i.e. that

> CLIL [...] has a major contribution to make to the Union's language learning goals. It can provide effective opportunities for pupils to use their new language skills now, rather than learn them for use later. It opens doors on languages for a broader range of learners, nurturing self-confidence in young learners and those who have not responded well to formal language instruction in general education. It provides exposure to the language without requiring extra time in the curriculum.[2]

The model employed by the VBS is essentially an English/German bilingual one, promoting English as the international language and German as the national one. The schools are state-run and follow Austrian school curricula. Both native speakers of English and of German are employed at VBS schools and team-teaching is explicitly favoured, although (presumably given restrictions in resources) for some subjects, lessons might take place alternatively in German or English. Not only is instruction at the VBS bilingual, the original intention was also to have equal groups of English- and of German-speaking children in each class in order to encourage informal language learning from one another. In reality, given the demographic situation of Vienna and the existence of private English-only

---

1.   For details see information provided by the Vienna School Board (http://www.stadtschulrat.at/bilingualitaet/catid18/detid4).

2.   Cf. European Commission, Directorate-General for Education and Culture. 2004. "European Label Awarded to Innovative Projects in Language Teaching and Learning: European priorities for the 2005 Label Campaign" (http://www.saaic.sk/eu-label/doc/EL_2005_PRIORITY_EN.DOC).

schools, the so-called "English-speaking" group comprises children from very diverse language backgrounds and only very few native speakers of English. As most children are more competent users of German than English, the first year of secondary school, i.e. year 5, usually involves more English-medium instruction in order to support their English language development. Some explicit targets for the foreign language are formulated in terms of the *Common European Framework of Reference*, i.e. A2+ (writing and speaking) and B1 (reading and listening) by the end of the fourth year of secondary school, i.e. year 8.

An important factor is that most schools offering VBS programmes have only one strand per year (about 30 children) that is bilingual and several regular strands that offer all education in German. Children are selected for the VBS strand, following an interview that aims to assess their problem-solving and communicative abilities. In general, three groups of children are eligible for the VBS strand of secondary schools, i.e. German-speaking children with previous knowledge of English or a specific interest in English; children who use English either as first language or a 'language of communication'; and children who attended a VBS primary school. Thus, the bilingual groups are both self-selected and school-selected, possibly allowing for higher levels of motivation among the children involved.

3.2   Participants and data collection

The participants in this study were 44 children with German as their L1 in year 7 (i.e. age 12–13), 22 each in the CLIL and in the non-CLIL strand respectively, in two VBS secondary schools, matched for socio-economic background. The children in the non-CLIL strand had 3 to 4 hours of EFL teaching per week, following a communicative approach; the children in the CLIL strand additionally received English medium instruction in most other subjects, excluding German and sports. The data collected consisted of audio-recordings of oral narratives based on the wordless picture story 'Frog where are you?' (Mayer 1969), which constitutes a widely used prompt for research in narratives (cf. Bamberg 1987; Berman & Slobin 1994; Bennett-Kastor 2002; Kang 2003 and others). The children were given time to familiarise themselves with the picture story and were then recorded individually. No translations of any terms were offered, but children were advised to try and paraphrase if they did not know a particular word in English. The participants were then asked to narrate the story to one researcher in German (their L1) and only then asked to tell the story again in English (L2) to another researcher, having been told that this person spoke no German. Allowing children to first narrate the story in their L1 provided us with comparative data in the L1, which is helpful in deciding whether particular features of the narratives are due to children being learners of the genre of oral narrative or of being language learners. Additionally, this research set-up should ensure that the children had the opportunity to make themselves genuinely familiar with the various plot elements of the story, and that the English version represented the children's best possible performance.

The elements of narrative competence were classified into macro-level ('thematic coherence') and micro-level ('linguistic cohesion') elements. To be more precise, the macro-level encompasses issues of genre awareness, including the explicit mentioning of the elements of the story (i.e. complication, unfolding of the plot, solution), the ability to shift perspective, using explicit framings of the story, and adapting the story to schematic expectations, e.g. regarding an 'ideal' ending. The micro-level includes mastery of the language system, comprising adherence to conventionalised tense forms for the narrative and the ability to produce grammatically well-formed utterances, the use of appropriate lexis and lexical density, as well as the use of communicative strategies.

In the following discussion of the findings, it will become apparent that in some areas more marked differences between the two groups could be observed than in others, but that in most areas investigated CLIL children performed better than children attending the regular programme.

4. Findings

Overall, the initial motivation for using oral narratives as a tool for eliciting data appeared to be justified, since the chosen genre indeed provided rich and informative language data from the group of learners investigated. As regards L2-specific narrative development, our results seem to indicate that depending on the particular competence aspect, both general cognitive maturation and influences of language proficiency may be responsible for explaining similarities and differences between L2 and L1 narrative production (see e.g. results on shifting perspective in 4.1.).

4.1 Macro-level (creating coherent narratives)

With regard to the stage of narrative competence reached (i.e. stage 3: employing merely local narrative structuring vs. stage 4: including global structuring devices, see Section 2.1), both groups show good abilities in creating their narratives globally coherent in the sense of realising all three core plot elements of the story, i.e. the onset or problem (the boy realises that his frog has disappeared), the unfolding (the boy looks for his missing frog) and the resolution (the boy finds the frog he has lost), thus appearing to have (almost) reached the final stage of narrative competence in this respect. There are slight differences between the groups as regards the first and the final plot elements, where only one CLIL pupil did not explicitly mention the problem at the onset as opposed to three pupils of the standard group, and two pupils of the standard group did not explicitly mention the resolution of the story, which all CLIL pupils did.

The children whose narratives had a clear ending did not always conform to the ending suggested by the pictures in the story.[3] This ending, i.e. that the boy finds the frog he has lost, was given by 23% of the CLIL and 18% of the standard group. The majority view in both groups, however, was that the story ends with the boy taking a different frog home, which was proposed by 41% in both groups. The third type of resolution offered deviated quite clearly from the suggested ending in that the boy leaves the frog in the forest. 27% of the children in the CLIL group and 18% of the children in the standard group proposed this ending. We can interpret this adaptation as an indication of the children adapting the genre-expectation of a resolution to their story to their more specific schemata regarding a 'happy end' of the story. Possibly due to changing attitudes towards wildlife, it seems that for some children in this study a happy ending excludes keeping animals that live in the wild as pets. The adaptation of input to schematic expectations can be considered a general feature of human minds to order their perception of the world and, indeed, already Bartlett (1932) observed that British students adapted Native American stories to their expectations of the ways in which a story should unfold. In some of the cases observed here, the adaptations not directly related to the information provided in the pictures towards the children's ideal solutions involved quite elaborate comments up to the inclusion of an explicit 'morale' to the story. However, what is noticeable is that more elaborate deviations from the information provided in the pictures in order to conform to relevant schemata of happy endings and idealised children's stories were produced by children in the CLIL group, arguably as they possessed the linguistic means in English to formulate these adaptations. Thus, in Example (1) we find the child framing the story quite explicitly to convey her morale of the story. The beginning of her story indicates a negative value judgement of the boy protagonist due to his catching animals, an activity clearly not considered good behaviour by the narrator. It is worth noting that none of this information is implied in the first picture of the story, which

---

3.   As regards variety in story endings, the German versions were basically identical to the English versions for each pupil.

shows a smiling boy looking at an equally smiling frog in a glass jar. The storyline involves the boy finding his frog reunited with its family and taking it back home with him. However, in this example the girl changed this ending to the protagonist leaving the frog with its family and the boy having learnt a lesson, namely that 'wild' animals should not be used as pets. The precise wording is given below:

(1)   Beginning:
       Fritzi was a very bad child (.) he always caught different kind
       of animals (.)
       End:
       he found a family of frogs and he watched them a few minutes (.) and he decided
       just to let them there and li- so they can live in peace and now he is a good child
       and comes to them every day and visits them

Despite the fact that examples like this do not conform to the frame given by the pictures, they suggest strong schemata of what an ideal story ending should be like. In that, they seem to indicate familiarity with the genre of children's stories and the relevant schemata of happy endings and the desire to make a slightly deviant storyline fit into the more expected one.

One important feature in the development of narrative competence (be it in the L1 or the L2) is the ability to shift perspective, i.e. to make explicit the difference between the states of knowledge of a protagonist in the story and the omniscient view of the narrator. In the picture story investigated here, there is one such situation in which the boy protagonist mistakes the antlers of a deer for branches of a tree and subsequently is carried off by the deer and thrown into a pond. The children narrating this story, who had already had time to look at the pictures beforehand, had an omniscient view of this misunderstanding whereas the protagonist only had a limited view of the matter. Making such a misunderstanding explicit is one way of showing the ability to shift perspective, i.e. to contrast what a character in a story thinks or knows at a particular moment in the story with what the narrator knows. Our data clearly show that narrating this sequence posed serious problems to both groups in both the L1 and the L2, indicating that such a shift in perspective presents a primarily cognitive problem. Thus, many children did not mention this misunderstanding and let the deer appear rather suddenly on the scene, as is indicated in Example (2), a typical instance of an unsuccessful rendering of this shift in perspective.

(2)   *they searched in every hole or yah erm where the frog maybe*
       could be. erm but then a big animal came

In sum, only five of the children in each group related this misperception explicitly in their German versions, indicating that this shift in perspective is cognitively still difficult at this age. There is, however, one marked difference between the two groups when it comes to relating these diverse perspectives in the English versions. In the CLIL group, all five children who made this shift in perspective in German also did so in the English versions of their stories. In the standard group, however, only two children made this contrast explicit in their English versions compared to the five who did so in German, suggesting that for three children who are cognitively able to make this shift and therefore formulate it in their L1 German, gaps in their foreign language competence arguably stop them from doing so in their L2 English. The pictures highlighting the misunderstanding are given below.

Figure 1. Misinterpretation of "branches" in pictures 14 and 15 (Mayer 1969)

As regards some established story-telling conventions, many children, i.e. 10 in the CLIL and 12 in the standard group, named at least one character of the story. Mostly, this was the boy protagonist, who often got typically German names like *Patrick, Lukas, Hannes, Peter, Florian, Maxi* or *Fritzi* and only sometimes English names like *Jimmy, James* or *Tom*. The dog, which was second in the frequency of being named, mostly got typical pet-names such as *Flipsy, Struppi, Fluffy, Bello* or *Lucky*. In the one instance where the frog got named this was as *Quaxi*. No clearly distinct patterns in naming could be observed for the two groups. Additionally, all children frequently attributed emotions to the protagonists in the story, e.g. *the owl wasn't very friendly* or *the boy is very angry with the dog*, and some children also verbalised thoughts and reasoning of the protagonists, e.g. *he saw a piece of wood and thought, well, this is a good place for frogs, I think I can find Quaxi [the frog] here*. Also for these patterns, however, no clear group differences could be observed.

One more feature of conventionalised story-telling could be observed in the realisations of the typical English formula *Once upon a time*. This was used three times by children in the CLIL group and once by a child in the non-CLIL group. Additionally, there was one form of *there once was a boy* used in the CLIL group and the non-target-like form *Once upon day* by one child in the standard group. Such a use of genre-specific framings arguably indicates an awareness of specific genre conventions. Other typical forms, such as *they lived happily ever after* were, however, not at all used by the children.

In sum, we can see that all children show clear familiarity with the genre of the oral narrative; the CLIL group, however, is clearly better equipped at dealing with shifts in perspective and in making all elements of the plot structure explicit.

4.2   Micro-level (mastering the language system)

With regard to micro-level features, two selected aspects of the verb system will be dealt with in detail since these are central features of narratives which are also focused on in teaching materials: firstly the use of an anchor tense in narratives, and secondly the verb form errors in both groups. As regards tense choice, narrators can generally decide to position their stories either in the present or in the past, resulting in the use of an anchor tense, that is to say, the tense form used predominantly, i.e. to 80–90% of all verb forms, in a narrative (cf. Bamberg 1987: 123); awareness of temporal anchoring thus also constitutes a feature of narrative competence according to Berman & Slobin (1994). In our study, a pronounced difference in the ability to consistently use one tense was observed: in the CLIL group, anchor tense consistency amounted to 94% whereas in the standard group it amounted only to 81%.

Furthermore, in the standard group this usually involved switching between tenses with no clear motivation and at several occasions in the story.[4] Example (3) illustrates this phenomenon: Here, the narrator's anchor tense appears to be past tense at the outset (and for most of the narration) while at random intervals, various obviously unmotivated switches to present tense can be observed (see, e.g. *don't find, look around, is, looks*). In contrast, in all instances in the CLIL group concerned, the switches from past to present tense use occurred at one point in the story, which had the effect of creating a lively narrative, rather than reflecting insecure tense use. This can be seen in the two narration extracts provided in example (4). In (4a), the narration starts out in the past and then switches to present tense at the unfolding of the plot, i.e. as the search for the frog begins, continuing in the present until the end. In (4b), in turn, the narrator uses past tense for almost the whole story and the switch to present tense occurs at the resolution element when the boy finally finds his frog, the narration from then on remaining in the present.

(3)   unmotivated tense switches – standard group
       *there was a child with two pets, a dog and a frog. and once and once a time, the frog jumped out of his bottle and run away and the child search (.) searched all (.) around his room and, but he **don't find** the frog and the dog put his head into a bottle and then he became it not (.) he don't became it out. and then he jumped out of the window and the bottle broke down, broked. and the child **is** very happy, and they searched weiter (.) searched (.) around and **look around** and they saw the house of beens and the child looked in a hole but there **IS** a hamster and the dog jumped to the house of the beens and the house fall down. and the dog ran away and the beens after him and the child **looks** in a in a hole of a tree ...*

(4)   motivated tense switches (2 narrators) – CLIL group
       a.   *so there was a boy and a dog and they erm in the in the evening they they found a frog and put him into a glass sh- glass [just a glass. yah.] yah and then they went to sleep and didn't didn't care didn't really erm know if the frog could escape. but he could. actually. and then he escaped and they erm the dog and the boy erm re- **realise** it at the morning and they **search** in the whole room in the boots and in the glass. and then they **see** that the window was open. and that and then they they **search** outside. [story continues with present tense]*
       b.   *[story starts with past tense] and the boy the little boy fell into a lake. and then there in the lake he there **is** a tree erm a part of a tree and the boy erm **looks** over the tree. and there and there he **sees** his frog and a frog erm woman. and and (then) he also **sees** the little babies they've got. and then he he ta- he **takes** one of the babies.*

---

4.   In the examples given, tense switches are indicated in bold.

An area of even more marked difference was the ability of children to produce error-free tense forms; thus the rate of verb errors amounted to 4% in the CLIL group compared to 20% in the standard group. In the standard group, verb errors mostly, i.e. in 72% of all instances, involved the use of the base form instead of either 3rd person present tense or a past form. The origin of these mistakes might lie in problems with the -s marker of the present tense or in a more general strategy of using base forms only. In this regard, we can see that the CLIL group with only 4% verb form errors does seem to have a clear advantage as regards competence in verb formation and use.

With respect to the overall length of the stories, group differences can be considered irrelevant, with the CLIL group averaging at 273 words and the regular group at 278 words. As regards lexical range and density, differences between groups are also small. As various verbs of motion were required to describe the protagonists' actions in the narrative, one aspect investigated for lexical range included the type/token ratio concerning verbs of motion. Here, the CLIL group (64%) showed a slight advantage over the standard group (57%). Type/token ratios for the entire stories appeared fairly similar in both groups, again yielding slightly better results for the CLIL group (38% vs. 35% in the standard group).

Although not equally pronounced on all levels, the differences described above interestingly indicate advantages of pupils in the CLIL strand also in areas that are generally not focused on in CLIL classes, such as grammatical accuracy. Given the research base here, it cannot be stated unambiguously whether this is related to CLIL instruction or an effect of group-selection.

4.3   Communicative strategies

In this study there were several lexical items relevant to the story in the pictures story that were not expected to be known to all pupils, and therefore were considered possible targets for communicative strategies, such as *beehive, antlers, mole* and *deer*. Although some children, especially in the CLIL group, knew the target lexical items, most did not. As we postulated the awareness of a problem as a requirement for the definition of any non-target-like form as a communicative strategy (see Section 2.2), only those realisations were considered that showed flagging devices, such as hesitations, fillers, or direct questions and comments regarding the sought-after word. Although the effectiveness of a particular communicative strategy depends to a large extent on its precise realisation, as a further layer to the divisions proposed in Section 2.2., we categorised strategies as 'unhelpful' in those cases where they were considered to not aid understanding if the listener understood no German. These include the linguistic strategies of transfer and the interactive strategy of appealing for assistance in German. The efficient use of communicative strategies that are understandable to the interlocutor, i.e. conceptual ones, was considered to be an indication that pupils were able to cope with their linguistic gaps and maintain an interaction.

A purely quantitative analysis of communicative strategies is difficult, as most children of the CLIL group were familiar with all the target lexical items, and so required overall a lesser use of communicative strategies. On a qualitative level, however, decided differences could be observed in the specific strategies employed. Firstly, the 'unhelpful' L1-based strategies, i.e. using a language switch to German or asking for help in German, were used much more frequently in the standard than in the CLIL group, with 20 switches to German in the standard groups contrasted with 2 in the CLIL group, and no occurrences of asking for help in German in the CLIL group compared to 3 occurrences in the standard group. The examples below illustrate the German-based strategies of the standard group:

(5)   Language switch
       suddenly there came a. hirsch (DEER)[5]

(6)   Appeal for help in German
       he looked into holes and erm. was ist bienenstock (WHAT IS BEEHIVE)

Both of these examples show that for a non-German speaker there would be serious problems of understanding what the speakers intended to say. This is contrasted in the example below, which presents a mixture of appeal for help in English and a conceptual strategy produced by a child in the CLIL group for the same target as the speaker in example (6), i.e. *beehive*, which is easily comprehensible to a non-German speaker.

(7)   Appeal for help in English combined with conceptual strategy
       a bee-, how's it called, it's ca – a bee – erm ja halt (WELL) where bees live

In the case of conceptual strategies in the L2, which were used by both groups, the circumlocutions and paraphrases used by children in the two groups showed marked differences, with the CLIL children better able to produce linguistically correct descriptions with fewer hesitations. Also, the CLIL children offer overall more specific circumlocutions and paraphrases, partly due to what appears to be a wider lexical range, allowing for such paraphrases for *beehive* as *colony of bees* or *cocoon of wasps*. This contrasts markedly with the very general *house of bees*, the most typical communicative strategy in the standard group, or the rather idiosyncratic *bee pocket*. The examples below illustrate this difference by target item:

---

5.   Translations of German words used are given in capital letters in brackets immediately following the German word or phrase.

(8)   L2-based communicative strategies
   a.   Target *mole*:
         CLIL group:
            'something like a a mouse but it's not a mouse (.) I think it's like it lives in the ground and erm it's small'
            'a hedgehog or something'
            Standard group:
            'a little animal'
            'a little mouse'
   b.   Target *beehive*:
         CLIL group:
            'a colony of bees' and later *'their home'*
            'a cocoon with wasps'
            Standard group:
            'house of bees'
            'bee pocket'

The differences in the use of communicative strategies seem to point towards a greater ability in the CLIL group to manipulate the code in order to still achieve the communicative aim even when the most direct means of doing so is unavailable to the speaker due to a lack of vocabulary knowledge. Arguably, this increased flexibility is furthered in CLIL classrooms where both teachers and pupils are often seen to struggle with specific terminology and resort to circumlocutions, paraphrases or approximations, while continuing to use English. This has been observed for instance by Dalton-Puffer (2007: 133) in similar CLIL settings, e.g. in the following example.

(9)   Teacher: *what are witnesses*
       Pupil: *witwe, oder* (WIDOW, ISN'T IT)
       Teacher: *witnesses are people who can say.aahm.who can say I've seen it. I can swear that this is the truth*

In contrast to this, the behaviour of the standard group seems to indicate that switching to the L1 is an accepted, nearly default way, of dealing with lexical difficulties and that non-task-related interactions with teachers are normally conducted in German, such as appeals for assistance.

5.   Conclusion

The study reported here supports the use of oral narratives in gathering language data from children by showing how rich and yet comparable the data so gathered is. With regard to the comparison between children attending CLIL versus regular strands of schooling, the findings reported here tentatively suggest quantitative and qualitative advantages as regards English language competence of the children in the CLIL group compared to those in the standard group in all the areas investigated, although not all areas are equally affected. The most marked differences can be found in the more complex elements, i.e. to use language to describe shifts of perspective or to apply communicative strategies *without* resorting to the L1. Especially the latter might indeed be traced to the use of CLIL in classrooms where arguably the focus on 'getting meaning across' is higher than on producing accurate lexical or grammatical items. Moreover, in the sample investigated, the advantage of the CLIL pupils was generally not restricted to the level of macro-elements or lexical flexibility, but could also be observed with regard to micro-level features (e.g. tense consistency and accuracy). We can thus interpret our results as encouraging for the programme in so far as CLIL pupils seem to be more successful both in the more communicative and functional use of language and in the production of lexically and grammatically accurate utterances. Given the small size of our sample, further research is, however, clearly required in that a more systematic and larger investigation of the success levels of CLIL students ought to be attempted, addressing also other areas of language use, notably writing, where the differences might be less marked than in speaking.

While the study results reported here present noticeable group differences, two aspects might still be worth remembering: firstly, the children in the CLIL groups were not randomly selected, but their parents chose this particular form of teaching and enrolment interviews were in place at both schools. This might suggest the existence of further variables contributing to the higher performance of the CLIL pupils than only the CLIL programme, e.g. parental support, motivation or language aptitude. Secondly, individual cases within both CLIL and standard groups are highly divergent, with high performers in the standard and low performers in the CLIL group. Especially the latter raise the important question of whether there might be groups of pupils for whom CLIL classrooms do not represent the ideal language learning environments, which clearly calls for further systematic research.

References

Bamberg, M.G.W. 1987. *The Acquisition of Narratives: Learning to Use Language.* Berlin: de Gruyter.

Bartlett, F.C. 1932. *Remembering.* Cambridge: CUP.

Bennet-Kastor, T. 2002. The 'frog story' narratives of Irish-English bilinguals. *Bilingualism* 5: 131–146.

Bensoussan, M. 1990. EFL reading as seen through translation and discourse analysis: Narrative vs. expository texts. *English for* Specific Purpuses 9: 49–66.

Berman, R. & Slobin, D. (eds). 1994. *Relating Events in Narrative: A Crosslinguistic Developmental Study*. Hillsdale NJ: Lawrence Erlbaum Associates.

Bialystok, E. 1990. *Communicative Strategies: A Psychological Analysis of Second Language Use.* Oxford: Basil Blackwell.

Boueke, D. & Schülein, F. 1991. Kindliches Erzählen als Realisierung eines narrativen Schemas. In *Kindliches Erzählen – Erzählen für Kinder*, H.H. Ewers (ed.), 13–41. Basel: Belz.

Boueke, D., Schülein, F., Büscher, H., Terhorst, E. & Wolf, D. 1995. *Wie Kinder erzählen: Untersuchungen zur Erzähltheorie und zur Entwicklung narrativer Fähigkeiten.* München: Fink.

Cain, K. & Oakhill, J. 1996. The nature of the relationship between comprehension skill and the ability to tell a story. *British Journal of Developmental Psychology* 14: 187–201.

Dalton-Puffer, C. 2007. *Discourse in Content-and-Language-Integrated Learning (CLIL) Classrooms* [Language Learning & Language Teaching 20]. Amsterdam: John Benjamins.

Dalton-Puffer, C. & Smit, U. (eds). 2007. *Empirical Perspectives on CLIL Classroom Discourse* [Sprache im Kontext 26]. Frankfurt: Peter Lang.

Dannerer, M. 2004. Können Kinder keinen Konjunktiv? Eine empirische Untersuchung mündlicher und schriftlicher Erzählungen. *Informationen zur Deutschdidaktik. Zeitschrift für den Deutschunterricht in Wissenschaft und Schule* 28(4): 29–40.

Dörnyei, Z. & Scott, M.L. 1997. Communication strategies in a second language: definitions and taxonomies. *Language Learning* 47(1): 173–210.

Ellis, R. 1994. *The Study of Second Language Acquisition.* Oxford: OUP.

Faerch, C. & Kasper, G. 1983. *Strategies in Interlanguage Communication.* London: Longman.

Fitzgerald, J. & Spiegel, D.L. 1983. Enhancing children's reading comprehension through instruction in narrative structure. *Journal of Reading Behavior* 15: 1–17.

Georgakopoulou, A. 1997. Narrative. In *Handbook of Pragmatics*, J. Verschueren, J.O. Östman, J. Blommaert & C. Bulcaen (eds), 1–19. Amsterdam: John Benjamins.

Hüttner, J. & Rieder-Bünemann, A. 2007. The effect of CLIL instruction on children's narrative competence. *VIEWS. Vienna English Working Papers* 16(3): 20–27.

Kasper, G. & Kellerman, E. (eds). 1997. *Communication Strategies: Psycholinguistic and Sociolinguistic Perspectives.* London: Longman.

Kang, J.Y. 2003. On the ability to tell good stories in another language: analysis of Korean EFL learners' oral "Frog story" narratives. *Narrative Inquiry* 13(1): 127–149.

Kang, J.Y. 2006. Producing culturally appropriate narratives in English as a foreign language: A discourse analysis of Korean EFL learners' written narratives. *Narrative Inquiry* 16(2): 379–407.

Kupersmitt, J. & Berman, R.A. 2001. Linguistic features of Spanish-Hebrew children's narratives. In Verhoeven & Strömqvist (eds), 277–317.

Lasagabaster, D. 2008. Foreign language competence in content and language integrated courses. *The Open Applied Linguistics Journal* 1: 30–41.

Martin, J.R. & Rose, D. 2008. *Genre Relations: Mapping Culture.* London: Equinox.

Mayer, M. 1969. *Frog, where are you?* New York NY: Penguin.

Mc Cabe, A. & Peterson, C. 1991. Getting the story: A longitudinal study of parental styles in eliciting narratives and developing narrative skill. In *Developing Narrative Structure*, A. McCabe & C. Peterson (eds), 217–254. Hillsdale NJ: Lawrence Erlbaum Associates.

Mewald, C. & Spenger, J. 2005. Die Auswirkungen von EAA auf die allgemeine Sprachkompetenz in Englisch. Erste Bilanz einer empirischen Studie. In *Professionalisierung in pädagogischen Berufen*, A. Kowarsch & K. Pollheimer (eds), 191–201. Purkersdorf: Verlag Brüder Hollinek.

Myles, F. 2003. The early development of L2 narratives: A longitudinal study. *Marges Linguistiques* 5: 40–55.

Ordóñez, C.L. 2004. EFL and native Spanish in elite bilingual schools in Colombia: A first look at bilingual adolescent Frog stories. *International Journal of Bilingual Education & Bilingualism* 7(5): 449–474.

Poulisse, N. 1990. *The Use of Compensatory Strategies by Dutch Learners of English*. Dordrecht: Foris.

Ruiz de Zarobe, Y. 2007a. CLIL in a bilingual community: Similarities and differences with the learning of English as a Foreign Language. *VIEWS. Vienna English Working Papers* 16(3): 47–52.

Ruiz de Zarobe, Y. 2007b. CLIL and foreign language learning: A longitudinal study in the Basque country. *International CLIL Research Journal* 1(1): 62–74.

Schmidlin, R. 1999. *Wie Deutschschweizer Kinder schreiben und erzählen lernen*. Tübingen: Francke.

Tarone, E. 1977. Conscious communication strategies in interlanguage: A progress report. In *On TESOL '77*, H.D. Brown, C.A. Yorio & R.C. Crymes (eds), 194–203. Washington DC: TESOL.

Verhoeven, L. & Strömqvist, S. (eds). 2001. *Narrative Development in a Multilingual Context* [Studies in Bilingualism 23]. Amsterdam: John Benjamins.

Viberg, Å. 2001. Age-related and L2-related features in bilingual narrative development in Sweden. In Verhoeven & Strömqvist (eds), 87–128.

Villareal Olaizola, I. & García Mayo, M.P. 2008. Does CLIL improve the acquisition of L3 tense and agreement morphology? Paper presented at the *CLIL Fusion* Conference, Tallinn, Estonia, October 2008.

Wolff, D. 2007. CLIL: Bridging the gap between school and working life. In *Diverse Contexts – Converging Goals: CLIL in Europe*, D. Marsh & D. Wolff (eds), 15–31. Frankfurt: Peter Lang.

Zydatiß, W. 2007. *Deutsch-Englische Züge in Berlin (DEZIBEL): Eine Evaluation des bilingualen Sachfachunterrichts an Gymnasien*. Frankfurt: Peter Lang.

Using a genre-based approach to integrating content and language in CLIL

The example of secondary history

Tom Morton
Universidad Autónoma de Madrid, Spain

This chapter proposes that a genre-based pedagogy could provide at least a partial framework for a language curriculum in CLIL. It starts from the idea that an important aspect of learning an academic subject is that of being a user of the different text types or genres through which the subject knowledge is construed. In a genre-based pedagogy, teachers and students jointly construct content knowledge along with the textual and linguistic forms in which it is packaged, thus linking the oral discourse through which knowledge is construed with the written genres which students may have to produce. Such an approach is particularly relevant for CLIL, as it provides a way of genuinely integrating content and language instruction. The chapter provides examples from secondary CLIL history lessons, but it is argued that a genre-based approach can be suitable across subject areas, and is compatible with the 4 Cs perspective on CLIL.

1. Introduction

One of the problems facing current CLIL practice is the need for specific curricula for language development across the various subjects taught. As Dalton-Puffer (2007) argues, the most urgent need is that for the identification and implementation of written and spoken academic language skills and functions. She claims that these should include not only such functions as describing, defining and explaining, but also "a progression of narrative, descriptive, informative, argumentative, and persuasive *texts*" (ibid. 295, italics added). In the approach to the literacies of school subjects based on systemic functional linguistics (e.g. Cope & Kalantzis 1993; Martin 1999; Schleppegrell & Colombi 2002; Schleppegrell 2004) such texts are referred to as 'genres'. The aim of this chapter is to show some ways in which this systemic-functional notion of genre (Martin & Rose 2008; Martin 2009) can provide a framework for the development of language curricula in CLIL, and for informing classroom practices. The examples are taken from one commonly taught CLIL subject, history, but it is suggested that the approach described can be applied, with modifications, to other CLIL subjects.

The chapter begins with some background on the notion of genre, and on how a genre-based pedagogy has been used in other educational contexts. In the central part of the chapter, data drawn from a study of CLIL classrooms in Spain are used to illustrate how elements of a genre-based pedagogy might be of benefit in CLIL instruction in secondary history. The chapter concludes by showing how using elements of a genre-based pedagogy can be linked to a 4 Cs approach to CLIL (Coyle, Hood & Marsh 2010). The main argument is that an understanding of genres can both show what it is that CLIL students have to achieve in terms of mastering discipline-specific texts, and provide a scaffolding structure for the joint construction of meaning in CLIL classrooms. While the focus of genre-based pedagogy has generally been on the production of written texts, it is argued that the process of joint construction of meaning as part of the "learning-teaching cycle" (Rothery 1996) can guide the production of oral discourse in CLIL classrooms.

2.   Genre and subject-specific literacy

As Luke, Freebody and Land (2000: 111) point out, disciplines such as science, history and social studies do not exist as we know them independently of their texts. In this way, they claim, the study of an academic discipline is a discourse practice. By participating in the practices typical of the subject and adopting the appropriate roles, for example by examining and analysing the veracity of sources in history instruction, students gain a "grasp of practice" (Ford & Forman 2006). In participating in such disciplinary practices, students will be positioned in the role of "text user" (Freebody 1992). They should be able to use texts functionally by

> knowing about and acting on the different cultural and social functions that various texts perform both inside and outside school and knowing that these functions shape the way texts are structured, their tone, their degree of formality and their sequence of components.   (Luke, Freebody & Land 2000: 29)

However, using subject-specific texts functionally presents certain challenges in second and foreign language contexts in which "knowledge of the language in which genres are composed cannot be assumed" (Martin 2009: 16). Martin goes on to point out that, in these contexts, "discussing the relation of lexis, grammar, and discourse structure to genre is inescapable – since the lower level resources have to be brought to consciousness and taught" (ibid.). This call for explicit teaching of lexicogrammar in relation to discourse structure contrasts with 'language bath' approaches to CLIL in which language learning is simply assumed to happen by osmosis.

Some of the arguments put forward in support of CLIL, at least as far as the second 'L' is concerned, would seem to suggest that it is influenced by what Bernstein (1996) described as a "competence" approach to pedagogy, in which learning is seen as a tacit process, with weak framing of the selection, grading and pacing of content (in this case, the 'content' being language). In this approach, teachers' main role is to facilitate the learning process and manage the learning context (Leung 2001: 42). As Leung (2001) and Creese (2005) point out, this approach has proved problematic in other contexts in which learners study subject matter in an additional language, such as schools in England in which English as an additional language (EAL) learners are mainstreamed into content classes. Byrnes (2009) shows that another approach that attempts to integrate content and language learning, content-based instruction (CBI) in the United States, "has often drawn on experiential knowledge that is short on principled approaches to language learning and teaching" (ibid. 1).

One principled way in which attention can be focused on the texts intrinsic to the practices in school subjects taught through CLIL is to use the concept of genre as developed in systemic functional linguistics. According to Martin and Rose, genres are

> staged, goal oriented social processes. Staged, because it usually takes us more than one step to reach our goals; goal oriented because we feel frustrated if we don't accomplish the final steps (…); social because writers shape their texts for readers of particular kinds.   (Martin & Rose 2008: 6)

They go on to point out that genres "enact the social practices of a given culture" (ibid.). In the case of learning academic subjects, including in CLIL contexts, an important aspect of 'culture' is that of the discipline being studied. In learning school science, for example, students may have to understand and/or produce genres such as different types of reports (descriptive, classifying and compositional) or procedural recounts which report on observations or experiments (Martin & Rose 2008). These genres cannot be seen in isolation from the oral language through which the content and procedural knowledge they express is construed. As Gibbons (2006: 32–36) explains, learners working in an L2 move along a "mode continuum" from more context-embedded spoken language to written texts which are more distanced from the original events in which they participated (see also Martin 1984). Thus, for example, CLIL learners may carry out a science experiment in which they use oral discourse as part of the activity, but may later have to produce a written procedural recount of the same experiment.

In order to be competent 'text users' of these genres in Freebody and Luke's terms, students will need, following the definition of genre above, to have a grasp of their purposes, the stages through which they are constructed and how they

are variously shaped for different audiences. For example, in producing a procedural recount in school science, students need to be aware of these three aspects
of the genre: its purpose in reporting on the steps of an investigation to an audience who was not present; the different stages (purpose, equipment and materials ∧ method ∧ results ∧ (conclusion))[1]; and the shaping for the audience involved
in the use of 'impersonal' or 'agentless' types of language such as passives.

3. Genre-based pedagogy

Proponents of a genre approach to school literacy in the 'Sydney School' of systemic functional linguistics have been developing a pedagogy for increasing
students' awareness and control of a range of genres important to their learning of school subjects such as history and science since the late 80's and 90's
(e.g. Cope & Kalantzis 1993; Johns 2002; Martin 1999, 2009; Martin & Rose
2008). The main objective of this pedagogy is to make explicit the stages and
linguistic features of key school genres and guide students in the production of
these important text types.

An important principle in this pedagogy is that such school genres are keys to
powerful and prestigious discourses in society, and that by denying students access
to them by, for example advocating certain types of progressive, constructivist or
process pedagogies, we may be doing a disservice to disadvantaged students (see
Martin & Rose 2008: 226–229 for a recent discussion of these issues). The present chapter, while acknowledging this sociopolitical dimension of genre pedagogy,
emphasizes more the importance of scaffolding English language learners' access
to the relevant text types in the subjects they are studying in CLIL, and integrating
language work within this framework. In this sense, it builds on previous work
which has highlighted the importance of an awareness of genre and rhetorical
features of texts and the language used to construe knowledge in CLIL classrooms
(for an example see Morgan 1999).

The genre-based pedagogy developed by the Sydney School researchers
(Martin 1999, 2002; Rothery 1996) consists of a 'teaching/learning cycle' in which
students are guided towards control and a critical appreciation of genres through
the stages of deconstruction, joint construction and independent construction.
In the deconstruction stage, students' awareness is raised of the purposes, stages
and linguistic features of the genre. In the joint construction phase, students
and teacher together build a representative example of the genre in question.

---

1. In genre notation, the symbol ∧ means 'followed by'.

Throughout this process, teacher and students are jointly building 'field knowledge', i.e. the relevant content that will be 'packaged' in the genre under construction. In the independent construction stage, students prepare their own examples of the genre. While this can be seen as a temporal, three-stage process, Martin (1999: 127) points out that this instruction can begin at any point, depending on the needs of the students.

Importantly for CLIL contexts, a genre-based approach provides a framework for the types of productive teacher-student (and student-student) spoken interaction which it is hoped will take place in CLIL or content-based instruction, and which may not always occur (Dalton-Puffer 2007; Musumeci 1996). A key concept is "guidance through interaction in the context of shared experience" (Martin 1999: 126). Throughout the processes of building field knowledge, and deconstructing and constructing relevant genres, teachers and students will be involved in interactions in which they explore not only the meanings relevant to the specific content being studied, but also the forms in which this content can best be communicated. Analysing such interactions according to the three register dimensions of field, tenor and mode (Martin 1999: 133–141; Martin & Rose 2008: 11–16) can throw light on the ways in which such interaction can be productive for learning in CLIL.

In terms of field, students and teachers gather information and move from commonsense to uncommonsense knowledge about disciplinary content. Information, rather than being organised in 'horizontal' or loosely organised structures (Bernstein 1999) may be organised according to taxonomies which can involve classification or composition (Martin 2007). In terms of tenor, or the interpersonal dimension of language use, the teacher can shape the ongoing construction of knowledge by the use of certain linguistic and interactional options such as asking questions, pausing, or providing prompts and cues. The mode dimension can best be understood as conscious attention to the role of language and discourse in packaging the information, for example in moving along the mode continuum from the more context-embedded spoken forms to the expression of academic knowledge in writing (Gibbons 2006).

Thus, a genre-based pedagogy informing a language curriculum for CLIL pays attention not only to the formal features of the text types which constitute disciplinary knowledge, but by also incorporating the notion of register, allows us to focus on the processes through which content learning is scaffolded (Hammond & Gibbons 2005; Sharpe 2006) as teachers and students engage in spoken discourse in the classroom. In the classroom data presented later in this chapter I will show how such processes already take place to a certain extent in the secondary CLIL history classrooms I observed, but will argue that such instruction could be enhanced with a more explicit focus on the purposes, stages and linguistic features of relevant history genres, and a greater understanding of the classroom discourse processes through which this knowledge is scaffolded with CLIL students.

4. Genres in secondary school history

Over the last two decades, linguists working from a systemic functional perspective have developed detailed descriptions of the genres and registers of history as an academic discipline (Coffin 2004, 2006a, 2006b; Eggins, Wignell & Martin 1993; Martin 2002; McCabe 1999; Schleppegrell & de Oliveira 2006; Schleppegrell, Achugar & Oteíza 2004; Veel & Coffin 1996). These studies have largely focused on history genres in English-speaking contexts, and thus must be treated with caution when discussing other educational and national cultures. However, evidence from the materials used in the CLIL classrooms reported on in this study shows that similar genres were in operation, if only tacitly.

Recently, functional linguists have worked with history teachers to raise their awareness of the importance of language in learning the subject. In one example, Coffin (2006a) shows how concepts from functional linguistics enabled history teachers to explore how language is used to build the key genres of the subject and to develop an approach to teaching these genres explicitly. According to Coffin, this collaboration had encouraging results in that the history teachers were positive about this approach and their students showed improvement in organising the history texts they had to write, and showed an increased ability to recontextualise ideas in meaningful ways rather than copying text (Coffin 2006a: 427). In other work with history teachers, Schleppegrell, Achugar and Oteíza (2004) and Schleppegrell and de Oliveira (2006) focused in more detail on the linguistic realisations of history genres. The results were positive in that there was improvement in the quality of students' classroom discussions of history topics, particularly with students who were English Language Learners (ELLs).

Coffin (2006a) uses a functional perspective to show how the linguistic demands of the secondary history curriculum become more complex as students move upwards through the secondary grades. In the earlier grades (approximate ages 11–13), the key text types are 'recording genres' whose main purpose is to retell events from the past. Examples are personal and biographical recounts which focus on the events in an indvidual's life, and historical recounts which focus at a more general level on historical events. A more complex genre in this category is the historical account, which also retells events from the past but adds to this some explanation of why they took place in this sequence.

Moving up the secondary history curriculum (ages 14–16), the key text types are 'explaining' genres, which involve explanations of the factors that led to a particular historical outcome, or consequences of a particular event. In the final years of secondary schooling (ages 16–18), the level of sophistication increases, with students expected to manipulate 'arguing' genres, which involve putting the case for or against one or more points of view on an important historical issue or event.

Along with these shifts in genre, students are expected to manage linguistic resources of increasing sophistication and complexity, with an increase in generalization, abstraction and the use of subject-specific lexis (Coffin 2006a: 420). One important linguistic resource is that of 'nominalisation', in which processes which are normally expressed as verbs, or logical connections typically expressed as conjunctions, are re-packaged as nouns. According to Martin (2007: 48–55), this process of grammatical metaphor is the 'gatekeeper' or the key to unlocking the kinds of vertical discourse through which knowledge is construed in academic subjects in secondary schools.

5.   Three examples of classroom practice in secondary CLIL history

In this section I present three examples of CLIL practices in bilingual departments in two secondary schools in Madrid, Spain. The schools are part of a bilingual education project led by the Spanish Ministry of Education and the British Council, with social sciences (history and geography), natural sciences (biology and geology) and technology being taught in English to students who mostly come from a bilingual primary school in the school's catchment area. One school is in a relatively prosperous middle class area, and the other is in a more working class area. In both, there is a generally high degree of enthusiasm for the bilingual project among staff, parents and pupils.

The data extracts come from audio and video recordings which were made as part of a multiple case study of the discursive practices and cognitions of five teachers working in the two schools. Three lessons for each teacher were recorded and transcribed and examples of materials used and students' work were collected. Teachers were interviewed both before and after the recordings in order to generate accounts of their planning processes and to elicit video stimulated comments on their classroom practices.

In none of the classrooms observed was there any explicit focus on the stages or linguistic features of history genres, either as texts to be understood or deconstructed or as texts to be produced by the students. Interestingly, however, the geography and history textbook used by the classes in the study required students to use a variety of genres in written exercises. In the list of activities from the textbook below, we can see that a range of genres is implicated:

1. Write a text *explaining* who the Yanomami people are and how many people there are and how they live. (From unit on prehistory: 143)
2. Search for information in an encyclopaedia and write a *tale* about the life of any of the great patriarchs or kings of Israel (Abraham, Moses, Joshua, Solomon, David). (From unit on the first civilizations: 157)
3. Write a similar *biography* on another character from ancient Greece. (From unit on Greek civilization: 199)
4. Out of all the peoples that inhabited the Peninsula in Antiquity, which one has left the deepest mark? Where is this noticeable? (From unit on the Iberian Peninsula in Antiquity: 242).   (Etxebarría et al. 2002 – italics added)

In the textbook there is no explicit guidance or instruction about *how* to construct the relevant genres, and the terminology is not always consistent, as in the first example above where an "explaining" text is asked for where the relevant genre is a report. So, while the characteristics of genres may not be referred to explicitly in the textbook, they are most definitely there in the tasks that students are asked to do. Even when specific text types are mentioned in curricular guidelines, as in the UK curriculum guides which inform the integrated curriculum used in the schools in the study, they are not normally the focus of explicit instruction. Spanish CLIL students, like many other CLIL and non-CLIL students around the world, may simply be expected to cope as best they can. And, as they move upward through the curriculum, the demands become more complex. Indeed, even in this first year secondary textbook, they are asked to produce arguing texts, as in the fourth example above.

Activities which involve literacy may therefore place high demands on CLIL students without offering the kinds of scaffolding they would need to complete them effectively. Alternatively, and this was often the case with the textbook discussed here, many classroom or homework tasks only required very short (often one word) answers, a practice which seems difficult to justify in a pedagogy such as CLIL which is intended to have a dual focus on content and language development. There is evidence that this situation may be more general in CLIL practices in Europe. For example, Dalton-Puffer (2007) found little attention to writing in her corpus of Austrian CLIL lessons, something which reflected the situation in Austrian non-CLIL contexts as well.

In the history lessons from the lower secondary years, there was little evidence of the recording genres, which, according to Coffin's work, would be expected at this level. A possible explanation may lie in the possible differences in genres across national and educational cultures, as mentioned above. For example, some of the teachers in the present study stated the opinion that narrative recounts of events were not really 'history' and that the Spanish curriculum focused more on causes and consequences. In fact, there was quite frequently a focus on cause and effect in teacher-led classroom discourse, but there was no evidence of any attention to the kinds of cause-effect written genres identified by Coffin. The most commonly used genre in the early secondary classes observed was the report, which is a genre used for making generalised descriptions (Martin 1993; Martin & Rose 2003: 209). This genre was used particularly in oral presentations of information that the students had researched, as will be described below.

5.1   Classroom Examples 1 and 2: building field knowledge together

The first extract from the classroom data is taken from near the beginning of a second-year secondary history lesson (students are 13–14 years old). The teacher is going over work they had done in previous lessons and for homework on the Emperor Justinian and his wife Theodora. In this sequence, she is attempting to establish the importance of the Empress Theodora's role in possibly expanding women's rights. The sequence is given in full here:

Sequence 1. What Theodora did for women

T: OK very good. And something about Theodora? Did she do something important?

S: (inaudible)

T: Yes, something very very important did she do anything?

S: (inaudible)

T: Yes, what?

S: (inaudible)

T: What did she do?

S: In the year 552 took place in Constantinople a resurrection and Theodora put it down.

T: Ah OK, so she had a very important role when there was a riot, there was a riot as she participated as she (…) There the role she developed she had a very very important thing to do there because er Justininian had real problems. Remember we mentioned religious problems? Yeah? So that day there was a riot and she was very very strict and she said she backed her husband, she backed the emperor and that was very very important. OK. And something about (…) Did she do anything good for women? Did she? What? What did she do? Remember her background? What was her job? What has she worked in? She was…?

S: An actress.

T: An actress. Where?

SS: In the hipódromo.

> T: OK hipódromos. Because her father had -
> S: He was a bear keeper ((pronounced *beer*)).
> T: A bear ((correct pronunciation)) keeper very good. Bear keeper. Yes, very good. OK, so? What has what was her job?
> S: An actress.
> T: An actress correct. Did she do anything for women do you think?
> S: That the women could eh be an actress too.
> T: OK women could be actresses too could participate or something else?
> S: They had eh democracy.
> T: They had democracy where?
> S: In (…)
> T: OK so we're talking about a women – woman. Did she do anything good for women? Remember she had been an actress and suddenly there was an opposition a strong opposition for Justinian to marry her but they had to change the law so he could marry her and then (…) Do you think she did something good for women?
> S: Yes.
> T: Yes? what type?
> S: They women had more power in economy and -
> T: OK women could have more power and her rights. What about her rights do you think she worked for women's rights?
> S: They could marry.
> T: They could marry more easily, yes. What else?
> S: With eh with anybody.
> T: With anybody. Yeah. About …
>   ((interruption as someone knocks door))
> T: OK, so. Probably she did a lot for women. Ok so ah we're going to stop there and we're going to start on something different. Could you please open your textbooks on pages 134 and 135?

In terms of field knowledge, in this sequence the teacher seems to be pushing towards a general and perhaps more abstract understanding of Theodora's possible role in expanding women's rights. The students are relatively successful in providing possibly relevant but perhaps rather isolated facts about Theodora's life, rather than encapsulating the important idea about what exactly Theodora's achievement for the benefit of women was. The end of the sequence seems rather inconclusive as the teacher decides to move on to another topic.

In terms of tenor, the teacher uses a range of questioning and elicitation techniques to attempt to build a common understanding with the students. There are examples of cued elicitation, which Mercer (2001: 46) describes as "a way of drawing out from learners the information they (the teachers- TM) are seeking – the right answers to their questions – by providing visual clues and verbal hints as to what answer is required". For example, when the teacher asks "What was her job? What has she worked in? She was…?" she gives a verbal hint by leaving the sentence unfinished for the students to complete, which one student duly does by saying "an actress".

Elsewhere, the teacher simply asks for information by using 'wh'-questions, such as "What did she do?" and "What was her job?". As the teacher already knows the answers she is looking for, these are 'display' questions. According to Zwiers (2008: 105), such questions can have a variety of useful functions: quickly showing what students already know before teaching a topic, bringing up facts, concepts, and ideas needed for discussion, and helping teachers quickly find out what students have learned. In the sequence above, the display questions and cued elicitations may have the double function of checking on what the students have learned, and bringing up the relevant facts about Theodora's life upon which can be built the more conceptually advanced generalisation of "what Theodora did for women".

However, the rather inconclusive ending to the sequence, perhaps contributed to by the interruption near the end, may have reduced the effectiveness of this dialogue in building a shared understanding of what it was that Theodora did for women. Mortimer and Scott (2003: 44–45) show that by carrying out such specific interventions as selecting and marking key ideas and ending dialogic sequences with more authoritative summarising statements of important ideas, teachers can more effectively build shared understanding in the classroom. Using a genre-based approach may provide a framework and a clear purpose for carrying out such interventions, as they would be clearly linked to the pedagogical purposes of not only building field knowledge, but of shaping the appropriate form or genre through which this knowledge can be communicated.

One way to provide such a focus for the spoken discourse would be to use the 'biographical recount' genre (Coffin 2006a: 418; Martin & Rose 2008: 100–105). The purposes and structure of biographical recounts are set out in Table 1:

Table 1. Biographical recount genre (Coffin 2006a: 418; Martin 2002: 110)

Genre (staging)	Purpose	Key linguistic features
Biographical recount [orientation ^ record ^ (evaluation of person)]	To retell the events of a person's life	Setting in time; 3rd person (specific); other specific and generic participants

Reworking this sequence as the building of field knowledge in the context of the joint construction of a biographical recount of Theodora's life would have the effect of contextualising the more isolated facts about her life in the chronological sequence of events, and of providing a purpose for the evaluation of the importance of her role. There would be a focus on the significance of events in the whole experience of her lifetime, and this would mean moving from serial to episodic time, with location in time expressed as circumstances in clauses as opposed to conjunctions (Martin & Rose 2008: 103).

In terms of mode, whatever it was that "Theodora did for women" would need to be expressed in an appropriate form of words, jointly constructed by the students and teacher, that would encapsulate the shared knowledge constructed in the classroom about the importance of Theodora's role. The 'raw data' built up by the students and teacher could then be 'packaged' in the relevant generic form, with perhaps some attention paid (either by the CLIL history teacher, or an English teacher working in collaboration) to the linguistic features of the genre, for example the organisation of time as circumstances at the beginning of clauses. Thus, through the teaching/learning cycle, the teacher could scaffold the students' linguistic trajectory as they move along the mode continuum from the spoken forms through which the knowledge was built, to forms more appropriate to the register of history.

The second classroom data extract shows an example of how CLIL history instruction can be moved in this direction. In this example, a CLIL history teacher, in a lesson about Oliver Cromwell, used a scaffolding process in which the language which students were exposed to in a reading text moved along a mode continuum before it was written on the board in a form which highlighted the structure of an 'argument' genre – whether Cromwell was a hero or a villain. Throughout the episode, the teacher skilfully managed various students' language production in two ways: by getting them to express the meanings in the text more flexibly in their own words (see Lemke 1990, on the importance of students expressing the 'thematics' and not just the 'wordings'), and by 'translating' ideas into a more 'academic' register (Mohan & Beckett 2003) which would be appropriate to an argument genre. In sequence 2 we see how she 'upgrades' one student's contributions to a more academic register.

Sequence 2. Oliver Cromwell

    T: Any other reason why he was a hero? Marta?
    S: Threw the corrupts member members of parliament awa-off.
    T: Can you say that in your own words?
    S: ((long pause)) He took out the corrupt people of the parliament.
    T: So he erm removed corruption from parliament ((writes on board)) corruption from Parliament okay.

In this extract the teacher asks the student to give an idea from the text to support the thesis that Cromwell was a 'hero'. In spite of the teacher's instruction to say it in her own words, the student in fact has already changed the wording in the original text, which was "He took 30 soldiers to the House of Commons and threw the corrupt MPs out". The teacher then moves the discourse along the mode continuum towards a more academic register in two ways. She first replaces the more everyday expression 'throw out' with the more academic 'removed', and secondly modifies the adjective 'corrupt' to the grammatical metaphor 'corruption'. Thus there is clear evidence of movement along a mode continuum in which the thematic meanings undergo a trajectory from the original reading text through the student's and teacher's rewordings to the version in the blackboard table (Table 2).

Table 2. Mode continuum in 3rd year history activity

Text 1 (reading)	Text 2 (student's version 1)	Text 3 (student's version 2)	Text 4 (teacher's reformulation on board)
He took 30 soldiers to the House of Commons and threw the corrupt MPs out	Threw the corrupts member members of parliament awa–off	He took out the corrupt people of the Parliament	He removed corruption from Parliament

As a result of such re-engineering of the wordings from the original texts, the students' contributions and the teacher's modifications, the information was organised as a table on the blackboard (Table 3).

Table 3. Contents of blackboard in 3rd year history lesson on Cromwell

Hero	Villain
He was the most powerful ruler of the time	He didn't deserve power
He meant to improve the country by the abolition of parliament	He betrayed the parliament
He helped the Protestants in Ireland	He punished the Catholics in Ireland
Protestants and Catholics showed the same cruelty	Burning of Catholic people alive
He removed corruption from parliament	He entered parliament by force

Although this teacher was not explicitly using a genre-based pedagogy, this example shows the close connections between the joint construction of field knowledge and the linguistic and structural realisations of this knowledge in text types such as exposition genres. It can be seen from the features of such a genre as identified by Coffin (Table 4) that the example of classroom practice described here would work well as a construction of field knowledge phase on the way to the joint construction of an example of this genre. With the main ideas collected on the board, the teacher and students together could construct an example of an exposition genre in which the writer defended one of the two theses: Cromwell as hero or villain. Again, as in the previous example, either in the history class, or in

English lessons, the students could be introduced to the purposes, stages and key linguistic features of the genre. Such practices are already common in L1 history teaching in the UK for example, where teachers in history lessons make repeated references to how the content is to be organised in essays.

Table 4. The exposition genre in secondary history (Coffin 2006a: 418; Martin 2002: 110)

Genre (staging)	Purpose	Key linguistic features
Exposition – one sided [thesis ^ arguments]	To put forward a point of view or argument	Use of evidence rather than chronology to organise text; internal conjunction; generalised, abstract nouns; nominalisation

5.2   Classroom Example 3: Student presentations

The third example comes from a first year CLIL history class (12–13 years old), in which the topic is life in prehistory. This whole lesson was taken up with three student group presentations. The first was about a visit to an archeological theme park, the second was about different hunting tools and the making of fire, and the third was about a sculpture from prehistoric times. The data presented here are from the first presentation, in which a group talk about their visit to an archeological theme park and what they had done and learned there.

Sequence 3. School outing

S1:   We are going to talk about the our school outing to Arqueopinto. First of all what we did there. Here's some pictures of a – of the prehistoric men and some people painting their faces ((points to photos on blackboard)). Here are Marta and Ana who were volunteers to paint their faces. The painting were eh doing mixing up water and some stones of the prehistorian age. Then we started our guided visit to the park. The first eh thing we saw was the Australopithecus eh which was the first the first ant – eh antecesors of us. And Jaime dressed up with a – with a Australopithecus mask.

S2:   Then Jaime dressed with a mask to imitate the Australopithecus. After the Australopithecus there was the Homo habilis which we didn't see eh but started making sorts of stone.

S1:   After that there was the Homo – Homo habus Homo erm habilus and then the Homo erectus which was like the Homo habilis but he had a greater technological advance. They start living in the southern part of Europa and Asia. This was the Homo erectus and this is Carlos ((laughter)). Then there was the Homo sapiens who appeared a hundred thousand ye- years ago and is divided into two sub-types the Homo sapiens neanderthalensis and the Homo sapiens sapiens. The Homo sapiens neanderthalensis started living in the northern part of Asia and Europe, in Oceania and in the western coast of

America. The Homo sapiens sapiens appeared thirty-five thousand years ago and is the species we belong to. He he lives in all the – all the world because he arrived into America.

In this extract, the students display competence in giving the audience a lively and engaging account of what they did and learned at the theme park. There is evidence that they had designed the presentation with their audience in mind, with a skilful mix of information about their own and their classmates' activities and what they learned there. They also signpost the presentation by announcing what they are going to talk about and by signalling the fact that they will first deal with their own activities there, before signalling the change of topic to the guided visit with the use of *then*.

The first part of the presentation, "what we did there" can be related to the personal recount, which is a genre found in some educational contexts to be relatively common in primary school and in the lower years of secondary school. Aspects of the second part, what they learned in the guided visit, can be linked to a genre less frequently found in history but often used in science – the report (Martin & Rose 2008: 3).

Table 5. The personal recount genre (based on Martin 2002: 110)

Genre (staging)	Purpose	Key linguistic features
Personal recount [orientation ∧ record]	To retell events, what happened to me	Sequence in time; 1st person; specific participants

Features of the personal recount genre (see Table 5) can be clearly identified in the extract from the students' presentation shown here. In the first line we find the orientation stage ("We are going to talk about the our school outing to Arqueopinto"). This is followed by the record of events, although the multimodal nature of this presentation, with the students pointing to and making deictic references to their pictures with *here's* and *here are* mean that the description of their activities is less explicitly coded by using material verbs in the past tense. However, elsewhere there is plenty of evidence of the key linguistic features of this genre, with events being sequenced in time with *first of all, then, the first thing we saw,* and the use of the first person plural and identification of specific participants (her classmates on the outing).

In the second part of this extract, the generic features seem to shade into those of another genre, that of the report, which has the main functions of classifying and describing things (Martin & Rose 2008: 142). Table 6 shows the features of this genre.

Table 6. The report genre (based on Martin 2002 and Martin & Rose 2003)

Genre (staging)	Purpose	Key linguistic features
Report [classification ∧ description of aspects of entity]	To make generalized descriptions	Relational verbs (being, having, existing); technical terminology; nominalisation

Student 1 orients to the report genre in her first turn when she says "The first thing we saw" and thus begins to provide descriptions of features or activities of the different hominids they had seen at the park. There is clear evidence of classification ("the Homo sapiens who appeared a hundred thousand ye- years ago and *is divided into two sub-types* the Homo sapiens neanderthalensis and the Homo sapiens sapiens") with descriptions of different aspects of the entities classified, such as where they lived ("The Homo sapiens neanderthalensis started living in the northern part of Asia and Europe, in Oceania and in the western coast of America").

This section of the presentation also displays many of the key linguistic features of the report genre. There are many examples of relational or existential verbs (*there was, was, had, was, there was, is divided into*), the use of technical terminology (*Australopithecus, Homo habilis, Homo erectus, Homo sapiens neanderthalensis, Homo sapiens sapiens*) and nominalisations (*a greater technological advance*). However, while the presentation as a text displays elements of the genres described, and many of their linguistic features, it cannot be said that it consists of 'canonical' examples of these genres. Rather, semantic and linguistc elements are knitted together in a text, which, while not representing any one genre, has a 'flavour' of at least two. A third may even be present by the end of the extract with the shift to verbs expressing material processes (*started, appeared, lives, arrived*) characterising another school history genre, the historical recount (Coffin 2006a; Martin & Rose 2008).

By describing the text these students produced in terms of its generic features, we can begin to build a richer description of the competences the students were displaying here. Given the complexity of the different genres, with their purposes, components and linguistic features, the students' performance looks quite impressive. They are doing two quite different things at once: using elements of a personal recount genre to relate their trip to the theme park (i.e. what they *did* there) and using features of the report genre with perhaps elements of an historical recount to describe and classify what they *learned* there.

However, in the data shown here, and throughout the data set, there were marked differences in the ease with which students were able to produce the language and texts they needed to construct knowledge and gain a 'grasp of practice' of history. In the example discussed here, we can see that student 1, while not producing a canonical form, seems to manage the features of the genres she is using quite well. In contrast, student 2 does not seem to deal with the complexities quite so well. Her contribution is rather short compared to student 1's, and it seems to mix up rather confusingly what one classmate did with a mask and what Homo habilis did with stone.

As with the discussion of Examples 1 and 2, the sequence of activities culminating in the class presentations could be reworked to allow some explicit teaching of the purposes, stages and language of whichever genres were identified by the teacher as relevant to the pedagogical purposes of the activity. For example, students could be introduced to the 'report' genre and a range of linguistic structures for identifying, defining and classifying phenomena. This can be carried out at a relatively simple level, for example the use of 'being' and 'having' verbs. Students could also be introduced to the key features of recounts, such as the organisation of events in time. In preparing their presentations, there could be a 'division of labour' in which groups would work on either 'what we did' or 'what we learned' and be encouraged to present it in appropriate generic forms. This would help improve the overall clarity of the presentations, and may have equipped student 2 with a clear framework within which to package her contribution using appropriate linguistic features. Such a reworking could be done in the context of the history content being taught, thus enhancing and not drastically changing what was already an activity in which students were able to display competence in producing complex texts.

6.   Genre and the 4 Cs approach to CLIL

Coyle, Hood and Marsh (2010) propose a '4 Cs' approach to CLIL, in which the elements content, cognition, communication and culture are taken into account in planning for CLIL instruction. Such a holistic approach, in which culture permeates the other elements, can reinforce CLIL as a type of instruction which fuses the best of subject matter and language teaching pedagogies. In this section of the chapter I suggest how adopting elements of a genre-based pedagogy can enhance CLIL practices in relation to each of the 4 Cs.

In thinking about the content dimension, an advantage of a genre approach, and indeed approaches based on SFL, is that it works against any artificial separation of content and language. Functional descriptions of genre and register portray a rich picture of how meaning is made in social situations, and of how language is the main symbolic tool for learning (Halliday 1993; Vygotsky 1987). Content in any subject is likely to be packaged in ways which are specific to the academic culture, and unlocking these packages, or genres, may also provide access to the knowledge and skills which are at the heart of attaining a grasp of the practices of the discipline. In the context of the study reported here, much historical knowledge was wrapped in rather dense texts. Deconstruction and reconstruction of examples of these texts, along with a critical orientation to them, would be likely to empower students to get at the knowledge construed through them.

In terms of communication, a genre-based pedagogy need not involve the addition of an extra layer of language instruction over and above the content instruction. Rather, it would provide an opportunity for genuinely integrated language and literacy work in CLIL. Instructing students in the forms and functions of text types they will have to use in the course of their science, history or geography studies can be seen as a natural extension of such work and not an add-on that distracts from the history content (Coffin 2006a: 424). In this way, a genre-based pedagogy would contribute to language learning in CLIL by providing a principled way of enhancing the written production of CLIL learners. As Coffin reports (2006a: 427), using a genre approach with native speaker students enhanced their ability to organise texts, and reduced copying. In so far as written production is given importance in any CLIL context, it would seem imperative for the texts students produce to conform to the purposes, stages and linguistic features of the text types through which the discipline is built.

A genre approach could also contribute to enhancing CLIL instruction in the oral aspects of the 'C' of communication. In terms of the processes through which language and content learning takes place through the mediation of classroom discourse, it is hoped that the brief analysis above using the SFL concept of register and the suggested reworkings have gone some way to showing how a genre-based approach could enhance the negotiation of meaning through talk in the CLIL classroom. Episodes of joint knowledge construction would be given clear purposes such as building biographical detail or constructing an argument, and work could be jointly carried out on making the appropriate mode adjustments so that the language reflected the register of the subject being taught. A genre approach can also be compatible with Lyster's (2007) recommendations for a counterbalanced approach, in that raising CLIL learners' awareness of the organisational and particularly the lexicogrammatical features of the genres they use can be seen as enhancing input through noticing and awareness activity (Lyster 2007: 135).

A genre-based approach could also enrich instruction in the 'C' of cognition. Genres used in academic disciplines are strongly linked to thinking processes and knowledge structures (Mohan 1986) associated with different subjects. For example, one thinking process of great importance in secondary history is that of cause and effect (see Zwiers 2008). The secondary history genres of historical accounts and explanations move students away from chronology in organising events in the past towards explanations of causes and consequences (Coffin 2006a). Moving further up the secondary history curriculum, argument genres that require students to argue for or against or even balance different points of view require critical thinking and understanding of the role of bias in history. In this way, the use of genres as tools can provide frameworks and linguistic realisations for the knowledge structures and thinking processes typical of the subjects taught through CLIL.

A genre-based approach is also relevant to the fourth C, culture. Coyle, Hood and Marsh point out that incorporating a focus on intercultural competence in CLIL is "not an option, it is a necessity" (2010: 64). This view of culture puts the emphasis on CLIL as a means of developing intercultural understanding in the context of global citizenship, rather than seeing CLIL practices as directed towards national cultures associated with the CLIL language. In the functional perspective on language and meaning taken in this chapter, genres are ways in which particular cultures organise meanings, and a culture itself can be defined as "a system of genres" (Martin 2009: 13). Different cultures may choose to configure meanings in school subjects such as history in different ways. As Morgan points out, this need not be an obstacle, but a catalyst for work in intercultural understanding:

> When teaching in an environment where there is concern for intercultural understanding, and where this is seen as one of the purposes, texts from the L2 culture can provide a useful source not only of access to the genre vocabulary in that language, but also to the specific genre approach of that culture.   (1999: 46)

However, Morgan also warns of the danger of assuming that "key linguistic elements and approaches which belong to the genre of history teaching/ learning (…) are always shared universally across cultures." (ibid. 45). In this sense, implementing CLIL may raise questions about the cultural assumptions inherent in using approaches and teaching materials which are products of societies and communities outside the local teaching context. For example, the schools in the study presented here have an integrated curriculum, in which subject areas from both the Spanish and the English National Curriculum are taught. There is also a growing trend to enter students for international examinations such as the Cambridge IGCSE. In order to be successful in such examinations, students need to be equipped to deal successfully with a range of text types which may not be common in the local educational culture. In Luke, Freebody and Land's terms, students in these contexts will need to gain understanding of the "different *cultural* and social functions that various texts perform" (2000: 29, italics added).

A genre-based pedagogy, if adapted to the different contexts and disciplines within which CLIL is implemented, could provide a principled framework for scaffolding students' knowledge of and ability to act on these texts as cultural artefacts. The aim would not be to see the texts as representing any particular national culture, but to enhance awareness of them *as* cultural and social artefacts with their specific purposes, staging and linguistic realisations. This would mean that a genre approach to CLIL for developing intercultural competence and awareness would need to emphasise a critical orientation to genres and their discourses (Martin 1999: 130).

7.   Genre and CLIL teacher education

A final observation is that adopting versions or elements of a genre-based pedagogy in CLIL would have implications for teacher education and development. The discussion of classroom sequence 2 above and more general observation of the secondary history CLIL classrooms in the study provide anecdotal evidence that some teachers were aware of the importance of subject-specific literacies and took steps to explicitly teach aspects of this to their students. For example, in one school, CLIL and language teachers were working on a 'writing framework' which aimed to specify the types of texts and writing needs throughout the secondary history curriculum. Coming into contact with a genre-based pedagogy in professional development sessions run by the author enabled them to specify in more detail the different text types and their linguistic realisations. One CLIL history teacher reported that after this professional development he was implementing ideas from the genre approach in his history classes taught in the L1, Spanish.

In the professional development work on genre-based pedagogy in CLIL with these teachers there was ample evidence of their openness to such practices. They found useful an approach which lays out, for them and their students, how important disciplinary texts work and the language needed to produce them. However, this was a first acquaintance with genre-based pedagogy. More sustained professional development and research would be necessary to investigate the impact of learning about genre-based pedaogy on CLIL teachers' cognitions and practices, and ultimately, on their learners' development of discipline-specific literacies.

For a genre-based approach appropriate to CLIL to take root, CLIL teachers in general would require more formal knowledge of the genres they already use and knowledge of a wider repertoire of genres relevant to their subjects. This raises questions about the kinds of knowledge about language (KAL) that CLIL teachers need to use, and has implications for pre and in-service education for CLIL teachers and language teachers who work with them (see Carter 1990 and Christie 2006 for discussions of KAL in general education, and Andrews 2007 for KAL in second language teaching). Martin (2009: 12) points out that in L1 educational contexts,

> [g]enre theory provided teachers with KAL that was relatively easy to bring to consciousness and did not immediately demand a costly induction into knowledge about functional grammar and discourse semantics.

As argued here, using 'popularizations' (Martin 2009: 14) of genre theory with CLIL teachers and language teachers who work with them offers a route towards a more principled integration of language and content. Making such work relevant to CLIL and language teachers should be feasible, as the relations between genre and lexicogrammar provide "a natural context for learning words and structures in second language development" (ibid.18).

8.   Conclusion

In this chapter I have argued that adopting aspects of a genre-based pedagogy could go some way towards meeting the need for more specifically defined language curricula in CLIL. Such a pedagogy would counteract a view of CLIL in which the first 'L' is, in Bernstein's terms, weakly framed, with little explicit selection, grading and pacing of what subject-specific language is to be learned. As Martin (2009: 19) suggests, the practical power of a genre-based model has yet to be fully explored in second language contexts, particularly in renovating pedagogy in two areas: the teaching of grammar and lexis and the focus on spoken discourse. This chapter has aimed to show how a genre-based pedagogy has potential for renovating or stimulating CLIL instruction by integrating with content a focus on subject-specific texts, their grammar and lexis, and the spoken discourse involved in their construction. Although the examples in the chapter focus on history, it is hoped that practitioners will see the potential of the approach to other CLIL subjects. Above all, it is hoped that the chapter has gone some way towards suggesting how a genre-based model of language combined with a teaching/learning cycle adapted to CLIL could provide a principled basis for the design of language curricula for CLIL and a framework for informing classroom pedagogy across CLIL contexts.

References

Andrews, S. 2007. *Teacher Language Awareness*. Cambridge: CUP.
Bernstein, B. 1996. *Pedagogy, Symbolic Control and Identity*. London: Taylor and Francis.

Bernstein, B. 1999. Vertical and horizontal discourse: An essay. *British Journal of Sociology of Education* 20(2): 157–173.

Byrnes, H. 2009. Systemic-functional reflections on instructed foreign language acquisition as meaning-making: An introduction. *Linguistics and Education* 20: 1–9.

Carter, R. (ed.). 1990. *Knowledge about Language and the Curriculum: The LINC reader.* London: Hodder & Stoughton.

Christie, F. 2006. Literacy teaching and current debates over reading. In *Language and Literacy: Functional Approaches*, R. Whittaker, M. O'Donnell & A. McCabe (eds), 45–65. London: Continuum.

Coffin, C. 2004. Learning to write history: The role of causality. *Written Communication* 21(3): 261–289.

Coffin, C. 2006a. Learning the language of school history: The role of linguistics in mapping the writing demands of the secondary school curriculum. *Journal of Curriculum Studies* 38(4): 413–429.

Coffin, C. 2006b. *Historical Discourse: The Language of Time, Cause and Evaluation.* London: Continuum.

Cope, B. & Kalantzis, M. (eds). 1993. *The Powers of Literacy: A Genre Approach to Teaching Writing.* London: Falmer Press.

Coyle, D., Hood, P. & Marsh, D. 2010. *Content and Language Integrated Learning.* Cambridge: CUP.

Creese, A. 2005. Is this content-based language teaching? *Linguistics and Education* 16(2): 188–204.

Dalton-Puffer, C. 2007. *Discourse in Content and Language Integrated Learning (CLIL) Classrooms* [Language Learning and Language Teaching 20]. Amsterdam: John Benjamins.

Eggins, S., Wignell, P. & Martin, J. 1993. The discourse of history: Distancing the recoverable past. In *Register Analysis: Theory and Practice*, M. Ghadessy (ed.), 75–109. London: Pinter.

Etxebarría, L., Grence, T., Moralejo, P. & Ramírez, D. 2002. *Geography and History 1.* Madrid: Santillana.

Ford, M.J. & Forman, E.A. 2006. Redefining disciplinary learning in classroom contexts. *Review of Research in Education* 30: 1–32.

Freebody, P. 1992. A socio-cultural approach: Resourcing four roles as a literacy learner. In *Prevention of Reading Failure*, A. Watson & A. Badenhop (eds), 48–60. Sydney: Ashton-Scholastic.

Gibbons, P. 2006. *Bridging Discourses in the ESL Classroom.* London: Continuum.

Halliday, M.A.K. 1993. Towards a language-based theory of learning. *Linguistics and Education* 5: 93–116.

Hammond, J. & Gibbons, P. 2005. Putting scaffolding to work: The contribution of scaffolding in articulating ESL education. *Prospect* 20(1): 6–30.

Johns, A.M. (ed.). 2002. *Genre in the Classroom: Multiple Perspectives.* Mahwah, NJ: Lawrence Erlbaum Associates.

Lemke, J.L. 1990. *Talking Science: Language, Learning, and Values.* Norwood NJ: Ablex.

Leung, C. 2001. English as an additional language: Distinct language focus or diffused curriculum concerns? *Language and Education* 15(1): 33–55.

Luke, A., Freebody, P. & Land, R. 2000. *Literate Futures: Review of Literacy Education.* Brisbane: Education Queensland.

Lyster, R. 2007. *Learning and Teaching Languages through Content: A Counterbalanced Approach* [Language Learning & Language Teaching 18]. Amsterdam: John Benjamins.

Martin, J.R. 1984. Language, register and genre. In *Children Writing: A Reader*, F. Christie (ed.), 21–30. Geelong: Deakin University Press.

Martin, J.R. 1993. Life as a noun: Arresting the universe in science and humanities. In *Writing Science: Literacy and Discursive Power*, M.A.K. Halliday & J.R. Martin (eds), 221–267. London: Falmer.

Martin, J.R. 1999. Mentoring semogenesis: 'Genre-based' literacy pedagogy. In *Pedagogy and the Shaping of Consciousness: Linguistic and Social Processes*, F. Christie (ed.), 123–155. London: Continuum.

Martin, J.R. 2002. Writing history: Construing time and value in discourses of the past. In *Developing Advanced Literacy in First and Second Languages: Meaning with Power*, M.J. Schleppegrell & M.C. Colombi (eds), 87–118. Mahwah NJ: Lawrence Erlbaum Associates.

Martin, J.R. 2007. Construing knowledge: A functional linguistic perspective. In *Language, Knowledge & Pedagogy: Functional Linguistic and Sociological Perspectives*, F. Christie & J.R. Martin (eds.), 34–64. London: Continuum.

Martin, J.R. 2009. Genre and language learning: A social semiotic perspective. *Linguistics and Education* 20: 10–21.

Martin, J.R. & Rose, D. 2003. *Working with Discourse: Meaning beyond the Clause*. London: Continuum.

Martin, J.R. & Rose, D. 2008. *Genre Relations: Mapping Culture*. London: Equinox.

McCabe, A. 1999. Theme and Thematic Patterns in Spanish and English History Texts. Ph.D. dissertation, Aston University.

Mercer, N. 2001. Language for teaching a language. In *English Language Teaching in its Social Context*, C.N. Candlin & N. Mercer (eds.), 243–257. London: Routledge.

Mohan, B. 1986. *Language and Content*. Reading MA: Addison-Wesley.

Mohan, B. & Beckett, G.H. 2003. A functional approach to research on content-based language learning: Recasts in causal explanations. *Modern Language Journal* 87(3): 421–432.

Morgan, C. 1999. Teaching history in a foreign language: What language? In *Teaching through a Foreign Language*, J. Masih. (ed.), 37–52. London: CILT.

Mortimer, E. & Scott, P. 2003. *Meaning Making in Secondary Science Classrooms*. Buckingham: Open University Press.

Musumeci, D. 1996. Teacher-learner negotiation in content-based instruction: Communication at cross-purposes? *Applied Linguistics* 17(3): 286–325.

Rothery, J. 1996. Making changes: Developing an educational linguistics. In *Literacy in Society*, R. Hasan & G. Williams (eds), 86–123. London: Longman.

Schleppegrell, M.J. 2004. *The Language of Schooling: A Functional Linguistics Perspective*. Mahwah NJ: Lawrence Erlbaum Associates.

Schleppegrell, M.J., Achugar, M.J. & Oteíza, T. 2004. The grammar of history: Enhancing content-based instruction through a functional focus on language. *TESOL Quarterly* 38(1): 67–93.

Schleppegrell, M.J. & Colombi, M.C. (eds). 2002. *Developing Advanced Literacy in First and Second Languages: Meaning with Power*. Mahwah NJ: Lawrence Erlbaum Associates.

Schleppegrell, M. & de Oliveira, L.C. 2006. An integrated language and content approach for history teachers. *Journal of English for Academic Purposes* 5(4): 254–268.

Sharpe, T. 2006. 'Unpacking' scaffolding: Identifying discourse and multimodal strategies that support learning. *Language and Education* 20(3): 211–231.

Veel, R. & Coffin, C. 1996. Learning to think like an historian: The language of secondary school history. In *Literacy in Society*, R. Hasan & G. Williams (eds), 191–231. London: Longman.

Vygotsky, L.S. 1987. An experimental study of concept development. In *Problems of General Psychology*, Vol. 1: Collected Works of L. S. Vygotsky, R.W. Rieber & A.S. Carton (eds), 121–166. New York NY: Plenum.

Zwiers, J. 2008. *Building Academic Language. Essential Practices for Content Classrooms.* San Francisco CA: Jossey-Bass/International Reading Association.

Effects of CLIL on a teacher's classroom language use

Tarja Nikula
Jyväskylän yliopisto, Finland

This chapter reports on a case study on the effects of CLIL on a teacher's language use. The data consist of biology lessons by a teacher both in his L1, Finnish, and in English. Analysis focuses both on what the teacher says and how he uses language in the two settings. In line with its discourse-pragmatic orientation, the chapter pays special attention to social and interpersonal dimensions of language use. The findings suggest that patterns of interaction differ across the two contexts, lessons in Finnish containing more teacher monologues than CLIL lessons. However, when teaching in Finnish, the teacher has at his disposal a wider repertoire of subtle means to construct and negotiate the teacher–student relationship and its power asymmetries.

1. Introduction

As elsewhere in Europe, CLIL entered the Finnish educational scene in the early 1990's, once the changes in educational laws made this form of education possible. The first years of its existence showed a rapid spread to different parts of the country, usually in the form of small-scale experiments started by inspired teachers (Nikula & Marsh 1996). The emergence of CLIL in Finland was thus very much a grassroots phenomenon. A decade later, many of the smaller experiments no longer exist, yet CLIL has established itself in Finnish education, especially in bigger towns and cities, which are better able than small towns and municipalities to cater for continuity for CLIL students from one level of education to another (Lehti et al. 2006). The overall number of schools offering CLIL may have decreased, but the schools continuing with it are usually very dedicated to this form of education. As regards research on CLIL, the same applies to Finland as to other contexts: research efforts have largely concentrated on learners and learning outcomes, and the effects of CLIL e.g. on target language learning, subject-specific skills, and mother tongue development (e.g. Järvinen 1999; Jäppinen 2005; Seikkula-Leino 2007). This focus is understandable given that the rapid spread has also given rise to many controversies and debates and much of CLIL research, explicitly or implicitly, has addressed the question whether and on what grounds CLIL can be regarded as a fruitful educational approach. Although results of CLIL research are somewhat heterogeneous because of the diversity of contexts studied, it is probably safe to argue that they have managed to show that when skilfully administered, CLIL has the potential of leading to favourable outcomes.

Although research on CLIL in Europe has grown steadily during the recent years, less attention has been paid to classroom practices and the details of language use in CLIL classrooms, be it from the perspective of classroom interaction or how learning and teaching as discursive processes are accomplished in actual instructional situations (Dalton-Puffer & Smit 2007: 14). This situation is, however, gradually changing as the number of studies on classroom discourse in CLIL settings is on the increase (e.g. Dalton-Puffer 2007; Dalton-Puffer & Nikula 2006; Dafouz et al. 2007; Llinares & Whittaker 2008; Nikula 2008a; and Maillat, Morton and Smit this volume). While these studies have revealed important insights into the nature of teacher-student interaction and the characteristics of teacher talk, the question about how a switch over to a foreign language affects teachers' language use has not been studied much (but see Nikula 2002; Nikula 2008b). This question is addressed by the present chapter, which explores the very same teacher's discourse practices both in CLIL (instruction in English) and non-CLIL classrooms (instruction in Finnish). It has to be pointed out at the outset that the focus is not on the teacher's foreign language skills but rather on whether using a foreign language affects his interactional and instructional style. Such information is needed because it can highlight aspects that need to be taken into account in CLIL teacher training and when developing CLIL pedagogies, both areas that are in need of further development as pointed out e.g. by Lorenzo (2007) and de Graaff et al. (2008). At a more general level, exploring teachers' performance in their two languages is useful because, apart from helping to understand features of CLIL teaching better, it may also reveal something about the connections between foreign language use and identity, an area of second language research that has attracted increasing attention over the last years (e.g. Block 2007; Norton 2000).

The importance of paying attention to teachers' language use partly derives from a feature that distinguishes CLIL from many other forms of bilingual education: CLIL teachers are usually non-native speakers of the target language, which makes this form of education challenging not only for students but also for teachers. Furthermore, although teacher qualification and professional background is one of the distinguishing features across contexts, it is still the case that the majority of European CLIL teachers are subject specialists rather than language specialists, which entails that they often have limited experience with matters of language proficiency and its development. There are some indications in earlier research that teaching in a foreign language may give rise to concerns about whether teachers are able to make full use of their professional competence. For example, in a study by Nikula & Marsh (1997: 54), CLIL teachers interviewed were concerned about not being as good teachers in English as in Finnish, an observation that resembles Harder's (1980) notion of the 'reduced personality' of foreign language speakers, i.e. that they may be unable to express themselves to the full when using a foreign language. Similarly, Moate's (2008) study shows that instructing through a foreign language easily gives rise to feelings of stress among CLIL teachers. Moreover, some of the teachers interviewed by Moate (2008: 44–45) also commented on CLIL having an adverse effect on their teacher personae; as examples of this the teachers mentioned the absence of humour and feeling 'distant' from students during CLIL lessons. It is, therefore, worthwhile to explore whether such sentiments carry over to teachers' language use in CLIL, perhaps making it different from teachers' L1 performance in ways that affect the social and interpersonal dimensions of language use.

2. Theoretical approach, data and methods of analysis

Theoretically, the case study reported in this chapter is grounded in pragmatics and discourse analysis, also drawing insights from sociocultural research on language learning (e.g. Hall & Verplaetse 2000; Lantolf & Thorne 2006). The ensuing discourse-pragmatic approach means that its analytical focus will be on features of classroom interaction rather than on formal aspects of language as a system. That is, rather than studying whether or not the teacher uses English 'correctly' as a formal system, attention will be paid to the teacher's ways of 'doing being a teacher' when teaching in English and in Finnish and in exploring the social consequences of his language use (e.g. in terms of involvement, politeness or participation).

The data derive from a larger data pool of classroom interaction collected at the University of Jyväskylä, which contains video recordings of EFL and CLIL classrooms as well as of subject lessons taught in Finnish. The data for this chapter consist of the same teacher's biology lessons in Finnish and English. The school where the recordings were made is a regular, state-owned lower secondary school in a mid-sized Finnish town. The school has a CLIL strand in which students' participation is voluntary. In this strand, instruction during the three years of lower secondary education is in English almost throughout, with the exception of lessons on Finnish language and literature. Before entering this strand, most CLIL students have, however, gone through their entire six-year primary education in Finnish.

The teacher under scrutiny is a biology teacher in his thirties, who has taught his subject in English for some years. He does not have formal qualifications as a language teacher, which is the typical case for CLIL teachers in Finland: double qualification is rare. He has a good command of English mainly through using the language frequently in his free time: he travels abroad extensively and has many friends with whom he uses English as a lingua franca. Originally, data was collected in his CLIL lessons in 2003 when he was teaching 9th graders in English. The main topic during the lessons recorded was human reproduction and the size of the group was rather small, 9 students. In this connection the teacher was also interviewed about his experiences as a CLIL teacher. As the research process proceeded, a need arose for data with the same teacher's instruction in Finnish in order to better understand how using a foreign language affects his teaching style. Consequently, the second set of recordings of his biology lessons, this time in Finnish, was collected two years later, 2005. Unfortunately, this time the teacher did not teach biology for 9th graders, which is why the lessons in Finnish are biology lesson for 7th graders, with water ecosystems as the main topic. The group size during the lessons in Finnish was also bigger than in CLIL classrooms, 17–18 students (depending on absences). There is an equal amount of data in both English and in Finnish: three so-called 'double lessons', that is two 45-minute lessons held consecutively, with only a brief break in between.

Table 1 summarizes the data analysed. As pointed out above, there are other contextual differences apart from the language of instruction that need to be taken into account in the analysis: differences in group size, topic area and students' age, perhaps also the fact that the recordings were made with a two years' interval. Therefore, the present observations need to be taken as preliminary, with full awareness of intervening contextual differences. However, I do believe in the usefulness of exploring the same teacher's lessons in Finnish and English because it helps to highlight aspects of both that might remain hidden if only focusing on one at a time. At the very least, the observations will hopefully provide some useful guidelines for further enquiries in this area.

Table 1. Overview of the data

	CLIL – biology in English	Biology in Finnish
Grade	9th (15 year-olds)	7th (13 year-olds)
Group size	9 students	17–18 students
Topic area	human reproduction	fresh water ecosystem
Number of lessons	3 double lessons (90 min)	3 double lessons (90 min)
Year of recording	2003	2005

The method of analysis is classroom discourse analysis, which involves close attention to the details of interaction, both in terms of content (*what* the teacher says) but especially in terms of *how* the teacher uses language in the two settings: what kind of words and structures are deployed, what kind of interactional patterns emerge in interactions between the teacher and the students. As the study has its theoretical underpinnings in pragmatics, special attention will be paid to social and interpersonal dimensions of language use (see also Nikula 2005, 2008a).

3. Findings

3.1 Different patterns of interaction

When interviewed about his own perceptions and experiences as a CLIL teacher, the teacher expressed the opinion that he teaches in a similar way both in Finnish and in English, i.e. unlike the teachers in Moate's (2008) study, he was not concerned about CLIL having an adverse effect on his professional integrity. The analysis lends support to the teacher's view in that both his CLIL lessons and lessons in Finnish share an easy-going, non-threatening atmosphere: the teacher is very skilful, whichever language he uses, in creating humour and in enlivening his teaching by forging connections between topics taught and the everyday experiences of either the students or himself. From a social-interactional perspective, he thus succeeds in creating involvement (e.g. Daneš 1994) and in portraying an easy-to-approach image of himself in both languages. This is illustrated by Extract 1 from a CLIL lesson, in which the teacher, while the class is discussing the function of tonsils, chooses to personalize the topic by telling a story about his own child (for transcription conventions, see Appendix):

(1)

T	fo- for example they may um (.) collect in them too much amount of bacteria and it (.) um can (x) (lead) to many many infections into ears and and these things.
?	(great)
T	yeah so um they are taken away if they cause problems. like they um (.) took them away from from our son. (.) last august when when he was about three years old. (.) he had problems with breathing. when he was sleeping. (.) he was snoring like an grown up man.

Despite the similarities in the overall classroom ethos, also differences emerge in the teacher's language use in English and Finnish, the most noticeable one relating to the amount of teacher talk which, by listening to the recordings, seems to occupy a much larger proportion of classroom time during the lessons in Finnish. This difference is borne out in quantitative terms in Table 2, which lists the number of turns in teacher-fronted whole-class activities during the three double lessons delivered in Finnish and in English (turns during group work activities are not included in calculations because students' contributions in these were only partially captured by the video recordings. As the table shows, the teacher produces fewer turns during whole-class activities when instructing in Finnish. Given the same length of lessons this means, in essence, that his turns are longer when he is instructing in Finnish, something that will be shown later in this section to indeed be the case when analyzing the data qualitatively.

Table 2. Number of turns by the teacher (T) and students (S) during whole-class activities

Lessons	Instruction in Finnish		Instruction in English	
	T	S	T	S
1	166	135	201	402
2	174	142	324	746
3	203	200	426	1410
Total	543	477	951	2558

Another noticeable difference lies in the relationship between the teacher's and the students' turns: during lessons in Finnish, the number of students' turns is rather close to that by the teacher, whereas in CLIL lessons the overall number of students' turns clearly outnumbers that by the teacher during all CLIL lessons. This suggests that CLIL classroom practices consist of more varied patterns than question-answer sequences with alternating teacher's and students' turns (see also Nikula 2007).

In the following, representative data extracts and their qualitative discourse-pragmatic analysis are presented in order to shed more light on these overall findings relating to turn distribution. For example, while the turn count in Table 2 reveals little about the qualitative features such as the length or distribution of turns, discourse analysis of the data shows that the teacher opts for much longer turns of speech during the lessons in Finnish, whereas similarly long stretches of teacher talk are practically non-existent during CLIL lessons. In other words, the teacher's style is much more monologic in Finnish. Long teacher monologues occur during all of the three double lessons in Finnish, Extract 2 serving as an illustration. For reasons of space, the extract displays only a section of the monologue, which is much longer in its entirety (rather than being idiomatic English, the translations seek to reflect as closely as possible the teacher's word choices).

(2)

T   *kaupungin kaikki jäte- jätevedet johdetaan tota viemäreitä pitkin*
        'all the waste waters of the town are led along the sewers over
        tuonne (.) tuota [nimi] jätevedenpuhdistamolle (.) ja siel
        there (.) to waste water treatment plant of [name](.) and there

ne puhistetaan ne vedet (.) ja sit ne päästetään takaisin järveen siitä
the waters get purified (.) after which they let the water flow back to the lake
siitä (xx) (.) nin nin tota ((someone shuts close a door))
there (xx) I mean like
vaikka niitä välttämättä niit kaikkia ravinteita mitä siellä on (.) ei saadakaan
although all the nutrients that it contains (.) may not be gotten rid of
ihan ehkä pois siis niit ravinteita tulee sinne (.) sinne vaikka
quite completely I mean nutrients get there (.) for example
vaikka niinkun sillä tavalla kun kotitalouksissa vaikka pestään astioita
for example when dishes are washed in households
nin nin sieltä voi jotaki (.) tulla sen niistä astioista sillä tavalla
then that may result in some (.) those dishes may yield
kasvinkin kannal- kannalta käyttökelpoisia juttuja
some things that are useful for plants
joitakin ((coughs)) vaikka fosforia ja typpeä ja tämmössiä aineita
some ((coughs)) like phosphorus and nitrogen and stuff like that
ja tämmössii samanlaisii aineita vesistöihin joutuu sitten myös
and those similar kinds of stuff then end up in water systems also
maatalouden seurauksena eli tota kun isännät
as a result of agriculture I mean like when farmers
lannottaa peltojaan nin nin tota (.) aina vähäsen kuitenkin sitä
fertilize their fields then you know (.) always a little bit of that
sitä tota (.) sadeveden mukana sitä lannotetta joutuu sinne järveen
like (.) with the rain water also fertilizers end up in the lake
vaikka nykyään pellot onkin sillä tavalla salaojitettu
despite the fact that nowadays fields have these subsurface drains
että ne jätevedet ei ei meekään suoraan järveen ja sitten aika usein vielä
so that the waste waters do not flow directly to the lake and then quite often
tai nykyään täytyy vielä niinkun (.) pellon ja järven välissä olla
or nowadays it's compulsory to have like (.) between the lake and the field
semmonen semmonen tota muutamien kymmenien metrien suojavyöhyke
such a such a I mean like a safety zone of some tens of meters
että mihkä sitä lannoitetta ei saa laittaa
into which you are not allowed to put fertilizers
mut siitä huolimatta niitä pikkasen joutuu aina (.) aina vesistöihin
but in spite of this a little of it ends up always (.) in water systems
näitä kasviravinteitakii ja ne kasviravinteet siellä vedessä tekee
those plant nutrients and those plant nutrients in water then do
sitte järvessä ihan saman jutun kun ne tekee vaikka siinä pellolakin
in the lake exactly the same they do for example in the field
että ne saa aikaan semmosta että kasvit kasvaa paremmin
I mean they make plants grow better
myös semmosissa paikoissa missä niitten ei tarttis kasvaa paremmin
also in such places where they wouldn't need to grow better
elikkä järven rannassa vaikkapa
I mean by a lake shore for example'

In the extract, the teacher is lecturing to students about how nutrients end up in water systems. He stands in front of the classroom, using an electronic whiteboard onto which he projects pictures of different kinds of lakes. The pupils listen, without verbally participating in this whole-classroom discourse. Lecturing is, of course, an effective way to simultaneously address a large group of students and it is likely that the bigger group size in the Finnish lessons is a contributing factor to the teacher more often opting for monologues and a lecturing style. However, it is worth bearing in mind that classroom settings are also contexts where pupils are socialised into specific structures of interaction and learn about their social role in relation to the teacher. In this respect, long teacher monologues may be problematic in that they position students in the role of listeners, which conveys a hidden message that their active participation may not be desired.

When teaching in English, the teacher does not opt for long monologues to the same extent, even though also the CLIL lessons contain numerous teacher-led activities, in which the teacher has the institutionally defined position of power and the right to orchestrate talk and action (see Dalton-Puffer & Nikula 2006). Despite this, the students in CLIL classrooms take more initiatives. Extract 3 serves as an example: it is from a teacher-fronted activity during which the teacher is lecturing about delivery. He is sitting on a chair in front of the students, holding a colourful book with photographs of different phases of delivery so that the pictures face the students while he is lecturing.

```
(3)
 1    T        they are taking very good care of the mother and the baby (.)
 2             an:d for example (.) they put (.) this kind of a (1.0)
 3             >what it is< (.) receptor thing electronical receptor thing
 4             on a baby's head. (.) to um (.) look look at the baby's um
 5             heart beat. (1.0) because they can tell many things about the
 6             baby's condition in- by just (.) watching the [heart beat]
 7    Liisa    [näytä tänne] (2.5)
               'show here'
 8             is her ear like sticking through the mo- mother's •(belly)•
 9    T        yeah this is a sort of a tube that you can hear the heart beats
10             of the baby through [the [mother's] tummy]
11    Rowan                        [feels   (x)   ]
12    Liisa                         [   ((laughs))  ] (3.5)
13    Reetta   °I don't think that it's (disgusting)° (1.5)
14    T        yeah. (.) and here are this um (.) several things to get the pains
15             away. for example this (.) woman here is hanging from (.)
16             the ((short laugh)) neck of of his husband [so so some    ]
17                                                         [ ((laughter))]
```

18	Ope	[women feel] that it takes the pains away.
19		[((laughter))]
20	?	she's gonna crack his spine. ((laughter))

While the teacher is lecturing, Liisa asks him at first in Finnish (line 7) to turn the book in her direction and then switches into English to make a clarifying question (line 8). The teacher gives a response (lines 9–10), which gives rise to a dialogic exchange between him and the students, reminiscent of the give-and-take of everyday conversation. Liisa's question thus serves as a trigger that turns the teacher's lecturing into a dialogue. From an interactional perspective, this is a very different situation socially compared to extract 2 above with no student participation and explains, in part, why the overall count of student turns is so much bigger in CLIL lessons (see Table 2).

That students in CLIL lessons more often adopt an active role as questioners and commentators is further illustrated by Extract 4, which is from a situation where the teacher is explaining different phases of foetus development with a set of pictures and where, within a short time, four different students contribute to the talk: first Reetta comments on a picture (line 2) and Aino reacts to this by supportive laughter (line 4) and finally both Rowan (line 5) and Aapo (lines 7–10) direct clarifying questions to the teacher.

(4)

1	T	yo- you can see the tail here↑](.) [a: nd]
2	Reetta	[looks like] it was boxing=
3	T	=this is [heart.]
4	Aino	[((laughs))]
5	Rowan	how can it change to that in just one week
6	T	um it grows very very fast. (.) [u:m]
7	Aapo	[if we] grew that fast right
8		now (.) how much do we grow. (1.5) (xx)
9	T	pardon me
10	Aapo	if we were growing still that fast how much would we grow.
11	T	um (.) I'm: afraid I can't (.) I'm not able to answer that
12		(.) question but um if we if we were thinking about this
13		growing and the dividing process of cells. (.) um never after
14		this (.) it is we- we are never growing as fast as we are we are
15		doing in this stage.
16	?	(x) definitely (x[x)]
17	T	[and if] we would continue that kind of a
18		growing we could be •th- three• metres tall a- or or so
19	Rowan	cool

The reasons for dialogic teacher-student exchanges being more common in CLIL lessons may be manifold: firstly, the smaller group size perhaps makes it easier for the students to participate. Secondly, it may well be that the topic at hand, human reproduction, is of greater interest to students than water ecosystems, which partly explains their eagerness to pose questions. Yet the language of instruction may also be at issue, in two ways at least. From the teacher's point of view, it is probably more difficult for him to produce sustained monologues in English which, in its turn, opens up opportunities for the students to contribute and to steer talk towards dialogue. As regards the students, it is important to realise that long teacher monologues during lessons in Finnish are as much of their making: having been socialized for years into classroom practices in which their role is constructed as that of passive receivers, there is probably very little incentive on their part to change things from this status quo. Instruction in English may thus function as a trigger that fractures the expected discourses of education by casting the teacher and student roles into a new light: although the teacher's content area expertise remains, the use of a foreign language seems to somewhat restrict the teacher's opportunities to act as an all-round expert and makes the interactional give-and-take more symmetrical as also students have their share of expertise in English. This may be one of the reasons contributing to the greater student activity in CLIL lessons, as also reported elsewhere (Nikula 2005).

The above extracts thus indicate that, as far as interactional patterns are concerned, the teacher tends towards a more monologic style when teaching in Finnish and a more dialogic one in English. Rather than resulting from language choice alone, this difference may also reflect the fact, reported for example by teachers in a study by Nikula & Marsh (1997), that CLIL instruction requires more careful planning and attention to the details of lesson structure. Consequently, when teaching through a foreign language, teachers may more consciously focus on providing students with opportunities to participate in classroom interaction, in order to help them to practice and learn the target language. As regards teaching in the mother tongue, it may more easily allow for free flow of teacher talk, with the result that teacher talk in fact takes up most of the classroom time during lessons in Finnish, something that is in line with what research has indicated about the predominance of teacher talk in classrooms (e.g. Cazden 2001). I have shown elsewhere (Nikula 2008b) that often this free flow of talk manifests, for example, in the teacher's greater tendency to provide ongoing commentary of his own actions in a 'thinking aloud' manner when teaching in Finnish.

Drawing far-reaching conclusions based on a single case study is obviously difficult, yet longer teacher monologues in L1 teaching is a phenomenon that is well worth further research as it has both pedagogical and social implications. There are earlier suggestions (e.g. Guazzierri 2007) that CLIL teaching benefits from practices that encourage student involvement. This is something that teachers ought to be made aware of and research findings such as these, which exemplify how the teacher's different strategy choices affect classroom interaction, could be used for purposes of awareness raising in CLIL teacher education.

3.2   Subtle means of meaning making used differently

The section above suggests that CLIL has an impact on this particular teacher's interactional patterns in that he opts for a more dialogic style when teaching in English. While this can be interpreted as a feature in favour of CLIL in that the teacher's dialogic strategies allow students more room to participate in the construction of classroom discourse, the findings also indicate that there are other areas of language use where teaching through English seems to narrow down the teacher's potential to express pragmatic meanings, i.e. using Finnish provides him with a much richer set of resources for meaning making. Quite often, this relates to the teacher having at his disposal means to convey meanings that allow him to regulate aspects of the institutionally defined teacher-student relationship, with its inherent power asymmetries. One such resource of meaning making is language-internal variation. In the present data, language-internal variation concerns speakers' choices between informal and formal registers in particular. A common way to conceptualise formality is to draw attention to different contexts requiring different levels of formality, e.g. official meetings versus casual chats with friends. However, speakers may also vary the degrees of formality within one context to convey social meanings. While there are several studies that have paid attention to language variation in the form of code-switching in classrooms and its relationship to levels of formality (e.g. Liebscher & Dailey-O'Cain 2004; Simon 2001), less is known about the functions of language-internal variation in classrooms (but see Knöbl 2006).

In the present data, the teacher uses a rather colloquial style throughout when teaching in Finnish. This is not exceptional, as the variety that could be called 'spoken Finnish' (as opposed to standard Finnish) is commonly used in most everyday encounters in Finland, including workplace interactions and classroom contexts. The informal style is illustrated by Extract 5. Typically for informal style in Finnish, there are various phonological reductions such as dropping word endings (e.g. colloquial variants *miks* ('why', line 6) and *sit* ('then', line 12) instead of standard forms *miksi* or *sitten*), diphthongs changing into short vowels (e.g. colloquial *tonne* ('there', line 1) instead of standard *tuonne*). The teacher also deploys word choices of informal register (e.g. informal *tiiäkkö* ('do you know', line 6) instead of standard *tiedätkö*, informal *varmaan* ('for sure', line 6) instead of standard *varmasti* and the very informal word *ällöttävää* ('yucky', line 12). The informal style choices are marked by underlining in the following:

(5)

1	T	*tonne ni sitte voi lähteä uimaan (.) kuka lähtis tekemään näin*
		'like there you could go swimming (.) who'd be ready to do so
2		*vetää tosta ton kaislikon läpi*
		just rush through those reeds
4	Kalle	*sinä*
		you
5		((laughter))
6	T	*miten niin minä (.) en varmaan lähtis (.) tiiäkkö miks*
		what do you mean I (.) I wouldn't for sure (.) y'know why
7	Kalle	*no*
		well (why)
8	T	*ensinnäkin (.) semmosissa pehmeepohjaisissa järvissä on must*
		firstly (.) in such lakes with soft bottoms I reckon it's
9		*kerta kaikkiaan ällöttävää kun (.) sinne sinne niiku (.) siellä kävelee*
		just so yucky when (.) there there like (.) you walk along there
10		*siellä pohjassa ni (.) muta tirsuaa varpaiden välistä*
		on the bottom an' (.) mud oozes from between your toes
11	LL	((laughter))
12	T	*ja sit on nilkkoja myöten siinä mudassa ja yööä (.) en tykkää yhtää*
		and then you're up to your ankles in the mud and yuck (.) I don't
		like it one bit'

The use of such informal style helps create an impression of a relaxed and easy-going teacher who does not want to maintain too distant a relationship with his students by making use of standard forms that, on many occasions, tend to be interpreted by Finns as somewhat 'bookish' and pedantic.

Although the teacher mainly uses the informal spoken variant, there are also occasions when he uses a more careful and formal style. Interestingly, this usually happens in situations in which the institutionally more powerful role of the teacher is emphasised. Extract 6 serves as an illustration. It is from a situation towards the end of a lesson when the teacher is closing off the lesson and gives students homework. On this occasion, he resorts to forms of standard Finnish: for example, he uses full forms instead of reduced ones (e.g. standard *ja sitten* ('and then', line 4) instead of informal *ja sitte*) as well as verb forms that retain both the personal pronoun and the personal verb ending which usually are dropped in informal style (e.g. standard *me lopetamme* ('we will stop', line 6) instead of the passive form *lopetetaan* more usual in colloquial style). It is noteworthy that the teacher uses this more formal style when giving students instructions, as if to emphasise his position of authority in the institutional context. However, perhaps to prevent too formal an impression, he also uses some colloquial forms (underlined) alongside the more formal ones (in boldface).

(6)

1	T	_joo_ (.) _hyvä_ ((claps hands))
		'right (.) good
2		_ei se mitään_ **lopetamme** _tähän_ (.) _läksynä on <u>öö tota</u>:_ (.)
		it doesn't matter **we will stop** here (.) as homework <u>erm well</u> (.)
3		_lukekaa vielä kerran se <u>eka</u> kappale ja <u>nää</u> vihkomuistiinpanot._
		read once more that <u>first</u> chapter and <u>these</u> notes in your notebooks
4		(.) **ja sitten** (.) <u>_tota_</u>: (.) _tehkää siitä_ (.) **vieläkin** _parempi_ (.)
		(.) **and then** (.) <u>well</u> (.) make it (.) **even better** (.)
5		_siitä_ **teidän** _kasvijutusta_ **kun se nyt jo on** (.) **seuraavaksi kerraksi.**
		that plant thing **of yours as it is now** (.) **for the next time**
6		_eli keskiviikkona._ (.) **me lopetamme** _tähän_
		that is next Wednesday (.) **we will stop** here'

Although the changes in style are rather subtle, they are also an effective means of conveying shifts in the teacher's interpersonal orientations, from interpersonally more involved to interpersonally more detached. When teaching in English, the teacher does not resort to similar style changes. In CLIL lessons, he opts for a relatively informal style throughout, and there are no instances of him using formal register to underline his position of power. There are occasions when he asserts his authoritative role but that happens through means other than style changes. The following extract is from a situation where students are involved in a lengthy disagreement as to when the class was supposed to have a test. In a humorous attempt to end the dispute, the teacher describes himself as 'the dictator' (line 4) which, however, does not seem to have a similar distancing effect as his choice of formal register in Finnish, which is perhaps a reason why the students continue the dispute for quite a while longer until the teacher finally ends it by announcing the date for the test (line 11).

(7)

1	Aapo	yes he said wednesday >I've prepared for today I'm not
2		gonna read twice.<
3	T	yeah yeah but the only only thing which count here is me
4		because I'm the dictator.
5	Aapo	yeah
6	Liisa	⟨no⟩
7	Aini	I don't remember what you said so I'm not going to
8		go on anybody's side
9		[…] ((several student turns during which they continue the dispute))
10	T	after all I want to be mister nice guy (.) so (.) I I do a
11		compromise. we have thirty minute test. (.) tomorrow.

Language-internal stylistic variation thus seems to be a strategic resource that is available when teaching through the mother tongue but more difficult to deploy when using a foreign language, something that also earlier studies on sociolinguistic competence of second language speakers have indicated (e.g. Nadasdi et al. 2005;

Rehner et al. 2003). Another, related difference is that when speaking Finnish, the teacher has access to other subtle means alongside stylistic variation with which to regulate the pragmatic impact of his messages. For example, the Finnish language is rich in pragmatic and clitic particles, with which speakers can for example convey power differences implicitly. In extract 8, the teacher uses a clitic *-pa* with an imperative verb form (lines 4 and 6). This small clitic adds an element of power differential to the meaning as it implies a relationship in which the speaker has more social power than the hearer (e.g. Carlson 1993). This is why imperatives with the clitic *-pa-/pä* are quite common in teacher talk or when parents address their children; in interactions with intimates it can also take on the meaning of solidarity. In contrast, if students used the clitic when addressing the teacher it would most likely be interpreted as arrogant or impertinent. In extract 8, the clitic in essence conveys the message that the teacher's directive for Ville to take off his cap is not something that can be negotiated; this is emphasised by the teacher adding another particle *nyt* (line 6) to the directive, which further adds to its pragmatic impact (roughly: do take it off now).

(8)

1	Ville	*hei meil ei oo saksia (xxx)* ((inaudible))
		'hey we don't have scissors (xxx)
2	T	*mitä*
		what
3	Ville	*mää joudun koko ajan (xx)*
		it's me who all the time has to (xx)
4	T	*te ootte sopinu tämän asian sillä lailla (.) otappa pipo pois päästä.*
		that's how you've agreed about it (.) take+pa the cap off your head
5	Ville	*sä sanoit (xx)*
		you said (xx)
6	T	*otapa nyt pois (pipo)*
		take+pa nyt (part.) [the cap] off
7	Matti	*noi saa syödä karkkia mut mä en saa pitää pipoo päässä*
		they're allowed to eat candy but I can't wear my cap
8	T	*karkin syönti on eri asia ku pipon päässä pitäminen*
		eating candy is different from wearing a cap'

Mastering subtle pragmatic means of meaning making is more difficult in a foreign language (cf. Nikula 2002; see also Bardovi-Harlig 2001 for an overview of the usual shortcomings in language learners' pragmatic performance) and the teacher indeed quite rarely uses for example discourse markers to convey interpersonal meanings. Instead, when discourse markers such as *I mean* or *okay* are used, their function is to regulate discourse organization rather than to orient to interpersonal dimensions of talk. For example, in extract 9 the teacher uses discourse markers to steer the discussion back to the day's topic, signalling the shift of topic with both *okay, now* and *I mean*:

(9)

T	okay now before this is going to get out of hand
	[(.) I mean] I mean this whole lesson please take
Rowan	[(((laughs))]
T	the page one hundred and fifty seven.

In terms of pragmatic meanings, then, the teacher's language use seems more 'straightforward' in English than in Finnish in that there are fewer means with which to express subtle nuances. In sum, where CLIL lessons are more symmetric than lessons in Finnish in terms of interactional patterns, at the level of verbal choices instruction in Finnish is stylistically and pragmatically more varied. In the following, the implications of these findings will be discussed in more detail.

4.   Concluding remarks

This chapter has focused on a teacher's performance when teaching in Finnish and in English, a parallel analysis unravelling aspects of classroom interaction characteristic of each. When considering the findings from the perspective of language learning in CLIL classrooms, various points of interest emerge. Firstly, the teacher and the students seem to construct different understandings of their roles in CLIL classrooms and in classrooms taught in Finnish. While in the former the students are on a more equal footing with the teacher as far as the right to participate in classroom discourse is concerned, in the latter students are positioned in a rather passive role as recipients of teacher talk. CLIL classrooms thus seem to offer good opportunities for students to practice ways of conducting social interaction in English. Secondly, the findings suggest that the greater sense of social symmetry between the teacher and the students in CLIL lessons may be due to the teacher lacking some of the language resources with which to contribute to subtle creation and re-creation of classroom power differentials in English. Consequently, students in CLIL classrooms are left with more space to act as interactional participants. This is potentially an empowering experience, especially when compared to other institutional contexts of foreign language learning such as EFL classrooms, in which discourse practices tend to be more teacher-centred (cf. Nikula 2005). In other words, a powerful impact of CLIL may lie in its ability to create fractures in the established, taken-for-granted discourses of education, which tend to position learners merely as recipients rather than active participants.

While in certain respects the effects of CLIL on the teacher's language use seem to be beneficial (in increasing students' interactional participation), the question that remains is whether the teacher's pragmatically less varied and less subtle language use may also have harmful effects on students' language learning. This question needs to be related to another, much broader one: what is set as the target for language learning in CLIL classrooms? If native-like competence is the goal, it might be argued that the teacher's way of using English falls short of such an ideal. However, language use in CLIL lessons resembles in many respects lingua franca interactions, especially in terms of their 'robustness' (cf. Firth 1996). Therefore, perhaps a goal better suited for CLIL than native-level proficiency is that of developing students' skills and courage to participate in social situations through a foreign language. In the light of the present findings, CLIL lessons have the potential to do exactly that, given that they seem to offer students more room for active engagement in classroom discourse than non-CLIL settings. While the question of language learning goals for CLIL education is obviously too broad to address in this chapter, it should be a crucial concern for any CLIL implementation, not least because realistic aims help to combat overly optimistic expectations for CLIL as a miracle solution to foster all-purpose language skills.

The question of whether the use of a foreign language affects the teacher's (professional) identity is difficult to answer on the basis of a single case study. While the findings point towards differences in the teacher's interactional and instructional style in L1 and L2, the extent to which these can be related to questions of identity construction merits more detailed research along the lines suggested by Block (2007: 202) when he argues for the importance of multiple sources of data such as a interviews, diaries and recorded interactions to explore the multifaceted nature of second language identities.

CLIL is a relative newcomer in the field of education. While its dedicated proponents may picture its effects in overly positive terms, and those sceptical of it easily succumb to alarmist notions about its impact, research on what happens at the level of actual classroom practices helps to put extreme notions into perspective. The present findings suggest that instructing through a foreign language has its effects on teachers' language use, but in ways that may be beneficial (i.e. increase students interactional participation) rather than harmful. While the full meaning-making potential may be neither at the teachers' nor the students' disposal when they use a foreign language, it is worth bearing in mind Blommaert's (2010) notion of 'truncated repertoires': more often than not, people in general and foreign language users in particular have repertoires that vary across contexts rather than remaining constant. Embracing the view of language competence as always partial might be beneficial for CLIL in liberating it from unrealistic expectations at times attached to it: rather than a panacea, CLIL is a form of education with both its merits and limitations. Finally, while the present findings provide some insights into the effects of CLIL on a teacher's language use, it is obvious that more research needs to be carried out in broader sets of data across culturally and linguistically diverse contexts before any definitive conclusions can be drawn. However, as Wiesemes (2007: 146) points out, case studies can serve as a fruitful "evidence base" for more comprehensive approaches. In this light, the present findings can hopefully serve as pointers for future research efforts seeking to unveil the effects of CLIL on classroom discourse practices.

References

Bardovi-Harlig, K. 2001. Evaluating the empirical evidence: Grounds for instruction in pragmatics? In *Pragmatics in Language Teaching*, K. Rose & G. Kasper (eds), 13–32. Cambridge: CUP.

Block, D. 2007. *Second Language Identities*. London: Continuum.

Blommaert, J. 2010. *A Sociolinguistics of Globalization*. Cambridge: CUP.

Carlson. L. 1993. Dialogue games with Finnish clitics. In *SKY 93: Yearbook of the Linguistic Society of Finland*, M. Vilkuna & S. Shore (eds), 73–96. Turku: Linguistic Society of Finland.

Cazden, C. 2001. *Classroom Discourse. The Language of Teaching and Learning*, 2nd edn. Portsmouth NH: Heinemann.

Dafouz, E., Núñez, B. & Sancho, C. 2007. Analysing stance in a CLIL university context: Non-native speaker use of personal pronouns and modal verbs. *International Journal of Bilingual Education & Bilingualism* 10: 647–662.

Dalton-Puffer, C. 2007. *Discourse in Content and Language Integrated Learning (CLIL) Classrooms* [Language Learning & Language Teaching 20]. Amsterdam: John Benjamins.

Dalton-Puffer, C. & Nikula, T. 2006. Pragmatics of content-based instruction: Teacher and student directives in Finnish and Austrian classrooms. *Applied Linguistics* 27(2): 241–267.

Dalton-Puffer, C. & Smit, U. 2007. Introduction. In *Empirical Perspectives on CLIL Classroom Discourse*, C. Dalton-Puffer & U. Smit (eds), 7–23. Frankfurt: Peter Lang.

Daneš, F. 1994. Involvement with language and in language. *Journal of Pragmatics* 22(3/4): 251–264.

de Graaff, R., Koopman, G.J. & Westhoff, G. 2008. Identifying effective L2 pedagogy in CLIL. A paper given at ReN Symposium: CLIL and immersion classrooms: Applied linguistic perspectives. The 15th AILA Congress, Essen, 24–29 August 2008.

Firth, A. 1996. The discursive accomplishment of normality: On 'Lingua Franca' English and conversation analysis. *Journal of Pragmatics* 26(2): 237–259.

Guazzierri, A. 2007. Participation in CLIL: Cooperative learning in CLIL. In *Diverse Contexts – Converging Goals. CLIL in Europe*, D. Marsh & D. Wolff (eds), 171–184. Frankfurt: Peter Lang.

Hall, J.K. & Verplaetse, L.S. (eds). 2000. *Second and Foreign Language Learning through Classroom Interaction*. Mahwah NJ: Lawrence Erlbaum Associates.

Harder, P. 1980. Discourse as self-expression. On the reduced personality of the second-language learner. *Applied Linguistics* 1(3): 262–270.

Jäppinen, A.-K. 2005. Cognitional development of mathematics and science in the Finnish mainstream education in content and language integrated Learning (CLIL) – teaching through a foreign language. *Language and Education* 19(2): 148–169.

Järvinen, H.-M. 1999. *Acquisition of English in Content and Language Integrated Learning at Elementary Level in the Finnish Comprehensive School.* Humaniora B/232. University of Turku.

Knöbl, R. 2006. Binnensprachliche Variation: Code-Switching und Mixing im Schwäbischen. In *Mehrsprachige Individuen – vielsprachige Gesellschaften*, D. Wolff (ed.), 59–86. Frankfurt: Peter Lang.

Lantolf, J. & Thorne, S. 2006. *Sociocultural Theory and the Genesis of Second Language Development.* Oxford: OUP.

Lehti, L., Järvinen, H.-M. & Suomela-Salmi, E. 2006. Kartoitus vieraskielisen opetuksen tarjonnasta peruskouluissa ja lukioissa ('Survey of content-based instruction in primary and secondary education'). In *Kielenoppija tänään* ('Language learner of today'). AFinLA Yearbook 64, P. Pietilä, P. Lintunen & H.-M. Järvinen (eds), 293–313. Jyväskylä: Finnish Association of Applied Linguistics.

Liebscher, G. & Dailey-O'Cain, J. 2004. Learner code-switching in the content-based foreign language classroom. *The Canadian Modern Language Review* 60(4): 501–525.

Llinares, A. & Whittaker, R. 2008. Writing and speaking in the history class: data from CLIL and first language contexts. A paper given at ReN Symposium: CLIL and immersion classrooms: applied linguistic perspectives. The 15th World Congress of Applied Linguistics, Essen, August 24–29, 2008.

Lorenzo, F. 2007. An analytical framework of language integration in L2 content-based courses: The European dimension. *Language and Education* 21(6): 502–514.

Moate, J. 2008. The Impact of Foreign-language Mediated Teaching on Teachers' Sense of Professional Integrity in the CLIL Classroom. MA thesis, University of Nottingham.

Nadasdi, T., Mougeon, R. & Rehner, K. 2005. Learning to speak everyday (Canadian) French. *The Canadian Modern Language Review* 61(4): 543–563.

Nikula, T. 2002. Teacher talk reflecting pragmatic awareness: A look at EFL and content-based classrooms. *Pragmatics* 12(4): 447–468.

Nikula, T. 2005. English as an object and tool of study in classrooms: Interactional effects and pragmatic implications. *Linguistics and Education* 16(1): 27–58.

Nikula, T. 2007. The IRF pattern and space for interaction: Observations on EFL and CLIL classrooms. In *Empirical Perspectives on CLIL Classroom Discourse*, C. Dalton-Puffer & U. Smit (eds), 179–204. Frankfurt: Peter Lang.

Nikula, T. 2008a. Learning pragmatics in content-based classrooms. In *Investigating Pragmatics in Foreign Language Learning, Teaching, and Testing*, E. Alcón & A. Martinez-Flor (eds), 94–113. Clevedon: Multilingual Matters.

Nikula, T. 2008b. Kieli vaihtuu, vaihtuuko opetustyyli? ('Language changes, how about style of teaching?') In *Kieli ja globalisaatio – Language and Globalization*. AFinLA Yearbook no 66, M. Garant, I. Helin & H. Yli-Jokipii (eds), 275–309. Jyväskylä: Finnish Association of Applied Linguistics.

Nikula, T. & Marsh, D. 1996. *Kartoitus vieraskielisen opetuksen tarjonnasta peruskouluissa ja lukioissa.* ('A survey on content and language integrated instruction in primary and secondary schools') Helsinki: The National Board of Education.

Nikula, T. & Marsh, D. 1997. *Vieraskielisen opetuksen tavoitteet ja toteuttaminen* ('CLIL in Finland: From aims to implementation'). Helsinki: The National Board of Education.

Norton, B. 2000. *Identity and Language Learning*. London: Longman.

Rehner, K., Mougeon, R. & Nadasdi, T. 2003. The learning of sociolinguistic variation by advanced FSL learners. The case of *nous* versus on in immersion French. *Studies in Second Language Acquisition* 25: 127–156.

Seikkula-Leino, J. 2007. CLIL learning: Achievement levels and affective factors. *Language and Education* 21(4): 328 – 341.

Simon, D.-L. 2001. Towards a new understanding of code switching in the foreign language classroom. In *Code Switching Worldwide II*, R. Jacobson (ed.), 311–342. Berlin: Mouton de Gruyter.

Wiesemes, R. 2007. Developing an expanded methodology for CLIL classroom research: CLIL classroom case studies. In *Diverse Contexts – Converging Goals. CLIL in Europe*, D. Marsh & D. Wolff (eds), 145–152. Frankfurt: Peter Lang.

Appendix

Transcription conventions

overlapping [speech] [text]	overlapping speech
(.)	a short pause that is not timed, less than a second
(2.5)	a pause, timed in seconds
text= =text	latching utterances
exte:nsion	noticeable extension of the sound or syllable
cut off wo-	cut off word or truncated speech
°high circles°	spoken more silently than surrounding utterances
·dark circles·	laughing voice
.	falling intonation
↑	rising intonation
<text>	spoken more slowly than surrounding utterances
>text<	spoken more rapidly than surrounding utterances
((text))	transcriber's comments
(text)	transcriber's interpretation of unclear word(s)
(x)	unclear speech, probably a word
(xx)	unclear speech, probably a phrase
(xxx)	longer stretch of unclear speech

Writing and speaking in the history class

A comparative analysis of CLIL and first language contexts

Ana Llinares & Rachel Whittaker
Universidad Autónoma de Madrid, Spain

This paper presents a comparative analysis of the language used by CLIL secondary school students of history and that of students following the same syllabus in their first language (Spanish). The data consists of spoken and written production: a whole-class end-of-topic summary session and short compositions by the same students on the same topic. Using a Systemic-Functional approach (Halliday 2004), we analyse a selection of features of the students' language in the two contexts. We focus on their expression of content: processes, participants, circumstances and clause complexes (Halliday's ideational function of language) and their use of modality (the interpersonal function). The results report differences between the two groups in the realization of the two functions.

1. Introduction

In the Spanish context, where knowledge of foreign languages, particularly of English, is a major priority, but results have remained below expectations, CLIL has been embraced by the educational authorities in many of the Autonomous Communities in Spain as the best way to face this challenge (Eurydice 2008; Pérez Vidal 2002). At the same time, studying in a foreign language throws into relief the problem of the role of language in learning. Research at secondary level has shown that, even in the mother tongue, some students have difficulties because of unfamiliarity with the language of the disciplines (eg. Christie 1998; Rothery 1996; Veel & Coffin 1996). Studies have shown how, at this level, language no longer represents events iconically and in everyday lexis but becomes much more abstract, more distanced from the events described, not only lexically but also grammatically (Halliday 1989; Halliday & Martin 1993). For students learning through a second or foreign language, the registers of the different subjects may pose an additional problem. If in the mother tongue a large part of learning a discipline is learning the language of that discipline, this is true to a much greater extent when learning in a foreign language, since it is not just a question of learning a new register for students who already possess the every-day terms to begin to talk about the topics. Since most CLIL teachers at secondary level are subject specialists with a good command of English, but with little or no linguistic training, it is important to provide them with information on the role language plays in the creation of disciplinary knowledge in their subjects, and the features of their written and spoken registers.

The UAM-CLIL project[1] started in 2005 with the aim of offering secondary school CLIL teachers some support in their new task by identifying the students' linguistic needs in specific subjects. There are some recent studies on CLIL which focus on CLIL students' spoken language (Dalton-Puffer 2005, 2007; Dalton-Puffer & Nikula 2006; Nikula 2007), but descriptions of written production are few (Vollmer et al. 2006; Ruiz de Zarobe this volume). In addition, most studies have focused on general language proficiency rather than subject-specific skills. In our project we set out to create a corpus of samples of CLIL students' language, both spoken and written, which would show how these pupils deal with the difficulties involved in expressing the content of a discipline in English. We wanted to know to what extent CLIL secondary students were able to produce spoken or written text on a subject, rather than just brief answers giving items of information, since such text production is both a means of learning the subject content, and evidence that the content has been learnt. The language of spoken classroom interaction is different from that of writing, and both modes are necessary for the learning/evaluation cycle. One of the fears of both teachers and parents is that content learning might be affected if this takes place in the L2, either because the content would have to be reduced and simplified or, if the subject is taught at the same level as in the L1, because it would be too demanding conceptually, and too complex linguistically for the students. While this remains a controversial area, research suggests that learning in a second language does not seem to affect content learning (Day & Shapson 1996; Jäppinen 2005). What is more, studies such as that of Van de Craen et al. 2007 on early bilingual learning show that CLIL students may even outperform their L1 counterparts when tested in the L1. However, despite the key role of language in learning, to our knowledge no study has been carried out yet comparing CLIL and L1 students' use of the spoken and written language necessary for specific genres and registers in their subjects.

1.   This project has received support from the Madrid Autonomous Community and the Universidad Autónoma de Madrid (09/SHD/017105, CCG06-UAM/HUM-0544, CCG07-UAM/HUM-1790).

2. Theoretical background: Genre and register

The genres and registers of school subjects have been studied for a number of years in the framework of Systemic Functional Linguistics, through different educational research projects led by disciples of Michael Halliday in Australia and elsewhere (see, for example, Cope & Kalantzis 1993; Hasan & Williams 1996; Whittaker et al. 2006; Morton this volume). Most teachers have certain implicit knowledge of the genres of their subjects, and of the expected register features, since they evaluate their students' written work, and, therefore, must be responding to such expectations. However, it is only through analysis of texts produced in different subjects that the genres and their registers could be described in detail.[2] Using this knowledge, teachers working in the Systemic framework have been able to make the language of their subjects explicit to their students, and help them produce texts appropriate for the different school tasks (for recent examples see Whittaker et al. 2006).

This work has been carried out mainly with students whose first language is English, or who use English as a second language. Our project is one of the few exploring its potential for CLIL contexts, in which English is a foreign language for students and most teachers, and was designed as a descriptive study of the registers and genres of social science in secondary school. In this chapter, we analyse a selection of linguistic features which make up the register required to respond to the prompt the students were given. The genre is that of historical account and explanation, in which historical events are reported and causes proposed (also see Morton this volume). This genre is found in early secondary school (Christie & Derewianka 2008; Coffin 2006a; Schleppegrell 2004). Other history genres are historical recounts, which simply present and organize events in time, and arguments, organized rhetorically rather than chronologically, which usually come in the later secondary years.

We analyse here a number of linguistic resources to present the content and indicate logical relations, the ideational metafunction in Systemic Functional grammar, and to show attitude towards that content, the interpersonal metafunction (Halliday 2004). We then look at the semantic classes of verbs, or process types, since the verb is central to the type of meaning made in a clause. Halliday distinguishes six classes of processes: material or action processes; relational or states of being and having; mental, including thinking, feeling and perceiving; verbal, expressing speech; behavioural, referring to human behaviour; and existential,

---

2. Genre has been defined by Martin (1992) as a staged, goal-oriented social process realised in register, which represents the linguistic features corresponding to a stage in a text.

predicating existence. Each process type requires different semantic classes of participants. Clauses are often expanded using circumstantial information: time, place, manner, cause, accompaniment, among others, and can be linked using markers of coordination and subordination, which carry information as to logical relations (addition, contrast, cause, condition, etc...). Information as to the probability or usuality of events, and about ability, obligation, permission – modality and modulation in Systemic Functional grammar – also plays an important part in the meaning of academic topics. These features were analysed in the clauses which made up the sample studied in this chapter.

3.   The study

This study is part of an on-going project in which we are following two CLIL groups through their secondary history classes, collecting spoken and written data on a topic from the syllabus once a year. We are also recording six students from each class individually, as they talk about the same topic, to follow their development. In this chapter we present a comparative analysis of the language used by four groups of early secondary school students of history (aged 13–14), two CLIL classes and two studying the same syllabus in their first language (Spanish) in the same two state schools. Drawing from previous studies that compare CLIL secondary school students' spoken and written performance in geography and history (Llinares & Whittaker 2006, 2007; Whittaker & Llinares 2009), we have designed this study to investigate whether language problems in constructing the required history genres were due to problems of performance in the foreign language, or whether they are also found when students carry out the same tasks in their L1, and so, perhaps, part of a more general process of development. Here, then, the interlanguage data is considered in the light of data from other students in the L1.

The two CLIL classes belong to a bilingual programme (British Council/ Spanish Ministry of Education) which offers an integrated curriculum in three subjects in a number of state schools. Our two groups belong to the second cohort in the programme, which started at pre-school level, and has just finished their fourth, and final, year of obligatory secondary schooling[3]. The data here come from a unit studied towards the end of the second year. The state schools are

---

3.   Our thanks to the teachers of the classes we are studying, Marcela Fernández and Joaquín Aparicio (Instituto de Enseñanza Secundaria Profesor Máximo Trueba) and Clara Mimbrera and Francisco Burgos (Instituto de Enseñanza Secundaria Joaquín Araujo), without whom this research would not have been possible.

situated in different areas of Madrid, an upper- and a lower-middle class area. The CLIL teachers have slightly different academic and professional backgrounds: one teacher is an expert in both English as a foreign language and history, the other is a history teacher with a good knowledge of English.

The data were collected in the following way: A unit from the syllabus was selected in consultation with the teachers, and a prompt designed to elicit the spoken and written production, first in an end-of-topic full-class summary session, preceded by group-work, and later in a written text. The topic was selected on the basis of the teachers' perception of students' interest and motivation. The prompt follows the requirements of the curriculum as to the focus and the genres expected in that topic. In the sample for this paper, the students' production on the topic "Feudal Europe" was collected from a CLIL group and an L1 group from each school. The recorded sessions, led by the teachers, lasted about half an hour. A few days later the texts were written in 20 minutes, in class and with no material available. A total number of 49 short compositions were collected from the two groups of CLIL students and 28 from the two L1 (Spanish) groups. The design of our data collection, where, previous to their writing, the students worked on the same prompt orally, meant that they devoted some time to activating their knowledge base (Bereiter & Scardamalia 1987). In a previous study, Llinares and Whittaker (2009) observed that such "register scaffolding" (from group work to whole class discussion to written text on the same prompt) had a positive effect on the students' written production.

The prompt for the class summary discussion and the written texts was as follows for the CLIL groups, with a Spanish version for the mother-tongue classes:

> We have been studying Feudal Europe. What were the characteristics of rural life in feudal Europe? Refer to the obligations and rights of the peasants. Why did cities grow? Compare them with the city where you live today. What were the causes and consequences of the plague?

For the second year of secondary education, in which the students are just moving into real disciplinary study, we decided to give a lot of help in the prompts. Students of this age are normally only asked to write short answers to factual questions, and are not used to producing texts of any length in the foreign language, or to speaking on a topic without supporting interaction from an interlocutor. The prompt was designed to cover all the sections of the topic in the syllabus. It should generate both *historical account* and *historical explanation*: recording facts, and explaining them, giving causes and consequences for states of affairs and events (Coffin 2006a, b; see also Morton in this volume for more on history genres). Apart from guiding the students to the information and the genre required for the different sections, the prompt used both the abstract language of the discipline of history, and direct questions in a more informal register. The reference to the present was included as a requirement of the curriculum, where one of the aims is for the students to reflect on the historical period they are studying in the light of their own experience.

4.   Analysis of the data

Using a Systemic-Functional approach (Halliday 2004), as pointed out before, we analysed a number of features in the students' productions, selected for their role in the construction of the content required by the prompt and the discipline. These were: processes, or semantic classes of verbs (actions, thoughts, states, existence etc.), types of circumstances used to expand the clause (time, place, manner, etc…), the way clauses were linked (logical relations and markers) and expressions of modality. We then mainly focused on the ideational function of language (the way language constructs the content). However, we were also interested in seeing whether learners were beginning to control some interpersonal resources in English, necessary to develop argumentation, hypothesis-making and other academic functions. In particular we focused on the use of modality (interpersonal function), found to be less developed in CLIL classrooms (Dalton-Puffer 2007).

We present the results for all these features, pointing out those for which differences were found. The spoken and written data are shown in different figures so that register differences can be seen. In the figures, each column in the bar graph corresponds to one of the four groups of students. On the right, the groups and the data collection session are identified. The two schools are referred to as SA and SB; CL and SP distinguish the language of instruction for each group, CL for the CLIL groups, and SP for the Spanish L1 groups. For each feature studied, the results are presented showing the distribution of that feature among the possible types.[4]

4.1   Process types

Figures 1 and 2 below show the distribution of the different process types. These are material processes (MA in the figure), existential processes, those which introduce new participants into the discourse using existential "there" (EXI), and relational processes, that is, processes representing states of being or having (REL).

---

4.   Those features which were very infrequent are not shown in the figures.

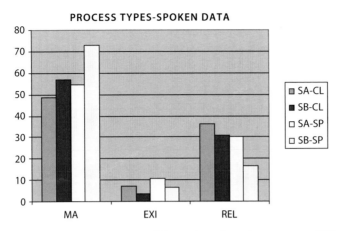

Figure 1. Percentage of process types out of the total number of processes in CLIL and L1 students' spoken data

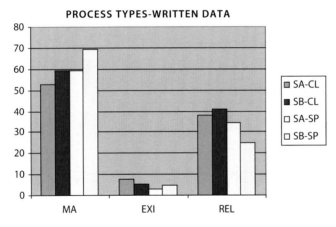

Figure 2. Percentage of process types out of the total number of processes in CLIL and L1 students' written data

Figures 1 and 2 show that, as regards the use of the different process types to represent the content, in general terms, the students were able to use the types of verbs expected for the task and genre in their spoken and written production. Both CLIL and L1 pupils selected mainly action verbs (material processes), of the sort found in Examples (1) and (2) from the class discussions (D), and Examples (3) and (4) from written texts (T), reproduced exactly as the students wrote them:

(1)   Most of the people <u>work</u> in farms and… Eh.. peasants <u>gathered</u> in villages. (SA-D-CL)

(2)   *También <u>hacían</u> el pan, también <u>cultivaban</u> las legumbres, las judías.* (SA-D-SP) 'They also made bread, they also grew pulses, beans.'

(3)   Cities <u>grew</u> because people who <u>lived</u> in rural areas <u>came</u> to cities <u>looking</u> for better lives. (SA-T-CL)

(4)   *Al producir más de lo que consumían, la gente se fue a vender esos productos a las ciudades, ahí se crearon las ferias y los mercados.* (SA-T-SP)
'Producing more than they consumed, the people went to the cities to sell those products, there fairs and markets were created.'

The prompt also elicited relational processes, needed to describe the characteristics of rural life and to express the comparison with the students' experience of present-day cities. Examples (5) and (6) are from the class discussions:

(5)   the church is not, so powerful now. (SB-D-CL)
(6)   *La mayor parte de la población era campesina.* (SB-D-SP)
'Most of the population were peasants.'

Both groups produced rather more relational processes in writing (Figure 2) than in speech, which is an expected register difference (Halliday 1989). The CLIL students, however, used rather more in comparison with the other process types. They also used more of the different classes of relational processes, not distinguished in the graphs. They expressed the characteristics of the feudal system and of life at that time using attribution (descriptions), as in (7), identification (8) and possession (9), again both in their speech and in their writing:

(7)   In Medieval rural areas the society were mostly peasants who could own their own small lands or be serfs and work the lands of noblemen and aristocrazy. (SA-T-CL)
(8)   The consequences were that 5 million people died. (SA-T-CL)
(9)   Eh.. peasants live in small houses eh.. that only have one room and a sh-shed to ⟨x…x⟩ (SA-D-CL)

In the L1 data, while students also used some possessive (10) and identifying processes (11), a higher proportion of their relational processes were attributive (12):

(10) *Tenían una sola habitación con 2 espacios.* (SA-T-SP)
'They had only one room with 2 spaces.'
(11) *Los montones de paja servían de cama* (SB-T-SP)
'Heaps of straw were their beds.'
(12) *Eran autosuficientes.* (SA-D-SP)
'They were self-sufficient.'

Finally, both groups, in both registers, used a small proportion of existential processes, introducing new participants into their discourse:

(13) and in the streets there were lots of rats. (SB-T-CL)
(14) *La mayoría de la población de la aldea era campesina, pero también había algunos artesanos.* (SB-T-SP)
'The majority of the population of the village were peasants, but there were also some craftsmen.'

In process types, then, similar choices were found in CLIL and L1 contexts, except in the case of relational processes. These appeared in a higher proportion, and were more varied in the CLIL groups' production. One of the reasons seems to be the higher use of possessive and identifying processes in the CLIL data. This might be due to the fact that both these process types allow description to be expressed using nouns, rather than adjectives. The lexis focused on in the CLIL curriculum includes a high proportion of terms in this word class, which might contribute to the CLIL students' linguistic resources being more based on nouns.

4.1.1 *Circumstances*

Moving now to the way the students expanded their clauses with circumstances, Figures 3 and 4 below show the distribution of the different types. Again, only the most frequent classes found in the data have been included. These were location-place (LO-PL), location-time (LO-TM), cause (CAU), and manner (MN).

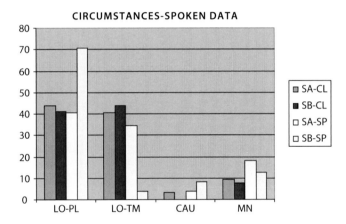

Figure 3. Percentage of circumstances in CLIL and L1 students' spoken data

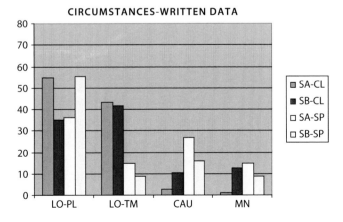

Figure 4. Percentage of circumstances in CLIL and L1 students' written data

Figure 3 shows that in three of the four groups studied, the circumstances used in the discussions are divided fairly equally between place and time, as expected, given the prompt. However, this focus on place and time is especially marked in the CLIL students' production. In their spoken answers, there is hardly any use of cause, and little of manner. Examples (15), (16) and (17) show expressions of time and place in the CLIL and L1 class discussions:

(15)   <u>in the Middle Ages</u> there were serfs and.. the agriculture was first.. the base of the economy. (SA-D-CL)

(16)   Most of the people work <u>in farms</u> and ⟨x…x⟩. Eh.. peasants gathered <u>in villages</u> that were eh.. that were houses surrounding a castle or a ⟨x…x⟩ (SA-D-CL)

(17)   *tenían que trabajar <u>en el campo</u> y tenían que trabajar <u>todos los días</u>* (SA-D-SP)
'They had to work <u>in the fields</u> and they had to work <u>every day</u>.'

In the written texts, the two CLIL classes still produce mainly temporal and location circumstances, while the L1 groups rarely use circumstances of time, but include cause (18) and manner (19):

(18)   *la población durante los siglos XI al XIII, creció <u>gracias a</u> una mejor alimentación <u>debida a</u> la mayor producción agrícola y <u>al</u> fin de las invasiones* (SB-T-SP)
'the population from the XI to XIII centuries, grew <u>thanks to</u> better food <u>due to</u> the increased agricultural production and <u>to</u> the end of the invasions.'

(19)   *como todo el mundo vivia <u>muy juntos</u> la peste se propago <u>con bastante rapidez.</u>* (SB-T-SP)
'as everybody lived <u>very close together</u> the plague spread <u>quite fast</u>.'

Here, then, the L1 students used a higher proportion and a greater variety of different types of circumstances, showing more developed awareness of the register of the discipline.

4.1.2   *Clause complexes*

Figures 5 and 6 below show the distribution of clause complexes. The main types found were addition and contrast in coordinated clauses, coded as extension-addition (EX-AD) and extension-contrast/adversative (EX-AV), cause and condition, coded as enhancement-cause (EN-CAU) and enhancement-contingency (EN-CO), clauses introducing indirect speech or thought, coded as projection (PR), and the use of non-defining relative clauses, coded as elaboration (EL).

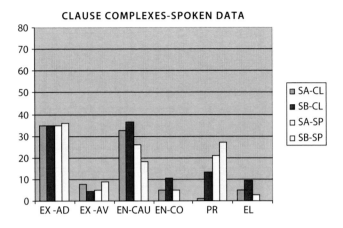

Figure 5. Percentage of clause complexes in CLIL and L1 students' spoken data

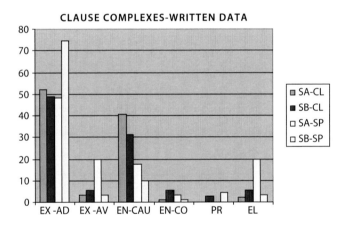

Figure 6. Percentage of clause complexes in CLIL and L1 students' written data

It is clear from these bar graphs that resources for clause-linking in both the CLIL and the L1 spoken and written data were limited to a few types. We found mainly addition (EX-AD) and cause (EN-CAU) in both registers and these were used considerably more frequently in the compositions than in the class discussions. In the spoken data, and especially in the L1 groups, projection (PR) was also quite frequent. Some clauses of contrast, condition and elaboration also appear in the data. Examples of the most common types are shown in (20) to (22). First, from a CLIL group, we see how the student strings a series of clauses together as he speaks using addition (20). The second CLIL Example, (21), is from a written text, where addition and contrast are shown, while Example (22), from an L1 composition, shows a number of clauses linked by addition markers:[5]

(20)   Ah no no no! Eh, for example, in that moments they were archers and warriors with swords <u>and</u> they were protect by walls, the cities <u>and</u>, for example, in Madrid, is no protect by, by nothing. (SB-D-CL)

(21)   Nowadays we are much more advanced in terms of medicine and architecture <u>&</u> today's population mayority isn't engaged to rural life and agriculture <u>but</u> work in offices and other terms. (SA-T-CL)

(22)   *La vida en las zonas rurales era muy simple, las casas estaban poco amuebladas <u>y</u> los campesinos cultivaban, tejian <u>y</u> hilaban, eran autosuficientes.* (SA-T-SP)
'Life in the rural areas was very simple, the houses had little furniture <u>and</u> the peasants farmed the land, wove <u>and</u> spun, they were self-sufficient.'

The logical relation of cause, important in the task, was very frequently expressed in subordinate clauses by CLIL students, both in speech and writing. Example (23) is from a written text:

(23)   There was a rebirth of cities <u>because</u> later the people in the forest don't like the type of living and they move to big cities and they can found more facilities of work. (SA-T-CL)

The L1 students also produced causal clauses but in a lower proportion. They tended to choose to express this logical relation in circumstances, especially in their writing, as Figure 4 above showed. Examples (24) and (25) below respectively show a clausal and a circumstantial realization of cause from L1 written texts:

(24)   *No podían salir de el pueblo <u>por miedo a que</u> se propagase más.* (SB-T-SP)
'They couldn't leave the town <u>for fear of</u> it [the plague] spreading more.'

(25)   *Las ciudades crecieron <u>por la tecnología agraria</u>* (SB-T-SP)
'The cities grew because of the farming technology.'

The high proportion of projection which appears in Figure 5 responds to the frequent prefacing of an answer with "*que*" (that), which is understood as complementing an elided projecting verb as in (26). This feature carries over to the CLIL groups' interlanguage (27):

(26)   *Pues <u>que</u>...los villanos eran hombres teóricamente libres, y los siervos pues no tenían derechos.* (SA-D-SP)
'Well, <u>that</u>... the villains were theoretically free men, and the serfs well they didn't have any rights.'

(27)   Eh, also <u>that</u>, eh, Middle Ages, em, there were a lot of invasions and ...(SB-D-CL)

---

5.   The L1 example from a composition uses juxtaposition as well as addition, a device not captured in our coding.

Though much less salient in the figures, it is interesting to see the use of elaboration as a clause-combining device. This is found in both groups' written and spoken discourse, where the students show some awareness of the need to display knowledge of the times they are writing about. Here we have two examples taken from compositions, the CLIL Example (28) showing formal errors in the use of the relative pronoun:

(28)   On the other hand, the peasants had to work very hard every day except Sundays, <u>that</u> were Holy days...Peasants had to pay the Church a tax called "tithe" <u>that</u> was a tenth of the harvest... (SB-T-CL)

(29)   *La vida en las zonas rurales en la Europa feudal, era una vida dura, los más desfavorecidos eran siervos, <u>que</u> no tenían parcelas para cultivar.* (SB-T-SP) 'Life in the rural areas in feudal Europe, was a hard life, the most underprivileged were the serfs, <u>who</u> had no pieces of land to cultivate.'

In the use of clause complexes, then, we also note differences between our two sets of data, particularly with respect to the expression of cause.

4.1.3   *Modality*

Our final feature studied here, the use of modality, as evidence of the students' control of the interpersonal function of language in their texts, produced few examples. Figure 7 shows the results of the analysis of modal expressions in the students' writing: modalisation-probability (MODA-PR), modalisation-usuality (MODA-US), modulation-readiness/ability (MODU-RE), modulation-obligation and permission (MODU-OB). We have not included a graph for the spoken data, since there we found even fewer instances. The modals tended to appear in the teachers' prompts and be elided in the students' responses.

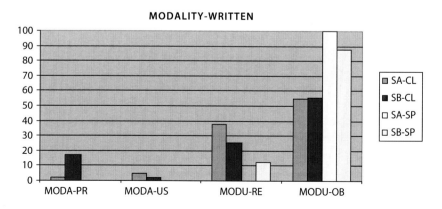

Figure 7. Percentage of modal expressions in CLIL and L1 students' written data

As always, the graph shows the distribution of the feature examined in the different types. More precisely, Figure 7 shows how, in the L1 data, the only type of modality found was in the expression of obligation, related to the prompt's question about the rights and obligations of the peasants, as in Example (30):

(30)   *El campesino __debía__ pagar al señor una parte de cosecha.* (SB-T-SP)
       'The peasant <u>had to</u> pay the lord a part of his harvest.'

While still presenting little modality, the CLIL groups' compositions showed a more frequent and more varied use than their L1 counterparts. The most frequent type was again the expression of obligation, referring to rights and duties:

(31)   they <u>had to work</u> very hard for money and they <u>had to pay</u>
       to the church. (SB-T-CL)

However, in the CLIL groups we also find the students' expression of ability:

(32)   Nowadays we have more rights than then, we <u>can</u> choose where we want
       to work. (SA-T-CL)

A different use, found in a small proportion, but interesting for its effect on the expression of the content, are the traces of modalisation, where some students make reference to the probability or usuality of the information they are recording, as in (33) and (34):

(33)   The houses were small <u>normaly</u> of one room and a shed. (SA-T-CL)
(34)   The Church had a lot of political, economical, cultural & <u>obviously</u> religious
       power. (SB-T-CL)

Thus, the few instances of modality in the data were concentrated, in the case of the L1 students, in the expression of obligation, while more variety was found in the CLIL groups, who also expressed ability and some probability and usuality. No modalisation was found in the L1 groups. This might be due to the way CLIL and L1 teachers focus on the content, since in our spoken data, we have found differences here. The CLIL teachers open up the discussion to a variety of points of view and relate the historical content to the students' personal experiences and views more than the L1 teachers. The appearance of modality contrasts with results from studies in other CLIL contexts and would need further research (Dalton Puffer & Nikula 2006).

5.   Discussion

Our analysis shows similarities and differences between the CLIL and the L1 samples. There are similarities in the distribution of process types, which are mostly action processes, as expected in a historical recount of events. However, the CLIL students produce a wider variety of processes mainly in the written register, with relational processes expressing identification, description/attribution and possession. Another similarity is the frequent use of addition to link clauses, the conjunction "and" in particular. This is common to both groups and both registers. The overuse of "and" in the students' written texts is a feature of orality and shows little register sensitivity, often found in this type of writer (Barrio 2004).

On the other hand, we also find interesting differences between the two groups. Firstly, many CLIL students seem to have a limited repertoire of circumstances, almost always using time and place. These students express cause through clauses in both registers whereas L1 students tend to use circumstances for this logical relation, especially in the written register. This difference seems to be related to the ability to use nominalisations, as Examples (35) and (36) from the L1 and the CLIL contexts show:

(35) Teacher: *¿Por qué creéis que se propagó tan rápidamente la Peste Negra? A ver, J.*
      'Why do you think the Black Death spread so rapidly. Let's see, J.'
      Student: *Por el hacinamiento* (SB-D-SP)
      'Due to overcrowding'
(36) Because the people are not clean (SA-D-CL)

While the L1 student answers with a prepositional phrase including an abstract noun, the CLIL student uses a clause and everyday lexis. According to Halliday (1989), this type of difference represents a key to academic language, as claimed in his description of spoken and written language. A number of studies on the language of history (Eggins et al. 1993; Martin 1993; Veel & Coffin 1996) have shown that, in this discipline, reasoning takes place within and not between clauses, which indicates that the L1 student's answer represents the language of written history while the CLIL student's does not.

At the same time, we find some examples in the data showing that the CLIL students are beginning to develop the register of the discipline. As Eggins et al. (1993: 75) show, "[i]n the process of arranging, interpreting and generalizing from recoverable facts [in historical discourse], people are effaced, actions become things, and sequence in time is replaced by frozen setting in time". Example (37) has some of these features:

(37) The cities grow because of the reactivation of trade and becaus the people
      of the country went to the city because there they payed better than in the
      country. (SA-T-CL)

Here, the first clause suppresses the human actors, gives agency to an inanimate city and includes the reasoning inside that clause. However, in the second and third clauses, the young writer reverts to a more oral style, introducing "the people" and

their activities, and linking the clauses with "because". Some of the CLIL students'
spoken language also shows features of the language of history, as in Example 38,
referring to the spread of the plague:

(38)   the filth of the cities promoted the expansion of it (SA-D-CL)

Here, there are no human actors, but a thing, "the filth", causing the plague to
expand; this action is expressed by a noun phrase, and the logical relation appears
inside the clause in the verb "promoted". Thus, while the L1 students show a
slightly greater distinction between their written and spoken registers and seem to
be more advanced in their development of the language of history, CLIL students
seem to be at a more unstable point in their interlanguage system as far as register
differences are concerned.

A second difference that emerges from the data is that in the CLIL classes
analysed there seems to be more space for individual students' views and interpretations and, thus, for what can be seen as more genuine communication (Dalton-
Puffer & Smit 2007). Dalton-Puffer's (2006) analysis of the complexity of CLIL
students' answers in relation to the type of questions posed by the teacher shows
that questions based on reasons, opinions and beliefs generate more complex
answers from the students. Our study points to similar conclusions, as shown in
the CLIL students' use of a more varied selection of linguistic resources. While
both groups use mainly material processes, the CLIL students produce more
relational processes and modal verbs of different types.

This could be related to a difference in focus taken by the L1 and CLIL teachers in our study, a focus related to the genre chosen by the teachers in their work in
the history classroom. The L1 teachers tended to require a historical recount, and
explanations based on accepted views, whereas teachers of the CLIL classes made
their students aware that the content they are learning is the result of generalising,
leaving open the possibility of other interpretations, as well as relating the topic to
their personal experience. This difference in focus might be due to the CLIL teachers' awareness of the students' difficulty in talking and writing about the subject
topic in a foreign language and, thus, they try to offer space for different types of
approaches to the content. With this focus, a double goal is achieved: through
the reference to students' socio-cultural experience they learn the content from a
different perspective, and they also have the chance to use the L2 for purposes
other than recounting and explaining known facts and events. Th is richer
approach, which we found in the class discussions, is later reflected in the written texts. In fact, some CLIL students' use of modality shows the beginning of
development towards the most complex of the history genres: argumentation
(Coffin 2006a). Example (39) shows students' creation of a hypothesis using strong
prediction modality:

(39)   Medicine has been improved a lot, in the Middle Ages took place The Black
        Death, a horrible disease that was transmited by rats in Eastern Europe to all
        Europe and killed 1/3 of the worlds population, <u>now this will not happen</u>
        <u>because of the hygiene and vacunes, the Black Death will be stoped.</u> (SB-T-CL)

Interestingly enough, this type of examples was not found in the L1 students' writing. Since both groups had the same prompt, and had studied the same content, this may reflect a different approach to the teaching of history, with the CLIL teachers using a variety of materials prepared for the British curriculum. These differences need to be further investigated with more data and in different classroom tasks and contexts.

6. Conclusions and pedagogic implications

The results from our study suggest some implications for CLIL teacher training and pedagogy. Firstly, if CLIL students need to learn the language of academic discourse in a discipline, their teachers need training in order to become aware of the linguistic features required for the representation of content in their subject, in a variety of genres and both in the written and spoken registers. Such a focus on language would take advantage of students' communicative needs, bringing in work on the lexis and grammar they require to express their meanings. This explicit and functional approach to the language of the disciplines has been found to be successful (for research and examples of practice, see chapters in Carter 1990; Hasan & Williams 1996; Johns 2002; Schleppegrell 2004; Schleppegrell & Colombi 2002; Whittaker et al. 2006). The teachers also need to know how best to integrate this focus on specific linguistic features into their teaching of their content subject. Coyle (2007), in her 4Cs framework, argues strongly for such integration of content and communication, which, together with cognition and culture, are presented as the key elements in CLIL.

Secondly, the CLIL classes studied here have been shown to provide a more open context than the L1 classes for approaching content from different perspectives. This was also found by Nikula (2007), in her comparison between CLIL and EFL classes, where the CLIL context was again seen as providing the learners with more space for interaction. Our comparative study of CLIL and L1 learning contexts suggests that offering the learners the possibility of using different academic functions in the class has implications both in the way the content is learned and in the language used to express this content. We believe this has important implications for both content and language learning: the students learn the content in different ways as they do not only display accepted knowledge but they also discuss it from a number of points of view, and relate it to their own experience.

To do this they need to use the L2 in different ways to convey these different functions. This may have a positive effect not only on their development of the target language, since they use different resources in their work on the content, but also on the development of different ways of learning.

References

Barrio, M. 2004. Experimental Study of Textual Development in Spanish Students of English as a Foreign Language. In *"segundo de bachillerato"*: Features of Written Register in Compositions of Argumentative Genre. Ph.D. dissertation, Universidad Autónoma de Madrid.

Bereiter, C. & Scardamalia, M. 1987. *The Psychology of Written Composition*. Hillsdale NJ: Lawrence Erlbaum Associates.

Carter, R. 1990. *Knowledge about Language and the Curriculum: The LINC Reader*. Sevenoaks: Hodder and Stoughton.

Christie, F. 1998. Learning the literacies of primary and secondary schooling. In *Literacy and Schooling*, F. Christie & R. Mission (eds), 47–73. London: Routledge.

Christie, F. & Derewianka, B. 2008. *School Discourse: Learning to Write across the Years of Schooling*. London: Continuum.

Coffin, C. 2006a. *Historical Discourse*. London: Continuum.

Coffin, C. 2006b. Reconstructing 'personal time' as 'collective time': Learning the discourse of history. In Whittaker et al. (eds), 207–232.

Cope, B. & Kalantzis, M. (eds). 1993. *The Powers of Literacy: A Genre Approach to Teaching Writing*. London: Falmer Press.

Coyle, D. 2007. Content and Language Integrated Learning: Towards a connected research agenda for CLIL pedagogies. *International Journal of Bilingual Education and Bilingualism*, 10(5): 543–562.

Dalton-Puffer, C. 2005. Negotiating interpersonal meanings in naturalistic classroom discourse: Directives in Content-and-Language-Integrated classrooms. *Journal of Pragmatics* 37: 1275–1293.

Dalton-Puffer, C. 2007. *Discourse in Content and Language Integrated Learning (CLIL) Classrooms* [Language Learning & Language Teaching 20]. Amsterdam: John Benjamins.

Dalton-Puffer, C. & Nikula, T. 2006. Pragmatics of content-based instruction: Teacher and student directives in Finnish and Austrian classrooms. *Applied Linguistics* 27: 241–267.

Dalton-Puffer, C. & U. Smit. (eds.) 2007. *Empirical Perspectives on CLIL Classroom Discourse*. Frankfurt: Peter Lang.

Dalton-Puffer, C. & Smit, U. 2007. Introduction. In Dalton-Puffer & Smit (eds), 7–24.

Day, E.M. & Shapson, S. 1996. *Studies in Immersion Education*. Clevedon: Multilingual Matters.

Eggins, S., Wignell, P. & Martin, J.R. 1993. The discourse of history: Distancing the recoverable past. In *Register Analysis*, M. Ghadessy (ed.), 75–109. London: Pinter.

Eurydice. 2008. *Key Data on Teaching Languages at School in Europe*. Brussels: Education, Audiovisual and Culture Executive Agency.

Halliday, M.A.K. 1989. *Spoken and Written Language*. Oxford: OUP.

Halliday, M.A.K. 2004. [1985]. *An Introduction to Functional Grammar*. 3rd edn. Revised by C. Matthiessen. London: Edward.

Halliday, M.A.K. & Martin, J.R. 1993. *Writing Science: Literacy and Discursive Power.* London: Falmer.

Hasan, R. & Williams, G. (eds). 1996. *Literacy in Society*, Longman: London.

Jäppinen, A-K. 2005. Thinking and content learning of mathematics and science as cognitional development in Content and Language Integrated Learning (CLIL): Teaching through a foreign language in Finland. *Language & Education* 19(2): 148–169.

Johns, A. (ed.). 2002. *Genre in the Classroom. Multiple Perspectives.* Mahwah NJ: Lawrence Erlbaum Associates.

Llinares García, A. & Whittaker, R. 2006. Oral and written production in social science. *VIEWS. Vienna English Working Papers* 15(3): 28–32.

Llinares García, A. & Whittaker, R. 2007. Talking and writing in the social sciences in a foreign language: a linguistic analysis of secondary school learners of geography and history. In *Models and Practice in CLIL*, F. Lorenzo, S. Casal, V. Alba & P. Moore (eds), 83–94. RESLA. Volumen monográfico. Seville: University Pablo de Olavide.

Llinares García, A. & Whittaker, R. 2009. Teaching and learning history in secondary CLIL classrooms: From speaking to writing. In *CLIL across Educational Levels: Experiences from Primary, Secondary and Tertiary Contexts*, E. Dafouz & M. Guerrini (eds), 73–88. Madrid: Richmond Publishing.

Martin, J.R. 1993. Life as a noun: Arresting the universe in science and humanities. In *Writing Science: Literacy and Discursive Power*, M.A.K. Halliday & J.R. Martin (eds), 221–267. London: Falmer.

Martin, J.R. 1992. *English Text. System and Structure.* Amsterdam: John Benjamins.

Nikula, T. 2007. The IRF pattern and space for interaction: Comparing CLIL and EFL classrooms. In Dalton-Puffer & Smit (eds), 179–204.

Pérez Vidal, C. 2002. Spain. In *Modern Languages across the Curriculum*, M. Grenfell (ed.), 114–130. London: Routledge.

Rothery, J. 1994. *Exploring Literacy in School English. Write it Right Project.* Erskineville: Disadvantaged Schools Program, Department of School Education.

Rothery, J. 1996. Making changes: Developing an educational linguistics. In Hasan & Williams (eds), 86–123.

Schleppegrell, M. 2004. *The Language of Schooling. A Functional Linguistics Perspective.* Mahwah NJ: Lawrence Erlbaum Associates.

Schleppegrell, M. & Colombi, C. (eds). 2002. *Developing Advanced Literacy in First and Second Languages. Meaning with Power.* Mahwah NJ: Lawrence Erlbaum Associates.

Veel, R. & Coffin, C. 1996. Learning to think like an historian: The language of secondary school history. In Hasan & Williams (eds), 191–231.

Van de Craen, P., Lochtman, K., Ceuleers, E., Mondt, K. & Allain, L. 2007. An interdisciplinary approach to CLIL learning in primary schools in Brussels. In Dalton-Puffer & Smit (eds), 253–274.

Vollmer, H.J., Heine, L., Troschke, R., Coetzee, D. & Küttel, V. 2006. Subject-specific competence and language use of CLIL learners: The case of geography in grade 10 of secondary schools in Germany. Paper presented at the ESSE8 Conference in London, 29 August 2006.

Whittaker, R. & Llinares, A. 2009. CLIL in social science classrooms: Analysis of spoken and written productions. In *Content and Language Integrated Learning. Evidence from Research in Europe*, Y. Ruiz de Zarobe & R. Jimenez Catalán (eds), 215–234. Bristol: Multilingual Matters.

Whittaker, R., O'Donnell, M. & McCabe, A. (eds). 2006. *Language and Literacy. Functional Approaches.* London: Continuum.

Language as a meaning making resource in learning and teaching content

Analysing historical writing in content and language integrated learning

Heini-Marja Järvinen
Turun yliopisto, Finland

This article reports on a study of written production in content and language integrated learning (CLIL) with special emphasis on the ways linguistic resources are used in constructing historical meaning. The study utilizes the systemic functional framework (SFL) and its data consist of essays written in English (language of instruction) and in Finnish (students' first language and language of instruction) by ten CLIL students and in English (the only language of instruction, students' first or second language) by nine peers in international school (all grade 8 students, about 14 years of age).

The discussion addresses the following questions: What are some of the features emerging in the written productions that reflect the use of language in constructing historical meaning in the light of systemic-functional linguistics? In particular, what characteristics of grammatical metaphor realized in terms of syntactic intricacy and thematic organization are observed in the English and Finnish essays of the CLIL students? The article concludes with a discussion of future research and pertinent pedagogical implications to CLIL environments.

1. Introduction

The research reported on in this article focuses on the integration of language and content in bilingual instruction. More specifically, it explores how students involved in content and language integrated instruction (CLIL) use language to construct historical meaning. The research investigates features of scientific discourse, such as nominalization, and other characteristics of grammatical metaphor, a central concept in Systemic Functional Linguistics, reflecting the development of scientific language. The experimental group data consists of ten 14-year-old

Finnish CLIL students' essays on the causes of the Finnish Civil War. The study is set in the framework of Systemic Functional Linguistics (SFL) and is guided by its functional and integrative approach to language and content.

This article focuses on the *integration* of language and content in CLIL. It is typical but often problematic (Davison & Williams 2001) that concepts such as learning, language, content and integration are mostly defined at a general and a technical level. For example, CLIL is defined as "an educational approach" in which a language which is not the students' native language is used "for the teaching and learning of subjects other than the language itself " (Marsh & Langé 2000: iii), often "by professionals who teach on courses other than languages" (Marsh et al. 2001, 13). Further, "CLIL is a multifaceted approach which is implemented to reach specific outcomes which enhance the learning of field specific education alongside" (Marsh et al. 2001, 20). These definitions describe the *forms* of implementation at the institutional level rather than the *"how"* and *"why"* of integration of content and language in terms of learning outcomes.

Research into learning in CLIL draws on the approaches and methods of either applied language study (e.g. Dalton-Puffer 2007) or content disciplines, primarily constructivist approaches to learning (see, e.g. Dantas-Whitney 2002; Kaufman & Crandall 2005). Typically, the focus is on content with content-embedded language as part and parcel of content instruction. Thus, learning content matter is the primary and learning language the secondary goal. Therefore, explicitly stated language learning goals are often missing, especially when the teacher lacks a formal language education and has little or no knowledge of language learning and teaching. Even in cases where a balanced emphasis on content and language is the goal, the implication is that language (form) and content (meaning) are kept separate (Schleppegrell & de Oliveira 2006).

To achieve true integration of language and content in the content classroom necessitates more than a double focus on language and content. What is needed is an emphasis on language in the content classroom with a functional focus on the meanings created by the language in order to develop the content, thus enabling an amalgamated view on language and content and a simultaneous focus on form and meaning. This article presents one such approach, systemic functional linguistics, and discusses the possibilities which SFL offers for integrating language and content in the CLIL classroom.

Below, a more detailed discussion of the framework of this study is provided. The empirical study investigates the use of language in the construction of historical meaning from the viewpoint of text construction (syntactic intricacy and thematic structure) and language development in the light of grammatical metaphor.

2. Systemic functional theory

There are a number of reasons why the SFL approach is compatible with a theoretical framework that is applicable to content and language integrated instruction. One is the way in which systemic functional theory combines and allows for interaction between content and language at three levels (strata): the level of semantics (content), the level of discourse (content-typical textual conventions), and the level of language production (spoken or written texts) (Halliday 1994). Another is the emphasis on academic literacy, especially writing, and yet another but related reason is dialectical learning. The latter refers to the learning processes that the learner is involved in when s/he is reading content-specific texts, learning new content-typical discourse from them and reproducing the newly learned discourse in writing (Byrnes 2009b). An important aspect of the systemic functional approach is its pedagogical potential (Halliday 2007a,b), which can be used to facilitate language teaching in content instruction by providing tools for content teachers in particular, but also for language teachers, to teach students how to study and learn the academic language of content (for history teaching, see, e.g. Schleppegrell & Achugar 2003; Schleppegrell et al. 2004).

The systemic functional account of language development posits a gradual progression from congruent (typical, unmarked) forms of language that are typical of oral language towards more incongruent (marked) and indirect forms of language, typical of written language with emphasis on the nominal phrase (Halliday 1993). The development from congruent forms to incongruent forms of language is called grammatical metaphor in Hallidayan SFL (Halliday 1994). Two aspects of grammatical metaphor are relevant for the present study. One relates to syntactic features at the clausal and interclausal levels, and the other concerns the semiotic features that are pertinent to the ways in which language participates in the process of meaning making.

2.1   Grammatical metaphor

As the name reveals, grammatical metaphor is a metaphorical expression for a process in which meanings are reconstructed by means of language (Hood 2008). Typically, this means a more compressed expression; verbs are replaced by nouns to achieve the kind of "abstract thinginess" that scientific writing is characterized by.

The following examples serve as illustrations of the development of grammatical metaphor. The sentence *The runner texted his coach* (Martin 2008: 802) shows a congruent relation, i.e. a matching relationship between semantics and lexicogrammar as is shown below.

semantics	participant	process	participant
	the runner	*texted*	*his coach*
grammar	nominal	verbal	nominal

The *runner* is a nominal and a participant. Similarly, *texted* is a verbal element referring to a process at the semantic level, and the final element *his coach* is another nominal (grammar) participant (semantics).

Written academic language, however, abounds in nominalizations in which the lexicogrammatical form does not match the discourse semantic meaning. The following example (Martin 2008: 803) may serve as an example of incongruent nominalization:

semantics	process	process	manner	process
	the argument	*is made*	*through*	*the use of nominalization*
grammar	nominal	verbal	preposition	nominal

The nouns *argument, use* and *nominalization* are derived from corresponding processes *arguing, using* and *nominalising* and the logical connection between the constituents is made through a preposition instead of a conjunction. Martin (2008: 803) suggests the following congruent reading of the example: *they argued by using language which nominalised verbs.* In this congruent configuration, the semantics and grammar match, whereas in the incongruent example *The argument is made through the use of nominalization* they are in tension with each other. This tension is created by grammatical metaphor and it is something that all "functionally literate members of post-colonial societies" (Martin 2008: 803) will have to learn to manage.

To quote Martin (2008: 803), mastery of stratal tension "comes from a successful apprenticeship into disciplinary and administrative discourse in institutionalized education – typically secondary school". In CLIL contexts (as well as in mainstream education), the secondary school curriculum is (more explicitly than the preceding primary school curriculum) divided into subjects taught by subject specialists. The focus is on subject-specific study, which requires from the students that they have adequate literacy skills to tackle the subject-specific discourse. To achieve discipline-specific literacy skills in the first language is a challenge to many mainstream learners, so learners in CLIL are likely to need support in dealing with stratal tension in a non-native subject-specific discourse.

The following Example (1) from the present data is an example of congruent language form. The (invented) Examples (2) and (3) are incongruent reformulations of (1).

(1)   Because there were food less and less, the prices was rising.
      They doubled in four months. (congruent) (learner data)

(2)   Due to the increasing shortage of food, the prices rose, doubling
        in four months. (incongruent) (reformulation)
(3)   The increasing shortage of food led to the price level doubling in four months.
        (incongruent) (reformulation)

In (2) and (3), the congruent expressions of (1) have been replaced by more incongruent, nominalised versions:

> because there were food less and less (1) >due to the increasing shortage of food
> (2) >the increasing shortage of food (3)

In addition to nominalizations, progression from the congruent stages of language development contains other manifestations of grammatical metaphor, for example embedded constructions exemplified in (2) and (3):

> They doubled in four months (1) > doubling in four months (2 and 3).

2.1.1   *Syntactic intricacy*

According to Halliday (2002), there is a development of language from an oral variety to a written one which takes place not only in individual language development but also at the phylogenetic level, observable as increasing nominalization in the development of scientific language. The oral and written varieties differ from each other in a number of ways. With regard to syntax, the differences are apparent at interclausal level in the oral variety: ample use of paratactic and hypotactic and embedded constructions, whereas the written end of the continuum shows a rich and elaborate use of nominal phrases and accompanying lexical density (Halliday 1994: 349). In other words, the information in spoken texts tends to be distributed across a number of clauses, whereas the information in the written texts is packed within one clause. Thus, syntactic intricacy is expressed differently in spoken and written texts: the former display a high ratio of clauses per sentence, the latter display high lexical density.

2.2.2   *Thematic organization*

Thematic organization refers to the cohesive development of a text, more specifically to the flow of information conveyed by themes (topic, focus, old information) and rhemes (comment, new information) in a text. Typically, themes and rhemes follow each other in patterned sequences which are characteristic of certain text types.

The theme is usually defined as occupying the initial, most prominent position in the clause. Halliday (1994) identifies the theme with all the clause-initial elements including the first ideational (topical) element. In general, a clause-initial, unmarked theme coincides with the grammatical and topical subject.

The narrative-type extract (4) from the present data contains a number of unmarked themes, coinciding with grammatical subjects. These themes are in bold.

(4)   **The Finnish civil** war started in 1917 and ended in 1918. **It** was against the whites and reds. **The reds** wanted to take over and be independant. **They** already had about 20 % of the south of Finland. **The whites** were the rest of Finland and wanted to stay in power. **Russia** helped the reds and **the germans** helped the whites.

If the clause-initial element does not coincide with the grammatical subject of the clause, but instead contains elements other than the grammatical or topical subjects, it is called a marked theme. Marked themes consist of fronted elements, such as pre-posed adverbial groups or prepositional phrases. In SVO languages like English, marked themes signal special changes and turns in the discourse or in the real world circumstances, such as changes in time or place or rhetorical moves, but in languages with a relatively free word order, like Finnish, clause-initial themes (other than grammatical subjects) are less marked. Example (5) below is taken from the present data (CLIL En). Marked themes are in bold.

(5)   **In 1917, after getting the independence** there were many kinds of problems in Finland. There were different opinions about Finnish independence between rightist and leftist parties. **In the countryside** the poor people were disappointment in their situation is society. They didn't have many rights and in 1917 they really woke up and saw their situation. They wanted some rights for themselves. **In 1917** unemployment increased and there were a huge shortage of food. People were disappointment in senate's works. […] **In autumn** the Finnish social democratises publisher their program called "We Demand" It was their strike against senate. They really believed that there were no other ways to solve the situation than revolution. **In "We Demand"-program** they wanted many changes in society.

Certain thematic patterns seem to be discipline-specific. The historical writing of children and adolescents tends to favour personified themes and thematic progression that is typical of the narrative text type (Halldén 1986; Voss et al. 1994; Coffin 2004). Also circumstantial themes have shown to be more frequent in historical writing than in science and biology (Taylor 1983; Lovejoy 1991).

The remaining part of the article presents an analysis in the light of systemic functional theory. The data analysis will focus on the development of grammatical metaphor, syntactic intricacy and thematic organization.

3.   The study

The purpose of the study is to illustrate how the syntactic intricacy observed in the data reflects grammatical metaphor and how the thematic development is used to construct historical meaning. The analysis and interpretation of the data are guided by the following research questions derived from the theoretical discussion above:

1.   What features of grammatical metaphor are observable in the written productions?
2.   What features of syntactic intricacy are observed in the data?
3.   Which types of topical (unmarked) and marked themes are observed in the data?

The study analyses historical writing by 19 lower secondary-level students participating in English-medium teaching in Finland. Out of the total 19, ten are enrolled in a CLIL programme and speak Finnish as the first language. Nine are international school students, the majority of whom are native English speakers or speak English as a strong second language.

There were some commonalities and differences between the two groups that might have an impact on the results. The commonalities were school, age and grade level, language of instruction (English) and the history curriculum. The investigated students were 14 or 15 year-old grade 8 students taught in English at the same school (but in different programmes). At the time of the study, they were studying the same unit in Finnish history. The differences are the first languages, length, amount and type of exposure to the English language. The international school students' first or (strong) second language was English, and the CLILEn students' first language was Finnish. The international students had more exposure to English in informal as well as formal contexts, for example their entire curriculum was taught in English. The Finnish CLILEn students' exposure to English was more restricted at school: only part of the curriculum was taught in English. It is also safe to assume that their informal exposure to English was more infrequent than that of their international school peers'.

On the basis of the above theoretical discussion and the commonalities and differences between the groups, it is reasonable to hypothesise that the international school students' writing exhibits features that are characteristic of more advanced grammatical metaphor, such as nominalizations and subordination, whereas the CLILEn students would show more congruent features of grammatical metaphor, such as paratactic structures and active verbal constructions. It might also be anticipated that the international school students' essays would exhibit features that are related with more advanced language skills and more developed grammatical metaphor, which would show as higher lexical density and syntactic complexity (more complex T-units, fewer clauses per sentence). On similar grounds, it might be anticipated that the Finnish students' L1 writing would be more advanced than their English writing. In addition, it might be expected that some features of the first language would be reflected in the essays, for example the free word order in Finnish, which might show as a large number of marked themes in the English data (see Grammatical metaphor: thematic perspective).

4.   Methodology

The participants of the study were ten fourteen-year old students (five girls and five boys) in the 8th grade in a bilingual CLIL programme in lower secondary school and nine peers (six girls and three boys) enrolled in the international stream of the same school.

The study was carried out in the context of content and language integrated learning of history. Prior to the empirical data collection, the participants had finished the study of a unit in national history dealing with the Finnish civil war that had taken place at the time of the newly achieved independence of the country. The data base of the present investigation consists of three sets of essays, one written by both groups (the CLIL group and the international group) as a take-home assignment to be written in English. The other was written by the CLIL group in Finnish as part of a course-final exam three weeks after the home assignment was administered.

The topic of all essays was "Causes of the Finnish Civil War". The students were asked to write about the causes that led to the breaking out of the civil war in Finland in 1918. The CLIL students were not informed that the course-final test would include the same assignment as the home essay, this time in Finnish, which was the students' native language. The conditions of the two productions were thus different: more time and more resources were available for the home assignment, whereas the course exam was written as one assignment out of a total of three and the whole test had to be completed within one hour. The course-final test situation is obviously a more stressful one than that of a home assignment, but the English and Finnish essays can still be viewed as comparable for at least the following reasons: Firstly, the students had the opportunity to write in their first language in the test; secondly, they had had – relatively seen – ample time to learn the content (during a six-week history course) and construe a solid memory representation of the historical content, and thirdly, they were advised to study the unit and prepare for the test. They also knew that the language of the test would be Finnish. However, it is obvious that the different circumstances need to be considered in the data analysis and interpretation.

The history teachers of these groups later rated the home essays and the final exam essay by using the conventional scoring system of the subject. The author and a history specialist, who also functioned as a co-researcher, made the linguistic and historical analyses for the present study.

5.   Results

5.1   Grammatical metaphor: Syntactic perspective

The two indicators of syntactic intricacy, i.e. the ratio of clauses per clause complex and the degree of lexical density were measured by means of T-units, frequencies of clauses and content words in the data. A T-unit is a measure consisting of "a main clause plus all subordinate clauses and nonclausal structures attached to or embedded in it" (Hunt 1970 cited in Gaies 1980: 54) and it is commonly used to describe sentence-level syntactic complexity in written and spoken discourse. Table 1 below shows the numbers of words (N), T-units and clauses in terms of occurrences in the three sets of data.

Table 1. Means (M) and standard deviations (SD) for words, T-units and clauses in the data

Level	N	Words			T-Units			Clauses		
		M	SD	Total	M	SD	Total	M	SD	Total
CLIL En	10	273.20	82.94	2732	23.70	8.25	237	33.70	10.34	337
CLIL Fi	10	86.80	49.78	868	12.20	6.80	122	15.30	7.75	153
International school	9	253.00	68.92	2277	19.78	4.21	178	27.44	3.32	247

The table indicates that the two essays written in English are about the same length in terms of all measures above as compared to the considerably shorter Finnish essay. The difference in length is probably due to the writing context: the Finnish essay was written as one assignment out of three in a test situation during one hour. The smaller number of words in the Finnish essays is partially due to the synthetic quality of the Finnish language: words carry a great amount of grammatical information that analytical languages like English express by prepositions and articles (*Suomessa* 'in Finland', *sisällissodan aikana* 'during the Civil War) and also compounds are written as one word (*sisällissota* 'the Civil War'). The Finnish essays also display a great variation in the number of words (ranging from 27 to 160 words), whereas the international school group shows the least variation.

Table 2 shows the data for syntactic intricacy in the studied samples. The majority, about three quarters, of the T-units in the data consist of one main clause; about a quarter of the T-units in each sample consist of one main and one subordinate clause. The number of T-units with one main clause and two subordinate clauses is small: four in the CLILEn essays, one in the CLILFi essays and nine in the international school essays. The depth of embedding, that is the number of embedded constructions linked to the main clause, is a reflection of syntactic intricacy and grammatical metaphor. The total number of complex T-units is small, but the nine complex T-units in the international school data in particular may reflect a more advanced grammatical metaphor than the four in the CLILEn data. The CLILFi data consist of independent main clauses or main clauses with one subordinate clause (with only one occurrence of two subordinate clauses).

Table 2 shows that the clauses and T-units in the CLILFi sample are short and simple when compared to essays written in English. Again, this may be due to contextual constraints, such as shortage of time in the test situation or the teacher's instructions to focus on the core content in the exam. This is supported by content analysis: the majority of the Finnish essays consist of lists or linear and simple causal-temporal structures. However, given that Finnish is the CLIL students' first language and that they were prepared for the test both by writing an essay (in English) on the topic a couple of weeks earlier and by studying for the test, the occurrence of more elaborate syntactic structures might have been expected.

Table 2. Indicators of syntactic intricacy

Level	Mean length of T-unit (MLTU)		Mean length of clause		Clauses/T-unit (C/TU)	
	M	SD	M	SD	M	SD
CLIL En	10.55	1.49	8.15	0.96	1.29	0.09
CLIL Fi	6.92	1.77	5.46	0.95	1.27	0.26
International school	13.01	3.10	9.45	1.72	1.34	0.13

Figures 2 and 3 illustrate lexical density and syntactic intricacy respectively. Both measures reflect the centrality of the clause (Halliday 2002) in systemic functional theory. Lexical density refers to the number of content words per clause and grammatical intricacy is computed as the ratio of clauses per sentence. Applying these measures to the oral – written cline in the Hallidayan framework reveals that lexical density is high at the written end and low at the oral end, whereas the reverse concerns grammatical intricacy, which is high in the oral variety and relatively low in the written mode (Byrnes 2009a). In other words, lexical density increases when the number of nominalizations increases and the ratio of grammatical words to lexical words decreases, and the number of clauses decreases accordingly. Obviously, the above will have to be taken as a general trend reflecting the theoretical constructs of the development of grammatical metaphor from clause to nominalization. The trend may be less clear in a small data sample where individual variation affects the results as the box plots in Figures 2 and 3 show.

The comparison of lexical density between languages that are syntactically different, such as English and Finnish in the present data, may be problematic, especially if the applied measure is sensitive to the ratio of lexical (content) words and functional words. A common formula for calculating lexical density is to divide the number of lexical words by the number of total words (lexical words + functional words) in a sample and multiplying the result by 100 (see e.g. Crawford Camiciottoli 2007: 73–74). However, if lexical density is measured as the number of lexical words per clause, the number of function words does not have an effect on the result. Thus, the Finnish word *sodassa* counts as one lexical word, and so does the English equivalent *at war*. Another difference is the orthography of compound words. The Finnish language tends to treat compounds as one orthographic unit, whereas the English language tends to keep the components of a compound separate. In the present data, compounds have been counted as one lexical word, for example *sisällissota* and *civil war*.

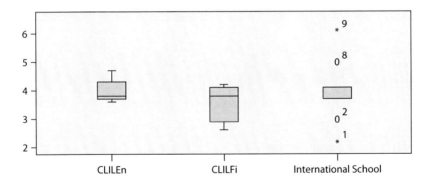

Figure 2. Variation of lexical density by language and group (content words per clause)

Figure 2 shows the box plots for the CLILEn, CLILFi and the International School data. The 'whiskers' indicate the sample minimum and maximum. The lower end line of the box denotes the first quartile (25 % of the observations are below this line). The line in the box is the median and the second quartile (50 % of the observations are below this line) and the upper line of the box is the third quartile (75 % of the observations are contained below this line). Circles and stars mark observations that are situated outside the box.

Table 3. Means and standard deviations for lexical density by language and group

	CLIL En	CLIL Fi	International school
Mean	4.07	3.62	3.80
SD	0.44	0.58	1.11

As can be seen in Figure 2 and Table 3, individual variation is the greatest in the International School group. The lowest (2.2) and the highest (6.1) values were found in this group. These, as well as the second lowest (3.0) and second highest (5.0), are shown as circles and stars in Figure 2. Apart from the four essays with high and low lexical densities in the international school data, more than half of the essays (5/9) were grouped relatively tightly around the mean (3.80).

The Finnish essays were the lowest in lexical density. It is possible that contextual factors are at play, such as time constraints in the test situation leaving little thinking time for search of appropriate nominalizations. It may also be that the students were ill prepared or even that the English language of instruction had had an effect on the Finnish of the essay. It may also be that the process of writing the English essay some three weeks earlier had not worked as preparation for the final exam, for example in the sense that it would have helped to build and consolidate the memory representation for the studied content or it may not have been understood as a learning opportunity and preparation for the final exam. The latter assumption gains some support from the comment that an International School student wrote at the end of his essay: "Please university don't tease us little poor children by your stupid tasks, because I've much more better use for my time". Comparing the content of the English and Finnish essays provides additional and more convincing support. The content is correct in one essay and incorrect in the other. This may concern details, but also core content, like in Examples (6) and (7) below, of which the former (English) essay (6) correctly reports that the Reds started the war, but the latter (Finnish) essay (7) suggests that the war was started by the Whites.

In general, there is more individual variation in the International School and CLILFi scores than in the CLILEn scores, and it also seems that students with low lexical density Finnish essays also wrote low lexical density English essays and vice versa, writers with lexically dense English essays also scored high on lexical density in the Finnish essays. Finally, the English essays (CLILEn) are the most homogeneous in terms of lexical density. Again, this may be due to contextual reasons. The English essay was written as a home assignment, and in spite of the fact that texts with clear signs of having been copied from the Internet or other sources were removed from the data at an early stage, it is possible that the sources that were available had an effect on the written output.

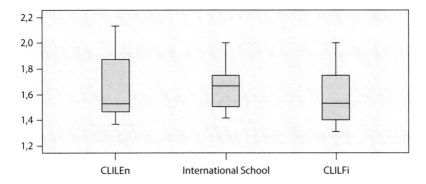

Figure 3. Variation in grammatical intricacy by language and group (clauses per sentence)

Table 4. Means and standard deviations for grammatical intricacy by language and group

	CLIL En	CLIL Fi	International school
Mean	1.63	1.70	1.73
SD	0.26	0.38	0.19

Figure 3 and Table 4 show the indices of grammatical intricacy in the data. As above, the results reflect the small size of the data and the impact of individual variation in the data as well as contextual and other factors discussed above.

To sum up, there is little difference between the three sets of data in terms of syntactic intricacy (T-units, number of clauses). The indices for lexical density show more variation, the International School group with the two highest values and the CLILFi group with the lowest values.

Syntactic and lexical indicators offer objective information about large datasets and the information they provide can be used to predict an overall trend. The information they provide is not complete and may even be misleading if the analysis and interpretation are not complemented with information from other sources. In the present study, historical content is an essential source of information. On the basis of content analysis (Virta & Järvinen, unpublished manuscript) conducted on the present CLILEn and CLILFi data, the essays were classified into additive (lists of facts), causal-temporal (chain of events, few linguistic indicators of causality) or analytic (abstract and structural causes, evaluation and problematization of causes) categories. Examples (6) and (7) show that content and linguistic analyses do not always match. Both essays scored high on both syntactic complexity and lexical density, but neither of them scores high on historical content. The Finnish essay (7) gained one point on a scale of 1 to 5 in the history test (rated by the history teacher) and the English essay (6) was analysed as a simple narrative (an additive type of essay) rather than an exposition analysing the causes of a historical event.

(6)   At 1917 the emperor died and to finland came a temporary government.
Because of that the population divided to two groups. One was called the reds
and the other one was the whites. The other group was like: "We need to change
the power from Russia to finland." So they, the social democratic's showed their
idea and it started to call "power law". Power law got accepted at July in 1917.
And because they wanted to make crofters situation better and chance the
landowner's situation other people didn't like the power law. Also the temporary
government from Russia didn't like the new law, so they made a new election,
where the social democratics lost their majority position. After that the violence
just kept going in Russia and it spread to finland also.
So one day the reds started revolution. At first the reds was controlling the war,
but then the whites made surprise attack to the reds camp. Then Finland
divided to two. At south finland was the reds and the other piece from
finland was controlled by the whites. Then the whites asked help from germany,
but Mannerheim didn't like it so he commanded his troop for a big attack to
Tanpere, wich was thereds the most important city. And they had two days long
fight at Tampere. But in the end the whites won the war.

(7)   Venäjällä oli valta vaikuttaa suomen asioihin ja jotkut suomalaiset eivät
halunneet asian olevan niin, joten he päättivät tehdä asialle jotain ja perustivat
puolueen. He olivat valkoiset. Punaisia ei haitannut että Venäjä hallitsi suomea.
Valkoiset aloittivat kapinan että valta siirtyisi suomelle ja punaiset lähtivät
sotaan mukaan.

English translation:

Russia had the power to influence Finland's affairs and some Finns did not want
this to happen, so they decided to do something about it and founded a party.
They were the whites. The reds were not bothered about Russia ruling Finland.
The whites started a rebel so that the power would transfer to finland and the
reds joined the war.

Because syntactic analysis alone does not do full justice to the description of the
data, the following discussion will centre on the semantic perspective of grammatical metaphor. The chapter discusses the quality of the themes as they appear
in the unmarked and marked positions in the data.

5.2   Grammatical metaphor: Thematic perspective

Thematic organization in the data consists of unmarked and marked themes.
Unmarked themes are usually subjects of sentences, whereas marked themes
precede the unmarked, topical theme. The marked or orienting themes can be
found in three meanings: textual, experiential and interpersonal. Textual themes
(conjunctions, conjunctive adjuncts, such as *but, and, however, as a result*) link
the clause to the surrounding text. Interpersonal themes include expressions
of modality (modal adjuncts) and reflect the writer's stance towards the textual
content. The definition of the third category, experiential themes, follows North's

(2005) definition: experiential themes are marked themes that do not fall into participant roles (e.g. subjects, predicate verbs, objects), typically circumstantial adjuncts. The following example (North 2005: 438) illustrates the textual, experiential and interpersonal marked themes in a sentence.

Orienting theme

Textual	Experiential	Interpersonal	Topical theme	Rheme
However,	given the political climate of the seventeenth century	it seems unlikely that	Descartes	would deliberately challenge the Church.

The majority of the themes in the data are unmarked topical themes in subject position in the sentence. The most common unmarked themes are listed below.

Table 5. Frequency of topical, unmarked themes in the English data

Topical Theme	CLIL En (N_{ALL}=249) n (%)	International school (N_{ALL}=173) n (%)
They	26 (10.4)	32 (18.5)
(The) Reds, The Red Guards	30 (12.0)	19 (11.0)
(The) Whites The White Guards/ Forces, The White Army, The White Terror	25 (10.0)	24 (13.9)
The (Finnish) Civil War	8 (3.2)	10 (5.8)
People	17 (6.8)	4 (2.3)
It	11 (4.4)	5 (2.9)
Total	117 (46.9)	94 (54.3)

Table 6. Frequency of topical, unmarked themes in the Finnish data

Topical Theme (in Finnish)	(English translation)	CLIL Fi N_{ALL}=113 n (%)
Punaiset (punakaartilaiset)	The Reds (Guards)	16 (14.2)
He	They	10 (8.8)
Valkoiset	The Whites	8 (7.1)
Suomi	Finland	3 (2.7)
(Suomen) sisällissota	The (Finnish) Civil War	3 (2.7)
Ihmiset	People	3 (2.7)
Total		43 (38.1)

As Tables 5 and 6 indicate, most topical, unmarked themes in the data are personalized themes closely related to the topic of the essay. Typically, such themes are found in thematic patterns in which the same themes are repeated, each followed by different rhemes providing items of new information which are not linked to another theme or rheme in the discourse. This type of thematic progression resembles the thematic progression typical of narratives. This is in line with earlier research on historical writing (Halldén 1986, 1997, 1998; Voss et al. 1994), which has found that young students' and adolescents' historical writing is characterized by personification of causes and narrative structure.

The English CLILEn Example (8) and the Finnish CLILFi example (9) below serve to exemplify theme-theme progression and unmarked thematization of primarily single-word subjects.

(8)   **There** were two kind of parties in Finland. The Red Guards and the White Guards. **Their task** were to make law and order. **The government** named Mannerheim to the commander of the White Guards. **The Reds** took Helsinki to control in Jan. 28 when the senate escaped to Vaasa. **The Whites** controlled the northern Finland and the Reds the southern Finland. **The Reds** were the poor workers, **and The white Guards** were the local societys leaders. **The Red's situation** get worse when the Jäger troops arrived to Vaasa. **The Reds and the Whites** had a bloody war in Tampere. **The White Guards** won it. **The Reds** escaped from Tampere to Russia with railway. (CLIL En)

(9)   **Sisällissota** alkoi 1918, koska ei ollut poliiseja ja armeijaa. **Punaiset Punakaartilaiset** olivat työläisiä vasemmistolaisia ja halusivat oikeuksia. **Valkoiset Suojeluskuntalaiset** olivat rikkaita tehtaanomistajia ja oikeistolaisia. **Ihmisillä** oli elintarvikepulaa. (CLIL Fi)

English translation:
The Civil War started in 1918, because there were no police or army. The Reds were leftist workers and wanted rights. The Whites were rich factory owners and right-wing people. People suffered from shortage of food supplies.

There were individual differences in the use of unmarked themes related to the thematic progression: narrative type essays tended to repeat the same theme, usually a single-word pronoun or noun. An obvious difference between the three groups was a more elaborate use of multi-word unmarked themes in the International School group when compared to the CLIL English and Finnish essays. The Finnish data showed least variation in the unmarked themes. Examples (10) and (11) are taken from the International School data:

(10)   Industrial workers, tenants from the countryside and members from the lower social group (*theme*) supported the Reds (*rheme*). (International school)

(11)   But (*marked, textual*) then (*marked, experiential*) the "break out" of this Civil War in Finland (*theme*) was, after the involvement of Germany and the loss of Tampere the situation became hopeless for the Reds (*rheme*). (International school)

In (11), the rheme contains two instances of grammatical metaphor: *involvement* and *loss,* but the rest of the rheme fails to maintain the same level of nominalization.

The data contain a small number of similar examples in the CLIL data, for Example (12)–(14).

(12)   The main reasons for the war were unemployment, shortage of food and **that Finland didn't have any police and military forces.** (CLIL En)

(13)   So, the unemployment, **that there were not enough food, cause the situation in the big cities got worse,** and **food being so expensive,** was too much for the workers. (CLIL En)

(14)   Suomen sisällissota alkoi vuonna 1918. Maailman **ollessa** sodassa Suomi kärsi siitä Venäjän takia. Suomeen tuli ruokapulaa ja ihmiset eivät olleet tyytyväisiä. **Tyytymättömyys** kasvoi edelleen ja työttömyyskin alkoi lisääntyä. Ruuan **ollessa** lopussa niiden hinnat kasvoivat. (CLIL Fi)

English translation:
The Finnish Civil War broke up in 1918. The world **being at war** (literal translation) Finland suffered from it due to Russia. Finland suffered from shortage of food and people were not satisfied. **Dissatisfaction** increased further and unemployment started to increase. Food **being at the end** (literal translation) their prices rose.

The marked, orienting themes were classified into textual, experiential and interpersonal themes. No interpersonal themes were found in the data. The most typical marked themes were experiential themes describing the circumstances (frequent in history, Taylor 1983; Lovejoy 1991), such as time or place. Typical examples are *during the civil war, in May 1918, in November, in the south of Finland.* Subordinated constructions, mainly subordinate clauses, were also frequent (*When the Reds saw that they were losing, Because the Whites did not know what to do with all of the "Red" prisoners*). The repertoire of textual themes in the data was narrow: the majority of them consisted of the conjunctions *and* and *but*.

Table 7 shows the occurrences of marked themes in the data. The number of marked themes differs in the three groups, with the CLILEn essays exhibiting the greatest percentage of marked themes out of all the themes (45%) as compared to the other two groups: 36% and 28% for the International school group and CLILFi data respectively. Textual themes are somewhat more frequent than experiential ones in the data (24%/22% for the CLILEn, 20%/16% for the international school and 16%/12% for the Finnish data).

Table 7. Distribution of marked themes in the data by language and group

	No (%) textual	No (%) experiential	No marked (N total)	N (%) of marked themes (% unmarked)
CLIL En	59 (24)	54 (22)	113 (249)	45 (55)
International school	34 (20)	28 (16)	62 (173)	36 (64)
CLIL Fi	18 (16)	14 (12)	32 (113)	28 (72)

To sum up, the results seem to be consistent with the earlier findings that marked historical themes are circumstantial expressing place and time (Taylor 1983; Lovejoy 1991). In the majority of instances, these themes marked the beginning or the end of an era or an important year or date, relating the discourse to the narrative or descriptive genre (Coffin 2004). Table 7 shows that the percentage of marked themes is the highest in the CLILEn data: almost half of the themes are marked, whereas one third of the themes are marked in the international school data. The small number of marked themes in the Finnish data is interesting. In comparison with the English language, which is a relatively fixed S(ubject) – V(predicate verb) – O(bject) language, the free word order of Finnish allows for a variety of (marked) clause-initial elements to be placed before the subject, that is, there is a wide range of thematic choices in Finnish (Shore 2008). Reasons for the use of the different strategies for conveying thematic organization in the English and Finnish essays can only be speculated upon, but it would be tempting to relate the ample marked thematization in the CLILEn and International School data to a narrative function in which the unfolding events are signalled by marked themes of place and time (recount, Coffin 2004). The Finnish essays would be linked to a re-telling function, the purpose of which is to pour out as many facts and details as possible within the limited time frame of the test situation. Examples (15) and (16) illustrate the occurrences of marked and unmarked themes in one CLIL student's English (15) and Finnish (16) essays. (The examples are identical to (6) and (7) above, bold print is added to indicate the marked themes).

(15)   **At 1917** the emperor died and to finland came a temporary government. **Because of that** the population divided to two groups. One was called the reds and the other one was the whites. The other group was like: "We need to change the power from Russia to finland." **So** they, the social democratic's showed their idea and it started to call "power law". Power law got accepted at July in 1917. **And because** they wanted to make crofters situation better and chance the landowner's situation other people didn't like the power law. **Also** the temporary government from Russia didn't like the new law, so they made a new election, where the social democratics lost their majority position. **After that** the violence just kept going in Russia and it spread to finland also.

      So one day the reds started revolution. **At first** the reds was controlling the war, but **then** the whites made surprise attack to the reds camp. **Then** Finland divided to two. **At south finland** was the reds and the other piece from finland was controlled by the whites. **Then** the whites asked help from germany, but Mannerheim didn't like it so he commanded his troop for a big attack to Tanpere, wich was thereds the most important city. And they had two days long fight at Tampere. **But in the end** the whites won the war.

(16)   **Venäjällä oli** valta vaikuttaa suomen asioihin ja jotkut suomalaiset eivät halunneet asian olevan niin, joten he päättivät tehdä asialle jotain ja perustivat puolueen.

He olivat valkoiset. **Punaisia ei haitannut** että Venäjä hallitsi suomea. Valkoiset aloittivat kapinan että valta siirtyisi suomelle ja punaiset lähtivät sotaan mukaan.

English translation:
Russia had the power to influence Finland's affairs and some Finns did not want this to happen, so they decided to do something about it and founded a party. They were the whites. The reds were not bothered about Russia ruling Finland. The whites started a rebel so that the power would transfer to Finland and the reds joined the war.

It should be noted that the grammatical subjects of the Finnish Example (16) are *valta* and *että Venäjä hallitsi suomea*, which is why the themes *Venäjällä* and *Punaisia ei haitannut* are viewed as marked. It is, however, uncertain whether these themes are to be viewed as unmarked rather than marked, because it is not easy to find an unmarked alternative to both of them, especially to the latter *Punaisia ei haitannut että Venäjä hallitsi suomea*. Turning the *that*-clause into a sentence-initial subject makes the clause more marked than the original version: *Venäjän Suomen hallitseminen ei haitannut punaisia* (Russia's ruling Finland did not bother the reds), which sounds awkward to a native speaker of Finnish. Starting the former example *Venäjällä oli valta vaikuttaa suomen asioihin* (Russia had the power to influence Finland's affairs) with the grammatical subject *Valta vaikuttaa Suomen asioihin oli Venäjällä* changes the thematic organization from the original version. In general, it seems that the Finnish language needs a more extensive definition of themes in systemic-functional theory, which would allow for themes such as the ones above be treated as unmarked themes (For a discussion of the definition of theme in the Finnish language and for a systemic-functional account of the Finnish language, see Shore 1992).

An additional aspect concerning grammatical metaphor is the intricacy of topical themes observable especially in unmarked themes. Multi-word themes are typical of the International School group essays but they also occur in some CLILEn productions. Multi-word themes consist of heads modified by embedded structures, exemplified below:

> *One of the main causes/Another important thing /All of theses things, mensoned arlier /Industrial workers, tenants from the countryside and members from the lower social group/A large part of Northern and central Finland as well as the province of Ostrobothnia/The last resistance of the Reds*

Multi-word topical themes are examples of how grammatical metaphor can be utilized to pack information in creating scientific discourse. For example, the heads of the multi-word themes in the first (*One of the main causes*) and the last (*The last resistance of the Reds*) examples above are abstract nominalizations modified by specifying elements (*one of, main, the last, of the Reds*). These types of complex noun phrases are typical of grammatical metaphor in written formal (often scientific) text. Their occurrence in learners' texts may be taken as an indicator of the acquisition of disciplinary-specific grammatical metaphor.

6.   Discussion

The aim of this article has been to discuss the construction of historical meaning as evidenced by three sets of history essays written in two languages by 19 secondary school students. The research relies on systemic functional linguistics, more specifically grammatical metaphor, which is explored by analysing the data for syntactic intricacy and thematic organization.

The purpose of the research was to describe the features of grammatical metaphor that were observed in the three sets of data. The specific components of grammatical metaphor under investigation were syntactic intricacy and thematic organization. A number of tentative hypotheses were presented which suggested some variation in grammatical metaphor in the data. It was anticipated that advanced language proficiency would be related to the realization of grammatical metaphor in written historical text. Thus, the more advanced English group (the International School group) might exhibit more elaborate grammatical metaphor than the CLIL English group. Similarly, it might have been expected that the CLIL Finnish L1 group might evidence developed use of grammatical metaphor.

The data analysis indicated that there is some evidence that may be interpreted as supporting the hypotheses presented above. The essays of the International School group were more intricate than those of the CLIL English group. The international school students' essays were syntactically more embedded (complex T-units), lexically denser and they had fewer clauses per sentence than the CLIL English group. The hypothesis for similar results in the CLILFi group was not confirmed. Of all the groups, the Finnish essays were the least intricate (simple T-units, low lexical density and a relatively great number of clauses per sentence).

One possible explanation of the results might be found in contextual factors, of which the most important are time and resources that were available at the time of writing of the Finnish essay. It is also possible that contextual factors had an effect on the writing of the English essays. The students had access to sources and they had time, but it seemed that not all of them used essay writing as an opportunity to learn but rather as an extra task that had been imposed on them.

It was noted above that the writing of the English essay might have had a facilitating effect on writing the same content after a couple of weeks in the final exam in the students' first language. However, in seven essays out of the total ten, the content structure of Finnish essay was less advanced than that of the English essay, one essay had improved (from causal temporal to analytic treatment) and the remaining two had the same content structure in both essays (Virta & Järvinen, unpublished manuscript). The simple linguistic structure of the Finnish essays (simple embedding with numerous independent main clauses and main clauses with one embedded structure, a relatively large number of clauses per sentence, few marked themes or multi-word themes) may reflect the simplicity of the content.

Grammatical metaphor can provide a linguistic angle on language use which is a more accurate measure of development in a long-term (Byrnes 2009a) than in a cross-sectional perspective. The interpretation of grammatical metaphor in a cross-sectional study and its relevance to teaching depend on complementary accompanying semantic analysis. For example, lexical density may not be a valid indicator of the use of register-typical grammatical metaphor unless the lexical items are assessed in terms of appropriateness, that is, how typical they are in the register of the genre. If lexical density is calculated mechanically as the ratio of content items per clause (or as the percentage of content items of the sum of content and functional items), high values may be achieved for a text that is not consistent with the conventional register-typical lexis. The present data are a case in point: the essays were written by students with inadequate knowledge of the register-typical linguistic expressions, both in the second and first languages.

On the basis of the results of the present study and existing literature, it may be useful to discuss the pedagogical implications, that is how to take grammatical metaphor into account in content and language integrated teaching. The present results indicate that learners of language and content are not aware of the linguistic conventions and devices that are necessary to be able to use the language of the subject in writing. There may be a number of reasons for this, but one may be lack of suitable pedagogical texts for language and content learners. Another may be content teachers' inadequate language knowledge (rather than language skills) that would inform them about appropriate ways to teach the subject in a foreign language and the language of instruction at the same time. Yet another may be the lack of pedagogy for content and language integrated teaching.

There are pedagogical implications to teaching history in the framework of systemic-functional theory that refer to learning history in the first language (e.g. Schleppegrell & Achugar 2003; Schleppegrell et al. 2004; Achugar & Schleppegrell 2005; Schleppegrell & de Oliveira 2006; Coffin 2006), but which can be applied to CLIL contexts. The basic idea is to start with providing the learners with ample input of discipline-typical texts and raise their awareness of the language that is used to "make meaning" in the specific discipline. Deliberate and intentional noticing of the linguistic expression is considered important in language learning (Schmidt 1990). Thus the linguistic devices that are used to express core content in the discipline are prime candidates for focused learning. In teaching grammatical metaphor, noticing might involve the comparison of incongruent and congruent expressions, such as (1)–(3) above, and the comparison of informal and formal varieties and speech and writing. Other examples of focused practice of grammatical metaphor would be "unpacking" congruent forms: turning nominalizations to clauses and vice versa, "compressing" clauses into nominalizations. Useful practice is also available in student productions, such as the present data. Student-generated texts might be used as examples of how topical and marked themes are built and what happens when pre- and post-modifiers are added to topical heads.

The present study is part of a content and language integrated research project. The present account represents the linguistic, more specifically systemic-functional angle. The other part (Virta & Järvinen, manuscript in preparation) comprises a content-focused approach to the essays. Some research implications from on-going research have already been referred to above, such as the structural analyses of historical content and how language reflects historical content. Some links are obvious. For example, simple syntactic structures (independent short main clauses, unmarked topics) were used in all the essays that involved lists of facts or fragments (simple additive structure). Other links are less obvious. For example, it was not always clear what was assessed in the essays. The assessment of essays with few cohesive devices but with reasonably correct content expressed primarily by main clauses may be problematic, because the assessor on the basis of her/his background knowledge may add more coherence to the text than the writer had intended. This is a common problem in the assessment of essay-type answers in any language. In CLIL, however, the inadequate language skills make assessment even more difficult.

Further research would be needed on the relation of writing, learning and assessment. There is some evidence in the present data that the writing of the English essay had little effect on the content of Finnish essays. In addition, problems related to essay-type answers in tests with restricted time were evident. Research into the mutual relation of the instructional languages is needed.

Due to the short life of content and language integrated programmes, there is as yet little longitudinal research on language development in Europe. One option to study the development of "language in making meaning" is to track the development of grammatical metaphor, using both longitudinal research and qualitative case studies covering a variety of content areas and disciplinary discourses.

References

Achugar, M. & Schleppegrell, M.J. 2005. Beyond connectors: The construction of cause in history textbooks. *Linguistics and Education* 16: 298–318.

Byrnes, H. 2009a. Emergent L2 German writing ability in a curricular context: A longitudinal study of grammatical metaphor. *Linguistics and Education* 20(1): 50–66.

Byrnes, H. 2009b. Systemic-functional reflections on instructed foreign language acquisition as meaning-making: An introduction. *Linguistics and Education* 20(1): 1–9.

Crawford Camiciottoli, B. 2007. *The Language of Business Lectures: A Corpus-assisted Analysis* [Pragmatics & Beyond New Series 157]. Amsterdam: John Benjamins.

Coffin, C. 2004. Learning to write history: The role of causality. *Written Communication* 21: 261–289.

Coffin, C. 2006. Learning the language of school history: The role of linguistics in mapping the writing demands of the secondary school curriculum. *Journal of Curriculum Studies* 38(4): 413–429.

Dalton-Puffer, C. 2007. *Discourse in Content and Language Integrated Learning (CLIL) Classrooms* [Language Learning & Language Teaching 20]. Amsterdam: John Benjamins.

Dantas-Whitney, M. 2002. Critical reflection in the second language classroom through audio-taped journals. *System* 10(4): 543–555.

Davison, C. & Williams, A. 2001. Integrating language and content: Unresolved issues. In *English as a Second Language in the Mainstream*, B. Mohan, C. Leung & C. Davison (eds), 51–70. Harlow: Pearson Education.

Gaies, S.J. 1980. T-Unit analysis in second language research: Applications, problems and limitations. *TESOL Quarterly* 14(1): 53–60.

Halldén, O. 1986. Learning history. *Oxford Review of Education* 12: 53–66.

Halldén, O. 1997. Conceptual change and the learning of history. *International Journal of Educational Research* 27(3): 201–210.

Halldén, O. 1998. Personalisation in historical descriptions and explanations. *Learning and Instruction* 8(2): 131–139.

Halliday, M.A.K. 1993. Towards a language-based theory of learning. *Linguistics and Education* 5: 93–116.

Halliday, M.A.K. 1994. *An Introduction to Functional Grammar*, 2nd edn. London: Edward Arnold.

Halliday, M.A.K. 2002. Spoken and written modes of meaning. In *On Grammar*, J.J. Webster (ed.), 323–351. London: Continuum.

Halliday, M.A.K. 2007a. A language development approach to education. In *Language and Education*, J.J. Webster (ed.), 368–382. London: Continuum.

Halliday, M.A.K. 2007b. On the concept of educational linguistics. In *Language and Education*, J. J.Webster (ed.), 354–367. London: Continuum.

Hood, S. 2008. Summary writing in academic contexts: Implicating meaning in processes of change. *Linguistics and Education* 19: 351–365.

Kaufman, D. & Crandall, J. 2005. *Content-Based Instruction in Primary and Secondary School Settings* [Case studies in TESOL practice series]. Alexandria VA: TESOL.

Lovejoy, K.B. 1991. Cohesion and information strategies in academic writing: Analysis of passages in three disciplines. *Linguistics and Education* 3: 315–43.

Marsh, D. & Langé, G. 2000. *Using Languages to Learn and Learning to Use Languages*. Jyväskylä: University of Jyväskylä.

Marsh, D., Marsland, B. & Stenberg, K. 2001. *Integrating Competencies for Working Life–Unicom*. Jyväskylä: University of Jyväskylä.

Martin, J.R. 2008. Incongruent and proud: De-vilifying 'nominalization'. *Discourse Society* 19(6): 801–810.

North, S. 2005. Disciplinary variation in the use of theme in undergraduate essays. *Applied Linguistics* 26(3): 431–452.

Schleppegrell, M.J. & Achugar, M. 2003. Learning language and learning history: A functional linguistics approach. *TESOL Journal* 12(2): 21–27.

Schleppegrell, M.J., Achugar, M. & Oteíza, T. 2004. The grammar of history: Enhancing content-based instruction through a functional focus on language. *TESOL Quarterly*, 38(1): 67–93.

Schleppegrell, M. & de Oliveira, L.C. 2006. An integrated language and content approach for history teachers. *Journal of English for Academic Purposes* 5: 254–268.

Schmidt, R. 1990. The role of consciousness in second language learning. *Applied Linguistics* 11(2): 129–158.

Shore, S. 1992. Aspects of a Systemic-functional Grammar of Finnish. Ph.D. dissertation, Macquarie University. <http://www.helsinki.fi/hum/skl/english/dept/shore_aspects.pdf >.

Shore, S. 2008. The textual organization of clauses. *Virittäjä* 112(1): 24–65.

Taylor, C.V. 1983. Structure and theme in printed school text. *Text* 3(2): 197–228.

Voss, J.F., Carretero, M., Kennet, J. & Silfies, L.N. 1994. The collapse of the Soviet Union: A case study of causal reasoning. In *Cognitive and Instructional Processes in History and Social Studies*, M. Carretero & J.F.Voss (eds), 403–429. Hillsdale NJ: Lawrence Erlbaum Associates.

The CLIL differential

Comparing the writing of CLIL and non-CLIL students in higher colleges of technology

Silvia Jexenflicker & Christiane Dalton-Puffer
FH Wiener Neustadt, Austria/Universität Wien, Austria

This chapter examines the effects of CLIL provision on different aspects of written language competence in order to determine which of these areas profit more and which are possibly unaffected by the experience of subject matter teaching in a foreign language. For this purpose we analysed the written work of students who followed either a traditional EFL curriculum or enjoyed additional CLIL provision. The data were obtained in a double case study at two higher technical colleges in Austria where students were asked to complete a free writing task. The bottom line of the analysis shows the CLIL students clearly ahead of their EFL-only peers on the basis of overall scores, but on closer inspection results tell a more complex story: in the area of lexico-grammar the CLIL students show significant advantages throughout, as they do in vocabulary range and orthographic correctness. On the level of discourse competence and textual organization, however, differences are difficult to discern with the general competence level in this area leaving a great deal of room for improvement. Several explanations for these results suggest themselves.

1. Introduction

The fact that oral language use has been and continues to be at the centre of interest for empirical CLIL research does not need extra justification: firstly, formal education is to a large extent located in the oral sphere, which is especially true of its crucial and defining event 'the lesson'. Secondly, when reference is made to the language learning effects which CLIL provision apparently has 'communicative competence' (cf. Dalton-Puffer 2009 for a critique) in the limited sense of 'oral fluency' (cf. Hüttner 2009) is the most common observational category. Nevertheless, writing is an important aspect of language competence. Given that CLIL research has started to take a stronger theoretical interest and to explicitly refer to current models of language competence and second language learning, it has become obvious that the written mode needs to have its place in a full appreciation of CLIL potentials and problems. While this may seem obviously pertinent to the language learning side of the CLIL enterprise, we believe that writing also plays a role in the construction of subject-specific competence (e.g. Zydatiß 2007; Schmölzer-Eibinger 2008; Zwiers 2008; Coetzee-Lachmann 2009). Students need to learn curricular concepts, facts and skills not only by rote memorization but by interacting with them in order to make them their own. Alongside palpable activities like experiments, cognitive-linguistic manipulation clearly plays a central role in such processes of appropriation and it is self-evident that writing is an important form of this kind of manipulation, even if it is not greatly exploited in some classroom traditions (more on this below).

Far removed from such considerations on the role of language in learning, the participants themselves see the salient feature of CLIL in its effect on their foreign language competence. This view became evident in a recent study of CLIL in upper secondary engineering colleges in Austria (Dalton-Puffer et al. 2008). In one part of this study CLIL and non-CLIL alumni were asked for a self-evaluation of their speaking, reading, writing and listening skills in English (ibid.: 100f.). In other words, the study did not try to obtain an objective measure but attempted to gauge the students' own perception. Results show that alumni who had experienced CLIL self-evaluated significantly higher on all four skills than regular alumni who had gone through the normal EFL curriculum only.[1] The data also show that receptive skills were rated better than the productive skills speaking and writing.

That teaching content subjects through the medium of a foreign language significantly improves foreign language skills is largely undisputed in the research literature (cf. Section 2 below). Despite the overwhelmingly supportive evidence, the assumption that CLIL education fosters all aspects of language competence in equal measure should be treated with caution. The present chapter, then, takes a closer look at the written production of learners with CLIL experience and compares them with non-CLIL peers. The following questions have served to focus our inquiry:

–   What is the effect if any of CLIL provision on students' writing performance?
–   Which components of writing ability profit most?
–   Are there any conclusions to be drawn from this for the conceptualization of CLIL and the design of CLIL programmes?

---

1.   This kind of approach has been criticized by Airey (2004) as unreliable evidence in terms of representing a true proficiency measure. We agree with this criticism and want our results to be read strictly as the subjects' own perception (which, however, may have a significant impact on their objectively measurable proficiency all the same).

2. Literature review on CLIL writing

In the literature CLIL students are regularly attested with a higher command of the target language than their non-CLIL peers (cf. Klieme 2006; Wesche 2002; Wode 1994). Haunold (2006) showed that 18-year old Austrian CLIL students reached the required B2 (CEFR) level on the written part of the Oxford Placement test significantly more often than their non-CLIL peers, who had followed only the conventional EFL curriculum. Hellekjær (2004) studied the Academic English reading skills of Norwegian CLIL and non-CLIL students and found the former to be far better equipped for studying through the medium of English at tertiary level. Lexical learning at secondary level has been targeted by Sylvén (2004) in Sweden and in Seregély's (2008) partial replication study in Austria. Both authors found significant advantages of CLIL students regarding vocabulary size and range. Comparable overall results were obtained by Mewald (2007) when testing the oral performance of lower secondary CLIL students and non-CLIL controls: the oral production of CLIL students was not only "more accurate but also more resourceful" (p.168).

Most studies to date have been based on a closely circumscribed understanding of 'language competence' either given through the adoption of a specific standardised test or via focussing on a specific skills area. Recently, two comprehensive studies (Lasagabaster 2008; Zydatiß 2007) have aimed at implementing a more differentiated and arguably more complete view of foreign language competence in the study of language learning outcomes in CLIL education.

Lasagabaster (2008) studied 198 Spanish secondary students (14–16 years of age) by means of a test battery comprising grammar, listening, speaking and writing. The author concludes that "CLIL exerts a positive influence on all the language aspects measured" in the study including writing and pronunciation (p.36); two areas which other researchers have claimed to be indeterminate or unaffected (e.g. Dalton-Puffer 2008; Varchmin 2008). The writing component of the test consisted in a letter to an English family with whom the students were supposed to stay in the summer. Test evaluation was carried out by means of a five-scale matrix consisting of the dimensions content, organisation, vocabulary, language usage (=grammar), and mechanics. The results presented show statistically significant advantages of the CLIL group on all five dimensions.

Zydatiß's (2007) study of 180 secondary students (16 years of age) in Berlin is almost identical in sample size to Lasagabaster's but even more comprehensive in terms of test range, as it includes not only grammatical, lexical and communicative competences but also subject-matter literacy. Zydatiß's overall results likewise attest a significantly higher overall language competence of CLIL students. The difference is so substantial, in fact, that Zydatiß argues that the usual norm-referenced grading used in the German education system is unable to do justice to the superior proficiency level of CLIL students and may actually disadvantage them in the competition for university placement (Zydatiß 2007: 220–226).

The writing component of the Berlin test battery consisted of three genre based tasks (note taking, letter to the editor, picture composition) encompassing expository-informative, subjective-commentary and narrative functions. Test evaluation was carried out on the basis of several quantitative measures (e.g. number of propositions, text length, error rate). The findings of the study suggest that the advantages of CLIL students over their peers are particularly visible with regard to lexical and grammatical range and accuracy, as well as degree of propositional richness and syntactic maturity (ibid.: 196–198). The CLIL advantage in direct comparison with the controls should not, however, obscure the fact that the CLIL students, too, had considerable difficulty with expository and argumentative writing which was based on subject-matter content materials. Zydatiß (2007: 313) argues that this reflects the low degree of experience German secondary students have with this kind of activity in their content subjects. His line of reasoning is substantiated by the findings of another German research project (e.g. Coetzee-Lachmann 2009; Vollmer et al. 2006) which investigated the subject-specific discourse competence of German 10th graders in geography. In this study comparisons were made not only along the CLIL-non-CLIL dimension but also between productions in L2 (English) and L1 (German). The results were such that participants showed considerable deficiencies in academic literacy in both languages in terms of encoding sufficiently complex conceptualizations as well as with regard to the use of subject-specific terminology and style. In this context it should be stressed that similar to Germany Austrian didactic traditions in non-language subjects put very little emphasis on student writing. Nevertheless, one has to assume that there would be a certain transfer from CLIL students' (presumably) higher general language skills, leading to improved writing ability.

The impact of the activities experienced in the CLIL content classroom on the writing skills demonstrated in test situations becomes obvious if we compare the above-mentioned German studies to another Spanish study: there, 7th graders were found "beginning to acquire some of the register features of their discipline [the social sciences]" (Whittaker & Llinares 2009: 234) with a distribution of certain common discipline-related words paralleling their textbooks. In our view this is a direct consequence of the greater emphasis put on writing in Spanish content lessons.

3. The case study: Sample and method

As mentioned before, the case study to be discussed in this chapter formed part of a research project on the effects of CLIL instruction on English language skills in upper-secondary engineering schools in Austria. The purpose of the case study was to compare the general level of language competence of 11th-grade students (around 16 years of age) who had undergone CLIL instruction with their EFL-only peers, with particular emphasis on writing skills. A two-part written test was administered to students attending one of two upper-secondary engineering colleges in Austria (henceforth College A and College B), with a total sample of 86 students. Overall, 39 students had received CLIL instruction in addition to their regular EFL classes, while 47 had not. The hypothesis to be tested was that CLIL students would exhibit a higher level of general language competence and would also outperform non-CLIL students in terms of writing skills.[2]

The writing test was designed to meet the requirements of communicative testing (see for example, Morrow 1979; Weir 1990: 10–14) in so far as students were put into a realistic communicative situation and had to freely compose a piece of writing to meet a particular communicative purpose. The task chosen consisted in the students writing a letter or e-mail to a host family in New York where they were going to spend two weeks.[3] It was assumed that students of the given age and grade level would be familiar with this situation so that it could be regarded as an 'authentic' task from their point of view. While it was basically a free-writing task, several suggestions were made as to the content of the letter or e-mail, including personal information and previous stays abroad but also questions to be put to the host family and a positive conclusion.

The texts were then assessed according to an analytic rating scale (see appendix). While a holistic scale would undoubtedly have been more economical in terms of time and effort expended on the marking process, an analytic scale was given preference to allow for the fact that learners do not necessarily develop all aspects of writing ability at the same rate, resulting in differences that are glossed over if only one global score is used (e.g. Hughes 2003: 100–103). In our case it was felt that a more differentiated approach would be more beneficial and that valuable insights might be gained from analysing different sub-skills.

3.1 A model for rating writing ability

The categories used for the rating scale had to reflect what was seen as key components of writing ability. While different models have been suggested (e.g. Bachman 1990; Canale & Swain 1980), there seems to be a consensus view that a good writer

---

2. General language competence was focused on in the first part of the test in the form of a C-test, a variant of the cloze test which involves reconstructing mutilated texts and which provides a global statistic reflecting students' overall language ability (e.g. Grotjahn et al. 2002; Sigott 2004)

3. An almost identical task was set in the test reported by Lasagabaster (2008).

must have good language skills, textual competence (i.e. the ability to compose a coherent and cohesive text) and sociolinguistic or pragmatic competence (i.e. the ability to use language in a contextually appropriate manner). The rating scale chosen for the case study was largely based on the scale developed for the new common school-leaving exam in Austrian grammar schools (Friedl & Auer 2007), consisting of four equally-weighted aspects of (written) language competence, i.e. task fulfilment, organisation, grammar and vocabulary. For every category, potential scores ranged from 0 to 5. In the field of lexico-grammar, the qualitative assessment was complemented by a few quantitative ratios.

Task fulfilment

In this field, some adaptations had to be made to the original rating scale. In particular, those descriptors referring to factual knowledge or the quality of the arguments used had to be eliminated as they did not suit the text type. The remaining aspects were:

–   The degree of task fulfilment
–   Relevance (with regard to the task given)
–   Appropriateness in terms of text format, length and register

With regard to task fulfilment the texts were evaluated according to the degree to which the points listed in the instructions had been covered and elaborated, taking into account that these points had been worded as suggestions and that not all the points were always applicable (e.g. previous stays abroad). In addition, it was assessed whether the texts were relevant and the format appropriate (e.g. suitable opening and closing, register). Finally, an important aspect in evaluating the texts was the extent to which the writer had managed to build rapport with the host family, which can be seen as the main communicative purpose of this type of text. The assessment thus took into account whether the test persons were aware of the communicative purpose of the text and whether this purpose was achieved. A high score in this category consequently required that a text covered (most of) the points mentioned, was relevant and appropriate, and helped to fulfil the communicative purpose by building rapport with the addressees. Finally, it should be added that task fulfilment was seen as a 'veto category'. Two texts which did not fulfil the task at all were thus rated 0 and eliminated from the sample.

Text organisation

This category was designed to measure the textual competence of the writer, assessing the overall structure of the text, the use of paragraphs as a structuring device and, generally, the extent to which the student had managed to write a cohesive and coherent text. To achieve a high score in this category, a text thus had to exhibit a coherent structure, good use of paragraphing and good use of connectives.

Grammar

The main aspects addressed by this category were, on the one hand, the accuracy with which the student applied grammatical rules and forms and, on the other, the variety and complexity of the structures used. It seems important to consider both aspects together as there is often a trade-off between accuracy and the complexity of the structures used (e.g. Ellis & Barkhuizen 2005: 144). A high score in this field consequently required the accurate use of a variety of structures, including complex ones, as well as high accuracy in terms of categories such as verb forms, tenses, plural, word order, prepositions etc.

Vocabulary

This category assessed the range of vocabulary and the appropriateness of the words chosen by the student, his or her ability to go beyond the use of rather basic vocabulary as well as formal accuracy and correct spelling. A high score in this category thus required the accurate and appropriate use of a wide range of vocabulary, with few orthographic errors.

4.   Findings

The general language ability test (Jexenflicker 2010) showed a highly significant advantage for the CLIL students. Out of a maximum of 120 obtainable points the CLIL students reached an average of 87.41 (about 73% of the total), while the non-CLIL students reached 74.47 (about 62% of the total). As for the free writing task, which this chapter focuses on, let us first consider the global results. Table 1 below provides an overview of the average scores achieved (out of a total of 5 for each category), by CLIL and non-CLIL students. The individual results will then be discussed by category of assessment.

Table 1. Average scores, total sample

	Average scores CLIL	Range CLIL	Average scores Non-CLIL	Range non-CLIL
Task fulfilment	3.897	1–5	3.021	1–5
Organisation and structure	2.949	2–5	2.404	1–4
Grammar	3.564	2–5	2.511	1–5
Vocabulary	3.718	2–5	2.936	1–5
TOTAL	14.128		10.872	
Number of test persons	39		47	

The overall impression at this point is that the results of the free-writing part confirm those of the general ability test as the CLIL students achieved higher averages throughout. However, the extent to which these differences are significant depends on which competence one focuses on, as will be explained below. Moreover, the rather wide range suggests considerable variation in student performance, with the CLIL students slightly more homogeneous than the non-CLIL ones on this global level.[4]

4.1   Task fulfilment

The dimension of task fulfilment is summarised in Table 2 below. The difference in average scores between the CLIL and non-CLIL groups is highly significant for the total sample as well as for the College A groups, but not significant for the B groups. In other words, the College A CLIL group clearly outperformed not only the non-CLIL group from the same school but also both groups from College B.

Table 2. Task fulfilment, total sample

	No of test persons	Range	Average scores	Standard Deviation (SD)	T value
Total CLIL	39	1–5	3.897	1.119	3.697**
Total non-CLIL	47	1–5	3.021	1.073	

**Difference highly significant (level of significance p = 0.01)

A more detailed analysis shows differences between the CLIL and non-CLIL groups in terms of appropriateness of text format, length and register as well as in the ability to build rapport with the host family. For example, in College A 90% of the CLIL group, but only 40% of the non-CLIL group, used an appropriate opening (salutation), while this gap was less striking in College B. In both cases there were differences in the students' ability to close the text appropriately, which was, however, linked to the fact that the non-CLIL students seemed to have more problems with writing a text of the required length (150–200 words) in the time given and thus more of them ended their text abruptly (see appendix, sample texts 3–5). Clear differences emerged in terms of register, with only 8% of the non-CLIL students in College B showing adequate register throughout the text, while this percentage was around 50%

---

4.   It should, however, be added that there was also a clear difference between the schools analysed, with CLIL students in College A clearly outperforming those in College B. For a discussion of possible reasons for these differences see Jexenflicker (2010).

for the other groups. In general, the content points were (mostly) covered by all the groups, with some variation in the students' willingness to come up with questions to the host family. There did not seem to be any systematic difference between CLIL and non-CLIL students in this respect, however. While in College A the CLIL students were more likely to include questions, 40% of the CLIL students in College B neglected this point.

A major dissimilarity can, however, be identified in the extent to which the communicative task of establishing rapport was fulfilled. In terms of the communicative purpose of the given text type this seems highly relevant as the main rationale for writing to a prospective host family is to start building a harmonious and positive relationship at an early stage. Typical examples of strategies contributing to positive rapport management would be, for example, thanking the host family for the opportunity to stay with them (e.g. "So I'm very honoured, that I can stay at your place"), saying how much you look forward to seeing their country (e.g. "I have never been to NY before, so I'm looking forward to stay there. It was a dream of mine since I was a young boy to go to the USA to see all the sights and landscapes…") or showing interest in them as a family (e.g. "I hope we will have two wonderful weeks together. It would be very nice if you tell me something about your family"). Derogatory remarks about any members of the family, US Americans in general or US politicians, on the other hand, will have the opposite effect and will harm relationships from the start (e.g. "A question which I will ask is why so much people had choosed Bush").

While over half of the CLIL students managed this communicative task well, this was true of less than a quarter of the respective non-CLIL groups. The overall impression was that the CLIL students were much more likely to identify the communicative purpose of the task whereas the non-CLIL students tended to simply work through the points listed in the instructions without giving too much thought to the communicative goals to be achieved. (See, for example, appendix, sample text 5).

Overall, it can be said that the CLIL students clearly outperformed their non-CLIL peers in terms of text format, length and register and, in particular, with regard to meeting the communicative task of building a relationship with the host family. For some reason, which cannot be explored here, the B CLIL group seemed less prepared to bring in their own ideas and limited themselves rather strictly to the points explicitly mentioned in the instructions.

4.2 Organisation

Table 3 summarises the results with regard to the dimension of text organisation and structure. On the whole, the differences seemed less marked in this field.

Table 3. Organisation, total sample

	No of test persons	Range	Average scores	Standard Deviation (SD)	T value
Total CLIL	39	2–5	2.949	0.887	3.158**
Total non-CLIL	47	1–4	2.404	0.712	

**Difference highly significant (level of significance p = 0.01)

While the score differences were highly significant for the total sample, only the A groups showed significant internal variation on this dimension. What is perhaps even more striking is the generally low level of achievement in the area of text organisation and structure, with only the A CLIL group reaching an average score above 3.

Generally speaking it can be said that all groups showed deficiencies in overall structure, the shortcomings being even greater among the non-CLIL groups. For example, transitions between the different parts of the text were often not clearly marked and abrupt. Another striking feature was that in all the groups the majority of students failed to integrate questions to the host family into the text in an appropriate manner. (For an obvious example, see appendix, sample text 4. In fact, all of the sample texts in the appendix are, to varying degrees, deficient in this respect as questions are either missing or have not been integrated well.) Overall it can be said that a coherent structure throughout the text was only found with a minority of test persons. The best performers in this respect were the A CLIL students, where about one quarter of the texts can be seen as coherent throughout, while none of the texts in the B non-CLIL group can be characterised as such. Moreover, 25% of the B non-CLIL texts were found to lack completely in structure and coherence.

Paragraphing was another weakness in all groups, with few consistent patterns emerging that would point to a systematic difference between CLIL and non-CLIL students. In fact, the B CLIL group was, at a rate of 33%, the most likely not to use this structuring device at all, while the percentage was about 20% for all the other groups. In terms of connectives, however, the situation is quite as expected again, with the non-CLIL group performing considerably less well in both schools. Generally speaking, it can be said that the CLIL students were more likely to go beyond the most basic connectives (*and, but, because*) and use a wider range (including, for example, *also, then, however, although, therefore*), while about half of the non-CLIL students at College A and the vast majority (96%) of the non-CLIL group at College B used simple connectives only. In particular, the conjunction *and* was often overused (see, for example, appendix, sample text 5).

4.3 Grammar

On the grammar dimension the differences in performance between CLIL and non-CLIL groups were highly significant throughout, with the most marked differences to be identified in the field of accuracy. While both groups were quite willing to use a variety of structures, the CLIL students tended to use them more accurately. Table 4 below summarises these results:

Table 4. Grammar, total sample

	No of test persons	Range	Average scores	Standard Deviation (SD)	T value
Total CLIL	39	2–5	3.564	0.882	5.353**
Total non-CLIL	47	1–5	2.511	0.930	

**Difference highly significant (level of significance p = 0.01)

If we take a closer look at accuracy, we can observe that well over 50% of the CLIL students used grammatical forms and structures accurately or mostly accurately. By contrast, none of their non-CLIL peers reached the highest score ('accurately') in this category. At the other end of the performance spectrum, only 2 CLIL texts (9.5%) but 52% of the non-CLIL texts from College A were highly inaccurate, with frequent morphosyntactic errors. In College B even 70% of the non-CLIL group fell into the 'highly inaccurate' category, but in this case also the CLIL-group had a much higher incidence of errors than the CLIL-group of College A.

Given the limited scope of this chapter only a few examples of the errors committed can be mentioned. The most frequent problem in the A CLIL group concerned the present tense (present simple vs present progressive). 19% of this group had problems choosing the right form, while the corresponding figures were 61% in the A non-CLIL group, 33% in the B CLIL group and 46% in the B non-CLIL group. Other mistakes that occurred in all groups were the use of the present simple instead of a future form and problems in using the present perfect correctly. The non-CLIL groups tended to overuse the present simple, substituting it for the present perfect and past tenses, while some students belonging to the B non-CLIL group also substituted the past tense for the present. In this group, some students showed a rather erratic use of tenses, while others limited themselves to using present tense and future simple. Problems with word order were rather infrequent in the A CLIL group (4.8%), but relatively prominent in the B CLIL group (39%), the corresponding figures for the non-CLIL groups being 26% and 29% respectively. Finally, the percentage of students using incorrect verb forms (e.g. "I want to knew", "will made") was considerably higher in the B non-CLIL group (25%), while it was below 10% in all other groups.

In the field of grammar, the qualitative assessment by means of rating scales was supplemented with quantitative measures, i.e. morphosyntactic errors per 100 words, number of different verb forms as well as sentence length (in number of words) and number of subordinate clauses per 100 words as measures of syntactic complexity. The analysis of the total sample showed highly significant differences between CLIL and non-CLIL students for all these indicators except for the number of subordinate clauses. If we analyse the schools separately, we see that the differences in errors and sentence length are more highly significant for College A, while the difference in the number of verb forms is only significant in the B groups.

To sum up, we can conclude that the groups analysed were found to differ mainly with regard to the accurate use of grammatical forms and structures. While the non-CLIL groups were prepared to use subordinate structures to a similar extent as the CLIL-groups, they tended to have greater difficulties using them correctly.

4.4   Vocabulary

As for the previous three dimensions of writing ability, the differences identified between CLIL and non-CLIL students are highly significant for the total sample also in the field of vocabulary and expression (see Table 5 below).

Table 5. Vocabulary, total sample

	No of test persons	Range	Average scores	Standard Deviation (SD)	T value
Total CLIL	39	2–5	3.718	0.857	4.561**
Total non-CLIL	47	1–5	2.936	0.704	

**Difference highly significant (level of significance p = 0.01)

As was the case with the other three categories, again the A CLIL group showed the best performance. What is remarkable is that the range of vocabulary and the accuracy of its use were rated at least 'adequate' (corresponding to a score of 3) for all members of this group. More than half the students in this group (57%) obtained the highest or second highest score on range of vocabulary, meaning that it was rated good or very good. There were few problems due to L1 transfer in this group and students rarely resorted to simple expressions such as *other things* or did not use them at all. There were practically no communicative problems due to wrong use of lexis. The B CLIL group showed a more varied performance, ranging from the highest score to the second lowest ('limited range of vocabulary and frequent mistakes'): 33% had a good or very good range of vocabulary, which they mostly used correctly. 22% did not perform adequately, using simple words such as *nice* and *big* repeatedly.

The control group (non-CLIL, both colleges) not only performed on a lower level overall, but also showed more varied results. Slightly over half of the group used an adequate range of vocabulary and used it appropriately, but over a quarter of the non-CLIL texts were characterised by a limited range of vocabulary, i.e. the vocabulary used was fairly basic (e.g. "I want to see the big buildings there"). The writing also showed clear deficiencies in orthography, which in some cases could interfere with understanding (e.g. "hoppies" for *hobbies*, "ettendig" for *attending*, "quescens" for *questions*, "coutrie" for *country*, "handy-caped" for *handicapped*, "expenciev" for *expensive*, "jears" for *years*). In one case such mistakes even concerned fairly simple words (e.g. "appel", "aske"). In addition, the non-CLIL students were more likely to use simple words such as the adjective *big* (e.g. "lives in a big house", "I like big cities"). In some cases students simply took over German words (e.g. "Maschinenbau", "matura", "Familie") which would be difficult for the recipients to interpret.

Again, a number of quantitative ratios were calculated in addition to the qualitative rating scale, i.e. the percentage of the 1000 and 2000 most frequent words (K1 and K1+K2), the type-token ratio (per 50-word segment; TTR) and average word length. The results showed significant or highly significant differences in the percentage of K1, the type-token ratio and word length if the two groups are considered together, suggesting that the CLIL students used the most frequent words less often, showed more lexical variation and tended to use longer words.

5. Conclusion

The purpose of this study was to assess and compare the different components of the writing ability of CLIL students and non-CLIL students at two upper-secondary engineering colleges in Austria. Part of the study not reported in detail in this chapter was a general language ability test that showed statistically significant advantages of the CLIL students both for the total sample and for the two schools analysed separately. Generally speaking, the results of the writing test support the underlying hypothesis that CLIL students outperform their EFL-only peers both in general language ability and writing skills, but it is also obvious that the results need to be considered in detail. In particular, they suggest that the extent to which CLIL students outperform non-CLIL students depends on the aspect of writing ability one focuses on. In most cases the study showed clear, statistically significant advantages of the CLIL students. However, it seems that CLIL instruction affects those areas most which concern purely linguistic skills (i.e. grammar and vocabulary). In these fields the differences were found to be highly significant and particularly marked in terms of accuracy, range of vocabulary and orthographic skills. The two other categories analysed, i.e. task fulfilment and organisation, however, demand textual and pragmatic skills. With regard to task fulfilment, the CLIL group clearly outperformed their non-CLIL peers by considering and realising the communicative purpose of the text and thus showing greater pragmatic awareness. This advantage was particularly significant in the A CLIL group. In the field of organisation and structure, the overall difference was smaller and it must be noted that, on the whole, these skills were not very well developed.

As discussed in the introduction, previous studies of CLIL writing have consistently shown significant differences between CLIL and non-CLIL students on all dimensions rated (such as content, organisation, vocabulary, use of language, mechanics; e.g. Ruiz de Zarobe, this volume; Lasagabaster 2008; Zydatiß 2007) and on this global level these results are also borne out by the present study. A more fi ne-grained analysis of the factor 'organisation and structure', however, shows that several aspects on this dimension represent a considerable challenge also for CLIL students. While the CLIL students seem to profit from their larger lexical knowledge in terms of disposing of a somewhat wider range of connectives for logically structuring their texts, awareness of the textual elements required by the genre 'e-mail to prospective host family' was not particularly high (though higher than in the non-CLIL control group). The same point can be made even more strongly for the use of paragraphing in structuring the text into distinct but coherent phases.

The results of the present study thus seem to suggest that the greatest advantages of CLIL students in terms of their writing skills result from their greater general language ability and also a greater awareness of the pragmatic demands of the task. The effects on textual competence, on the other hand, seem limited, which is not surprising in view of the fact that, apart from note-taking, very little writing is typically demanded in Austrian CLIL classrooms. As writing tasks may also help students come to terms with the concepts discussed (e.g. Lemke 1990: 168; Schmölzer-Eibinger 2008; Zwiers 2008), an opportunity to promote both an understanding of the content and the development of language skills may be lost in this way.

We would like to remind readers at this point that the writing task used in this study was of a general nature and did not require participants to show literacy skills which are specific to any particular content subject (a similar general task was, in fact, used in Ruiz de Zarobe, this volume; Lasagabaster 2008). Studies conducted in Germany have shown CLIL and non-CLIL students to have considerable difficulty with expository and argumentative writing based on subject-content materials (Coetzee-Lachmann 2006, 2009; Vollmer et al. 2006; Zydatiß 2007). Interestingly, these difficulties were language-independent, surfacing also in the students' L1 German, which led the authors to reason that the problems were due to the widespread absence of writing in content lessons and the ensuing lack of experience with this kind of activity on the part of the students. This absence of writing is an element in the culture of subject-didactics which Austria and Germany seem to share. By contrast, a series of studies conducted in Spain (e.g. Llinares & Whittaker 2006; Whittaker & Llinares 2009) shows a somewhat different picture: obviously, in keeping with different traditions in the teaching of content-subjects, Spanish CLIL students are shown to possess age-adequate subject-specific writing skills in their L1 while their subject-specific L2 writing skills obviously lag behind but are in the process of developing (see also Lorenzo & Moore; this volume). These observations point to an important factor which is generally neglected in the evaluation of CLIL programmes and their effectiveness: while it is often said that CLIL impacts on the didactics of the content subjects, the opposite effect namely the impact of subject didactic practices and traditions on CLIL pedagogy is equally true but rarely taken into account.

Finally, a caveat should be added with regard to general language ability. As there were no data available on the students' level of language competence at the start of the CLIL programme, it cannot be ruled out that the performance of the two groups (CLIL vs non-CLIL) was already significant at that time. Another important point is that there were noticeable differences not only between the CLIL and non-CLIL groups but also between the two schools, which makes it difficult to draw general conclusions about CLIL instruction. What would be needed to obtain greater insights into the effects of CLIL on language competence is a more broadly-based longitudinal study. Moreover, as CLIL programmes tend to differ greatly from one school to another, it would be interesting to investigate the effects of different types of programmes on the development of language competence in order to identify those factors which are most beneficial.

References

Airey, J. 2004. Can you teach it in English? Aspects of the language choice debate in Swedish higher education. In *Integrating Content and Language: Meeting the Challenge of a Multilingual Higher Education*, R. Wilkinson (ed.), 97–108. Maastricht: Maastricht University.
Bachmann, L.F. 1990. *Fundamental Considerations in Language Testing*. Oxford: OUP.
Canale, M. & Swain, M. 1980. Theoretical bases of communicative approaches to second language teaching and testing. *Applied Linguistics* 1: 1–47.

Coetzee-Lachmann, D. 2006. Eine Definition fachspezifischer Diskurskompetenz. In *Fremd-sprachenlernen und Fremdsprachenforschung: Kompetenzen, Standards, Lernformen Evaluation. Festschrift für Helmut Johannes Vollmer*, J.-P. Timm (ed.), 249–265. Tübingen: Gunter Narr.

Coetzee-Lachmann, D. 2009. Assessment of Subject-specific Task Performance of Bilingual Geography Learners: Analysing Aspects of Subject-specific Written Discourse. Ph.D. dissertation, University of Osnabrück.

Dalton-Puffer, C. 2008. Outcomes and processes in Content and Language Integrated Learning: Current research from Europe. In *Future Perspectives for English Language Teaching*, W. Delanoy & L. Volkmann (eds), 139–157. Heidelberg: Winter.

Dalton-Puffer, C. 2009. Communicative competence and the CLIL lesson. In *Content and Language Integrated Learning: Evidence from Research in Europe*, Y. Ruiz de Zarobe & R. Jimenez Catalán (eds), 197–214. Clevedon: Multilingual Matters.

Dalton-Puffer, C., Hüttner, J., Jexenflicker, S., Schindelegger, V. & Smit, U. 2008. *CLIL an Österreichs HTLs. Projektbericht*. Vienna: Bundesministerium für Unterricht, Kunst und Kultur.

Ellis, R. & Barkhuizen, G. 2005. *Analysing Learner Language*. Oxford: OUP.

Friedl, G. & Auer, M. 2007. Erläuterungen zur Novellierung der Reifeprüfungsverordnung für AHS, lebende Fremdsprachen. St. Pölten.

Grotjahn, R., Klein-Braley, C. & Raatz, U. 2002. C-tests – an overview. In *University Language Testing and the C-test*, J. Coleman et al., 93–114. Bochum: AKS-Verlag.

Haunold, C. 2006. English as a Medium of Instruction in Austrian Secondary Education. MA thesis, University of Vienna.

Hellekjær, G. 2004. Unprepared for English-medium instruction: A critical look at beginner students. In *Integrating Content and Language: Meeting the Challenge of a Multilingual Higher Education*, R. Wilkinson (ed.), 147–171. Maastricht: Maastricht University.

Hughes, A. 2003. *Testing for Language Teachers*, 2nd edn. Cambridge: CUP.

Hüttner, J. 2009. Fluent speakers-fluent interactions: On the creation of (co-)fluency in English as a lingua franca. In *English as a Lingua Franca: Studies and Findings*, A. Mauranen & E. Ranta (eds), 274–297. Newcastle: Cambridge Scholars Press.

Jexenflicker, S. 2010. A Comparative Study on Differences in Language Output between Mainstream and CLIL Students at two Austrian Colleges of Engineering, Crafts and Arts. MA thesis, University of Vienna.

Klieme, E. 2006. Zusammenfassung zentraler Ergebnisse der DESI Studie. Deutsches Institut für Internationale Pädagogische Forschung. <www.dipf.de/desi/DESI_Ausgewaehlte_Ergebnisse.pdf>.

Lasagabaster, D. 2008. Foreign language competence in content and language integrated courses. *The Open Applied Linguistics Journal* 1: 31–42.

Lemke, J.L. 1990. *Talking Science, Language, Learning, and Values*. Norwood NJ: Ablex.

Llinares, A. & Whittaker, R. 2006. Oral and written production in social science. *Current Research on CLIL. VIEWS* 15(3): 28–32.

Mewald, C. 2007. A comparison of oral foreign language performance of learners in CLIL and mainstream classes at lower secondary level. In *Empirical Perspectives on CLIL Classroom Discourse* [Sprache im Kontext 26], C. Dalton-Puffer & U. Smit (eds), 139–177. Frankfurt: Peter Lang.

Morrow, K. 1979. Communicative language testing: Revolution or evolution? In *The Communicative Approach to Language Teaching*, C.J. Brumfit & K. Johnson (eds), 143–157. Oxford: OUP.

Schmölzer-Eibinger, S. 2008. *Lernen in der Zweitsprache: Grundlagen und Verfahren der Förderung von Textkompetenz in mehrsprachigen Klassen.* Tübingen: Narr.

Seregély, E. 2008. A Comparison of Lexical Learning in CLIL and Traditional EFL Classrooms. MA thesis, University of Vienna.

Sigott, G. 2004. *Towards Identifying the C-test Construct.* Frankfurt: Peter Lang.

Sylvén, L.K. 2004. Teaching in English or English Teaching? On the Effects of Content and Language Integrated Learning on Swedish Learners' Incidental Vocabulary Acquisition. Ph.D. dissertation, Göteborg University.

Varchmin, B. 2008. Effects of Content and Language Integrated Learning (CLIL) on Final Devoicing and the Pronunciation of Dental Fricatives: A Case Study of German Speakers Learning English. MA thesis, Goldsmiths College/University of London.

Vollmer, H.J., Heine, L., Troschke, R., Coetzee, D. & Küttel, V. 2006. Subject-specific competence and language use of CLIL learners: The case of geography in grade 10 of secondary schools in Germany. Presentation at ESSE8 Conference in London 2006.

Weir, C.J. 1990. *Communicative Language Testing.* New York NY: Prentice-Hall.

Wesche, M.B. 2002. Early French immersion: How has the original Canadian model stood the test of time? In *An Integrated View of Language Development: Papers in Honour of Henning Wode,* P. Burmeister, T. Piske & A. Rohde (eds), 357–379. Trier: Wissenschaftlicher Verlag Trier.

Whittaker, R. & Llinares, A. 2009. CLIL in social science classrooms: Analysis of spoken and written productions. In *Content and Language Integrated Learning: Evidence from Research in Europe,* Y. Ruiz de Zarobe & R. Jimenez Catalán (eds), 215–233. Clevedon: Multilingual Matters.

Wode, H. 1994. *Analytische Auswertungen 2* [Bilinguale Unterrichtserprobung in Schleswig-Holstein]. Kiel: l&f Verlag.

Zwiers, J. 2008. *Building Academic Language. Essential Practices for the Content Classroom.* San Francisco CA: Jossey-Bass.

Zydatiß, W. 2007. *Deutsch-Englische Züge in Berlin: Eine Evaluation des bilingualen Sachfachunterrichts an Gymnasien. Kontext, Kompetenzen, Konsequenzen.* Frankfurt: Peter Lang.

Appendix

1. Rating scale used for assessment (adapted from Friedl/Auer 2007):

Task fulfilment: content and relevance; text format, length and register

5 Task fully achieved, content entirely relevant; appropriate format, length and register

4 Task almost fully achieved, content mostly relevant; mostly appropriate format, length and register

3 Task adequately achieved, some gaps or redundant information; acceptable format, length and register

2 Task achieved only in a limited sense, frequent gaps or redundant information; often inadequate format, length and register

1 Task poorly achieved, major gaps or pointless repetitions; inadequate format, length and register

0 Not enough to evaluate

Organisation: structure, paragraphing, cohesion and coherence, editing and punctuation

5 Clear overall structure, meaningful paragraphing, very good use of connectives, no editing mistakes, conventions of punctuation observed

4 Overall structure mostly clear, good paragraphing, good use of connectives, hardly any editing mistakes, conventions of punctuation mostly observed

3 Adequately structured, paragraphing misleading at times, adequate use of connectives, some editing and punctuating errors

2 Limited overall structuring, frequent mistakes in paragraphing, limited use of connectives, frequent editing and punctuation errors

1 Poor overall structuring, no meaningful paragraphing, poor use of connectives, numerous editing and punctuation errors

0 Not enough to evaluate

Grammar: accuracy/errors, variety of structures, readiness to use complex structures

5 Accurate use of grammar and structures, hardly any errors of agreement, tense, word order, articles, pronouns, etc.; meaning clear, great variety of structures, frequent use of complex structures

4 Mostly accurate use of grammar and structures, few errors of agreement etc., meaning mostly clear, good variety of structures, readiness to use complex structures

3 Adequate use of grammar and structures, some errors of agreement etc., meaning sometimes not clear, adequate variety of structures, some readiness to use complex structures

2 Limited use of grammar and structures, frequent errors of agreement etc., meaning often not clear, limited variety of structures, limited readiness to use complex structures

1   Poor use of grammar and structures, numerous errors of agreement etc., meaning very often not clear, poor variety of structures

0   Not enough to evaluate

Vocabulary: range and choice of words, accuracy, spelling, comprehensibility

5   Wide range of vocabulary, very good choice of words, accurate form and usage, hardly any spelling mistakes, meaning clear

4   Good range of vocabulary; good choice of words; mostly accurate form and usage, few spelling mistakes; meaning mostly clear

3   Adequate range of vocabulary and choice of words, some repetitions, some errors of form and usage, some spelling mistakes, meaning sometimes not clear, some translation from mother tongue

2   Limited range of vocabulary and choice of words, frequent repetitions, frequent errors of form and usage, frequent spelling mistakes, meaning often not clear, frequent translation from mother tongue

1   Poor range of vocabulary and choice of words, highly repetitive, numerous errors of form and usage, numerous spelling mistakes, meaning very often not clear, mainly translation from mother tongue

0   Not enough to evaluate

2. Sample texts:

Sample text 1: College A, CLIL student

Dear Mr and Mrs Ferguson,

My name is XXXX and as you know I am going to visit you in a few weeks. So I want to give you some personal information.

Sixteen years ago I was born in the hospital in XXXX. I still live in this nice city with my parents and my two sisters. I visit the HTL-XXXX, a technical school for automotive engineering. Many people think it is hard to be the only girl in a class with twenty boys, but I don't really have a problem with this situation. After school I often meet my friends to play poker, listen to music etc. I have not much hobbies but I like to play the piano or to sing.

I really look forward to visit you because I have never been in New York, but I have often stayed abroad for example in Greece, Turkey, England and some other countries in Europe. It is very exiting for me to visit such a big town in an other continent.

Now I would like to ask some question: What kind of school do Paul and Amanda visit? And is it a long way from your house to the city?

I really look forward to meet you and I am sure that we will have a good time together!
Yours
XXXX (222 words)

Sample text 2: College B, CLIL student

Dear Mr and Mrs Ferguson,

As you probably already know, me and my classmates are going to visit you next month. My name is XXXX, I'm 17 years old and my family consists of my parents my (sometimes) lovely sister and my two sweet little cats.

In my leisure time I play football, basketball and during the winter I do some skiing (as nearly every Austrian). At the moment I attend the XXXX, a technical school tomorrow's engineers. In the future I want to do something which combines both automation and networking.

My experience in english countries are a language week in England and a language week in Malta.

But, enough about me, let's talk about your city, New York, the "Big Apple". I'm very excited to visit Manhattan and its busy crowd and I'd love to see the Liberty Statue from close.

As a conclusion, I can say that I'm looking forward to our stay in your amazing country. Yours sincerely,
XXXX (163 words)

Sample text 3: College A, non-CLIL student

Hello,

My name is XXXX. I am 17 years old and live in the beautiful country Austria.

I am also excited to see you and our family. At this time I atend the HTL-XXXX in XXXXXXX. I am in the third class and want to improve my english. In the future I will be a konstructor, and I learn hard for it.

My Hoppies are skiing and swimming. I also spend a much of time with my friends. I hope that I will find friends in New York. That would very nice.

In New York I will see the life in the big city and (105 words)

Sample text 4: College B, non-CLIL student

Dear Mr and Mrs Ferguson,

My name is XXXX. I am 15 years old and I come from XXXX.

I attending the XXXX in Austria. I am like to play the drums and go out with friends. I also like to play soccer. I love to go on holiday.

I'm happy to go to New York because NY is is one of the biggest cities of the world and there are famous people. I will go to the Central Park.

What do you do in your Spare time?
How is the wheater like? (93 words)

Sample text 5: College A, non-CLIL student

Hello,

My name is XXXX. I'm 14 years old and I live in Austria.

    I have one mother and one father and two brothers. I'm attending the third year at the HTL-XXXXX. I want to finish school and want to gain wealth. My spare time activities are running, driving and eating. I'm happy about going to NY. because this happns (?) in school time. So I have not to learn for school. A question which I will ask is why so much people had choosed Bush. And I want to know if Amanda is a beautiful girl. (97 words)

Written production and CLIL

An empiricial study

Yolanda Ruiz de Zarobe
Euskal Herriko Unibertsitatea, Spain

This paper analyses the written competence attained by two groups of bilingual students that follow two different CLIL programmes, and another group enrolled in a traditional English as a Foreign language (EFL) programme. This study also analyses the longitudinal progression of these three groups to offer a more prolonged perspective on CLIL.

Our results show the CLIL groups score better in relation to the five categories analysed in written production: content, organisation, vocabulary, language usage and mechanics, which suggests there is a positive relationship between the amount of exposure through English and written foreign language proficiency.

Furthermore, the longitudinal evaluation of the results show that students enrolled on CLIL programmes outperform students on the EFL programmes, and this advantage increases with grade, confirming the effectiveness of the CLIL approach on written production outcomes. These results serve as evidence that CLIL can be more useful than traditional language teaching in promoting proficiency in the foreign language.

1. Introduction

In *Profiling European CLIL Classrooms*, Marsh, Maljers & Hartiala (2001: 14) distinguish five dimensions or reasons for the implementation of CLIL in Europe. These are briefly summarised below:

- *Culture dimension*: Building intercultural knowledge and understanding. Developing intercultural communication skills. Learning about specific neighbouring countries/regions and/or minority groups. Introducing the wider cultural context.
- *Environment dimension*: Preparing for internationalisation, specifically EU integration. Accessing international certification. Enhancing school profile.
- *Content dimension*: Providing opportunities to study content through different perspectives. Accessing subject-specific target language terminology. Preparing for future studies and/or working life.

- *Learning dimension*: Complementing individual learning strategies. Diversifying methods and forms of classroom practice. Increasing learner motivation.
- *Language dimension*: Improving overall target language competence. Developing oral communication skills. Deepening awareness of both mother tongue and target language. Developing plurilingual interests and attitudes. Introducing a target language.

These five dimensions show the breadth of European CLIL in relation to culture, environment, content, learning and language and its versatile nature, presenting different fields of reflection and development. The evidence on CLIL needs to be evaluated in light of the many variables that are at play, ranging from the impact of internationalisation and integration, the development of intercultural communication skills and greater levels of foreign language proficiency.

The traditionally most common reason for the introduction of CLIL in the educational system is to support foreign language education. The related set of objectives has been called the language dimension of CLIL (cf. Marsh, Maljers & Hartiala 2001), its aims being to improve overall language competence, including reading, writing, speaking and listening skills. Out of all these skills, communication skills, notably oral communication skills, have been given special importance. Yet, although in the last years the number of studies has increased significantly, there is still little research on language learning outcomes and L2 developing competence. An explanation for this lack of available evidence may lie in the diversity of programmes and approaches that sometimes do not allow for generalisations. Each community adopts different models to suit their needs and expectations, and programmes fall along more language-driven approaches, where language learning is the primary goal of education, to more content-driven approaches, where the content and the language are equally important. Despite the diversity in contexts and applications, all these approaches show a focus on language learning, which deserves further analysis.

Much of the linguistic research about the impact of teaching through the foreign language has been positive, although some areas of language competence seem to benefit more than others (Dalton-Puffer 2008). One of the language components that demonstrate the positive effects of CLIL is related to the lexicon. Studies suggest that CLIL students' vocabulary has in general more lexical richness and sophistication (Jiménez Catalán, Ruiz de Zarobe & Cenoz 2006; Jiménez Catalán & Ruiz de Zarobe 2009; Moreno 2009) and higher lexical variation (Ackerl 2007; Agustín Llach & Jiménez Catalán 2007). Another difference is related to lexical transfer. CLIL students show fewer instances of lexical transfer, and fewer cases of direct borrowing from the L1, while the number of lexical inventions (calques and coinages) is more frequent in CLIL (Celaya 2007; Celaya & Ruiz de Zarobe 2008; Agustín Llach 2009). As preceding studies show (Navés, Miralpeix & Celaya

2005; Celaya 2007), borrowings are characteristic of learners at earlier stages of acquisition while lexical inventions imply higher proficiency in the target language and are more common at later stages of the acquisition process.

However, other linguistic areas do not offer such clear gains, notably morphosyntax and phonetics. Although some studies show that CLIL students partially outperform non-CLIL in some morphosyntactic components, such as sentence complexity, affixal inflection or the use of placeholders, other properties, notably the use of null subjects, negation and suppletive forms, seem to remain unaffected (Martínez Adrián & Gutierrez Mangado 2009; Villarreal & García Mayo 2009). As regards the phonetic component, a study by Gallardo del Puerto, Gómez Lacabex and García Lecumberri (2009) suggests that CLIL students have a more intelligible and less 'irritating' foreign accent than non-CLIL students. However, there are no statistically significant differences in the degree of foreign accent between both groups, suggesting that results in this competence seem to be less uniform.

Another area that deserves special attention is the dichotomy between productive and receptive skills. As has often been pointed out, bilingual educational programmes in Europe have been inspired by Canadian immersion programmes, where anglophone students received subject-matter instruction through French. Research on those programmes (Cummins & Swain 1986; Genesee 1987; Swain & Lapkin 1995) indicated that students' comprehension ability was comparable to that of their native francophone peers, but Anglophone students did not reach full native-like competence in production skills. Research has tried to examine whether the same situation holds in CLIL. Some studies show a mismatch between receptive and productive skills in CLIL (Jiménez Catalán, Ruiz de Zarobe & Cenoz, 2006; Ruiz de Zarobe 2007) with better results on receptive skills, but still little research has looked at the differences between both productive skills. Some studies (Naiman 1995) suggest that CLIL students show lower inhibition levels when actually speaking the foreign language. CLIL students also seem to be more fluent and risk-taking, rating their abilities significantly higher than non-CLIL students (Sylvén 2006; Dalton-Puffer et al. 2009).

However, results in writing do not seem to be so definite. Although some studies confirm the benefits of CLIL in different skills of foreign language competence, including written competence (Lasagabaster 2008), others suggest there are deficiencies both in CLIL and non-CLIL classrooms in relation to writing (Llinares & Whittaker 2006; Vollmer et al. 2006). For instance, Vollmer et al., who analysed Grade 10 students learning geography in Germany through English, found that there were considerable deficiencies in academic literacy in CLIL classrooms as well as in L1 subject-classrooms and suggest there should be much more focus on developing academic language use and general writing competence of the learners in the classroom.

2.   The Basque Country and CLIL

CLIL is offered in a variety of forms in Europe. According to the Eurydice network on education in Europe, in the majority of countries, schools offer a form of CLIL in which subjects are taught in two different languages, the official state language and the foreign language. The situation in the Basque Country is somehow different, as it is a bilingual community where two official languages, Basque and Spanish, already form part of the curriculum.[1] Although the implementation of CLIL in Spain, particularly in the Basque Country, is relatively new, these programmes have benefited from the experience gathered in programmes for the normalisation of Basque as an official language. When the *Basic Law on the Standardisation of Basque* was passed in 1982, three linguistic models were established to ensure that every student had the possibility to learn in Spanish and/or Basque: (i) Model A: all subjects, apart from the Basque language and literature and modern languages, are taught in Spanish; (ii) Model B: both Spanish and Basque are used to teach all the subjects, and (iii) Model D: all subjects, except Spanish language and literature and modern languages, are taught in Basque.[2] The application of these models is currently under review to reorganise the education system for the purpose of achieving a system of higher quality. Nevertheless, research has demonstrated that Model D, which has become the most preferred model in the community, provides the best programme for balanced bilingualism (Cenoz 1991).

Apart from these models, the Department of Education of the Basque autonomous community has set up an experimental programme to implement CLIL models geared to:

1.   promote the knowledge and use of a foreign language, generally English, although there are some programmes with French.
2.   reach a better command of the foreign language.
3.   become proficient in three languages: Basque, Spanish and the foreign language.
4.   prepare students for a more international society.

---

1.   In the year 2006, 37.5% of the population of the Basque Autonomous Community were bilingual, 17.3% were passive bilinguals (they can understand Basque but they cannot speak it fluently) and 45.2% were classified as monolinguals in Spanish (IV Mapa Sociolingüístico 2006. Viceconsejería de Política Lingüística, Gobierno Vasco, Vitoria-Gasteiz, 2009 ISBN 978-84-457-2942-7).

2.   No Model C exists in the Basque educational system because there is no letter 'c' in the Basque alphabet.

The fact that CLIL is becoming a very popular and widespread practice in the Basque Country is reflected, for example, in the number of private Basque-medium schools that have adopted this approach in what has been termed the "Eleanitz (Multilingual)-English experience". Th is experience, which includes the early introduction of English (when pupils are 4 years old) and the teaching of at least one content subject through the English language, started from eight schools in 1991, with 600 students and 8 teachers, to 72 schools in 2008, with 25.000 students and 200 teachers involved.

In relation to the fi rst component, the introduction of English when pupils are 4 years old, previous research on the early start of the foreign language in instructed settings (see García Mayo & García Lecumberri 2003; Ruiz de Zarobe 2003, 2005; Muñoz 2006, among others) concluded that children's language proficiency does not benefit much from an early introduction that does not involve an increase in the number of hours and meaningful exposure to the language. Research suggests that the intensity and timing of exposure may be more important than exposure itself.

> Second language learning success in a foreign language context may be as much a function of exposure as of age. Exposure needs to be intense and to provide an adequate model. (Muñoz 2006: 34)

CLIL may offer more opportunities for higher exposure to the language and therefore better results, provided it is linked to other factors such as quality of teaching and time of learning.

As regards CLIL subjects and the number of hours per week, a number of centres in the Basque Country have begun to teach one or two non-language subjects in the foreign language. Any non-language subject can be taught in English, and subjects vary between schools; these subjects are very often from the social sciences and creative subjects such as music, arts and crafts and physical education. In public schools, the programme is generally implemented at the levels of compulsory secondary education (12–13 years old), where students learn seven hours a week through the foreign language. In post-compulsory secondary education (Baccalaureate), 20 to 25% of the subjects may be taught through the foreign language. However, as students need to participate in the national final examination (*Selectividad*) at the end of Baccalaureate, there is a tendency to offer fewer subjects through the foreign language at pre-university level.

Apart from that, although the general trend has been to offer 1 or 2 non-language subjects in the foreign language, there has been an increase in the number of individual institutions offering alternative CLIL curricula, with the integration of more subjects in the foreign language. This gives us the possibility to research how CLIL is being applied and, more importantly for this paper, to analyse the competence attained through CLIL compared to more conventional linguistic programmes, as we will see in the following section.

3. Hypotheses

Our research project poses a general question: Can CLIL lead to foreign language learning faster and/or better than a more traditional educational model as regards written production?

Based on the findings from previous studies in this field of research we present the following hypotheses:

1. Students enrolled on CLIL programmes will outperform students on the non-CLIL programme in all written production categories, as they do in oral production tasks (Ruiz de Zarobe 2008).
2. There will be a positive relationship between the amount of content-based instruction and the written production outcomes. In other words, the more content-based instruction there is, the better the results (more-content-is-better hypothesis).[3]
3. The participants on the CLIL programmes will obtain better results than the ones on the non-CLIL programme in the longitudinal evaluation of the results.

The question and hypotheses stated above led to the design of a study undertaken in the Basque autonomous community with the aim of exploring linguistic competence in different content-based programmes. In the next section we will explain the sample used for the research.

4. The study

4.1. Participants

The study was conducted in three school programmes in the Basque Country, selected to include different approaches to CLIL. In all three groups Basque was used as the main language of instruction. However, Spanish is the majority language in the community and all the students exhibited native levels in Spanish, thus, the participants were fully bilingual in Basque and Spanish. All of them had started learning English as their third language at school when they were eight years old.

---

3. We have paraphrased the 'more-English-is-better hypothesis', used in Genesee & Jared (2008: 141).

The sample was divided into three groups on the basis of the English programme.

1. The first group, the non-CLIL group, had received 3 hours of English per week, following a conventional English as a Foreign Language (EFL) programme. These participants did not receive any extra-English classes outside school.
2. The second group, CLIL1, had received instruction in EFL 3 hours per week. When they were 14 they entered a CLIL programme, in which one curricular subject (Social Science) was taught through English for 3 or 4 hours per week. The number of hours provided in Table 1 include their EFL classes and the CLIL classes. Unfortunately, we could not collect information for this group at pre-university level. The school was reluctant to allow external tests the year the students had to take the national final examination (*Selectividad*) to enter university.
3. The third group, CLIL2, who had also entered a CLIL programme when they were 14, had received, apart from the EFL classes 3 to 4 hours a week, two curricular subjects through English (Social Sciences: 3/4 hours a week and Modern English Literature: 2 hours a week).

Table 1 provides information about the student population participating in the research.

Table 1. Overview of type and size of participant population

	Secondary 3	Secondary 4	Pre-university (Baccalaureate)	Number of students per program
Number of students	Non-CLIL: 29 CLIL1: 24 CLIL2: 36	Non-CLIL: 18 CLIL1: 16 CLIL2: 17	Non-CLIL: 7 CLIL1: XXX CLIL2: 14	Non-CLIL: 54 CLIL1: 40 CLIL2: 67
Age during data collection	14–15	15–16	17–18	
Hours of instruction	Non-CLIL: 695 CLIL1: 875 CLIL2: 910	Non-CLIL: 792 CLIL1: 1120 CLIL2: 1155	Non-CLIL: 990 CLIL1: XXX CLIL2: 1453	

4.2 Instruments and procedure

In order to collect the data, participants were asked to complete a written production task: they were asked to write a letter to a host family with whom they were going to spend a month in England. In the letter they had to introduce themselves and their family, and provide information about their hobbies and interests. These compositions, which are considered a good measure to study overall written performance (Hughes 1989), were done in the natural classroom setting, within regularly scheduled classes and were run by their instructor.

The holistic approach by Jacobs et al. (1981), the ESL Composition Profile, was used to identify the students' written competence, based on five scales. These scales are used for a general evaluation of their proficiency level, although specific features of compositions are also involved.[4] Compositions were scored using the following categories: content (max = 30), organization (max = 20), vocabulary (max = 20), language use (max = 25), and mechanics (max = 5). These five scales were used to have an overall account of the written assignment:

a. Content (30 points): this category considers the development and comprehension of the topic as well as the adequacy of the content of the text.
b. Organisation (20 points): several factors are considered here, such as the organisation of ideas, the structure and cohesion of the paragraphs and the clarity of exposition of the main and secondary ideas.
c. Vocabulary (20 points): this category deals with the selection of words, expressions and their usage. The appropriateness of the register used is also taken into account.
d. Language usage (25 points): the use of grammar categories is taken into account, e.g. tense, number, subject-verb agreement, in addition to word order and the use of complex syntactic structures.
e. Mechanics (5 points): this category includes the evaluation of punctuation, spelling, and the use of capitalisation.

These five major writing components: content, organization, vocabulary, language, and mechanics have four rating levels of very poor, poor to fair, average to good, and very good to excellent. Each component and level has clear descriptors of the writing proficiency for that particular level as well as a numerical scale. For example, excellent to very good organisation has a minimum rating of 18 and a maximum of 20 indicating an organisation of the composition with the following profile: "fluent expression – ideas clearly stated/supported – succinct – well-organised – logical sequencing and cohesive", while very poor organisation has a minimum of 7 and a maximum of 9 indicating writing that "does not communicate – no organization OR not enough to evaluate". Similarly, good to average content has a minimum rating of 22 and a maximum of 26 indicating that there is "some knowledge of subject – adequate range – limited development of thesis – mostly relevant to topic, but lacks detail", while fair to poor content has a minimum of 17 and a maximum of 21 and indicates that there is "limited knowledge of subject – little substance – inadequate

---

4. It could be argued that the ESL Composition Profile (Jacobs et al. 1989) is partly holistic and partly analytic.

development of topic". The range for each of the writing skills are content 13–30, organization 7–20, vocabulary 7–20, language 5–25 and mechanics 2–5.

Each composition was double marked following the five scales provided, and the final grade was the average of the two raters' scores, who had been previously trained on the procedure of the Profile.

5. Results

Results are summarised first by an overall evaluation of written production in the three school programmes and then, by a description of the results in the three programmes according to the participants' grade and age, to account for the longitudinal distribution of results.

In Figure 1 the overall evaluation of written production based on the educational programme is presented. The overall results of written production in the three school programmes show that the CLIL groups outstrip the non-CLIL group in most of the scales analysed. The nonparametric tests[5] show that these differences are significant in relation to content (Chi-square = 6.348, p < 0.042) and vocabulary (Chi-square = 10.288, p < 0.006). In the rest of the scales, organization, language usage and mechanics, although the results are better in the case of CLIL2 students, these differences are not statistically significant.

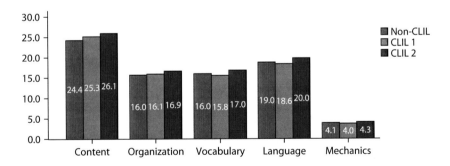

Figure 1. Overall evaluation of written production based on the educational programme

Figures 2, 3 and 4 below show the results for each of the three educational programmes depending on the participants' grade. These results show how in the third year of secondary education, the differences between CLIL1 and CLIL2

---

5. The Kolmogorov-Smirnov Test (K–S test) run for normality testing showed the sample did not have a normal distribution (p < 0.05). Thus, as the assumption of normality was not met, the Kruskal-Wallis non-parametric test was used to compare the three independent groups of sampled data.

groups are not significant. Unfortunately, the written test could not be collected for the non-CLIL group.

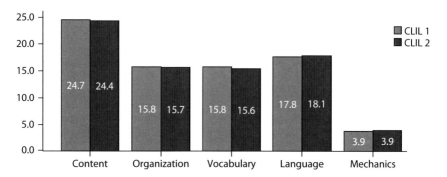

Figure 2. Written production based on educational programme in Secondary Year 3

Both groups score similarly in the five scales analysed in the third year of secondary education. Nevertheless, in the fourth year of secondary education the students enrolled in the more intensive CLIL programme (CLIL2) scored higher than the other groups. These differences are significant in three of the categories analysed: vocabulary (Chi-square = 11.622, p < 0.03), language usage (Chi-square = 6.677, p < 0.035), and mechanics (Chi-square = 15.613, p < 0.00). In the other two scales, content and organisation, even though the results are still more positive in the case of the two content-based groups, no statistical differences are found between them.

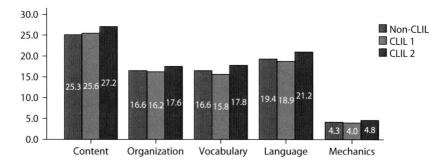

Figure 3. Written production based on educational programme in Secondary Year 4

As mentioned above, the participants enrolled in the pre-university grade only belonged to two groups:[6] non-CLIL and CLIL2. The differences between both

---

6. The Wilcoxon signed rank test for two related simples was used, as results were not obtained at pre-university level for group CLIL1.

turned out to be significant in all the categories: content (Chi-square = 15.066, p < 0.00), organisation (Chi-square = 12.423, p < 0.000), vocabulary (Chi-square = 13.201, p < 0.000), language usage (Chi-square = 7.240, p < 0.007), and mechanics (Chi-square = 6.429, p < 0.011), with the CLIL group scoring higher than the non-CLIL counterpart.

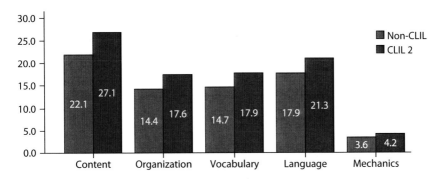

Figure 4. Written production based on educational programme in pre-university level

6.   Discussion

The general evaluation of both programmes, CLIL and non-CLIL as regards written production confirms the effectiveness of the CLIL approach. The results in the overall evaluation of written competence show that the CLIL groups surpass the non-CLIL group in most of the scales analysed, with significant differences in content and vocabulary. In this last scale, vocabulary, the difference between both approaches is highly significant (p < 0.006).

These results support previous research on vocabulary outcomes that demonstrated the positive effects of CLIL in relation to vocabulary acquisition (Jiménez Catalán, Ruiz de Zarobe & Cenoz 2006; Jiménez Catalán & Ruiz de Zarobe 2009; Moreno 2009). There is evidence once again that in CLIL lessons one of the linguistic aspects that shows significant gains is the lexicon which, on the other hand, is one of the very few that are explicitly taught in the classroom.

Our next step will be to see whether our first hypothesis is borne out:

Students enrolled on CLIL programmes will outperform students on the non-CLIL programme in all written production categories, as they do in oral production tasks (Ruiz de Zarobe 2008).

Our results show the positive gains that CLIL has in written production outcomes. Nonetheless, the written test does not seem to yield results as good as the ones obtained in oral productive competence (Ruiz de Zarobe 2008) with the same groups under discussion.

In Ruiz de Zarobe (2008), five categories were used for the purpose of the analysis on speech production:

a. Pronunciation (10 points): in this category phonetic accuracy and the communication effect of pronunciation are analysed.
b. Vocabulary (10 points): this category deals with the selection or words and their usage.
c. Grammar (10 points): accuracy and the use of different grammatical structures were considered in this scale.
d. Fluency (10 points): in this category the communicative effect of the oral production and continuity were analysed.
e. Content (10 points): the adequacy of the content was examined.

By and large the results indicated that the students in the CLIL programme outperformed the non-CLIL counterparts in all the categories analysed. The non-parametric tests showed that these differences were significant as regards pronunciation (Chi-square = 13.752, $p < 0.001$), vocabulary (Chi-square = 31.359, $p < 0.000$), grammar (Chi-square = 22.031, $p < 0.000$), fluency (Chi-square = 21.122, $p < 0.000$), and content (Chi-square = 17.545, $p < 0.000$).

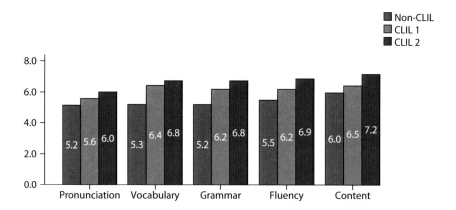

Figure 5. Overall evaluation of oral production based on the educational programme

The written test performed in this study shows that, although scores are better in the CLIL approach, the results are not statistically significant in all the scales (cf. Figure 1). This provides further evidence on the differences between skills and abilities depending on the approach. As was pointed out in the introduction, Canadian immersion programmes showed how students' French oral and reading comprehension skills (receptive skills) had evolved to almost a native-like proficiency while speaking and writing in the second language (productive skills) were not as developed and advanced. Previous research on CLIL (Jiménez Catalán, Ruiz de Zarobe & Cenoz 2006; Ruiz de Zarobe 2007), also suggested that this is the situation in some CLIL programmes, where there is a mismatch between receptive and productive skills, with better results on the side of the receptive skills.

The results presented here indicate that there is also a difference between both productive language skills: oral and written competence. As CLIL seems to stress face-to-face oral interaction and fluency in a meaningful and significant context (Brumfit & Johnson 1979; Ellis 2001), results in oral competence are favoured. These outcomes seem to be consistent with the language dimension presented in the introduction. One of the tenets of this dimension is to develop oral communication skills, together with characteristics such as the improvement of overall target language competence and the awareness of both the mother tongue and the target language. Our findings suggest that the CLIL approach has a clear impact on both communicative tasks, but preferably on oral communicative competence. CLIL provides more opportunities for students to speak and to practise oral skills when using the target language as a tool in the classroom. This fact supports the view that communicative competence is acquired more successfully as a medium of communication and not as an end in itself.

On the other hand, the results obtained in the written task in this study can be connected with previous research (Llinares & Whittaker 2006; Vollmer et al. 2006) on writing outcomes, notably, on post-teaching writing tasks in social science subjects. These studies, contrary to expectations, concluded that on a number of variables related to written performance such as discourse function, style and coherence and cohesion results were not as positive as had been in principle expected, due mainly to the lack of written competence also in the mother tongue. As Dalton-Puffer states:

> The explanations of these deficiencies in academic literacy take recourse to the kind of pre-scientific understanding of the subject which is visible from these texts, but also to the fact that the general writing competence of the learners is in need of development, particularly since parallel results were obtained on writing tasks completed in the mother tongue. What is at issue here is the role of writing in content-teaching in general, irrespective of the language it is conducted in.
> (Dalton-Puffer 2008: 7)

In view of such observations, it is clear that at a more general didactic level, literacy in the mother tongue and the foreign language are to be taught in parallel, with teachers cooperating to pace L1 and L2 instruction accordingly.

Let us turn now to the second hypothesis of our study:

There will be a positive relationship between the amount of content-based instruction and the written production outcomes. In other words, the more content-based instruction there is, the better the results (more-content-is-better hypothesis).

After looking at the data in the overall written task and the results by grade/age, our second hypothesis can be partially borne out. Our results confirm that there is a positive relationship between the amount of content-based instruction and the written production outcomes. Apart from the differences between non-CLIL and CLIL groups, both CLIL groups also present differences depending on the amount of content, with better results as content instruction increases. Despite these results, we still find that in the 3rd year of secondary education there are no significant differences between CLIL1 and CLIL2 groups. This fact may be due to the small difference in the number of hours between both CLIL programmes, which do not allow for differences to emerge, as previous research has already proposed (Ruiz de Zarobe 2007).

This finding bears directly on another issue that is often mentioned in relation to content-based instruction. It could be argued that the positive results on CLIL that this study and others (see Ruiz de Zarobe & Jiménez Catalán 2009 for a review of some of them) present are so by virtue of the CLIL approach having quite often more hours of exposure through the target language. It is true that in CLIL programmes the traditional English as a foreign language (EFL) lessons and CLIL instruction are linked together, which implies a higher exposure to the target language. However, this is one of the benefits of the CLIL approach, that is, the possibility it offers of increasing the number of hours of exposure to the target language in the curriculum which, linked to other factors such as quality of teaching and timing is conducive to language acquisition. In other words, if we learn a language by being exposed to it with a reasonable degree of intensity (Ellis 1984; Doughty & Long 2003), we may assume that an increase in the number of hours over the same period of time would also lead to more advanced levels of performance, which is one of the goals pursued via CLIL.

In view of these facts we could also compare the results provided by non-CLIL and CLIL students with a similar number of hours of instruction, but with a different educational approach: the former would basically have EFL instruction while the latter would have EFL plus content-based instruction.

If we look at Table 1 again, we see how the non-CLIL group in the pre-university grade and the CLIL2 group in the 3rd year of secondary education have similar, although not identical, hours of exposure to English, 990 and 910 respectively.

	Secondary 3	Secondary 4	Pre-university (Baccalaureate)
Number of students	Non-CLIL: 29 CLIL1: 24 CLIL2: 36	Non-CLIL: 18 CLIL1: 16 CLIL2: 17	Non-CLIL: 7 CLIL1: XXX CLIL2: 14
Age during data collection	14–15	15–16	17–18
Hours of instruction	Non-CLIL: 695 CLIL1: 875 **CLIL2: 910**	Non-CLIL: 792 CLIL1: 1120 CLIL2: 1155	**Non-CLIL: 990** CLIL1: XXX CLIL2: 1453

The results in the five scales of the written production task are presented in Table 2.

Table 2. Written production outcomes in CLIL and non-CLIL with similar exposure to English

	Secondary 3 CLIL 2	Pre-university non-CLIL
Content	24.4	22.1
Organisation	15.7	14.4
Vocabulary	15.6	14.7
Language	18.1	17.9
Mechanics	3.9	3.6

As can be observed, the CLIL group outstrips the non-CLIL group in each of the five scales of the writing test. CLIL students reach higher levels of written competence, despite the difference in hours of exposure (80 hours in a three-year span) and the age difference (the CLIL group is three years younger). Thus, we can conclude that CLIL offers a more effective approach to language learning, irrespective of the number of hours or the amount of content involved. However, it is necessary to take these results with caution, as the sample for this longitudinal evaluation is too small, although other research in the field (see, for example, Navés 2010) also seems to provide support for these conclusions.

According to our third hypothesis, the CLIL approach would provide better longitudinal results than the non-CLIL traditional approach:

The participants on the CLIL programmes will obtain better results than the ones on the non-CLIL programme in the longitudinal evaluation of the results.

The longitudinal evaluation of the results shows that the differences between programmes increase with grade and age. If in the 4th year of secondary education we find statistical differences between non-CLIL and CLIL in three of the five scales: vocabulary, language usage and mechanics, two years later (Baccalaureate) these differences are significant in the five scales analysed: content, organisation, vocabulary, language usage and mechanics. Furthermore, the non-parametric Friedman test for correlated values indicates that there is a positive relationship between grade and linguistic outcomes with significantly better results in higher grades. It needs to be pointed out that for the longitudinal evaluation of the study, the same students have been followed through the different levels. However, we have included some other students who were in the same group along the grades to obtain a statistically significant number. Despite this consideration, we can see how the number of learners has progressively fallen with respect to the number of the first group.

These results serve as new evidence on the longitudinal effects of CLIL and support some previous research (Alonso, Grisaleña & Campo 2008) that to my knowledge is still very limited. In their study, Alonso et al. analysed trilingual education in Secondary Education in the Basque Country. Their results showed how the CLIL group (the experimental group) surpassed the non-CLIL group (the control group) in the skills measured in the Cambridge ESOL exam. Furthermore, after two years the CLIL group obtained better results in all the tests, improving their linguistic competence and rate of learning with respect to the control group. Our results also show that in the three educational programmes once again the CLIL groups perform more accurately than their non-CLIL counterpart, and their gains are substantial in the longitudinal evaluation of the results. Thus, it can be concluded that CLIL results improve with grade, outstripping the non-CLIL counterpart in written language competence longitudinally.

7. Conclusions

The aim of this study has been to compare the written production outcomes in two groups following two different educational programmes: CLIL (CLIL1 and CLIL2) versus non-CLIL. Our results reveal that the former score higher than the latter in the five categories that make up the written production test (content, vocabulary, organization, language usage and mechanics) with significant differences in two of these scales, content and vocabulary. These findings are in contrast to results obtained in previous research in relation to oral competence, where there were statistically significant differences in all the scales under analysis. This leads us to conclude that there is an advantage in learning in the CLIL context, when there is an increased opportunity for learners to develop their communicative abilities in the foreign language, but this advantage is higher in oral productive competence than in written competence, where deficiencies both in CLIL and non-CLIL classrooms are found. In view of such observations, it is clear that at a more general didactic level, literacy in the mother tongue and the foreign language are to be taught in parallel, with teachers cooperating to pace L1 and L2 instruction accordingly.

Our results also confirm that there is a positive relationship between the amount of exposure to English and the linguistic outcomes. This suggests that students with more exposure to English achieve higher levels of proficiency on the written production task than students with less exposure to English, provided they receive sufficient exposure to the target language. Furthermore, when the number of hours is held constant in both groups the CLIL group reaches a higher level of written competence even though they are three years younger than the non-CLIL group. In other words, the written outcomes of younger learners in CLIL surpass those of older learners who have followed a traditional EFL methodology, which leads us to conclude that under CLIL the rate of acquisition is faster.

Finally, as regards the longitudinal evaluation of the results, the CLIL groups outscore the non-CLIL group in the different grades, with significantly better results in higher grades, suggesting once again that there is a positive relationship between grade, linguistic outcomes and the educational programme.

In sum, we can conclude that CLIL programmes offer the possibility of a more intensive exposure to the target language in the school curriculum and lead to foreign language learning faster and better than more traditional educational models as regards written production, which is one of the goals of the CLIL approach. Although further empirically driven research is necessary to confirm the benefits of the CLIL approach in different linguistic domains, this study serves as evidence that CLIL can be more effective than traditional language teaching in promoting proficiency in the foreign language.

Acknowledgement

The author acknowledges support of the grants HUM2006-09775-C02-01/FILO and FFI2009-10264 awarded by the Spanish Ministry of Education and Science, and the grant IT-202-07 awarded by the Department of Education, University and Research of the Basque Government.

References

Ackerl, C. 2007. Lexico-grammar in the essays of CLIL and non-CLIL students: Error analysis of written production. In *VIEWS. Vienna English Working Papers* 16: 6–11. (Special Issue: *Current Research on CLIL 2*).

Agustín Llach, M.P. 2009. The role of Spanish L1 in the vocabulary use of CLIL and non-CLIL EFL learners. In *Content and Language Integrated Learning: Evidence from Research in Europe,* Y. Ruiz de Zarobe & R.R. Miller (eds), 112–129. Clevedon: Multilingual Matters.

Agustín Llach, M.P. & Jiménez Catalán, R.M. 2007. Lexical reiteration in EFL young learners' essays: Does it relate to the type of instruction? *International Journal of English Studies* 7(2): 85–103.

Alonso, E., Grisaleña, J. & Campo, A. 2008. Plurilingual education in secondary education: Analysis of results. *International CLIL Research Journal* 1(1): 36–49.

Brumfit, C.J. & Johnson, K. (eds). 1979. *The Communicative Approach to Language Teaching.* Oxford: OUP.

Celaya, M.L. 2007. 'I study *natus* in English': Lexical transfer in CLIL and regular learners. Paper presented at the AESLA Conference, Murcia, Spain, 19–21 April 2007.

Celaya, M.L & Ruiz de Zarobe, Y. 2008. CLIL, age and L1 influence. Paper presented at the Asociación Española de Estudios Anglonorteamericanos (AEDEAN), Palma de Mallorca 13–15 November, 2008.

Cenoz, J. 1991. *Enseñanza-Aprendizaje del Inglés como L2 o L3*. Donostia: Universidad del País Vasco/Euskal Herriko Unibertsitea.

Cummins, J. & Swain, M. 1986. *Bilingualism in Education: Aspects of Theory, Research and Practice*. London: Longman.

Dalton-Puffer, C. 2008. Outcomes and processes in Content and Language Integrated Learning (CLIL): Current research from Europe. In *Future Perspectives for English Language Teaching*, W. Delanoy & L. Volkmann (eds), 139–157. Heidelberg: Carl Winter.

Dalton-Puffer, C., Hüttner, J., Schindelegger, V. & Smit, U. 2009. Technology-geeks speak out: What students think about vocational CLIL. *International CLIL Research Journal* 1(2): 17–25.

Doughty, C. & Long, M. 2003. *A Handbook of Second Language Acquisition*. Oxford: Blackwell.

Ellis, R. 1984. *Classroom Second Language Development*. Oxford: Blackwell.

Ellis, R. 2001. *Form-focused Instruction and Second Language Learning*. Malden MA: Blackwell.

Gallardo del Puerto, F., Gómez Lacabex, E. & García Lecumberri, M.L. 2009. Testing the effectiveness of Content and Language Integrated Learning in foreign language contexts: The assessment of English pronunciation. In *Content and Language Integrated Learning: Evidence from Research in Europe*, Y. Ruiz de Zarobe & R.R. Miller (eds), 63–80. Clevedon: Multilingual Matters.

García Mayo, P. & García Lecumberri, M.L. (eds). 2003. *Age and the Acquisition of English as a Third Language*. Clevedon: Multilingual Matters.

Genesee, F. 1987. *Learning through Two Languages: Studies of Immersion and Bilingual Education*. Rowley MA: Newbury House.

Genesee, F. & Jared, D. 2008. Literacy development in early French immersion programs. *Canadian Psychology* 49(2): 140–147.

Hughes, A. 1989. *Testing for Language Teachers*. Cambridge: CUP.

Jacobs, J.L., Zinkgraf, S.A., Wormuth, D.R., Hartfield,V.F. & Hughey, J.B. 1981. *Testing ESL Compositions*. Newbury MA: Rowley.

Jiménez Catalán, R.M., Ruiz de Zarobe, Y. & Cenoz, J. 2006. Vocabulary profiles of English foreign language learners in English as a subject and as a vehicular language. In *VIEWS. Vienna English Working Papers* 15(3). (Special Issue: *Current Research on CLIL 1*).

Jiménez Catalán, R.M. & Ruiz de Zarobe, Y. 2009. The receptive vocabulary of EFL learners in two instructional contexts: CLIL vs. non-CLIL. In *Content and Language Integrated Learning: Evidence from Research in Europe*, Y. Ruiz de Zarobe & R.R. Miller (eds), 81–92. Clevedon: Multilingual Matters.

Lasagabaster, D. 2008. Foreign language competence in Content and Language Integrated Learning. *The Open Applied Linguistics Journal* 1: 31–42.

Llinares, A. & Whittaker, R. 2006. The written language produced by Spanish learners of geography and history in two types of CLIL contexts. In *VIEWS. Vienna English Working Papers* 15(3). (Special Issue: *Current Research on CLIL 1*).

Marsh, D., Maljers, A. & Hartiala, A.K. 2001. *Profiling European CLIL Classrooms. Languages Open Doors*. Jyväskylä: University of Jyväskylä and European Platform of Dutch Education.

Martínez Adrián, M. & Gutiérrez Mangado, M.J. 2009. The acquisition of English syntax by CLIL learners in the Basque country. In *Content and Language Integrated Learning: Evidence from Research in Europe*, Y. Ruiz de Zarobe & R.R. Miller (eds), 176–196. Clevedon: Multilingual Matters.

Moreno, S. 2009. Young learners' L2 word association responses in two different learning contexts. In *Content and Language Integrated Learning: Evidence from Research in Europe*, Y. Ruiz de Zarobe & R.R. Miller (eds), 93–111. Clevedon: Multilingual Matters.

Muñoz, C. (ed.). 2006. *Age and Foreign Language Learning Rate*. Clevedon: Multilingual Matters.

Naiman, N. 1995. *The Good Language Learner*. Clevedon: Multilingual Matters.

Navés, T. 2010. How promising are the results of integrating content and language for EFL writing and overall EFL proficiency? In *Content and Foreign Language Integrated Learning: Contributions to Multilingualism in European Contexts*, Y. Ruiz de Zarobe, J.M. Sierra & F. Gallardo del Puerto (eds). Bern: Peter Lang.

Navés, T., Miralpeix, I. & Celaya, M.L. 2005. Who transfers more… and what? Cross-linguistic influence in relation to school grade and language dominance in EFL. *International Journal of Multilingualism* 2(2): 113–134.

Ruiz de Zarobe, Y. 2003. Instruction and age in the acquisition of negation in English as a third language. *Linguistica Atlantica* 24: 1001–1017.

Ruiz de Zarobe, Y. 2005. Age and third language production: A longitudinal study. *International Journal of Multilingualism* 2(2): 105–113.

Ruiz de Zarobe, Y. 2007. CLIL in a bilingual community: Similarities and differences with the learning of English as a Foreign Language. In *VIEWS. Vienna English Working Papers* 16(3): 47–53. (Special Issue: *Current Research on CLIL 2*).

Ruiz de Zarobe, Y. 2008. CLIL and foreign language learning: A longitudinal study in the Basque country. *International CLIL Research Journal* 1(1): 60–73.

Ruiz de Zarobe, Y. & Jiménez Catalán, R.M. 2009. *Content and Language Integrated Learning: Evidence from Research in Europe*. Clevedon: Multilingual Matters.

Swain, M. & Lapkin, S. 1995. Problems in output and the cognitive processes they generate. A step towards second language learning. *Applied Linguistics* 16: 371–391.

Sylvén, L.K. 2006. Extramural exposure to English among Swedish school students and the CLIL classroom. Paper presented at the ESSE8 Conference in London, 29 August 2006.

Villarreal, I. & García Mayo, M.P. 2009. Tense and agreement morphology in the interlanguage of Basque/Spanish bilinguals: CLIL versus non-CLIL. In *Content and Language Integrated Learning: Evidence from Research in Europe*, Y. Ruiz de Zarobe & HR.M. Jiménez Catalán (eds), 176–196. Clevedon: Multilingual Matters.

Vollmer, H.J., Heine, L., Troschke, R., Coetzee, D. & Küttel, V. 2006. Subject-specific competence and language use of CLIL learners: The case of geography in grade 10 of secondary schools in Germany. Paper presented at the ESSE8 Conference in London, 29 August 2006.

PART III

CLIL at the tertiary level

Metadiscursive devices in university lectures

A contrastive analysis of L1 and L2 teacher performance

Emma Dafouz Milne & Begoña Núñez Perucha
Universidad Complutense de Madrid, Spain

Drawing on Systemic Functional Linguistics, and especially, on the notions of genre (Martin 1985; Eggins 1994) and phase (Young 1990, 1994), the present paper pursues a two-fold objective: (i) to identify the type, function and linguistic realisation of the metadiscursive devices (MDs) used in the organisation of lectures; and (ii) to account for similarities and differences between the L1 and L2 and assess their implications for teacher training. The contrastive analysis of six lectures given by the same speakers in Spanish (L1) and English (L2) reveals differences regarding the types and realisations of MDs. Specifically, the Spanish data show more explicit signalling, a wider variety of stylistic choices, and a higher use of interaction devices and conclusion markers. These findings point to the need for precise language objectives (e.g. explicit focus on the role of MDs) in CLIL teacher education in university contexts.

1. Introduction

1.1 Aims and scope

In the internationalisation process that higher education is undergoing worldwide, the use of foreign languages, and more specifically English, as a means of instruction plays a vital role. Although learning through a foreign language (FL) in tertiary settings is hardly a new experience (see de Rydder-Symoens 1996; Wilkinson 2004), what is novel is the wide scale that this phenomenon has acquired. In the case of Spanish universities, three types of pro-CLIL stages can be identified.[1] The first type originated in the 1980s, when mainly private universities implemented

---

1. The term pro-CLIL is used here to refer to teachers' positive stance towards the use of a FL (mainly English) to teach content in tertiary contexts. Strictly speaking, in these CLIL practices the focus lies almost exclusively on content matters, rather than on the integration of content and language, as would be expected in "an ideal CLIL context".

international degrees for national students. These international courses offered a combination of studies in the home country and universities abroad, with a chance for immersion in the FL. The second type, already in 2000, involved teachers who individually decided to teach through English as a means to open up career opportunities and favour mobility. This initiative usually stemmed from teachers who had prior experiences abroad together with a high command of the FL and who were usually engaged in postgraduate courses. Finally, the third type currently in-progress refers to the official programmes, known as "bilingual" or "multilingual" degrees, offered by a number of public universities (see Lasagabaster 2008a; Fortanet 2008), and involves over thirty universities (i.e. approximately 50% of the official universities in Spain). These new undergraduate degrees normally cover the syllabi entirely through English, evaluate in the FL and issue a specific "bilingual/multilingual" certificate.

In general terms, these programmes pay scant attention to teacher education, especially as regards language teaching competences. In most cases, as observed in several institutions and reported in teachers' questionnaires and semi-structured interviews (see Dafouz et al. 2007; Dafouz & Núñez 2009), classes are indeed taught through English but lecturers usually receive little or no specific training in the linguistic (and methodological) characteristics of this new scenario. It is within this context that our research project aims to shed some light on the language used in university classrooms, with special reference to the language of lectures. In line with Lasagabaster, we believe that "observation of the teachers involved in CLIL programmes should occupy a leading position on the list of researchers' priorities" (Lasagabaster 2008b: 40).

Adopting a Systemic Functional approach and drawing on the notion of genre (Eggins 1994; Martin 1985), the present paper focuses on the contrastive analysis of the organisational and linguistic features of lectures.[2] Specifically, this study pursues a two-fold objective: (1) to identify the categories and functions of metadiscursive devices (hereinafter MDs) used by teachers in the organisation of lectures in Spanish (L1) and English (L2), and (2) to account for similarities and differences in the use of these MDs, which, hopefully, will provide useful guidelines for the development of a functional-metalinguistic repertoire for CLIL university educators.

In our opinion, this study may be of importance in the CLIL environment for two main reasons. Firstly, it describes in a contrastive fashion the linguistic and

---

2. This study is part of a larger project entitled Content and Language in University Education (CLUE at www.clue-project.es), which has been operating since 2007 and is principally based at the Universidad Complutense of Madrid (REF. GR58/08).

functional choices that non-native lecturers make in the delivery of content in their L1 and L2. Secondly, it raises awareness among university authorities, teachers and educational planners of some of the specific language needs that the tertiary level demands for a truly successful implementation of CLIL.

1.2   The data: Collection and description

The data presented here comprises six university lectures (about 46,000 words), delivered by the same teachers in English and Spanish. The lecturers, two males and one female, are native speakers of Spanish and permanent teachers in the Faculty of Aeronautical Engineering (*Universidad Politécnica de Madrid-UPM*). The three instructors are content experts with specialised knowledge of a specific area in Aeronautical Engineering and a high command of the technical language that the field demands. Their level of English ranges from intermediate to high intermediate (as self-reported in a questionnaire distributed prior to recording), and their earlier experience in teaching through a FL also varies, with only one teacher having previous practice in the use of English as the language of instruction.

The lectures delivered in English were part of a summer course on *Formula One Engines* that took place in July 2006. Twenty-six international students from the BEST programme (Board of European Students of Technology) attended this course. The lectures given in Spanish were part of the official degree in Aeronautical Engineering and were recorded between March & May 2008. These classes held on average 60 students per group, all native speakers of Spanish. An attempt was made to select those lectures whose topics were similar (i.e. metallic materials in engines, aerodynamic engineering and composite materials). These sessions were recorded in naturalistic conditions and cover sixty minute sessions. Both sets of lectures were simultaneously video- and audio-taped, so that the visual support enabled us to understand better the classroom dynamics (e.g. teachers' position and actions).

2.   Lectures from the perspective of systemic functional linguistics and genre theory

An approach that can shed light on the organisational features of lectures and the way they are linguistically signalled is Systemic Functional Linguistics (SFL), and, in particular, genre analysis. Broadly speaking, SFL "seeks to explain the nature of language by examining the ways in which it is used to transmit experiences, feelings and attitudes, because it views language as part of a social system" (Halliday in Young 1990: 3). In a functional approach the fundamental concern is to reveal the instrumentality of language in terms of what speakers/writers do with it in different social situations. In other words, speakers make linguistic choices according to the context of situation (cf. Halliday 1978). In the classroom context SFL emphasises the role of language in mediating the *construction* of knowledge, rather than in the pure transmission of it.

Adopting a SFL approach entails investigating how language is used and how it is structured for use (Eggins 1994: 25). Within SFL these two questions are examined through the concept of genre, understood as a goal-oriented purposeful activity organised into different stages leading to the achievement of that purpose (Martin 1985; Eggins, 1994 *inter alia*). In general, the task of the genre analyst is to "reveal something of the patterns of organization of 'genre' and the language used to express those patterns" (Dudley-Evans 1987: 1). In this sense, SFL places emphasis on the notion of language choices through which the boundaries between the different stages and the function of each stage are expressed.

2.1   Lectures as an educational genre: A functional view

SFL and genre analysis regard lectures as a type of educational genre (Eggins 1994: 27) and their interest has been mainly in the organizational features and in the role of discourse markers in lecture comprehension.[3] As far as structural patterns are concerned, within the SFL framework, Young (1994) carried out a functional analysis of lectures in terms of phases. From a genre perspective, phases can be interpreted as the different stages into which the activity of lecturing (i.e. lecturing event) is divided. In particular, as defined by Young (1994: 165) phases are "strands of discourse that recur discontinuously throughout a particular language event, and, taken together, structure the event". Phases encompass register choices in a specific discourse and are characterised by a high degree of consistency in meta-functional selections, which means that process types and associated participant roles have to be the same throughout occurrences of the phase and in the morpho-syntactic choices made (Young 1990: 42–47).

Young (1990, 1994) analysed the macro-structure of university lectures and identified six types of phases, arranged into two broad categories: metadiscoursal phases (which comment on the discourse itself) and non-metadiscoursal phases (which are loosely described as connected to the ideational content). Among

---

3.   From a different perspective, other studies have focused on the features of good lecturing skills (Leech & Svartvik 1975), on types of lecturing styles (Dudley-Evans & Johns 1981; Saroyan & Snell 1997), and on the correlation between lecturing styles and discourse comprehension (Dudley-Evans 1994; Flowerdew 1994; Crawford Camiciottoli 2005).

the metadiscoursal phases are the *Discourse Structuring phase*, in which the speaker announces the different directions of the lecture; the *Conclusion phase*, where the speaker summarises the main points covered in the lecture; and the *Evaluation phase*, in which the lecturer evaluates the information presented. Non-metadiscoursal phases also include three types: *Interaction phase*, which refers to the interpersonal strategies the lecturer implements to establish contact with the students and to ensure comprehensibility; *Theory or Content phase*, in which concepts, models and definitions of the subject are presented; and *Exemplification phase*, where lecturers illustrate theoretical concepts through concrete and practical examples. Young shows that these phases are characterised by the presence of certain linguistic devices: for instance, the Discourse Structuring phase tends to include markers such as "first", "another point", while in the Evaluation phase expressions such as "more importantly" or "it is interesting to notice that" are used (Young 1994: 166–172).

These devices have proved to be decisive in the successful delivery of lectures as well as in their accurate comprehension, both in a L1 and a L2 context. For example, Chaudron and Richards (1986) investigated the effect of discourse markers on the L2 comprehension of lectures and found that students recalled better lectures that contained mainly macro-markers, that is, "explicit expressions of the planning of the lecture information" (1986: 123) rather than those that combined both macro and micro-markers (that is, cohesive expressions at a lower level of information). Chaudron and Richards conclude that while the former are essential to follow main concepts and primary information, the latter are responsible for secondary levels of information. Inspired by this study, Aguilar Pérez and Arnó Maciá (2002) focused on the role of certain discourse markers (which they referred to as metadiscourse) in lectures addressed to a Spanish student audience. By metadiscourse these authors refer loosely to "any means the speaker uses to shape discourse or to express his attitude" (2002: 8). Their analysis indicates that metadiscourse appears to be more helpful for students with lower language skills than for proficient students, since explicit use of organisational markers helps lighten the cognitive load while concurrently activating the "existing schemata" (see Anderson 1977).

The importance of metadiscourse in lecture production and comprehension was also highlighted by our lecturers and their students in the interviews that we recorded. Without using the technical term "metadiscourse", teachers nevertheless agreed that lecturing in a FL demanded better organisational skills and a clearer structure than lecturing in one's L1:

> When I am teaching <u>in Spanish</u> I <u>only need to have the basic structure</u> because you have many resources, and if a new idea comes you can start talking about it (…) <u>In English</u> you cannot allow yourself to do that <u>unless you have the lesson</u>

<u>much better prepared, otherwise you get lost</u> (…) and there is always some
word that you miss and you try to remember and you never remember on time.
(Lecturer 2 interview, July 2006 – emphasis added)

Similarly, students revealed that they felt both frustrated and lost when unable to
follow lecture ideas clearly. They also perceived teachers who generally did not use
explicit organising markers as disorganised and, even as "less credible and reliable".

In sum, from the above observations it follows that good lecturers tend to structure their sessions in a clear way and to include a variety of metadiscourse items to
signal the different parts. In fact, it can be argued that metadiscourse allows for the
identification of the different phases in a lecture. From a genre-perspective, these
MDs can be said to represent the boundary features used by lecturers to move from
one phase to the other and to explicitly signal this change of move to the listeners.
Indeed, explicitness is a key feature of metadiscourse since it represents the writer/
speaker's overt attempt to create a particular discursive effect.

2.2   A metadiscourse taxonomy for lecture analysis

Before moving onto the classification of metadiscourse categories and functions, it
should be noted that the present analysis offers a revision of the phasal categories
originally proposed by Young (1994), as shown in Table 1.

Table 1. Comparison of phasal categories for the analysis of lecturing discourse

Young (1994)	Dafouz Milne and Núñez Perucha (2010)
Metadiscoursal	**Metadiscoursal**
Discourse Structuring	Discourse Structuring
Conclusion	Conclusion
Evaluation	**Interaction**
Non-Metadiscoursal	**Discoursal**
Interaction	**Evaluation**
Content	Content
Exemplification	Exemplification

As can be seen from the above table, our model adopts the term Discoursal
phase in place of Young's Non-metadiscoursal phase. This decision was mainly
motivated by the following reasons: Young's (1994: 166) definition of metadiscoursal phases as "strands which comment on the discourse itself" does not seem
to account for the well-established view of metadiscourse as involving interpersonal markers (cf. Crismore, Markannen & Steffensen 1993; Dafouz 2003, 2008;
Hyland 1998, 2005; Vande Kopple 1985 *inter alia*). According to Hyland (2005: 37)

metadiscourse represents the umbrella term for "the self-reflective expressions used to negotiate interactional meanings in a text, assist the writer (or speaker) to express a viewpoint and engage with readers [or listeners] as members of a particular community". On this basis, the Interaction phase (placed in the non-metadiscousral level in Young 1994) would fit better in the metadiscoursal plane, since it fulfils an interpersonal function.

Another difference concerns the classification of the Evaluation phase. It seems that in the lecturing event, evaluative devices tend to comment on the importance and relevance of the propositional material they accompany. That is, evaluation tends to be subordinated to the expression of content, and as such, should also be placed within the discoursal level.

It follows then that the study of metadiscourse in lecturing should account for those linguistic devices that are used to signal each of the metadiscoursal phases, namely, the Discourse Structuring phase ⟨DS⟩, the Interaction phase ⟨INT⟩ and the Conclusion phase ⟨C⟩. As metadiscourse studies have mostly focused on written texts (with counted exceptions such as the aforementioned Chaudron & Richards 1986; and Aguilar Pérez & Arnó Macià 2002), our study seeks to elaborate a metadiscourse classification that could be applied to spoken data. This classification of metadiscourse draws on two different sources: The first one is the deeply rooted and extensively used functional distinction between textual and interpersonal metadiscourse markers.[4] Textual markers refer to the organisational devices that hold the discourse together and make it reader/listener-friendly, while interpersonal markers reflect the writer/speaker stance towards both the propositional content and the potential addressee.[5] The second source for classification is the relationship and interdependence between macro-elements (phases) and the micro-linguistic devices used to signal a particular phase (i.e. metadiscursive devices or MDs). In this sense, we introduce a more refined level of analysis where each of the metadiscourse phases mentioned above is realised by a number of metadiscourse devices. The resulting taxonomy stemmed from the adaption of other existing classifications applied specifically to written texts (see for example Crismore, Markannen & Steffensen 1993; Dafouz 2003, 2008; Hyland 1998, 2005; Mauranen 1993; Vande Kopple 1985), and from some earlier data-driven analysis (Núñez Perucha & Dafouz Milne 2007) which dealt with lecture discourse.

---

4. See Hyland (2005) for a comprehensive summary of the notion of metadiscourse and its functions in a range of different types of text.

5. Some authors (see Hyland 2005, Hyland & Tse 2004) have put forth a stronger interpersonal view of metadiscourse advocating that all MDs are essentially interpersonal, since they take into account the reader/listener's knowledge, textual experiences and processing needs.

Table 2 displays our proposal of the types of metadiscourse categories identified for each phase:

Table 2. Phase analysis and its relation to metadiscourse categories and functions (Dafouz Milne & Núñez Perucha 2010)

Phases	Metadiscourse Category	Function of metadiscursive devices	Examples
Discourse structuring phase ⟨DS⟩	Openers	Signal the formal beginning of a class	*Today, we are going to talk...*
	Sequencers	Mark particular positions within a series	*First, then, next...*
	Topicalisers	Indicate introduction of new topics/topic shifts	*Another concept; what are F1 cars made of?*
	Prospective markers	Refer forwards to future topics/sections in the lecture/other lectures	*We will see later...*
	Retrospective markers	Refer backwards to previous topics/sections in the lecture/other lectures	*As I mentioned before...*
Interaction phase ⟨INT⟩	Questions	Requesting student participation/checking comprehension	*Who can answer this?*
	Commentaries (help to establish speaker/listener rapport)	Direct address to the audience/Inclusive expressions	*Remember; you know well...We all know; it is our decision ...*
	Apologetic comments	Apologise for some lack/deficiency	*I have to apologise for; sorry...*
	Contextual comments	Comment on situational features or aspects outside the actual content of the lesson.	*We are going to be recorded today; Is it too hot [in the classroom]?*
Conclusion phase ⟨C⟩	Closing markers	Indicate the formal closing of the lecture	*I will finish here*
	Recapitulation markers	Summarise the main ideas in the lecture	*Today we saw...*
	Prospective markers	Refer forwards to future topics to be dealt with in other lectures (placed towards the end of the lecture)	*Tomorrow we will cover...*
	Retrospective markers	Refer backwards to the previous topics/sections of the lecture (placed towards the end of the lecture)	*What we learned today was...*

3. Findings and discussion: Lecture performance in Spanish (L1) and English (L2)

This section examines the different subcategories of MDs that realise each of the aforementioned phases in both sets of data in order to account for similarities and differences in the lecturers' discourse in L1 and L2. In doing so, it refines and expands Núñez Perucha and Dafouz Milne's (2007) work, which focused primarily on the main phases of lecturing discourse in L2. By and large, Table 3 below yields the total findings:

Table 3. Number of phases in lecturers' discourse in L1 and L2

		Lect. 1	Lect. 2	Lect. 3	TOTALS (*n*)
DISCOURSE STRUCTURING	L1 (Spanish)	43	23	30	96
⟨DS⟩	L2 (English)	21	27	35	83
INTERACTION	L1 (Spanish)	21	5	42	68
⟨INT⟩	L2 (English)	10	22	15	47
CONCLUSION	L1 (Spanish)	4	11	9	24
⟨C⟩	L2 (English)	1	11	2	14

At a global level, as shown by Table 3, the three lecturers use more meta-discursive devices when delivering content in L1. Although in both sets of data discourse structure markers outnumber interaction and conclusion markers, differences emerge regarding the frequency of interaction and conclusion markers in L1 and L2. The following subsections analyse the specific types of meta-discursive devices used by the lecturers in each phase and try to account for possible reasons that may explain the similarities and differences found in the use of these markers.

3.1 Discourse structure markers

As mentioned above, the contrastive analysis shows that the Discourse Structuring phase (⟨DS⟩) is the most frequently used. The types of markers used in this particular phase are roughly similar in L1 and L2, except for the higher use of retrospective markers in Spanish.

Table 4. Discourse structuring MDs in lecturers' discourse in L1 and L2

⟨DS⟩		Lect. 1	Lect. 2	Lect. 3	TOTALS (*n*)
Openers ⟨DS-O⟩	L1 (Spanish)	1	1	1	3
	L2 (English)	1	1	1	3
Sequencers ⟨DS-S⟩	L1 (Spanish)	0	5	8	13
	L2 (English)	4	8	5	17
Topicalisers ⟨DS-T⟩	L1 (Spanish)	28	14	10	52
	L2 (English)	11	12	23	46
Prospectives ⟨DS-P⟩	L1 (Spanish)	9	2	5	16
	L2 (English)	1	5	5	11
Retrospectives ⟨DS-R⟩	L1 (Spanish)	5	1	6	12
	L2 (English)	4	1	1	6

Regarding some of the ⟨DS⟩ subtypes used, *openers* ⟨DS-O⟩ and *sequencers* ⟨DS-S⟩ appear to have the same form and functions in the English and Spanish corpora. In other words, *openers* initiate formally the beginning of the class and state the content objectives:

(1)   ⟨DS-O⟩ **Good morning,** (…) what **we will do during this day will** be first, we **will… look into the requirement for the structural design,** eh (…) for about twenty minutes… (…) to have a basic knowledge about Composite Materials. ⟨DS-O⟩ (L2).

(2)   ⟨DS-O⟩ Bueno, buenos días. **Empezamos** con la clase de hoy.
[*Well, good morning.* ***We start*** *with today's class*] ⟨DS-O⟩ (L3).

As for *sequencers*, a wide range of realisations is used to mark particular positions within a series when delivering content. In both corpora, typical devices are temporal markers, such as "primero" (*first*) and "por último" (*finally*), and noun phrases containing determinatives indicating order (e.g. "lo primero" (*the first thing*), "la siguiente idea" (*the next idea*). In Example (3) the order expressed by the *sequencer* is reinforced by means of the determinative "first" within a noun phrase functioning as a *topicaliser* device ("primer requisito funcional", *first functional requirement*). This case illustrates what we call a "metadiscursive chain", that is, a series of metadiscursive devices co-occurring within the same stretch of discourse. Such a mechanism seems to be a recurrent pattern in lecturing discourse.

(3)   ⟨DS-S⟩ Entonces **la primera idea** de diseño es, o **primera, primer requisito funcional** (*escribe en la pizarra*). [*Then,* ***the first idea*** *for designing is, or the first thing, the first functional requirement …(writes on blackboard)*] ⟨DS-S⟩ (L1).

(4)   ⟨DS-T⟩ What are the properties that we need in material … for an F1 car?)
       ⟨DS-T⟩ ⟨DS-S⟩ **The first one**, this material has to be light enough to allow for
       an optimum distribution ⟨DS-S⟩ ; ⟨DS-S⟩ **the second**, is that they must be able
       to cope with not just heat but also the colossal forces, very very high forces
       (…)⟨DS-S⟩. And ⟨DS-S⟩ **the third one** is that the car *completes* all the FIA
       safety standards. ⟨DS-S⟩ (L3).

Regarding *topicalisers* ⟨DS-T⟩, two recursive linguistic realisations can be distinguished in both sets of data: (i) presentative devices mostly under the form "we
have" (see (5) and (6)), and (ii) noun phrases functioning as a sort of heading that
encapsulates the main focus of the explanation (i.e. the topic), as in Examples (7)
and (8).

(5)   ⟨DS-T⟩ **Then we have** two other efficiencies: the volumetric efficiency and the
       mechanical efficiency ⟨DS-T⟩ (L1).

(6)   ⟨DS-T⟩ **Y lo que tenéis** son estas 3 opciones, bueno 4 ⟨DS-T⟩ [*And what you
       have here are these 3 options, well, 4]* (L1).

(7)   ⟨DS-T⟩ **The pistons.** Here **we have** the pistons of a V8 engine ⟨DS-T⟩ (L3).

(8)   ⟨DS-T⟩ **Fuel.** ⟨DS-T⟩ To obtain the fuel that you are giving to the engine you
       have to multiply by the efficiencies of the rest of the processes that we have. ;
       ⟨DS-S⟩The first one, for example, is the efficiency of the combustion ; ⟨DS-S⟩
       (…); ⟨DS-S⟩ Then we have to put here the thermal efficiency that takes into
       account thermodynamic… thermodynamic efficiency; ⟨DS-S⟩ (…) ;
       ⟨DS-S⟩And we have to calculate **now** the volumetric efficiency ; ⟨DS-S⟩ (L1).

Topicalisers are usually found to follow or precede *sequencers* in a stretch of discourse, as if embedded in a metadiscursive chain. This pattern helps to structure
the main ideas and present them in an orderly fashion to favour comprehension.
In Example (8) above, cardinal markers (*first*) are combined with temporal ones
(*then, now*) to signal smooth transition:
    Another typical device that is used with a *topicaliser* function is the use of
rhetorical questions, either in the usual pattern of question-answer or in the form
question-sequencer-answer. In all instances of our analysis, rhetorical questions are
distinguished from non-rhetorical (or interactional) ones in that there is no pausing for audience response and that it is the teacher himself/herself who answers.

(9)   ⟨DS-T⟩ **What is the main characteristic of the service conditions for
       pistons?** ⟨DS-T⟩ Heat and high pressure. So, we have to choose a material that
       supports high heat and mechanical laws and you should not forget also light
       constructions. (L3).

(10)   ⟨DS-T⟩ Bueno, **¿y hay alguna forma de asumir que el aceite va a llegar pero
       que no se quede en esta parte?** ⟨DS-T⟩ Es la siguiente… la siguiente idea….
       [*Well, **and is there any way of understanding that the oil is going to come but
       that it may not stay in this part?** It is the following…the next idea]*(L1).

Finally, regarding *prospective* and *retrospective* markers, the English corpus exhibits three linguistic realisations: (i) the verbal form "remember" to refer retrospectively to relevant information in the current or in past lectures, as in (11); (ii) the future tense + adverbial "later" to refer to prospective information, as in (12); and (iii), present tense constructions used with a prospective function, as in Example (13). In the latter instance the construction is the result of a direct transfer from the lecturer's L1 (e.g. "pasamos a hablar…" meaning "we move onto…"), which lends support to the role of mother tongue influence in the L2:

(11)   ⟨DS-R⟩ (…) **remember** that we have to use petrol because it is obligate… oblique…obliged by the regulations and for petrol we have a loss of a 2 % only ⟨DS-R⟩ (L1).

(12)   ⟨DS-P⟩ **we will see later**, eh, this advantage, eh, very big advantage is this one, eh, the second, that the manufacture on process allow for very complex shape ⟨DS-P⟩ (L2).

(13)   ⟨DS-P⟩ We left the engine and **we pass to talk** a bit about the chassis ⟨DS-P⟩. What is a chassis? (L3).

In the Spanish data, the future forms, especially "ir a" (*be going to*), and simple future forms are also very common realisations of *prospective* markers. They are mainly used to refer to sections to be covered within the same lecture or topics to be dealt with in another lecture. Example (14) includes different DS markers used within a metadiscursive chain:

(14)   ⟨DS-T⟩ Los precipitados que podemos obtener para reforzar las aleaciones pueden **ser de distintos tipos** ⟨DS-T⟩ ⟨DS-T⟩ **¿Cuál es el más importante?** ⟨DS-T⟩ El gamma-gamma. ⟨DS-P⟩ **Es en el que nos vamos a centrar hoy** ⟨DS-P⟩; ⟨DS-P⟩ **el martes que viene hablaremos** de aleaciones níquel-hierro, ⟨DS-P⟩ [*The precipitates that we can obtain to reinforce the alloys can be of different kinds. Which one is the most important? The gamma-gamma. This is the one we are going to focus on today; next Tuesday we will talk about the nickel-iron alloys*] (L3).

As regards *retrospective* markers, they show more elaborated realisations in the Spanish corpus, where they are mainly represented by manner clauses that refer to a past time, as in "como os comenté el otro día" ("as I mentioned the other day"). As Example (15) illustrates, this type of markers is likely to appear in combination with *prospective* markers (e.g. "como voy a comentar luego en un momento"/*as I will briefly comment later*):

(15)   ⟨DS-R⟩ ¿Este criterio para qué se usa? ⟨DS-R⟩ Este criterio **como os comenté el otro día** ⟨DS-R⟩, se usa para refinar el diseño del timón… ⟨DS-P⟩ como voy a comentar luego un momento ⟨DS-P⟩. [*What is this criterion used for? This criterion, **as I mentioned to you the other day**, is used to refine the design of the steering wheel, as I will briefly comment later*] (L2).

Regarding distribution, ⟨DS⟩ markers are mostly found at the beginning of lectures (with certain concentration in the initial part) but they also appear intermittently throughout the session when the speaker refers prospectively or retrospectively to certain information, or when he/she synthesises main ideas. Differences arise, however, in the degree of specificity in the expressions used to signal a shift within or across phases. More specifically, as regards *topicalisers*, the lecturers in the English data tend to use expressions such as "thing" or "idea", which belong to a set of nouns having generalised reference (see Halliday & Hasan 1976) while in Spanish they seem to show preference for narrower referential items such as *cuestión* ("issue/factor"), *tipo* ("type"), *motivos* ("reasons"), or *criterio* ("criterion"). Presumably, these narrower references would render the expressions more salient and accurate, thus favouring higher levels of lecture comprehension.

(16)   ⟨DS-T⟩ **The following thing** that I am going to do, the engine, the engine has a loss of around a 50%…15 ⟨**DS-T**⟩. (L1).

(17)   ⟨DS-T⟩ **Una segunda cuestión** sería familiarizarnos con las presiones de inflado (…) ⟨DS-T⟩ [*A second issue would be to get familiar with the inflation pressures*] (L2).

Concurrently, within *topicalisers*, lecturers show considerable repetition in the adjectives used to evaluate the new topics introduced both in English and Spanish in detriment of other possible collocations (e.g. essential, crucial, vital, etc), as the examples below show:

(18)   ⟨DS-T⟩ An, eh… **another important thing** was fibres have a diameter typically of ten microns ⟨DS-T⟩. (L2)

(19)   ⟨DS-T⟩ **Another important contribution** of the resin is for compression ⟨DS-T⟩ (L3).

This may support some research findings that hold that lecturers' academic speech is gradually becoming more closely connected to everyday language than to academic prose (see Biber 2006; Crawford Camiciottoli 2005). Also register differences, regarding spoken versus written modes of communication may come into play when using different lexical choices. From a cross-cultural perspective, the study by Bellés (2004), comparing an American corpus of lectures with a British corpus, suggests that the American lecturers prefer a lower level of formality than the British ones, pointing at the same time at a trend towards a more interactive type of lecture discourse in general (see Benson 1994).

3.2   Interaction markers

As far as the Interaction phase ⟨INT⟩ is concerned, MDs fall mainly into three categories: (i) questions (display and referential), typically realised by *wh*-questions, which refer to both previous or current content, or yes/no questions, which tend to address present content; (ii) commentaries containing imperatives to engage listeners or pronominal forms with an inclusive function ("we", "our"), and (iii) comments, either contextual or apologetic.

Table 5. Interaction MDs in lecturers' discourse in L1 and L2

⟨INT⟩		Lect. 1	Lect. 2	Lect. 3	TOTALS (*n*)
Questions ⟨INT-Q⟩	L1 (Spanish)	5	3	28	36
	L2 (English)	6	8	8	22
Commentaries ⟨INT-C⟩	L1 (Spanish)	13	0	10	23
	L2 (English)	2	10	2	14
Apologetic markers ⟨INT-A⟩	L1 (Spanish)	0	1	0	1
	L2 (English)	1	2	3	6
Contextual markers ⟨INT-CT⟩	L1 (Spanish)	3	1	4	8
	L2 (English)	1	2	2	5

Lecturers' questions fulfil two functions: they seek to activate students' thinking skills (as in Examples (20) and (21)), and check comprehension (as in (22)):

(20)   ⟨INT-Q⟩ Then, the situation is good or bad? For the volumetric efficiency? Try to answer. ⟨INT-Q⟩. ⟨INT-Q⟩ What is the good situation, to have a high temperature or a low temperature in the inlet pipes? Some ideas? Any idea about his? *(pause)* ⟨INT-Q⟩ You see something to say about this? (L1).

(21)   ⟨INT-Q⟩ L: ¿Por qué eso no puede ser? Ésa es la pregunta que está en el aire. ¿Alguna idea? (espera 15 segundos) ¿Alguna idea? ⟨INT-Q⟩ (espera 8 segundos) (L1).
       S: XX…XXX (inaudible).
       [*Why can't it be? This is the question that is up in the air. Any idea? (waits 15 seconds) Any idea? (waits 8 seconds).*
       S: *XX…XXX (inaudible)*].

(22)   ⟨INT-Q⟩ Do you understand, **kind of?** ⟨INT-Q⟩ Ok. (L3).

With regard to *comments*, there is a stark contrast in their use and presence in both corpora, with apologetic comments appearing mostly in the English data and contextual comments mainly in the Spanish corpus. *Apologetic comments* ⟨INT-A⟩ refer exclusively to lecturers' limited command of the FL and are common to all three teachers. A plausible explanation for this use of apologetic utterances, always situated at the beginning of the lecture, is linked to the specific teaching context, where all the international students are using English as a lingua franca and the teacher is self-conscious of his/her own level of the FL.

(23) ⟨INT-A⟩ **I must apologise** for my English but I'll try to do my best to… (unfinished sentence) ⟨INT-A⟩. (L3).

(24) ⟨INT-A⟩ Well, **I have to apologise** for my poor English. In fact, I tried to … eh… I stayed for a year in Stanford, I tried to improve it, I took a special lesson they have there for Japanese and Latin people to improve the accent and … what I have is the best I can have ⟨INT-A⟩. (L2).

Contextual comments ⟨INT-C⟩ appear in the Spanish corpus related to three situations: the actual fact of being recorded, the possibility of looking at real materials in the laboratory, and comments/questions about how students feel in the classroom. Example (25) illustrates well teacher-student rapport in the L1 class:

(25) L: ⟨INT-CT⟩ Cualquiera de esos tres casos provoca una inestabilidad de la fase gamma prima. **¿Tenéis mucho calor? ¿Queréis que abra aquí?** ⟨INT-CT⟩
SS: Sí (Pausa, abre la ventana)
L: ⟨INT-CT⟩ **Si tenéis frío me lo decís** ⟨INT-CT⟩. Ya es esto lo suficientemente duro como para que encima tengáis que estar sudando la gota gorda y goteando como los peces.
[L: *Any of these three cases causes instability in the gamma prima phase. Are you hot? Would you like me to open the window?*
SS: Yes (Pauses, L opens the window)
L: If you are cold, just tell me. This is already hard enough for you so as to be here sweating blood and feel dripping wet […]. (L3).

In English, there are fewer examples of *contextual comments*, which can possibly be associated with the lack of familiarity between teacher-students as it was a two-week course. On the other hand, this absence of contextual comments may also be related to teachers feeling more at ease with subject specific language than with interpersonal registers, as personal communications from a number of lecturers interviewed actually reported (see Dafouz & Núñez 2009: 104).

By and large, variation in interaction markers among the three lecturers in this study suggests that the individual lecturing style plays an important role in the use of these MDs. For instance, lecturer 3 uses a very high number of questions to engage students in her session and to check comprehension. By contrast, lecturer 2 uses more questions when lecturing in English than in Spanish (see Table 5). Speculatively, one could argue that the reason for the different use of interactive strategies may be linked to the lecturers' concern with content clarity (given the non-native condition of both speaker and audience) or, alternatively, it could be related to the different nature of the sessions analysed: while the Spanish data are drawn from compulsory regular classes taught within the official degree, the English data come from a non-compulsory summer course which, according to the organisers, aimed to represent an opportunity to bring together academic knowledge and cultural experiences. Whatever the reason, there is some evidence that extra-linguistic factors (such as situational classroom features, student profile or level of familiarity between participants, to mention a few) may have an influence on the interactional devices used during lectures.

3.3   Conclusion markers

As can be seen from Table 6, the Spanish data show a higher use of Conclusion ⟨C⟩ markers, retrospective markers being the most numerous. Such markers, which are absent in the English data, are used at the end of the session to refer back to issues covered in previous topics or parts of the lecture (e.g. "hemos hablado ya de la fase gamma (….)" / *we have already talked about the gamma phase*).

Table 6. Conclusion MDs in lecturers' discourse in L1 and L2

⟨C⟩		Lect. 1	Lect. 2	Lect. 3	TOTALS (n)
Closing ⟨C-C⟩	L1 (Spanish)	0	0	0	0
	L2 (English)	1	0	1	2
Recapitulation markers ⟨C-R⟩	L1 (Spanish)	2	2	2	6
	L2 (English)	0	2	1	3
Prospectives ⟨C-P⟩	L1 (Spanish)	2	2	0	4
	L2 (English)	0	6	0	6
Retrospectives ⟨C-RT⟩	L1 (Spanish)	0	7	7	14
	L2 (English)	0	0	0	0

An interesting finding concerns the use of recapitulation markers. Whereas recapitulation is explicitly conveyed in Spanish by means of verbs such as *summarise, recapitulate* or other markers such as *in brief/short, as a conclusion*, in the English data, when it exists, it is mostly implicit and partial. That is, recapitulation is basically presented as interspersed rephrasing of immediately previous points:

(26)   ⟨C-R⟩ **Recapitulando lo que hemos visto en la lección** desde el segundo apartado en adelante ⟨C-R⟩, para que el avión sea capaz de hacer frente al control sobre el mismo . . . [To *summarise what we've seen in this lesson from the second part onwards, for the plane to be able to control itself*. . .] (L2).

(27)   Imagine that you have a bicycle of carbon fibre and you just rock, so there is an impact. This small impact will create small micro-cracks inside and these small

micro-cracks have not change the stiffness of their structure but has produce a, eh, strong loads of the compressive strength, I mean, for every time you're doing that, you may, eh, produce even absolutely undetected, because from the outside is okay, but there are small micro-cracks inside that have lost more than fifty per cent of the original strength. ⟨C-R⟩ **This is currently the main limitation of composite materials** ⟨C-R⟩. (L2).

The examples above suggest that in the English lectures this type of metadiscursive markers is used rather as a micro-strategy to recapitulate certain parts of the lectures than as a macro-strategy to organise and summarise the whole speech event, as seems to be the case in Spanish.

4. Conclusions and implications

The contrastive analysis presented here has shown that, in general terms, the lecturers utilised similar types of MDs to structure their sessions, irrespective of the language of instruction or the audience addressed. In this connection, language transfer has been mainly observed in their choice of ⟨DS⟩ such as the use of prospective markers or topicalisers and in the linguistic realisations of these markers. In the latter case, however, some instances have emerged as functionally adequate but formally deviant from the native speakers' norm. These findings tentatively suggest, given the limited amount of data, that professors replicate their lecturing styles and transfer linguistic tools from L1 to L2.

As far as differences are concerned, lectures in L1 and L2 vary, however, in the degree of explicitness with which phase transition is signalled. While in the Spanish data lecturers overtly use specific MDs to move from one section to another, to anticipate information and to summarise main ideas, in the English data, these same lecturers often shift to the next move without explicit signalling. Moreover, stylistically speaking, in English there is less variety in the MDs employed as well as a lower level of specificity in the terms used to introduce a new topic. In the case of interaction markers, for example, differences are observed regarding the types of commentaries that lecturers make. The fact that apologetic comments are mostly present in the English data and that contextual ones appear mainly in the Spanish lectures lends support to the crucial role of contextual variables (e.g. the degree of familiarity with the audience or the lecturer's concern with his/her level of English) in motivating language choices and in shaping teacher-student relations. Finally, conclusion markers are more frequently used in the Spanish data with lecturers overtly summarising the main ideas developed in the class.

At a pedagogical level, we believe that the findings discussed above could have important implications for FL lecturers and for CLIL teacher education in university settings. Firstly, lecturers would benefit from becoming aware of the strong link between explicit MDs signalling and a clearer structure in lecture organization – a feature that was said to be highly valued by lecturers and students, especially in a L2 context. Secondly, by observing their own use of these MDs, FL lecturers could be encouraged to reflect on the extent to which teaching through a L2 may entail differences in their lecturing style which frequently go unnoticed.

On the whole, the results obtained from this small-scale analysis point to the fact that there seems to be a need for language-oriented teacher education in CLIL university contexts. In this sense, our taxonomy of MDs for lectures, as arranged into categories and metadiscoursal phases, could be a useful framework for a linguistic repertoire containing a set of L2 markers typically used for signalling phases (both discoursal and metadiscoursal), which could be of assistance to non-native lecturers in their teaching of content through a FL.

References

Aguilar Pérez, M. & Arnó Maciá, E. 2002. Metadiscourse in lecture comprehension: does it really help foreign language learners? *Atlantis* XXIV(2): 3–21.

Anderson, R.C. 1977. The notion of schemata and the educational enterprise. In *Schooling and the Acquisition of Knowledge*, R.C. Anderson, R.J. Spiro & W.E. Montague (eds), 415–431. Hillsdale NJ: Lawrence Erlbaum Associates.

Bellés. B. 2004. The Spoken Academic Discourse of Social Sciences: Discourse Markers within the University Lecture Genre. MA thesis. Universitat Jaume I, Castellón, Spain.

Benson, M.J. 1994. Lecture listening in an ethnographic perspective. In *Academic Listening: Research Perspectives*, J. Flowerdew (ed.), 181–198. Cambridge: CUP.

Biber, D. 2006. *University Language: A Corpus-based Study of Spoken and Written registers* [Studies in Corpus Linguistics 23]. Amsterdam: John Benjamins.

Chaudron, C. & Richards, J. 1986. The effect of discourse markers on the comprehension of lectures. *Applied Linguistics* 7(2):113–127.

Crawford Camiciottoli, B. 2005. Adjusting a business lecture for an international audience: A case study. *English for Specific Purposes* 24: 183–199.

Crismore, A., Markkanen, R. & Steffensen, M. 1993. Metadiscourse in persuasive writing. A study of texts written by American and Finnish university students. *Written Communication* 10(1): 39–71.

Dafouz, E. 2003. Metadiscourse revisited: A contrastive study of persuasive writing in professional discourse. *Estudios Ingleses de la Universidad Complutense* 11: 29–52.

Dafouz, E. 2008. The pragmatic role of textual and interpersonal metadiscourse markers in the construction and attainment of persuasion: A cross-linguistic study of newspaper discourse. *Journal of Pragmatics* 40(1): 95–113.

Dafouz, E., Núñez, B. & Sancho, C. 2007. Analysing stance in a CLIL university context: Non-native speaker use of personal pronouns and modal verbs. *International Journal of Bilingual Education and Bilingualism*. Vol. 10(5): 647–662.

Dafouz, E. & Núñez, B. 2009. CLIL in tertiary education: Devising a new learning landscape. In *CLIL across Educational Levels: Experiences from Primary, Secondary and Tertiary Contexts*, E. Dafouz & M. Guerrini (eds), 101–112. London: Richmond.

de Rydder-Symoens, H. (ed.). 1996. *A History of the University in Europe: Universities in Early Modern Europe*, Vol. 2. Cambridge: CUP.

Dudley Evans, T. 1987. Introduction. *ERL Journal* 1: 1–9.

Eggins, S. 1994. *An Introduction to Systemic-functional Linguistics*. London: Pinter.

Fortanet, I. 2008. Questions for debate in English medium lecturing in Spain. In *Realizing Content and Language Integration in Higher Education*, R. Wilkinson & V. Zegers (eds), 21–31. Maastricht: Maastricht University.

Flowerdew, J. 1994. *Academic Listening. Research Perspectives*. Cambridge: CUP.

Halliday, M.A.K. 1978. *Language as Social Semiotic. The Social Interpretation of Language and Meaning*. London: Edward Arnold.

Halliday, M.A.K. & Hasan, R. 1976. *Cohesion in English*. London: Longman.

Hyland, K. 1998. Persuasion and context. The pragmatics of academic discourse. *Journal of Pragmatics* 30: 437–455.

Hyland, K. 2005. *Metadiscourse. Exploring Interaction in Writing*. Oxford: Continuum.

Hyland, K. & Tse, P. 2004. Metadiscourse in academic writing: A reappraisal. *Applied Linguistics* 25(2): 156–177.

Lasagabaster, D. 2008a. El inglés como lengua vehicular en el ámbito universitario. Paper given at the XXVI AESLA International Conference, 3–5 April 2008. Almería: Spain.

Lasagabaster, D. 2008b. Foreign language competence in Content and Language Integrated Learning. *The Open Applied Linguistics Journal* I: 31–42.

Mauranen, A. 1993. *Cultural Differences in Academic Rhetoric*. Frankfurt: Peter Lang.

Martin, J.R. 1985. Process and text: Two aspects of human semiosis. In *Systemic Perspectives on Discourse*, Vol. I, J.D. Benson & W.S. Greaves (eds), 248–274. Norwood NJ: Ablex.

Núñez Perucha, B. & Dafouz Milne, E. 2007. Lecturing through the foreign language in a CLIL university context: Linguistic and pragmatic implications. *VIEWS. Vienna English Working Papers* 16(3): 36–42. (Special issue: *Current Research in CLIL* 2).

Saroyan, A. & Snell, L. 1997. Variations in lecturing styles. *Higher Education* 33: 85–104.

Wilkinson, R. (ed.). 2004. *Integrating Content and Language. Meeting the Challenge of Multilingual Higher Education*. Maastricht: Universitaire Pers.

Vande Kopple, W. 1985. Some exploratory discourse on metadiscourse. *College Composition and Communication* 36: 82–93.

Young, L. 1990. *Language as Behaviour, Language as Code: A Study of Academic English* [Pragmatics & Beyond New Series 8]. Amsterdam: John Benjamins.

Young, L. 1994. University lectures – macro-structure and micro-features. In *Academic Listening: Research Perspectives*, J. Flowerdew (ed.), 159–176. Cambridge: CUP.

Language matters

Assessing lecture comprehension in Norwegian English-medium higher education

Glenn Ole Hellekjær
Universitetet i Oslo, Norway

The present study examines lecture comprehension in English-medium (EM) courses, i.e. non-language subjects taught through English in higher education. It uses a questionnaire with self-assessment items to compare lecture comprehension in English and in the first language (L1). The sample comprises 391 respondents from three Norwegian institutions of higher education. Analysis shows that although the differences in comprehension scores between English and the L1 are not substantial, and the respondents experienced much the same difficulties in the L1 and English, a larger number of students have comprehension difficulties in the EM lectures. The main problems are difficulties distinguishing the meaning of words, unfamiliar vocabulary, and difficulties taking notes while listening to lectures. It concludes by arguing the need to take language difficulties seriously, through the use of effective lecturing behavior and improving the lecturers' as well as the students' English proficiency.

1. Introduction

The focus on internationalization in the 1999 Bologna Declaration on the reform and convergence of European higher education, and the resulting 2003 Quality Reform of Norwegian higher education resulted in a massive increase of English-Medium (EM) courses, i.e. non-language subjects taught in English. At the University of Oslo the number of these jumped from about 40 Masters level EM programs in 2003 to more than 800 separate courses and programs in 2009. However, a recent national report and several Nordic and Norwegian studies (Halvorsen & Faye 2006; Hellekjær & Westergaard 2003; Hellekjær 2007; Ljosland 2008; Räsänen 2000; Tella et al. 1999) reveal that implementation has suffered from a lack of awareness of the practical and pedagogical implications of using a foreign language, English, for instruction. This might be because it is taken for granted that lecturers will have few difficulties teaching in a foreign language. Norwegian students, or Danish or Swedish ones for that matter, are also expected to be able to understand lectures, take part in discussions and seminars, and write papers and examinations in English on the basis of their skills from upper-secondary education (Hellekjær & Westergaard 2003). That students do not necessarily agree is another matter, and Ljosland (2008) gives an example from the Norwegian University of Science and Technology where engineering students protested the compulsory use of English for examinations due to worries about their writing proficiency and the risk of poorer grades.

In fact, this protest mirrors the findings of several Nordic studies (Hellekjær 2004; Räsänen 2000; Tella et al. 1999) that show that students in EM courses experience language problems, in particular at the undergraduate level. While poor writing proficiency is the most serious problem, there are difficulties in other areas as well, including lecture comprehension. A recent qualitative study of 23 Swedish university level physics students comparing lecture comprehension and learning in English and Swedish, provides additional, and more detailed information (Airey & Linder 2006; Airey 2009). Interestingly, Airey and Linder (2006: 555) found that "the students initially report no difference in their experience of learning of physics when taught in Swedish or English" However, videos of the students during lectures, and "the students' own accounts of their learning experience during stimulated recall indicate a number of problems related to learning in English rather than Swedish" (Airey & Linder 2006: 555). One was difficulties taking notes during lectures, another the reluctance to ask and answer questions.[1] However, they also found that the students developed compensatory strategies. One was "that a number of students, though silent in the lecture, came forward at the end of each session to ask questions" (Airey, 2009: 79). Another was increased reliance on preparatory reading, and a third, that they engaged in follow-up reading and discussions to ensure comprehension. In fact, such a change in study habits, along with the possible improvement of English proficiency over time, can explain Klaassen's (2001) finding that Dutch engineering students over the period of a year manage to adapt to EM instruction. What remains clear, however, is that many students have initial problems with EM instruction that they may, or may not, overcome.

This makes it important to document whether, and to what extent university students in EM courses have difficulties understanding lectures, and second, in order to suggest improvements, identify factors that impact on their performance. This is also the goal of the present quantitative study of EM lecture comprehension

---

1. This differs from e.g. Nikula (2007), who found a higher level of teacher student interaction in Finnish upper secondary school level Content and Language Integrated Learning (CLIL) classes than in EFL. In my opinion, this contrast might be explained by differences in the teaching context, different levels of difficulty with regard to subject matter and language, and perhaps by student selection, i.e. how CLIL students are recruited.

with a sample comprising 391 (mostly undergraduate level) respondents from three Norwegian institutions of higher education.

The main aim of the study is therefore to examine whether, and to what extent students in Norway experience lecture comprehension problems in EM lectures that are due to language difficulties by comparing with their comprehension of L1 lectures. The second is to identify the main language variables affecting lecture comprehension. The third is to use the data to suggest what can be done to improve EM lecture comprehension. It should be mentioned that, given the reputation of Norwegians as being good in English, any lecture comprehension problems found should be of interest in other non-English speaking countries as well.

Towards a construct definition of academic English lecture comprehension
In the following, I give a brief description of the phenomenon being studied, namely academic English listening comprehension, drawing heavily upon Vandergrift (2007) and Buck (2001). This description, also known as a construct definition, was used to develop the items about lecture comprehension.

Listening comprehension is a process combining bottom-up and top-down processing. In bottom-up processing, listeners build meaning from aural input by combining information from the phoneme-level up to word and discourse-level features. Both vocabulary knowledge and word-segmentation skills, the latter being the ability to find word boundaries in spoken discourse, are particularly important at this level. In top-down processing, however, the listener uses context and prior knowledge to build, check or repair understanding. An example would be using knowledge of the topic in question to infer the meaning of unfamiliar words. This is also an example of the interaction between processing levels, of how the lack of comprehension at the word/bottom-up level can be compensated for by using top-down "compensatory mechanisms – contextual, visual or paralinguistic information, world knowledge, cultural information and common sense" (Vandergrift 2007: 193). The ability to compensate, however, is limited by the limited capacity and transient nature of the working memory, which means that interruptions longer than about 30 seconds to ponder the meaning of words or expressions can lead to the listener losing track of what is being talked about (Buck 2001; Rayner & Pollatsek 1989).

To return to the interaction between processing levels during listening, the bottom-up and top-down processes function in parallel, with the focus depending on the "purpose for listening, learner characteristics such as the level of language proficiency, and the context of the listening event" (Vandergrift 2007: 193). Variations in second language (L2) listening proficiency will therefore depend on language proficiency and strategy use. Less proficient listeners, for instance, often focus on the word level cues to build understanding, and some even attempt to translate what they hear to their first language. In contrast, more skilled and/or more linguistically proficient listeners will rely more on top-down compensatory strategies to infer what is not immediately understood. In addition, they will to a greater extent use cognitive and metacognitive strategies such as comprehension monitoring, that is to say checking whether they have understood correctly, and elaboration relating what they have heard to previous knowledge – to repair or enhance comprehension.

This brings us to the question of what to focus on when assessing listening proficiency, linguistic knowledge or strategy use. In *Assessing Listening*, Buck (2001) argues that although comprehension depends on the combination of strategic knowledge and language proficiency, variation in performance most often correlates with linguistic competence. He therefore argues that it "makes more sense to put the emphasis on testing language competence rather than strategic competence" (Buck 2001: 105).

Buck (2001:114) also proposes a default listening construct that can be adapted to different contexts. It describes listening as the ability to:

> (1) process extended samples of realistic spoken language, automatically and in real time; (2) understand the linguistic information that is unequivocally included in the text; and, (3) make whatever inferences are unambiguously implicated by the content of the passage.

In the present study, the context is academic lectures, and the respondents' actual experience is with real-time lectures in English (L2) and the L1. In accordance with the construct, the questionnaire uses a combination of items about low-level linguistic processing, such as difficulties distinguishing words or unfamiliar vocabulary, and items about higher-level processes such as content understanding. The items used are presented in the following section.

2. Method

The present questionnaire-based quantitative study uses a quasi-experimental, one-group, post-test research design, in this case a single questionnaire (see Shadish, Cook & Campbell 2002: 106–107).

The survey took place late in the 2008 spring and fall semesters. Four institutions were invited to participate, one of which declined to take part. Next, the institutional websites were used to identify undergraduate level EM courses at different faculties at the University of Oslo, BI Norwegian School of Management, and Oslo University College. I then contacted lecturers by phone or e-mail to ask for permission to survey their students. To ensure a reasonably high reply rate, paper questionnaires were handed out during lectures or groups. Table 1 provides an overview of the sample.

Table 1. Overview of the sample according to institution, faculty and level of study

Faculty and institutions	Undergraduate level	Graduate level	Total
Faculty of Mathematics and Natural Sciences, University of Oslo	123		123 (31%)
Faculty of Humanities, University of Oslo	70	32	102 (26%)
Faculty of Medicine, University of Oslo	57		57 (15%)
Faculty of Social Sciences, University of Oslo	49		49 (12%)
Bachelor of Business Administration, BI Norwegian School of Management	47		47 (12%)
Faculty of Engineering, Oslo University College		13	12 (3%)
Total	346 (88%)	45 (22%)	391(100%)

The majority of the respondents (88%) are undergraduate level students and the remaining (22%) graduate level. Almost all the respondents at lectures filled in the questionnaire, but in most cases less than half of the registered students were present. Of those who answered 227 (57.5%) were female and 166 (42.5%) male. The majority, 267 (68%) had Norwegian as their L1, 27 (7%) had English as their L1, and 97 (25%) had another L1. In the following statistical analysis the 27 respondents with English as a first language are excluded, which gives a sample of 364.

This sample does not meet the requirements of a random sample, which are extremely difficult to obtain in education-based research. It is better described as a purposive sample of typical instances, which entails some limits with regard to external validity (Ary, Jacobs & Razavieh 1996; Shadish, Cook & Campbell 2002). I would, nevertheless, argue that a sample of 364 respondents from three Norwegian institutions of higher education provides useful data about undergraduate level EM students in Norway.

The questionnaire comprises 61 multiple choice and two open ended items (see Appendix). It was designed to take about ten minutes to fill in at the end of lectures. This time limitation led to the use of self-assessment items to measure lecture comprehension instead of a listening test. There were also items about background variables such as education, prior experience with EM courses, motivation for EM courses. To return to the use of self-assessment items instead of a listening comprehension test, research shows that self-assessment in general gives reasonably valid information in low stakes situations such as this study (Harrington & Harrington 2001; Oscarson 1997). In validation studies of the self-assessment of language proficiency Marian, Blumenfeld, & Kaushanskaya (2007) and Ross (1998) also found self-assessment to be reliable predictors of listening proficiency. There is therefore good reason to expect the scores from the self-assessment items and indices used in the present study to provide a useful and valid comparison of student lecture comprehension difficulties in English and the L1. A firmer conclusion, however, would require a validation study where self-assessment item scores are correlated against a relevant listening test.

The self-assessment items used to measure lecture comprehension were designed to do so by tapping into different aspects of listening during lectures. These aspects were vocabulary, clarity of pronunciation/word segmentation, speaking speed, ability to follow the lecturer's line of thought, the speed of the presentation of information, difficulty in taking notes and finally, content understanding. There were identical items for the L1 and English, all of them using four point Likert scales with 1 indicating a high level of difficulty, 4 no difficulty. The seven items selected for English are presented below. The wording for the equivalent L1 items is almost identical.

> 48. Indicate on the scale **to what extent you find words and expressions in the English language** lectures **unfamiliar.**
> 49. Indicate on the scale to what extent **words and expressions are clearly pronounced and understandable in the English language lectures.**
> 50. Indicate on the scale to what extent you experience **that the lecturer in English language lectures speaks too fast.**
> 52. Indicate on the scale to what extent you can **follow the lecturer's line of thought during English** lectures.
> 53. Indicate on the scale **to what extent you understand the content of the English lectures.**
> 54. Indicate on the scale to what extent **the information in the English lectures is presented so quickly** that it hinders your understanding.
> 57. Indicate on the scale **how difficult you find taking notes** during English lectures.

Figure 1. Selected items from student questionnaire

Finally, there were a number of items designed to elicit whether students compensated for the use of English through preparatory reading or asking questions for clarification, as reported by Airey and Linder (2006). Statistical analysis was carried out using the Statistical Package for the Social Sciences (SPSS).

2.1   Dependent variables

As mentioned, the questionnaire comprised a number of items designed to elicit information about the listening comprehension construct. There were identical items for the L1 and English, and the L1 scores were intended to serve as a benchmark to measure to which extent the use of English affects comprehension.

Testing which items do, and do not measure the same underlying trait can be done using Cronbach's alpha or factorial analysis. In the present study, I used factorial analysis (principal axis factoring) to identify and select the items that loaded on the same (latent) variables, in this case language proficiency in the L1 and English respectively. The English versions of the seven items selected are listed above.

Factorial analysis shows that the seven English items that loaded on the same variable can explain 52% of the total variance in lecture comprehension scores, while the Cronbach's alpha coefficient for seven items was a = .84. For the L1 the explained variance was 43%, while the alpha coefficient was a = .76.

Since analysis confirmed that each of these seven items' measures loaded on the same variable, they could be merged into single additive indices and used as dependent variables for listening comprehension in the L1 and in English. In the following, these are designated L1Index for the L1, and EngIndex for English. Using additive indices simplifies analysis by making it possible to use one instead of several items as indicators of the same underlying trait. It also helps reduce the effects of possible measurement errors and improves both validity and reliability (Hellevik 1999: 303–310).

With regard to the validity of using self-assessment items' instead of a listening comprehension test, research shows that self-assessment in general gives reasonably valid information in low-stakes situations such as this study (Harrington & Harrington 2001; Oscarson 1997). In validation studies of the self-assessment of language proficiency Marian, Blumenfeld, and Kaushanskaya (2007) and Ross (1998) also found self-assessment to be reliable predictors of listening proficiency. There is therefore good reason to expect the scores from the self-assessment items and indices used in the present study to provide a useful and valid picture of student lecture comprehension difficulties.

3.   Results and analysis

To start with the indices, on a scale from 1 indicating high levels of difficulty and 4 no difficulties, analysis found a clear, but not dramatic difference in the mean scores with 3.4 (SD = .6) for the L1index and a somewhat lower 3.1 (SD = . 5) for Engindex. However, the comparison of the scores for L1Index and EngIndex presented in Figure 1 provides additional information.

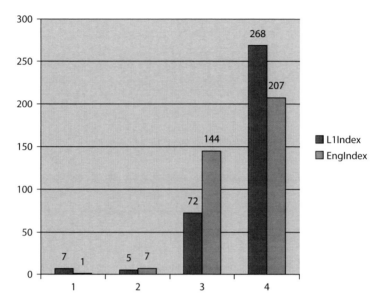

Figure 1. Comparison of the lecture comprehension scores for the L1 (L1Index) and English (EngIndex) (N = 364).

This comparison shows that while there is a ceiling effect with mostly high scores for the L1, this is not the case for English, where about 42% (144) respondents have a score of three or below. It is also interesting to note that 24% (84) have difficulties with L1 lectures as well. In other words, a number of students are experiencing lecture comprehension difficulties, but first and foremost in EM lectures.

To return to English, many EM lecturers in Norway assume that it is first and foremost the exchange students, not the Norwegians, who have comprehension difficulties (Hellekjær 2007). To examine this, I used an independent samples T-test to compare the EngIndex scores of the respondents with Norwegian as their L1 (N = 267) with those who had another first language than English (N = 97). The latter group comprises both exchange students and a number with language minority backgrounds. The T-test showed no meaningful difference between the groups, with a mean score of 3.14 (SD = .5) for those with Norwegian as their L1 and a mean of 3.17 (SD = .7) for those with another L1, and that this was statistically significant at the p < .01 level. In other words, and contrary to expectations, there seems to be little difference between the exchange students and those from Norway.

To return to the scores displayed in Figure 1, this shows that as many as 42% of the sample experience lecture comprehension difficulties in EM lectures, compared to 24% in the L1. The question is whether this is due to respondents' language skills, or due to the quality of instruction. I will therefore examine these lecture comprehension issues in further detail in the following.

3.1   Lecture comprehension issues

Table 2 displays the differences in mean scores between the L1 and English for the seven items that were included in the additive indices L1Index and EngIndex. These mean scores were 3.4 (SD = .6) for L1index and 3.1 (SD = .5) for Engindex. The higher the score, the better the comprehension.

Table 2. A comparison of the mean scores and standard deviation for the items tapping into lecture comprehension in the L1 and English. N = 364

Items and item numbers	L1		English	
	Mean	SD	Mean	SD
To what extent do you find words and expressions unfamiliar? (items 35, 48)	3.3	.8	3.0	.6
To what extent are words and expressions clearly pronounced and understandable? (items 36, 49)	3.4	.7	2.9	.7
To what extent does the lecturer speak too fast? (items 37, 50)	3.6	.7	3.4	.7
To what extent can you follow the lecturer's line of thought? (items 39, 52)	3.4	.6	3.1	.7
To what extent do you understand the content of the lectures? (items 40, 53)	3.5	.6	3.3	.6
To what extent is the information in the lectures presented so quickly that it hinders your understanding? (items 41, 54)	3.4	.7	3.3	.7
How difficult do you find taking notes during lectures? (items 44, 57)	3.4	.8	3.1	.8
Additive indices – L1Index & EngIndex	3.4	.6	3.1	.5

As can be seen, although there are lower scores for English for all the items, the largest difference is for words and expressions not being understandable, which might be due to unclear pronunciation or word segmentation problems. The next is unfamiliar words and expressions, although unfamiliarity with subject specific terminology and concepts can be a problem irrespective of language. After this, there are difficulties following the lecturers' line of thought, and then difficulties taking notes. Last, higher scores and smaller differences between languages indicate that speaking speed, how fast information is presented, as well as content understanding, are somewhat less problematic areas.

Another sign of comprehension difficulties during lectures is the extent to which the respondents feel the need to ask questions about language or content. Table 3 displays the correlations between L1Index and EngIndex and two items about the need to ask questions about language and content.

Table 3. Comparison of the correlations between L1Index, EngIndex and items tapping into the need to ask questions about language or content

Questions	L1Index		EngIndex	
	Correlation	N	Correlation	N
How often do you want to ask about unfamiliar words and expressions during lectures?	$-.38^{**}$	346	$-.47^{**}$	359
How often do you want to ask about unclear content during lectures?	$-.48^{**}$	344	$-.46^{**}$	357

**Correlation is significant at the 0.01 level (2-tailed).

The table shows that there are fairly strong, negative correlations between these items and L1Index and EngIndex. The negative correlations show that the lower the respondents' lecture comprehension scores, the greater is their desire to ask questions. What is interesting is that this is almost equally the case for the L1 as well as for English, which might argue the need to work with language issues such as key concepts and subject specific vocabulary and terms in L1 as well as in EM lectures.

Yet another sign of language problems or general difficulties with EM instruction is workload, i.e. to what extent the respondents find studying in English more laborious compared to in the L1. This is a question that involves more than lecture comprehension, and should be of interest for teaching as well as course design. The respondents' answers are presented in Table 4 below.

Table 4. How laborious attending a course in English is compared to in the L1. A score of 1 indicates the same as in L1 courses, 4 much more work

	1 Just like in the L1	2	3	4 Much more work than in the L1	N
How laborious is EM instruction?	35% (124)	24% (86)	27% (97)	12% (45)	352

As can be seen in the table, about 63% of the respondents find EM courses more laborious than in their L1, although to varying degrees. Interestingly, this item also has a negative correlation of r = -.40 (p < .01, N = 352) against EngIndex as a dependent variable. Again, this shows that the lower the respondents' EngIndex scores are, the more laborious they find EM instruction to be.

Another indication of language difficulties is the degree of dependence on visual aids to support comprehension. I therefore included an additional item on the importance of transparencies/PowerPoint slides for lecture comprehension. Table 5 below displays the importance the 364 respondents attribute to the lecturers' use of transparencies/PowerPoint slides for lecture comprehension in the L1 and in English.

Table 5. How important are the lecturer's transparencies/PowerPoint slides or other visual aids for your understanding of the lectures?

	1 Not important for understanding	2	3	4 Very important for understanding	N
L1 lectures	18% (61)	32% (110)	32% (109)	18% (63)	343
English lectures	13% (47)	25% (89)	30% (108)	31% (111)	355

This presentation of answers shows, that irrespective of language, the majority of the respondents find visual aids important, some even very important, for lecture comprehension. Furthermore, when the importance of visual aids for understanding in the L1 was correlated with L1Index, this gave a negative correlation of r = −.26 (p < .01, N = 343), compared to r = −.32 (p < .01, N = 355) with EngIndex. Again, this means that the lower the respondents' lecture comprehension scores are, in the L1 as well as English, the more they depend on visual aids to support comprehension.

3.2 Background variables

Airey (2009), Airey and Linder (2006) and Klaassen (2001) report that students in EM programs, despite initial difficulties, gradually adjust to teaching in English. In the survey I therefore included an item on whether the respondents had previously attended an EM course, to which 132 (38%) answered yes and 222 (62%) answered no. My expectation was that the 132 respondents with previous EM experience would have higher EngIndex scores. Rather unexpectedly, an independent samples T-test found no significant difference between the mean scores of the two groups. This might be because most of the courses surveyed were single subjects and not part of EM programs, which means far less exposure to EM instruction and the possibility of improved English proficiency. Alternatively, a single EM course might provide less reason to change study habits.

Another factor I expected to correlate positively with language scores was study experience; that is to say, the more experienced a student is, the better he or she will comprehend lectures. To check this, I correlated time of study with L1Index and EngIndex, but got very low, and non-significant results in both instances. Time of study in an English speaking country, however, gave a low but significant positive correlation with EngIndex, $r = .16$ ($p < .01$, N = 357).

As mentioned in the introduction, Airey and Linder (2006) found that some EM students compensated for comprehension difficulties by reading relevant course material either before the lectures or as a follow-up. I therefore included questions on the extent of reading in preparation for lectures in the questionnaire for the L1 and English. The answers are presented in Table 6.

Table 6. How often do you read in preparation for lectures?

	1 Never	2	3	4 For every lecture	N
L1 lectures	22% (78)	42% (148)	29% (102)	8% (27)	355
English lectures	16% (56)	34% (122)	32% (116)	18% (63)	357

This comparison shows that there is little difference between languages with regard to preparing for lectures. About 36 more respondents prepared regularly for EM lectures by reading up beforehand than for the L1 lectures. Furthermore, correlating this item against EngIndex gave only a low and non-significant correlation, $r = .07$, N = 356. In comparison, there was a low but significant positive correlation for the L1, $r = .18$ ($p < .01$, N = 351). This indicates that preparing for lectures by reading improves lecture comprehension in the L1, but not in English. This may well be because those who prepare extra in English do so to compensate for language difficulties, and/or that such efforts at best allow them to cope in English. Last, and as mentioned above, an isolated EM course may not provide sufficient motivation to change study habits.

Apart from previous experience with EM instruction, there were two other areas that were expected to correlate with higher levels of lecture comprehension, namely exposure to English, for instance through reading or the media, and attitudes to the utility of learning English. Examples of the latter would be feeling that English would be useful in future careers, or the desire to work in an English speaking country. Table 7 presents the correlations between items about the utility of English and EngIndex.

Table 7. Correlations between attitudes towards the utility of English
and EM lecture comprehension scores (EngIndex)

Questions	Correlation	N
How useful do you believe knowing English will be in your future career?	.23**	356
How interested are you in working outside Norway/your own country in your future career?	.16**	357
Are you interested in working in a job where English is your working language?	.17**	356
Do you think knowing English will be important for new jobs?	.12*	356
Is the extra work involved in taking an EM course worthwhile?	.21**	342

**Correlation is significant at the 0.01 level
*Correlation is significant at the 0.05 level

The low but positive correlations between items for motivation and EngIndex can be interpreted in two ways. One is that many of the most positive, or motivated respondents are among the more proficient in English. The other is that their belief in the utility of English for future careers or interest in working abroad enhances their efforts to master EM lectures. The latter might well be indicated by the positive correlation for the extra work involved in taking an EM course being considered worthwhile.

The next issue is how exposure to, or the respondents' use of English correlate with EngIndex scores. In Norway, for instance, exposure to English through the media is considered an important explanation for Norwegians' supposedly high levels of proficiency (Bonnet 2004; Ibsen 2004). Table 8 presents an overview of the correlations between different items on exposure to and use of English and EngIndex scores.

Table 8. Correlations between items for the exposure to and use of English, and EM lecture comprehension scores (EngIndex)

Questions	Correlations	N
How many English books do you read per year?	26**	359
How often do you read English periodicals, magazines or newspapers?	.26**	357
How often do you read English on the Internet?	.21**	357
How often do you watch English language movies, videos, or TV programs?	.08	357
How often do you speak English?	.26**	358
How often do you write English?	.26**	356

**Correlation is significant at the 0.01 level.

These correlations show that the active use of English, by reading, speaking or writing in English all correlate positively with lecture comprehension scores. In comparison, the very low and non-significant correlation for exposure to English through the media shows that this source of language input, contrary to expectations, does not covary with high levels of academic English listening proficiency. One reason might be that TV programs and films in Norway are subtitled in Norwegian. Another might be that the linguistic input from this source is minimal. What remains clear, however, is that media exposure seems to be of limited utility for the development of academic English listening proficiency for the respondents in this sample.

4.   Discussion

This section begins with a summary of the findings of the survey, continues with a brief discussion of their validity, and ends with suggestions about how to improve lecture comprehension in EM instruction.

As noted above, the gaps between the mean scores for lecture comprehension in the L1 and English appear to be low (see Table 2). However, a comparison of their distribution (see Figure 1), reveals that almost 42% of the respondents in this sample experience EM lectures as more difficult than in the L1. In other words, the present study shows that many respondents in EM courses experience varying degrees of lecture comprehension difficulties, to the extent that this must be taken seriously in lecturing and course design.

The most frequent source of difficulty appears to involve unclear pronunciation/word segmentation. This may reflect the respondents' listening proficiency and/or the lecturers' pronunciation. Other areas of difficulty are unfamiliar vocabulary, problems following the lecturer's line of thought, and difficulties taking notes. While the difference between L1 and English lecture comprehension scores displayed in Table 2 is not big enough to argue for the exclusive use of the L1, the findings show that a considerable number of respondents have difficulties.

One indication of this is that as many as 63% of the respondents find attending an EM course more laborious than in the L1, with statistical analysis giving a negative correlation of $r = -.4$ ($p < .01$, N = 352) against EngIndex as a dependent variable. In other words, the respondents who find EM instruction most laborious are those with the lowest EngIndex scores. The same is the case for the fairly high negative correlations between the items about the desire to ask questions about content and language and L1Index and EngIndex presented in Table 3. Again, the lower the scores for lecture comprehension, the greater is the need to ask questions. Yet another indication can be found in the negative correlation of $r = -.32$

(p < .01, N = 355) between EngIndex and how important the respondents feel that transparencies/PowerPoint slides are for their understanding. It was, however, interesting to note that this was the case for the L1 as well.

Next, and contrary to many lecturers' expectations, the difficulties were not limited to the exchange students. Indeed, an independent samples t-test found no significant difference in the EM lecture comprehension scores between students with Norwegian as their L1, and those with a different L1. In other words, both domestic and exchange students are experiencing difficulties with EM instruction.

4.1 Validity

The first issue is whether the difference between the comprehension scores for EM and L1 lectures is large enough to indicate that there is a problem with lecture comprehension. First, I would argue that when 42% of the respondents have scores indicating that they are experiencing difficulties with EM instruction, and that 24% have difficulties in the L1 as well, this clearly indicates that there is a problem. Second, statistical analysis also shows that respondents with low L1Index and EngIndex scores feel a greater need to ask questions about content and language, that they find following EM instruction more work than in the L1, and rely more on the lecturers' notes for comprehension. These are all signs of comprehension difficulties that are most probably due to poor language skills on the part of the students. Furthermore, much the same difficulties are found for L1 lectures as in English, but to a greater extent for the latter. In other words, the findings in this study clearly indicate the need to take students' language proficiency into consideration in EM instruction, and clear backing for the need to use effective lecturing behavior to improve lecture comprehension in EM and L1 lectures. This I will return to below.

Before continuing, the use of self-assessment in the present study needs to be addressed. As mentioned above, a number of studies indicate that self-assessment items can be valid predictors of listening proficiency. Of course, a firmer conclusion would be correlating these against listening test scores in a validation study. Such a test would also be useful to check construct validity, that is to say to which extent the scores in EngIndex and L1Index actually reflect lecture comprehension and not other variables (see for instance Messick 1996). It would also help determine at which level in the self-assessment scores the respondents are starting to have serious problems. In the present study, however, I would argue that research on self-assessment indicates that the self-assessment items and indices used in this low-stakes situation provide a useful picture of student lecture comprehension difficulties.

The next issue concerns external validity, the generalizability of the findings beyond the sample studied, which depends largely upon how the sample is selected. As mentioned, practical constraints made it difficult to select a random, representative sample from the relevant reference population, in this case all students receiving EM instruction at Norwegian institutions of higher education. Nevertheless, I would argue that a purposive sample of typical instances comprising 391 respondents from 14 courses and three different institutions should be adequate to provide useful insight into the extent and kind of difficulties many undergraduate level students in Norway have, or do not have, with EM instruction. In the following I will therefore point out some of the key implications.

4.2   Improving EM instruction

The main finding of the present study is that even Norwegian students in EM courses have language problems that impact on lecture comprehension. This means it is essential to address this issue in teaching and course design in Norway as well as in other countries. In doing so, however, it is important to keep in mind "that changing the lecturing language [may simply accentuate] communication problems that are already present in first language lectures" (Airey 2009: 84). Indeed, in the present study it was interesting to note that many of the problems found in English were also present in the L1 lectures. This means that the most important implication, irrespective of the language used, is the need to make use of effective lecturing behavior and to support lectures with visual aids (see Airey 2009; Airey & Linder 2006; Klaassen 2001; Vinke, Snippe & W. Jochems 1998). Indeed, Klaassen (2001) found that effective lecturing behavior could have a greater effect on Dutch students' lecture comprehension than the language used.

To return to the language difficulties found in the present study, the perhaps most important problem was that the respondents found that words and expressions used in the lectures were not clearly pronounced and understandable. This means it is important to help lecturers speak clearly and distinctly. On the one hand, it could mean working with pronunciation, stress and word segmentation; on the other it might mean screening EM lecturers with regard to their English proficiency.

The next issue concerns vocabulary, which seems to be a problem in the L1 as well as in English, although the answers may also reflect that university studies involve socializing students into domain-specific academic genres and registers with specialized vocabularies. One means of compensating for this problem would be if lecturers spent some time going through key terms and concepts before lectures as a pre-listening exercise, or explaining these during or afterwards. It would also be important, as Airey and Linder (2006) also suggest, to create extra space for clarification questions in connection with lectures, or in follow-up groups. This is because the figures in Table 3 show that respondents with low lecture comprehension scores have extra need to ask questions about language and content. Yet another option would be to encourage students to work together in preparation for lectures and groups, and as a follow up (see Airey & Linder 2006).

Next, in order to help students follow the lecturers' line of thought, it is important to ensure that lectures are well structured. It is also important that lecturers provide information about where they are and where they are going in their lectures. This is called "[i]nteractive discourse structuring – the use of metadiscursive [signposting] comments such as 'First, let's look at' or 'what I will do now is' – can also facilitate lecture comprehension, particularly for L2 listeners" (Vandergrift 2007: 202; see also Dafouz & Núñez this volume).

The present study also highlights the importance of the lecturers' use of well-made visual aids, since the analysis shows that weaker students rely heavily on the lecturers' visual aids to support their understanding (see Table 5). Airey and Linder (2006) also observed that students had problems simultaneously taking notes and listening to the lecturer, which suggests the utility of providing copies of the lecture notes beforehand, as many lecturers actually do. For instance, when listening to an EM lecture in a well-established program while carrying out the survey, I noticed that lecture notes had been made available to the students in a booklet, and that many students were annotating these during lectures.

A last point is to introduce language learning goals into EM courses to remind all parties of the extra value of learning content through an L2, as well as the need to take language issues into consideration when teaching and designing courses. It is also important to work actively to improve the students' language proficiency. One means of doing so would be requiring students to write papers and give presentations in English, and by assessing these for language quality as well as content, as is done at the University of Maastricht (Hellekjær & Wilkinson 2003). Doing so, however, will require the support of a language specialist, to teach language, sort out language problems, and to assist students in producing domain-specific texts and presentations. This also requires close cooperation between the subject matter lecturers and the language specialists to properly integrate content and language aims in teaching (Jacobs 2007).

5. Conclusion

To sum up, the present study shows that Norwegian students in higher education experience lecture comprehension difficulties when English is used instead of the L1. Given the Norwegian reputation for English proficiency, this means that this is most probably a problem elsewhere as well. For EM programs, ensuring quality will therefore require active efforts to improve lectures through effective lecturing behavior, to help students handle language difficulties during lectures, and to improve the students' as well as the lecturers' English proficiency.

References

Airey, J. 2009. Science, Language and Literacy. Case Studies of Learning in Swedish University Physics. Ph.D. dissertation, University of Uppsala.

Airey, J. & Linder, C. 2006. Language and the experience of learning university physics in Sweden. *European Journal of Physics*, 27(3): 553–560.

Ary, D., Jacobs, L.C. & Razavieh, A. 1996. *Introduction to Research in Education*. Fort Worth TX: Harcourt Brace College.

Bonnet, G. (ed.). 2004. *The Assessment of Pupils' Skills in English in Eight European Countries 2002*. The European network of policy makers for the evaluation of educational systems. <http://www.reva-education.eu/> (11 June, 2009).

Buck, G. 2001. *Assessing Listening*. Cambridge: CUP.

Halvorsen, T. & Faye, R. 2006. *Internasjonalisering. Evaluering av NIFU STEP: Kvalitetsreformen, Delrapport 8*. Oslo-Bergen: Norges forskningsråd, Rokkansenteret.

Harrington, T. & Harrington, J. 2001. A new generation of self-report methodology and validity evidence of the ability explorer. *Journal of Career Assessment* 9(1): 41–48.

Hellekjær, G.O. 2004. Unprepared for English-medium instruction: A critcal look at beginner students. In *Integrating Content and Language: Meeting the Challenge of a Multilingual Higher Education*, R. Wilkinson (ed.), 147–161. Maastricht: University of Maastricht.

Hellekjær, G.O. 2007. The implementation of undergraduate level English medium programs in Norway: An explorative case study. In *Researching Content and Language Integration in Higher Education*, R. Wilkinson & V. Zegers (eds), 68–81. Nijmegen & Maastricht: Valkhof Pers & Maastricht University.

Hellekjær, G.O. & Westergaard, M.R. 2003. An exploratory survey of content learning though English at Nordic universities. In *Multilingual Approaches in University Education*, C. van Leeuwen & R. Wilkinson (eds), 65–80. Maastricht: University of Maastricht.

Hellekjær, G.O. & Wilkinson, R. 2003. Trends in content learning through English at universities: A critical reflection. In *Multilingual Approaches in University Education*, C. van Leeuwen & R. Wilkinson (eds), 81–102. Maastricht: University of Maastricht.

Hellevik, O. 1999. *Forskningsmetode i sosiologi og statsvitenskap* (6 ed.). Oslo: Universitetsforlaget.

Ibsen, E.B. 2004. Engelsk i Europa – 2002. *Acta Dididactica*, Vol. 2. Oslo: University of Oslo.

Jacobs, C. 2007. Integrating content and language: Whose job is it anyway? In *Researching Content and Language Integration in Higher Education*, R. Wilkinson & V. Zegers (eds), 35–47. Nijmegen & Maastricht: Valkhof Pers & Maastricht University.

Klaassen, R. 2001. *The International University Curriculum: Challenges in English-medium Engineering Education*. Delft: Delft University of Technology.

Ljosland, R. 2008. Lingua Franca, prestisjespråk og forestilt fellesskap: Om engelsk som akademisk språk i Norge: Et kasusstudium i bred kontekst. Ph.D. dissertation, Norges teknisk-naturvitenskapelige universitet, Trondheim.

Marian, V., Blumenfeld, H.K. & Kaushanskaya, M. 2007. The language experience and proficiency questionnaire (LEAP-Q): Assessing language profiles in bilinguals and multilinguals. *Journal of Speech, Language, and Hearing Research* 50: 940–967.

Messick, S. 1996. Validity and washback in language testing. *Language Testing* 13(3): 241–256.

Nikula, T. 2007. The IRF pattern and space for interaction: Comparing CLIL and EFL classrooms. In *Empirical Perspectives on CLIL Classroom Discourse,* C. Dalton-Puffer & U. Smit (eds), 179–204. Frankfurt: Peter Lang.

Oscarson, M. 1997. Self-Assessment of foreign and second language proficiency. In *Language Testing and Assessment,* C. Clapham & D. Corson (eds), 175 – 187. Dordrecht: Kluwer.

Räsänen, A. 2000. *Learning and Teaching through English at the University of Jyväskylä,* No. 4. Jyväskylä: Jyväskylä University Language Centre.

Rayner, K. & Pollatsek, A. 1989. *The Psychology of Reading.* Englewood Cliffs NJ: Prentice-Hall.

Ross, S. 1998. Self-assessment in second language testing: A meta-analysis and analysis of experiential factors. *Language Testing* 15(1): 1–20.

Shadish, W.R., Cook, T.D. & Campbell, D.T. 2002. *Experimental and Quasi-experimental Designs for Generalized Causal Inference.* Boston MA: Houghton Mifflin.

Tella, S., Räsänen, A. & Vähäpassi, A. 1999. *Teaching through a Foreign Language: From Tool to Empowering Mediator,* Vol. 5. Helsinki: Publications of Higher Education Evaluation Council.

Vandergrift, L. 2007. Recent developments in second and foreign language listening comprehension research. (Review). *Language Teaching* 40(3): 191–210.

Vinke, A.A., Snippe, J. & Jochems, W. 1998. English-medium content courses in non-English higher education: A study of lecturer experiences and teaching behaviours. *Teaching in Higher Education* 3: 383–394.

Appendix

1.   Course _____

2.   University/college _____

SOME QUESTIONS ABOUT YOUR BACKGROUND

3.   Are you: ☐ Male   ☐ Female

4.   What is your first language?
     ☐ Norwegian/Swedish/Danish   ☐ English   ☐ Other

5.   Do you use English regularly in social situations?   ☐ Yes   ☐ No

6.   Do you use English regularly in job related situations?   ☐ Yes   ☐ No

7.   Did you attend high school in Norway?   ☐ Yes   ☐ No

8.   If yes to 7: What was the most advanced English course you completed in Norwegian high school.

     ☐ First year course   ☐ Second year course   ☐ Third year course

Have you received any other forms of English instruction in high school?
(You may give several answers)

9. ☐ yes   ☐ no   Instruction in a non-language subject, for example
                     History or Religion, in English?

10. ☐ yes   ☐ no   High school in an English speaking country
                     (6 months or more)

11. ☐ yes   ☐ no   Attended an English language high school, i.e. the
                     International Baccalaureate.

12. How many English books do you read per year? (Give only one answer)
    ☐ None   ☐ 1–3   ☐ 4–6   ☐ 6–12   ☐ 13 or more

13. How often do you read English periodicals, magazines or newspapers?
    (Give only one answer)
    Never   sometimes   monthly   weekly   daily
    ☐ 1   ☐ 2   ☐ 3   ☐ 4   ☐ 5

14. How often do you read English on the Internet? (Give only one answer)
    Never   sometimes   monthly   weekly   daily
    ☐ 1   ☐ 2   ☐ 3   ☐ 4   ☐ 5

15. How often do you watch English language movies, videos, or TV programs?
    (Give only one answer)
    Never   sometimes   monthly   weekly   daily
    ☐ 1   ☐ 2   ☐ 3   ☐ 4   ☐ 5

16. How often do you speak English? (Give only one answer)
    Never   sometimes   monthly   weekly   daily
    ☐ 1   ☐ 2   ☐ 3   ☐ 4   ☐ 5

17. How often do you write English? (Give only one answer)
    Never   sometimes   monthly   weekly   daily
    ☐ 1   ☐ 2   ☐ 3   ☐ 4   ☐ 5

QUESTIONS ABOUT YOUR UNIVERSITY LEVEL STUDIES

18. Have you studied in an English speaking country while at college or university?
    ☐ No   ☐ 1–6 months   ☐ 6–12 months   ☐ more than a year

19. How long have you studied so far?
    ☐ 1 year   ☐ 2 years   ☐ 3 years   ☐ 4 years   ☐ 5 years or more

20. Were any of your courses in English as a subject, such as English literature or grammar?   ☐ Yes   ☐ No

21. If yes to 20, please indicate how many credits (studiepoeng) of the subject English you have completed (30 credits = 1 semester).
    ☐ 2–30 credits   ☐ 31–60 credits   ☐ 61–90 credits   ☐ 91 credits or more

QUESTIONS ABOUT YOUR ATTENDING AN ENGLISH-MEDIUM COURSE OR PROGRAM
English Medium Instruction is the teaching of non-language subjects through English, such as Economics, Medicine or Political Science in English, to students for whom English is a foreign language. In the questionnaire I call these EM courses/programs.

22. Have you attended an English Medium course before this semester?
    ☐ Yes   ☐ No

Indicate your reasons for attending an English-Medium course:

23. ☐ yes   ☐ no   I am/was an exchange student.

24. ☐ yes   ☐ no   The course is part of an EM program with several subjects that are taught in English

25. ☐ yes   ☐ no   To improve my English

26. ☐ yes   ☐ no   I am/was interested in this specific course

27. ☐ yes   ☐ no   Other reasons _____

28. How useful do you believe knowing English will be in your future career?
    Not   Very
    at all   useful
    ☐ 1   ☐ 2   ☐ 3   ☐ 4

29. Are you interested in working outside Norway/your own country in your future career?
    Not   Very
    at all   interested
    ☐ 1   ☐ 2   ☐ 3   ☐ 4

30. Are you interested in working in a job where English is the working language?
    Not   Very
    at all   interested
    ☐ 1   ☐ 2   ☐ 3   ☐ 4

31. Do you think knowing English is important when applying for new jobs?

Not   Very
at all   important

☐ 1   ☐ 2   ☐ 3   ☐ 4

32. Do you think having completed English Medium courses will give you an advantage when applying for a job?

No advantage   A great
at all   advantage

☐ 1   ☐ 2   ☐ 3   ☐ 4

33. What is your opinion of the extra work involved in taking an English Medium course ?

It is not worth   It is worth
the extra effort   the extra effort

☐ 1   ☐ 2   ☐ 3   ☐ 4

QUESTIONS ABOUT YOUR UNDERSTANDING OF LECTURES IN YOUR FIRST LANGUAGE (SUCH AS NORWEGIAN). YOU MAY ANSWER ON THE BASIS OF COURSES YOU HAVE HAD EARLIER.

34. How often do you **read in preparation for lectures** in Norwegian/your first language?

Never   For every lecture

☐ 1   ☐ 2   ☐ 3   ☐ 4

35. Indicate on the scale **to what extent you find words and expressions** in the Norwegian/mother tongue lectures **unfamiliar.**

All the words are unfamiliar   All the words are familiar

☐ 1   ☐ 2   ☐ 3   ☐ 4

36. Indicate on the scale **to what extent words and expressions are clearly pronounced and understandable** in Norwegian/mother tongue lectures.

All words are   All words are
indistinctly pronounced   clearly pronounced

☐ 1   ☐ 2   ☐ 3   ☐ 4

37. Indicate on the scale to what extent do you experience that **the lecturer in Norwegian/mother tongue lectures speaks too fast.**

Too fast to   I have no difficulties
understand   understanding

☐ 1   ☐ 2   ☐ 3   ☐ 4

38. Indicate on the scale **how often you want to ask about unfamiliar words and expressions** during Norwegian/mother tongue lectures.

All the time   I never want to ask

☐ 1   ☐ 2   ☐ 3   ☐ 4

39. Indicate on the scale to what extent you can **follow the lecturer's line of thought during Norwegian/mother tongue** lectures.

The lecturer's line of thought   The lecturer's line of thought
is difficult to follow   is easy to follow

☐ 1   ☐ 2   ☐ 3   ☐ 4

40. Indicate on the scale to what extent you **understand the content of the Norwegian/ mother tongue lectures**.

Impossible to understand   Everything is understandable

☐ 1   ☐ 2   ☐ 3   ☐ 4

41. Indicate on the scale to what extent **the information** in the Norwegian/mother tongue lectures **is presented so quickly that it hinders your understanding**.

Too much information   I have no difficulties
to understand   understanding the
                                 information presented

☐ 1   ☐ 2   ☐ 3   ☐ 4

42. Indicate on the scale **how often you want to ask about unclear content** during Norwegian/mother tongue lectures.

All the time   I never want to ask

☐ 1   ☐ 2   ☐ 3   ☐ 4

43. Indicate on the scale **how important the lecturer's transparencies/ PowerPoint slide – or other visual aids** are for your understanding of Norwegian/mother tongue lectures.

Very important for   Not important for my
understanding   understanding

☐ 1   ☐ 2   ☐ 3   ☐ 4

44. Indicate on the scale **how difficult you find taking notes** during Norwegian/mother tongue lectures.

Impossible to take notes   It is easy to take notes

☐ 1   ☐ 2   ☐ 3   ☐ 4

45. Indicate on the scale if you **get the chance to ask questions** during and after the Norwegian/mother tongue lectures.

Difficult to ask questions   Easy to ask questions

☐ 1   ☐ 2   ☐ 3   ☐ 4

QUESTIONS ABOUT YOUR UNDERSTANDING OF LECTURES IN ENGLISH

46. Indicate in percent **how much of the lectures are in English:** _____ %

47. Indicate how often do **you read in preparation for lectures in English?**
Never   For every lecture
□ 1   □ 2   □ 3   □ 4

48. Indicate on the scale **to what extent you find words and expressions in the English language** lectures **unfamiliar.**
All the words are unfamiliar   All the words are familiar
□ 1   □ 2   □ 3   □ 4

49. Indicate on the scale to what extent **words and expressions are clearly pronounced and understandable in the English language lectures**
All the words are   All the words are
indistinctly pronounced   clearly pronounced
□ 1   □ 2   □ 3   □ 4

50. Indicate on the scale to what extent do you experience **that the lecturer in English language lectures speaks too fast.**
Too fast to understand   I have no difficulties
                                           understanding
□ 1   □ 2   □ 3   □ 4

51. Indicate on the scale how often you **want to ask about unfamiliar words and expressions** during English language lectures.
All the time   I never want to ask
□ 1   □ 2   □ 3   □ 4

52. Indicate on the scale to what extent you can **follow the lecturer's line of thought during English** lectures.
The lecturer's line of thought   The lecturer' line of thought
is difficult to follow   is easy to follow
□ 1   □ 2   □ 3   □ 4

53. Indicate on the scale **to what extent you understand the content of the English lectures.**
Impossible to understand   Everything is
                                           understandable
□ 1   □ 2   □ 3   □ 4

54. Indicate on the scale to what extent the **information in the English lectures is presented so quickly** that it hinders your understanding.

Too quickly to understand

I have no difficulties understanding

☐ 1   ☐ 2   ☐ 3   ☐ 4

55. Indicate on the scale how often **you want ask the lecturer about unclear content** during English lectures.

All the time

I never want to ask

☐ 1   ☐ 2   ☐ 3   ☐ 4

56. Indicate on the scale **how important the lecturers' transparencies/PowerPoint slides – or other visual aids** are for your understanding of English lectures.

Very important for understanding

Not important for understanding

☐ 1   ☐ 2   ☐ 3   ☐ 4

57. Indicate on the scale **how difficult you find taking notes** during English lectures.

Impossible to take notes

Easy to take notes

☐ 1   ☐ 2   ☐ 3   ☐ 4

58. Indicate on the scale if you **get the chance to ask questions** during and after the lectures in English.

Difficult to ask questions

Easy to ask questions

☐ 1   ☐ 2   ☐ 3   ☐ 4

59. Indicate **how much work you find attending a course in English compared to one in Norwegian/your first language (L1).**

Just like in Norwegian/your LI

Much more work than in Norwegian/your L1

☐ 1   ☐ 2   ☐ 3   ☐ 4

60. Which language will/did you use for **oral examinations/presentations** in your English language course(s).

☐ Norwegian/first language   ☐ English

61. Which language will/did you use for **written examinations/papers** in your English language course(s).

☐ Norwegian/first language   ☐ English

IF YOU HAVE TIME TO ANSWER:

62. What do you like best about your lectures in English? Answer in your own words (feel free to use the other side of the page):

_____

_____

_____

63. What do you like the least about your lectures in English? Answer in your own words (feel free to use the other side of the page):

_____

_____

_____

64. Do you have any further comments or things to add? Answer in your own words (feel free to use the other side of the page):

_____

_____

_____

CLIL in an English as a lingua franca (ELF) classroom

On explaining terms and expressions interactively

Ute Smit
Universität Wien, Austria

Based on a longitudinal study of an international educational programme in English as the participants' lingua franca, this chapter argues for 'interactive explaining' as a new construct that offers direct access to analysing content and language integrated learning at the micro-level. A detailed discourse-pragmatic analysis of twelve lessons spread over two years in this tertiary classroom community of practice has revealed distinct patterns of explaining subject-specific versus general terms and expressions. The results offer new and revealing insights into, firstly, the community-specific discursive 'principle of joint forces' and, secondly, the different activation of subject- vs. language expertise in discursively integrating new concepts into already shared knowledge.

1. Introduction[1]

As especially tertiary education focuses largely on imparting, developing or constructing knowledge, it amounts to a common-place that 'explaining' or "making (something) comprehensible" (*Collins Cobuild English Dictionary* 1998) is a central role of teaching. At the same time, explaining is also the skill learners are often required to perform in contributing to the lesson or in revealing their acquired knowledge. It seems, therefore, only logical that the ability to explain is generally regarded as a highly relevant asset for successful teaching and learning (e.g. Kiel 1999: 15ff). As illustrated in Quotes 1 and 2, the students of the study in question are no exception in this regard as they describe explaining as a crucial discourse function in constructing successful main classroom talk (Ehlich & Rehbein 1986).

---

1. Many thanks to the co-editors and reviewers for their critical suggestions which have helped me to clarify and improve on the contribution.

Quote 1. Interview (1st sem, 4th mth) [2]
Anns: I think it's [=the teachers' English] very good, I mean all the teachers are
       nice in speaking their language and explaining us.

Quote 2. Interview (1st sem, 3rd mth)
Suka: some are like they know it, but they cannot explain us. they are not able to
       explain us. I mean they just they are also in the middle and we are not even
       in the middle we are just down.

In contrast to such personal experiences and reflections on the relevance of explaining in education, classroom discourse research has shown interest in this discourse function rather sporadically, with only a handful of studies dedicated to it (Ehlich & Rehbein 1986; Kidd 1996; Kiel 1999; Lemke 1990; Mohan & Slater 2005). It is the aim of this contribution to strengthen the relevant research by underlining that explaining is not only crucial to the dynamic learning process in general, but it also offers real-time glimpses on instances of meaning making, of familiarising oneself with thus far new expressions and concepts. Explanatory exchanges offer 'analytical windows' (Antaki 1994: 1) on learners discursively (re)constructing their take on the topics in question. In educational programmes that are run in an additional language, such discursive reconstructions are likely to combine content and language issues; or, put differently, they can be seen as instantiations of content and language integrated learning or CLIL.

As expounded in more detail elsewhere (e.g. Introduction, this volume), CLIL is generally identified as a relatively new teaching approach in European primary and secondary schools, which entails teaching and learning through an additional language in pursuit of, amongst other motivations, the European policy of enhancing multilingualism (Dalton-Puffer & Smit 2007; Marsh & Wolff 2007). Given that similar considerations have also shaped educational language planning at the tertiary level, an increasing number of mainland European post-secondary institutions use an additional language as medium of instruction. While this recent development might have been sparked by other motivations as well, such as an increase in fee-paying international students, it has resulted in a considerable number of mainly English-medium tertiary programmes (e.g. Fortanet-Gómez & Räisänen 2008) attended by multilingual students to whom studying in English is a new, and often daunting experience (cf. also the recent literature on integrating content and language at tertiary level, e.g. Wilkinson 2004; Wilkinson & Zegers 2007).

---

2.   In order to respect the participants' anonymity, indications of time are given in relative terms only, by specifying the semester and month within the tertiary educational programme investigated. Furthermore, the students are referred to by arbitrarily chosen pseudonyms consisting of four-letter combinations, while upper-case three-letter ones are reserved for the teachers.

This is also the case in the educational setting under investigation in this paper. As will be explained in more detail in the next section, the respective educational programme is run in English in order to facilitate a truly international student intake. English is the only language all participants share, i.e. it is their 'lingua franca' and makes (classroom) communication possible. Therefore, and in contrast to CLIL at the primary and secondary levels, language learning is not considered a motivation for choosing the classroom language, as official documents, but also the participants themselves have made clear. As, however, motivation for language choice cannot be equalled with discursive practices, it would be hasty and, as this paper will show, mistaken to conclude that language learning does not take place. On the contrary, subject knowledge learning is largely a discursive process, which suggests that learning in an additional language subsumes both the respective subject topics as well as the classroom language.

This contribution approaches this issue on the micro-level by analysing explanatory exchanges of terms and concepts in the classroom talk of one tertiary programme (see Section 4). In preparation for this analysis and its interpretation (Section 5), the reader is first introduced to the study itself (Section 2) as well as to explaining as an interactive discourse process (Section 3).

2.   The study: Setting and methodology[3]

The investigation reported on here is a 'discourse-pragmatic ethnography' of classroom interaction, that is "a qualitative applied linguistic investigation that combines discourse analytical and pragmatic approaches with (educational) ethnography and aims at a principled analysis and informed interpretation of [...] classroom interaction". (Smit 2010: 87) Additionally, this approach understands formal learning as a social practice (e.g. Rampton 2006) that develops dynamically in temporary communities of practice (Corder & Meyerhoff 2007; Wenger 1998), in which, for a set period of time, students and teachers are united by their common endeavour and "develop and share ways of doing things, ways of talking, beliefs, values – in short, practices – as a function of their joint engagement in activity". (Eckert 2000: 35)

The tertiary setting in question is a two-year international hotel management programme set at a hospitality education centre in Vienna, Austria. While the programme leads to a diploma in hotel management and is thus job-oriented rather than academic, it is accepted as first part of respective BBA (Bachelors of Business Administration) programmes at other hospitality education institutions.

3.   This study has been made possible by a research grant of the Austrian Science Fund; the transcriptions have in part been financed by a grant of the 'Wiener Hochschuljubiläumsstiftung'.

Reflecting its practical nature, the programme offers a broad introduction to the various areas of expertise central to the hospitality industry, such as hotel management, accounting, marketing or public relations, as well as typical hospitality skills, such as serving, cooking or front office computer programmes. This is reflected in a dense study programme of on average 34 contact lessons per week. Additionally, students are required to do a three-month internship in a hospitality business of their choice between the first and second year of studies, thus gaining what is the first practical experience for most of them.

In accordance with the ethnographic research methodology, I accompanied one group and their teachers (henceforth HMP) for the whole duration of their studies, starting on their very first day and acting as non-participant observer throughout the four semesters until their graduation, all of which took place in the first decade of the 21st century (cf. Smit 2010 for the detailed study report). The student group was truly international: the 28 students had 14 different nationalities, reported to use 14 different home languages and eight further languages of communication, and had previously lived on all continents apart from Australia. The teachers involved in the study, on the other hand, reflected the local setting more clearly: apart from one native British teacher, they were Austrians with extensive international work experience. As regards English, however, teachers and students displayed similarly diverse backgrounds and kinds of experience. While some had used English extensively in education before, others had studied the language as a subject only and/or used it for professional or private reasons. The group can thus be described as heterogeneous in terms of lingua-cultures as well as English language proficiency levels.

The description of the setting already suggests that English functioned as classroom language in the HMP because of the practical necessity of relying on the one language all participants could communicate in. As the recent increase in publications on English as a lingua franca shows (e.g. Gnutzmann & Intemann 2008; Jenkins 2007; Prodromou 2008; Seidlhofer 2010; Smit 2010), applied linguistic research into the contemporary role(s) and function(s) of English has embraced this motivation for using English amongst speakers of various L1s and placed this research focus centre-stage (for an overview see Smit 2010: ch. 2.3). For the purposes of this study, ELF is conceptualised as "the use of English amongst multilingual interlocutors whose common language is English and who communicate in a country or area in which English is not used in daily life" (Smit 2005: 67). This entails that ELF communication is – typically, but not exclusively – situated outside English-speaking areas, that it is put into practice by multilinguals drawing on their linguistic repertoires who, furthermore, act as communicators and users of the language, rather than its learners. Furthermore, participants of ELF interactions have revealed a great deal of awareness of their different backgrounds and the little they usually share lingua-culturally when engaging in their communicational practices in English (e.g. Smit 2010). As remarked perceptively by House (2003), it is revealing to conceive of ELF communications as creating and shaping communities of practice, whose 'joint enterprise' is "to successfully negotiate on the content plane (reach a common goal) and on the level of linguistic (English) forms" (ibid.: 572). In view of the twofold relevance of the 'community of practice' notion for an educational ELF setting, the HMP is arguably well characterised as a classroom community of practice, in that it is an aggregate of students and teachers mutually engaged in the joint enterprise of co-constructing classroom discourse in order to meet educational aims with the help of the classroom language as developing shared repertoire (Smit 2010: 10–11).

In an attempt to analyse the discourse in the classroom community of practice in its diversity, dynamics and longitudinal developments, I observed more than 120 lessons spread over the two years of the hotel management programme, a tenth of which were chosen as data base for analysing explaining. As presented in Table 1, the 12 lessons were selected according to the three parameters time, subject and teacher. While the latter two aim at a balanced representation of the subjects and teachers involved, the former reflects the longitudinal character of the study. Based on the emic insights gained during the extensive pilot phase that preceded the study proper, three critical phases were singled out as especially relevant to the developing community:

T1: the short introductory phase of getting to know one another;
T2: the latter half of the first semester and familiarization with the subject content areas;
T3: the third semester, also building on the practical hotel experience gathered during the summer internships.

Table 1. Data base for 'explaining'

Phase	Lesson	Teacher	Mins	Words
T1	Hotel Management	LER	50	7017
(first	Austrian Law	XEN	43	5855
2 weeks)	Marketing	NER	47	10306
	Hotel Operations	OUL	49	4933
T2	Hotel Management	LER	46	8160
(2nd half	Austrian Law	XEN	49	6963
of sem.1)	Cooking – theory	RER	42	7423
	Human Resources	OPP	41	7728
T3	Hotel Management	LER	45	6823
(sem. 3)	Financial Management	TON	39	6015
	Marketing	NER	37	8108
	Public Relations	MER	45	8928
Sum			*533*	*88259*

This data base amounting to almost nine hours or 90 000 words has been scrutinised for the students and teachers engaging in 'interactive explaining'.

3.   On conceptualising 'interactive explaining'

While diverse research frameworks such as philosophy (e.g. Govier 1987), social studies (e.g. Antaki 1994), classroom pedagogy (Kiel 1999) or classroom discourse analysis (e.g. Lemke 1990; Mohan & Slater 2005) have been employed to elucidate explanatory communicational processes, the respective analyses display surprising overlaps in their conceptualisations. They agree that the central discursive function of explanations is "to account for, or show the cause of, a state of affairs" (Govier 1987: 159) in reaction to a knowledge deficit (Kiel 1999: 68). Put more discursively, the literature suggests that explaining is employed by interlocutors in order to make certain discourse topics, referred to as 'explananda', more easily comprehensible by connecting them with other, more familiar topics, or 'explanantia'.

This understanding implies that what is identified as explanandum is either assumed as in need of explaining or it is discursively established as such. The resulting distinction between assumed and established explananda specifies two basic motivations for instigating explaining in a classroom: on the one hand, teachers in their role as 'primary knowers' (Berry 1981) expect that certain topics are unfamiliar to students and thus treat them *a priori* as explananda. This contrasts with the cases when the ongoing classroom discourse identifies certain topics as in need of explanation and thus turns them into explananda *a posteriori*. While the former, didactically motivated explanatory exchanges, would undoubtedly be well worth analyzing, especially for their pedagogical merits (cf. Kiel 1999), it is the latter, the interactionally stimulated explanatory sequences that show how students and teachers spontaneously engage in explicating partly unsatisfactorily understood topics. They thus offer an 'analytical window' on the interactional processes themselves as well as on the discursive co-construction of new knowledge structures relevant to what Marton, Runesson and Tsui (2004) refer to as the respective 'object of learning'. Despite the static term chosen, 'object' is explicitly conceived of as a capability which combines action, such as, for instance, remembering or interpreting with "the thing or subject on which these acts are carried out" (ibid.: 4) such as, in the case of the HMP, hospitality qualification systems or taxation formulae. In other words, explanatory exchanges offer an 'analytical window' on the learning process itself.

Based on these considerations, the focus here is on 'interactive explaining' or, for short, INTEX. As illustrated in Figure 1, INTEX is conceptualised as integral to classroom discourse, which (re)constructs the respective social practice of, for instance, learning the principles of the Austrian legal system or the ground rules for a PR manager in a hotel. This is done in the classroom specific constellation of a group of students ('Student 1', 'Student 2' up to 'Student n') and one teacher per subject ('Teacher'), who acts by default as classroom organiser and manager (visualised in Figure 1 by 'Teacher' facing 'Students 1-n').

Most centrally, the figure presents INTEX or interactive explaining as an integral part of classroom discourse and specifies it as, firstly, focusing on specific topics turned explananda and, secondly, developing sequentially, mirroring the turn-by-turn nature of interaction. The individual steps reflect the generally accepted description of 'explaining' summarised above. As certain *explanantia* might lead to reformulations of the original *explanandum* and to further explanations, explaining can take place in loops (represented by the backwards arrow in the figure). At the same time, the labels given to the three basic steps point to 'interactive' as specific characteristic of INTEX in two ways: firstly, it is taken as a defining feature in that only those explaining exchanges are considered whose explanations follow on explananda that are interactively established. Secondly, this emphasis on interactive realisations as starting point of the analysis pays tribute to the potential discrepancy between 'knowledge deficits' that are cognitively experienced vs. those that are explicitly verbalised. As the latter is the only level accessible to participants in talk as well as the analyst, it is the one relevant here.

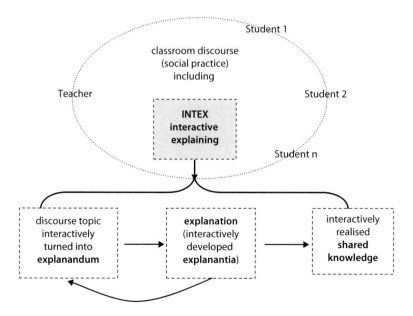

Figure 1. INTEX – 'interactive explaining'

For the sake of illustration, let us turn to Extract 1, taken from a Marketing lesson in the introductory phase (T1). While talking about the various departments of hotels, the teacher, NER, realises that 'stewarding' might be a new term to some of the students and turns it into an explanandum ('exm') in lines 2 and 3, asking the students for an explanans ('exp'). Kosk responds immediately and offers such an explanation (line 4), which the teacher acknowledges as correct (line 5).

Extract 1. Marketing (T1); 'clarifying *stewarding*'[4]

exm		1	NER	[...] even the stewarding (.) department
		2		you know what the stewarding department is, (1) in
		3		a hotel
exp	i.e.	4	Kosk	for dish-washing (.)
		5	NER	washing dishes. (2)

Besides such prototypical examples of teacher-led I:R:F (initiation- response-feedback) exchanges (cf., e.g. Nassaji & Wells 2000; Sinclair & Coulthard 1975), INTEX comes in highly diverse speaker constellations, such as in Extract 2, in which the roles of questioner and respondent are exchanged. In this Hotel Management class, it is the student who turns a term used by the teacher into an explanandum (line 3) and the teacher who offers an explanation (lines 3–6), which Kosk acknowledges as satisfactory in line 7.

Extract 2. Hotel Management (T2); 'clarifying *competitors*'

		1	LER	(2) and sometimes from your competitors and colleagues.
exm		2	Kosk	(1) competitors ? <SOFT> what's a competitor </SOFT>
exp	e.g.	3	LER	yeah, if you have a good relation with your
		4		competitor, and the er the general manager of the
		5		other hotel, (.) is a good friend of you, then you can
		6		ask him I need some new china, where do you buy it.
		7	Kosk	yeah.

In addition to changing participation patterns of who initiates explananda and offers explanantia, these examples underline another relevant criterion of description: the 'how' of INTEX or the main semantic and logical relations between explanandum and explanantia. Despite a potentially much wider range of relations (e.g. Dalton-Puffer 2007; Lemke 1990), the present data set displays only the employment of elaboration and of taxonomic relationships (see Figure 2).

---

4. For the transcription conventions see the Appendix.

In Extract 1, the student uses an exposition ('i.e.' in column 2), while the teacher in Extract 2 draws on exemplification ('e.g.').

Main relations between EXM (explanandum) and EXP (explanantia)	
Elaboration:	exposition (i.e.)
	exemplification (e.g.)
	clarification (viz.)
Taxonomic type/token:	glossing (glos)
	translating (tran)

Figure 2. 'How' of INTEX (cf. Lemke 1990)

Finally, the sample extracts illustrate the type of explananda focused on in this paper: lexical items in need of interactive explaining. While the detailed analysis of the 12 lessons has revealed various types of topic turned into explananda – such as institutions, regulations or personal experiences (cf. Smit 2010: ch. 7.3.3) – the following analysis will show that it is INTEX on terms and expressions that reveals the discursive processes of negotiating conceptual understanding in the HMP and how the participants managed to co-construct knowledge in their classroom community of practice.

4. Analysing INTEX on lexical items

While the research methodology applied here is mostly qualitative, a quantitative glance at the data offers a first overview of how often teachers and students explained topics interactively. As can be gleaned from Table 2, in the 12 lessons analysed, the participants engaged in interactive explaining 125 times, with more than a third of these episodes relating to lexical items in need of further explanation. When turning to the three critical phases, the relative frequencies (last column) reveal that lexical uncertainties triggered explanatory exchanges considerably more frequently right at the beginning of the programme. With time

Table 2. Instances of INTEX

Phase	INTEX in total	INTEX on lexical items	% of total
T1 (first 2 weeks)	30	18	60
T2 (sem. 1, 2nd half)	57	19	33
T3 (sem. 3)	38	8	21
Sum	125	45	36

progressing interactive explaining turned to other explananda, focusing on lexical items in only one out of five cases. Even though the data permit no statistical analysis, this numerical decrease could reflect a diminishing need in explaining lexical items with the students becoming familiar with the respective subject areas and their terminologies.

In elaboration of this tendency, the 45 instances of INTEX on lexical items have been analysed qualitatively, which has revealed that the lexical items explained fall into two distinct groups as regards their relation to the subject content in question or the respective 'object of learning' (Marton, Runesson & Tsui 2004): the lexical items being explained are either treated as directly linked to the respective object of learning, i.e. they are seen as discipline- or subject-specific, or they do not denote a subject-specific concept and, thus, fall into what is generally referred to as 'general English' (e.g. Basturkmen 2006: 15–17; Dudley-Evans & St. John 1998: 3–9). In other words, the analysis of INTEX reveals two different discursive constructions of explaining technical and semi-technical terms, on the one hand, and non-technical lexical items, on the other (cf. Nation 2001). While the latter refer to the vast group of "general language terms" (Hüttner 2007: 156), the former contain words which, in relation to a certain subject or its related discipline, are either "specific [… or] which are given different or more precise meanings" (ibid.).

4.1 Explaining subject-specific terms

As illustrated in Extract 1, subject-specific terms tend to be introduced by the teacher. The terms are discursively established as belonging to the respective subject topic and therefore identified as objects of learning. So, irrespective of whether it is the teacher or a student who turns a subject-specific term into an explanandum, it is the teacher's task to either provide or, at least, sanction the term and its explanation as correct.

A case in point is Extract 3 (a and b). Set in an Austrian Law lesson in the second half of the first semester (T2), it contains the dynamic, but teacher-led construction of *testimony* rather than *witness* as the technical term for someone testifying in courts of law.

Extract 3a. Austrian Law (T2); 'clarifying a witness's role, using *testimony*'

		1	XEN	(4) we need a testimony, who is a testimony? who is
		2		testimony? (3)
exm		*3*	Jenz	what? testimony?
		4	XEN	that's what does a testimony do?
exp	i.e.	*5*	Crek	attended the (.) happening and has to say the truth in
		6		front of the court. (.) <1> testimony </1>

		7	Jenz	is this <1> a (xxxx) </1>?
exm'				
	e.g.	8	XEN	no. (.) testimony. testimony, you for example,
		9		you have been out there (.) while the other guy
		10		crashed his car into the other car. (1) and you
		11		where there just waiting for the bus and you say,
exp		12		<QUOTATIVE squeaky voice> oh terrible, terrible,
		13		</QUOTATIVE> (1) and you saw the whole thing,
		14		with police came
	glos	15	Jenz	witness
		16	XEN	=to witness it.
exm"		17	Jenz	is called testimony,
		18	XEN	you come and give your testimony. (.) so you are (.)
	viz	19		erm asked to <QUOTATIVE> tell the truth, nothing
exp		20		but the truth </QUOTATIVE> (.) in front of your
		21		(god), (what) you've witnessed, (.) and not (.) tell a
		22		little better in another way to make it better for one
		23		of them. (1) so you're,
		24	Jenz	I do
		25	XEN	you d- you do it,
		26	Jenz	mhm testimony
		27	XEN	yeah testimony

The extract is taken from a lesson phase in which the teacher XEN describes the participant roles at court in preparation of staging the scenario in class. In line 1, XEN turns to the witnesses and asks for a student willing to play this role *(who is a testimony?)*. Unfamiliar with the term, Jenz, a Chinese student, turns it into an explanandum, which XEN rephrases (line 4). Crek, a German student, provides a partial definition (lines 5–6). This Jenz reacts to by offering an unfortunately inaudible gloss with which XEN is not happy. Instead, the teacher offers an exemplification (lines 8–14) which Jenz uses again to provide a gloss, this time audibly (line 15). XEN acknowledges the term *witness*, but only as a verb, which has the implicature of it not being a noun (see Jenz's comment in line 17). XEN implicitly agrees with Jenz's comment by describing the role of a witness at court (lines 18–23). Interestingly, she introduces this instance of clarification by using *testimony*, in systemic functional terminology (Lemke 1990: 222), as target and then sways from this use of the term, which would be 'correct' with regard to English first language norms, and uses it for the agent as well (line 27), establishing it as technical term for the person testifying at court.

As supported in Extract 3b, which takes place some six minutes later than 3a, *testimony* in this agentive sense has been accepted as appropriate term. When the classroom interaction returns to the topic of acting as witness at court, the term *testimony* is used in this meaning not only by the two students involved in the first exchange, Jenz (line 2) and Crek (line 10) and the teacher (line 16), but also by a further, this time Austrian, student, Anki (lines 14 + 17). *Testimony* referring to the agent providing a report on happenings important to the court case in question is thus established as the appropriate technical term in this group of Austrian Law students (and is used again in this meaning towards the end of that lesson).

Extract 3b. Austrian Law (T2); 'using *testimony*'

	1	XEN	who are you, (.) Jenz?
	2	Jenz	I am the **testimony** or the police and the (x).
glos	*3*	XEN	yeah, you are the one who witnessed anything, yeah.
	4	Jenz	hm
viz	*5*	XEN	okay? erm and sometimes if it's a criminal thing, you are
	6		the victim. (1) yeah? because the victim is only asked erm
	7		what happened, tell us, just like the policeman saw it, (1)
	8		yeah is it <QUOTATIVE> oh I saw it, I felt it, yeah? (2) I
	9		witnessed it (.) on my own body, </QUOTATIVE>
viz	*10*	Crek	there could be an additional (.) **testimony** as well,
	11	XEN	yeah sure, yeah, (2) there can be TEN of them, yeah? a
	12		doctor from the ambulance and (.) yeah. and you are the
	13		one, the cruel one. yeah?
viz	*14*	Anki	and is it possible to have a **testimony** too? as a criminal or
	15		not.
	16	XEN	you being the **testimony**?
	17	Anki	no, (1) if if I am the criminal to have a **testimony**,
	18	XEN	yeah
	19	Anki	yeah?
	20	XEN	yeah for sure, (.)

In sum, this case illustrates what the analysis of INTEX on subject-specific terms has shown: such explanations are either directed by the teacher or, if largely offered by students, require the teacher's sanctioning as appropriate. Furthermore, the thus established term and meaning meet with general acceptance within the classroom community of practice, even if contrasting with previously held understandings. In other words, the teachers' generally uncontested status as content experts extends to subject-specific terms and expressions.

4.2   Explaining general language terms

As can be expected from the distinction made here between technical and semi-technical vs. non-technical terms, INTEX on the latter has revealed a markedly different discursive construction. Put in a nutshell, terms or expressions associated with general English are explained as regards their local and temporal situatedness of use and provided by whoever can do so. This means that teachers and students offer community- and setting-specific explanantia, aiming for a collaborative explanation of the term identified as explanandum that is fully contextualised in the here and now.

Let me illustrate this interactive co-construction of explaining general lexical items by first returning to Extract 2, in which the term *competitor* is used by the Hotel Management teacher and then immediately identified as unknown by a student who requests an explanation (line 3). While elaborating on her previous statement, the teacher offers an explanans rather indirectly by describing the competitor she has in mind as *the general manager of the other hotel*. By way of such an exemplification ('e.g.' in Extract 2), the student can grasp the local, pragmatic meaning of *competitors*, but does not get a semantic clarification or definition of the lexeme (e.g. Widdowson 1996: 61–62).

As indicated above, explanatory help on general English terms is not only offered by the teacher, but also by students. Extract 4, for instance, is taken from one of NER's extended and lively narrations of personal experiences, during which he needs the English equivalent for *Umleitung*, i.e. 'diversion' (lines 3 to 5). Instead of attempting a paraphrase, he simply asks the listeners to help out, which Crek does extremely promptly (see the overlap in lines 5 and 6). NER briefly acknowledges the term and continues with his story.

Extract 4. Marketing (T3); 'translating *Umleitung*'

		1	NER	⟨relates a recently made experience⟩ and I have my map,
		2		(.) er (.) but at some stage I have an <GERMAN>
exm		*3*		Umleitung <GERMAN>. er (.) what do we call an
		4		<GERMAN> Umleitung </GERMAN>
		5		<1> in English? </1>
exp	tran	*6*	Crek	<1> a diversion.</1>
		7	NER	a diversion. right, (.)

Extract 5 is taken from a Hotel Management lesson from the third semester. Preceding the extract, the teacher describes a hotel, referring to the modern paintings in the reception hall (lines 1–2). When she halts in her description, a student immediately offers an unintelligible suggestion (line 3), which LER is eager to take up, thus asking for repetition (line 4). Another student offers *artist*, which LER acknowledges as appropriate, but not completely fitting to her intended word. In response to the German equivalent LER offers, the observer and the student provide the English translation that LER is happy to pick up (line 10) for her ensuing description of this hotel. In other words, this example shows that the moment the teacher hovers over a word (line 2) or indicates that a slightly different one is actually intended (lines 6–7) others 'jump in' verbally and try to help out.

Extract 5.   Hotel Management (T3); 'searching for the English equivalent of *Maler*'

		1	LER	(.) and there there where these huge paintings from a very
		2		modern Austrian (.) erm (2) bro-?
		3	SX-m	(xx)
		4	LER	\<GERMAN\> was ? \</GERMAN\>
	i.e.	5	SY-f	artist
exm		6	LER	artist yeah. @ I was thinking about \<GERMAN\> Maler
		7		\</GERMAN\>
	tran	8	US	\<1\> painter \</1\>
exp		9	SY-f	\<1\> painter \</1\>
		10	LER	painter. even if he is an artist he is a painter. @@

When it comes to non-technical, general English, the data has thus revealed that teachers neither act as those who by default know the appropriate terms, nor are they discursively required to do so. All the participants seem happy to help each other and their classroom talk along and, if possible, provide highly situated explanations of expressions which were interactively identified as in need of such. As can be expected from this collaborative approach, INTEX on general terms and expressions does not need the teachers as the ones 'sanctioning' the appropriate term and conceptual understanding, neither do they (expect to) act as primary knowers in language matters. Put more positively, explaining general language matters is undertaken by all community members who have something to contribute towards discursively acknowledged shared understanding. As this finding has found support in analyses of repair work and directing classroom talk (Smit 2007a, 2010), it illustrates an interactive principle in this community of practice, which for obvious reasons I suggest to call 'principle of joint forces'.

So far, the findings have been presented as if they were rather uniform; but this is far from the case. Due to the longitudinal methodology covering the community investigated for over two years, the findings actually gain in explanatory strength: in addition to general discursive patterns they also allow insights into time-dependent developments. As regards INTEX on lexical items, the analysis has revealed that interactive explanations of subject-specific terms are given in all three critical phases (T1, T2, T3), but those of non-specific terms appear with one exceptional case only after the introductory phase (see Table 3). As the one exception of interactive explaining on general language items took place at the end of the introductory two weeks, this instance supports the interpretation that it took students and teachers some time before they started to turn general lexical items into explananda and to respond to them by engaging in explanatory exchanges.

Table 3. INTEX on subject-specific vs. general lexical items

INTEX on lexical items	subject-specific	general	in total
T1 (first 2 weeks)	17	1	18
T2 (2nd half of sem. 1)	13	6	19
T3 (sem. 3)	3	5	8
Sum	33	12	45

While 45 items is a relatively small data base and interpretations have to be done with due caution, this appearance of INTEX on general terms practically exclusively during T2 and T3 might indicate that, at a time when most students were complete novices in the respective subject areas, subject-specific explananda were more numerous and maybe also considered more relevant, with non-specific terms going past undetected. Another reason might also have been that students and teachers were still strangers to each other, thus possibly finding the discursive activity required for interactive explanatory exchanges such as in Extract 5 too daunting an undertaking. In other words, it could be that interactive explaining required a certain degree of sense of community before it revealed the 'principle of joint forces' when dealing with non-technical explananda. Furthermore, the data also indicate a difference between T2 and T3 as regards students' discursive roles. While they were generally more hesitant to engage actively at T2 without any teacher invitation or call to do so, the examples from the third semester show the general openness of all students to interact (see Extracts 4 and 5). Familiarity within the community, but I wish to argue also with the respective subject matters seem to have had their impact on students' (self perceived) interactional roles in main classroom talk.

5. Conclusions

Based on the solid foundations of a detailed discourse pragmatic ethnography of one tertiary educational programme set in Austria but undertaken in English, this contribution has argued for a new analytical concept, i.e. interactive explaining or INTEX and its merits for analysing the interactional dynamics of explaining as a central discourse function of educational discourse. Reflecting the constructivist and practice approach prevalent in this study (cf. Smit 2010), INTEX describes discursive sequences, in which the teacher and/or students first raise an 'explanandum', i.e. a discourse topic that is considered to be in need of more satisfactory integration in the participants' understanding of the social practice in question. As long as interactionally deemed necessary, this topic is then enlarged upon in the ongoing interaction in the form of 'explanantia'. In other words, INTEX focuses on discursively constructed sequences of making sense of so far new or unclear topics and ideas and of integrating them into established knowledge structures (Mohan & Slater 2005). It thus suggests itself as an analytical approach to interactive sequences of discursively realised moments of learning. Given that in the present study the classroom language is an additional one for learners and teachers, interactive explaining can be argued as allowing micro-level insights on, as it were, 'content and language integrated learning' in the making.

The analysis of classroom talk recorded during the first and third semesters of a tertiary hotel management programme has revealed that lexical items form one category of discourse topics that is regularly and centrally turned into explananda in educational talk. In view of the international character of the educational setting and the fact that English functions as the participants' lingua franca, the centrality of lexical items as in need of explanation is less surprising; the analytical findings, however, are remarkable in at least two regards. Firstly, the longitudinal methodology applied has allowed insights into the developing relevance of the 'principle of joint forces', i.e. the readiness to contribute to the ongoing (explanatory) exchanges by whoever can do so. Instances of INTEX taken from the three critical phases analysed point out that the group of participants needed to develop into a community of practice before teachers and students could collaborate on supplying an appropriate and satisfactory explanation, bringing into the exchange whatever is interactionally necessary. After the introductory phase, the data have shown that if one explainer cannot produce the expected information, another participant will help out, irrespective of otherwise clearly observed teacher or student roles.

Secondly, the analysis has unearthed previously unacknowledged patterns of explaining that are related to the kind of lexical item explained. For subject-specific lexical items, i.e. technical and semi-technical terms pertaining to the subject content in question, explanatory exchanges are centrally 'orchestrated' by the teachers in their roles as classroom manager and uncontested subject expert. Thus, the teacher's suggestions of technical terms and their explanations are integrated into the verbal practices of a certain subject; even when that means changing a previously established understanding of the respective lexical item. General lexical items, on the other hand, receive their explanations in a markedly different way: they tend to be fully situated and contextualised in space and time (cf. Lea 2005; Smit 2007b) and constructed by whoever feels able to contribute to the exchange. As neither of the participants acts as – or is interactively made to be – the expert on general language issues, such interactive explanations are preferably achieved jointly, indicating a kind of joint expertise in language matters, to which community members are welcome to contribute.

While, as discussed elsewhere (e.g. Smit 2010), these two explanatory patterns reflect the function of English as a lingua franca in this community, these findings arguably hold insights for core CLIL settings at tertiary and secondary levels as regards the construction of content and language expertise as well as the dynamically developing roles of the social players involved. Such a transferability of findings suggests itself in view of the shared characteristic that the classroom language is, for most participants, an additional language which they command at varying levels of language proficiency. Consequently, it is likely that language expertise is not something to be found in the CLIL teacher alone, but rather to be of a more complex nature, comparable to the situation in the tertiary educational setting described here. As long as language issues fall into the subject in question, teachers can be expected to take on the expert role, but when the lexical problems are of a more general nature, expertise and thus linguistic appropriateness can be expected to develop into a community concern. This suggests that language learning in CLIL settings necessitates the active participation of all as they engage in the complementary processes of teacher-led subject-specific language learning, on the one hand, and community-driven general language learning, on the other. As the necessity of interactivity for language learning implies orality rather than literacy, this finding bears potentially revealing insights into the scarcity of literacy learning opportunities in such ELF educational contexts. Taken in combination with the emic evaluations of the HMP students who explicitly denied any improvements in their written language abilities (Smit 2007b), the question of literacy learning in such educational contexts is definitely well worth further investigations. At the same time and given the distribution of language expertise over all social players, it can be argued that CLIL settings allow for the otherwise relatively stable power differential between teacher and students to open up towards a more flexible and dynamic give-and-take (cf. Nikula 2007). On a speculative note, the resulting dynamic power relations might be one of the reasons for the generally attested success of CLIL for language learning.

In conclusion, the study has argued for interactive explaining as a discourse function that allows direct and micro-level access to discursive learning processes. In view of the analytical value this investigative approach holds for actual instances of CLIL, it is hoped that the initial findings presented here will soon be complemented by comparable investigations in other educational settings integrating content and language learning.

References

Antaki, C. 1994. *Explaining and Arguing: The Social Organization of Accounts*. London: Sage.
Basturkmen, H. 2006. *Ideas and Options in English for Specific Purposes*. Mahwah NJ: Lawrence Erlbaum Associates.
Berry, M. 1981. Systemic linguistics and discourse analysis: A multi-layered approach to exchange structure. In *Studies in Discourse Analysis,* M. Coulthard (ed.), 120–145. London: Routledge.
Collins Cobuild English Dictionary. 1998. London: Harper Collins.

Corder, S. & Meyerhoff, M. 2007. Communities of practice in the analysis of intercultural communication. In *Handbook of Intercultural Communication, HAL 7*, H. Kothoff & H. Spencer-Oatey (eds), 441–461. Berlin: Mouton de Gruyter.

Dalton-Puffer, C. 2007. *Discourse in Content and Language Integrated Learning (CLIL) Classrooms* [Language Learning & Language Teaching 20]. Amsterdam: John Benjamins.

Dalton-Puffer, C. & Smit, U. (eds). 2007. *Empirical Perspectives on CLIL Classroom Discourse.* Frankfurt: Lang.

Dudley-Evans, T. & St. John, M.J. 1998. *Developments in English for Specific Purposes.* Cambridge: CUP.

Eckert, P. 2000. *Linguistic Variation as Social Practice.* Malden MA: Blackwell.

Ehlich, K. & Rehbein, J. 1986. *Muster und Institution. Untersuchungen zur schulischen Kommunikation.* Tübingen: Narr.

Fortanet Gómez, I. & Räisanen, C. (eds). 2008. *ESP in European Higher Education. Integrating Language and Content* [AILA Applied Linguistics Series 4]. Amsterdam: John Benjamins.

Gnutzmann, C. & Intemann, F. (eds). 2008. *Globalisation of English and the English Language Classroom.* Tübingen: Narr.

Govier, T. 1987. *Problems in Argument Analysis and Evaluation.* Dordrecht: Foris.

House, J. 2003. English as a Lingua Franca: A threat to multilingualism? *Journal of Sociolinguistics* 7(4): 556–578.

Hüttner, J.I. 2007. *Academic Writing in a Foreign Language. An Extended Genre Analysis of Student Texts.* Frankfurt: Peter Lang.

Jenkins, J. 2007. *English as a Lingua Franca: Attitude and Identity.* Oxford: OUP.

Kidd, R. 1996. Teaching academic language functions at the secondary level. *The Canadian Modern Language Review/La Revue Canadienne des Langues Vivantes* 52(2): 285–303.

Kiel, E. 1999. *Erklären als didaktisches Handeln.* Würzburg: Ergon.

Lea, M.R. 2005. 'Communities of practice' in higher education. In *Beyond Communities of Practice. Language, Power and Social Context*, D. Barton & K. Tusting (eds), 180–197. Cambridge: CUP.

Lemke, J.L. 1990. *Talking Science. Language, Learning and Values.* Norwood NJ: Ablex.

Marsh, D. & Wolff, D. (eds). 2007. *Diverse Contexts – Converging Goals. CLIL in Europe.* Frankfurt: Peter Lang.

Marton, F., Runesson, U. & Tsui, A. 2004. The space of learning. In *Classroom Discourse and the Space of Learning*, F. Marton & A. Tsui (eds), 3–40. Mahwah NJ: Lawrence Erlbaum Associates.

Mohan, B. & Slater, T. 2005. A functional perspective on the critical 'theory/practice' relation in teaching language and science. *Linguistics and Education* 16: 151–172.

Nassaji, H. & Wells, G. 2000. What's the use of 'triadic dialogue'? An investigation of teacher-student interaction. *Applied Linguistics* 21(3): 376–406.

Nation, I.S.P. 2001. *Learning Vocabulary in Another Language.* Cambridge: CUP.

Nikula, T. 2007. The IRF pattern and space for interaction: Comparing CLIL and EFL classrooms. In *Empirical Perspectives on CLIL Classrooms Discourse*, C. Dalton-Puffer & U. Smit (eds), 179–204. Frankfurt: Peter Lang.

Prodromou, L. 2008. *English as a Lingua Franca. A Corpus-based Analysis.* London: Continuum.

Rampton, B. 2006. *Language in Late Modernity. Interaction in an Urban School.* Cambridge: CUP.

Seidlhofer, B. 2010. Forthcoming. *Understanding English as a Lingua Franca.* Oxford: OUP.

Sinclair, J. & Coulthard, M. 1975. *Towards an Analysis of Discourse. The English Used by Teachers and Pupils.* Oxford: OUP.

Smit, U. 2005. Multilingualism and English. The lingua franca concept in language description and language learning pedagogy. *Favorita Papers* 4: 66–76. (Vienna: Diplomatic Academy).

Smit, U. 2007a. ELF (English as a Lingua Franca) as medium of instruction. Interactional repair in international hotel management education. In *Empirical Perspectives on CLIL Classroom Discourse*, C. Dalton-Puffer & U. Smit (eds), 227–252. Frankfurt: Peter Lang.

Smit, U. 2007b. Writing in English as a lingua franca (ELF) in international higher education. In *Researching Content and Language Integration in Higher Education*, R. Wilkinson & V. Zegers (eds), 207–222. Maastricht: University Language Centre.

Smit, U. 2010. *English as a Lingua Franca in Higher Education. A Longitudinal Study of Classroom Discourse*. Berlin: Mouton de Gruyter.

Wenger, E. 1998. *Communities of Practice. Learning, Meaning, and Identity*. Cambridge: CUP.

Widdowson, H. 1996. *Linguistics*. Oxford: OUP.

Wilkinson, R. & Zegers V. (eds). 2007. *Researching Content and Language Integration in Higher Education*. Maastricht: Universitaire Pers.

Wilkinson, R. (ed.). 2004. *Integrating Content and Language. Meeting the Challenges of a Multilingual Higher Education*. Maastricht: Universitaire Pers.

Appendix

Transcription conventions

3-letter pseudonyms (in capitals)	refer to teachers
4-letter pseudonyms	refer to students
(.)	pause shorter than a second
(2)	pauses, timed in seconds
exte:nsion	noticeable extension of a syllable or sound
cut off wo-	cut off word or truncated speech
.	falling intonation
?	rising intonation
,	level intonation
CAPITALS	stressed syllables, words
<1> </1>, etc	overlapping speech
<SOFT>text</SOFT>	text spoken in a soft voice
<QUOTATIVE>text</QUOTATIVE>	speaker quoting somebody else
<GERMAN> Text </GERMAN>	German words or expressions
[…]	deletion of text
<text>	added explanations
(xxx)	inaudible speech, 'x' stands for approximately one syllable
text	translation from the original German
text (in Excerpts)	material which is currently under discussion
@	laughter

Language use and language learning in CLIL

Current findings and contentious issues

Christiane Dalton-Puffer, Tarja Nikula & Ute Smit
Universität Wien, Austria/Jyväskylän yliopisto, Finland/Universität Wien, Austria

1. Summary of findings

The contributions to this volume have approached the subject matter from different theoretical and methodological perspectives, based, however, on the common understanding that the institutional setting is *a*, if not *the*, crucial factor in determining how teachers and learners *use* language in CLIL lessons. As a consequence, the institutional context also crucially co-determines the language *learning* that will take place.

By and large, CLIL research has emphasized the effects of CLIL on language performance, especially speaking and, more recently, writing; overall, interpretive abilities in listening and reading have received little attention. In this sense, Hellekjær's chapter with its focus on listening represents a new departure (cf. also Jiménez Catalán & Ruiz de Zarobe 2007). Not only do Norwegian university students find CLIL lectures more difficult to comprehend than lectures in their L1, their responses also reveal a considerable level of comprehension difficulties in their L1, suggesting that certain genres or text types may be intrinsically challenging irrespective of the language of instruction. In an analogous line of reasoning, Llinares & Whittaker and Lorenzo & Moore show that the performances of CLIL students cannot be fully explained by mere reference to their limitations in the L2 but clearly interact with their overall cognitive development and general academic language ability (CALP) in the L1 (cf. also Jäppinen 2005; Vollmer et al. 2006).

The studies dealing directly with face-to-face classroom interaction underline the nature of CLIL classrooms as a context of situation with specific discursive practices (Hall 1993) for language use. Overall, they confirm that CLIL teaching offers relatively more interactional space for students (e.g. Llinares & Whittaker, Maillat), affording them with a range of communicative intentions that are not typical of most EFL lessons. Because the language of instruction is usually L2 for both learners *and* teachers an enhanced discourse space seems to be possible on the basis of which both teachers and students can renegotiate their respective roles. That is, students' more active role in CLIL lessons as compared to L1 or EFL lessons may reflect their ability to appropriate for themselves a certain level of expertise in language matters vis a vis their instructors (Nikula, Smit).

Although teachers are rarely explicitly in focus, their oral language use turns out to differ depending on whether they teach in their L1 or an L2. It seems that the L1 allows for more stylistic variability and discursive flexibility (Dafouz & Núñez, Nikula). In their L2, by contrast, teachers tend to use a smaller stock of discursive devices, at times doing so in potentially misleading ways. This characteristic also appears in Hellekjær's aural comprehension study, inasmuch as students tend to find L2 lectures more demanding not only in terms of lexical difficulties, but also as regards lecture structuring. Additionally, L2 pronunciation seems to cause some comprehension problems; a finding which is echoed in studies into English used as a lingua franca (cf. also Jenkins 2000; Smit 2007).

As regards oral production, the chapters of this book comparing CLIL students with traditional EFL students (Hüttner & Rieder, Maillat, Ruiz de Zarobe) underscore the results of Ruiz de Zarobe's (2008) quantitative survey, which showed CLIL students ahead on all dimensions of speaking ability, thereby corroborating self-reports regarding student's perceived speaking confidence (Dalton-Puffer et al. 2008). Hüttner & Rieder and Maillat concur in ascribing CLIL students greater flexibility and listener-orientedness in the use of communication strategies: CLIL students appear more self-assured in getting their intended meanings across in the L2 even if they momentarily lack linguistic resources (see also Nikula 2008). CLIL students also show more experience in dealing with the requirements of spontaneous conversational interaction (Maillat) and are more adept at implementing macro-level structuring devices as well as micro-level features like maintaining tense consistency in narratives (Hüttner & Rieder). However, the minimum instructional time in CLIL necessary for producing favourable effects remains an open issue, though, according to Ruiz de Zarobe (2007), 210 hours (2 school years of CLIL in one subject) did not produce significant differences between CLIL and non-CLIL learners. Nevertheless, evidence from this volume and other publications now appears robust enough to conclude that CLIL fosters spontaneous L2 speaking abilities, with pronunciation being the dimension least affected. At the same time, it is worth bearing in mind that in addition to general language skills, spoken skills in CLIL also need to be considered in relation to subject-specific genres and their conventions, a point raised both by Llinares & Whittaker and Morton.

This volume includes several contributions that deal with writing, a hitherto underexplored area in CLIL research. An interesting observation that feeds into the pool of evidence which grants CLIL students significant levels of strategic competence (see section on speaking above) is made by Lorenzo & Moore: they find that

CLIL students are able to successfully convey content notions at an early stage, even though their linguistic resources are still limited. The studies in the volume comparing CLIL and non-CLIL writing (Jexenflicker & Dalton-Puffer, Ruiz de Zarobe) concur in finding that CLIL students have at their disposal a wider range of lexical and morpho-syntactic resources, which they deploy in more elaborate and more complex structures. Particularly surprising, given the focus on meaning and not on form in CLIL, is the fact that CLIL students also show a higher degree of accuracy in their written production, including not only features such as the use of tenses but also adherence to spelling conventions. The greater pragmatic awareness of CLIL students shows in their better fulfilment of the communicative intentions of writing tasks. There are, however, areas of writing on which CLIL experience seems to have little or no effect. These are the dimensions that reach beyond the sentence level, i.e. cohesion and coherence, discourse structuring, paragraphing, register awareness, genre and style. Comparable results were obtained in contexts where writing tasks are a standard component of content-subject methodology (Spain) and contexts where they are not (Austria). What might contribute to this puzzling finding is the fact that in both countries features of text and discourse grammar are either presented in confusing ways via textbook writing prompts with misleading genre labels (Morton) or not explicitly taught at all.

Following on from the last statement, significant insights have also been gained by comparing CLIL-students' L2 writing with their writing in the L1 (Llinares & Whittaker, Lorenzo & Moore, Järvinen; cf. also Vollmer et al. 2006). Perhaps surprisingly, L1 writing has not necessarily been found to surpass CLIL-L2 writing in every respect. The areas of convergence between CLIL writing and L1 writing are exactly the same as the ones mentioned above, namely those concerning the textual level. Interesting practical as well as theoretical implications may be derived from this: might we be justified in postulating some kind of general level of writing development which has an impact on how learners deal with a writing task independently of whether it is in L1 or in L2? This is an issue that needs to be developed further with reference to current discussions on literacy (e.g. Prinsloo & Baynham 2008).

2. Contentious issues

As summarized above, the research studies presented in this volume show CLIL lessons to provide an educational context that affords participants with a range of opportunities for language use and language learning. Some of these contextual conditions coincide with those also present in traditional foreign language lessons (roles of teachers and learners, discourse rules of classroom interaction), others go beyond them (redistribution of expertise, more semantic focus because of content), while some seem more limiting (e.g. role flexibility, exclusion of personal topics). On the whole, however, and despite the reservations and limitations formulated by individual authors, the picture emerging with regard to language use and language learning in CLIL is positive, warranting the high degree of face validity and 'street credibility' that CLIL tends to receive from the public. However, considering the contributions in their totality also raises numerous issues, both conceptual and with regard to research practice. Next, we highlight those we consider to be worthy of particular attention.

2.1   Dilemmas of comparison and implications of research for practice

Two dilemmas exposed both in contributions to this volume and in CLIL research in general relate to doing comparative classroom-based research and to its relevance for educational practice. While both are seemingly inherent to educational research, they are particularly prominent in the CLIL context because of its fundamental reliance on the nature of language practices in class and on comparisons. A central question is this: what is the common ground against which comparisons are entertained? For research into the effects of CLIL, the obvious and undisputed 'common ground' is instructed language learning. But it is well known that education is far from monolithic, instead coming in a myriad of realizations, influenced by factors as diverse as educational goals, financial means available, parental interests and support, teachers' abilities and aptitude, and individual differences between the learners themselves. Consequently, it is hardly possible to find two learner groups with 'similar backgrounds' that would allow an uncontestable comparison of their educational achievements. To make matters even more complicated, CLIL programmes tend to be voluntary all over Europe, which means that in most cases CLIL students are not randomly selected. On the contrary, students tend to have gone through a selection process of some kind, be it because of parental choice or meeting certain intake criteria, thus very often forming some kind of elite (cf. de Mejiá 2002). Additionally, CLIL teachers are special in that they are willing to take on a considerable amount of extra work, which usually implies higher levels of motivation and pedagogical interest than teachers taken more generally. Given these special 'CLIL circumstances', straightforward comparisons between CLIL and mainstream teaching and learning are clearly fraught with difficulties. At the same time, making such comparisons is unavoidable if researchers want to accumulate more detailed descriptions and gain a deeper understanding of what a CLIL approach means for the actual content and language learning taking place in the field. Like all dilemmas, this one cannot be solved, but it can and should enter research designs. Contributions to this volume suggest, among other possibilities, focusing on the same group of learners (a) in their L1 and FL (Hellekjær, Järvinen, Llinares & Whittaker, Lorenzo & Moore, Maillat) or (b) at different moments in time (Ruiz de Zarobe, Smit); (c) on the same teachers (Dafouz & Núñez, Nikula); or (d) at different learner groups from the same school (Hüttner & Rieder-Bünemann, Jexenflicker & Dalton-Puffer). While such comparisons hold many factors stable, the author's cautious interpretations provide clear evidence that they are aware that other factors may yet have a biasing effect on the outcome. Readers would therefore be wise to take such cautionary comments at face value and interpret the respective findings accordingly.

As regards the second dilemma, namely whether CLIL research findings can contribute to enhanced practice, there exists little difference to the findings derived from any other educational setting: the relationship between research and practice is never straightforward so that research findings would automatically present recipes for good practice. It is inherently difficult to arrive at generalizations when studies may well have different analytical foci, make use of different types of data, and come from contextually very different situations. This is not to deny the relevance of contextualized research itself and of the relevance of its findings for practice. Rather, it points to the necessity of finding patterns and tendencies across a considerable number of studies. Here, many of the volume's contributions point towards implications for CLIL teacher education and suggest recommended forms of practice. For example, several studies find that mastering subject-specific conventions of language use is a challenge for students (Järvinen, Llinares & Whittaker, Morton), thereby signalling to CLIL teachers and teacher trainers the importance of paying attention to matters of language in CLIL in general and to its subject-specific aspects in particular, i.e. to make content and language integration a central concern also in teacher training. While suggestions for good CLIL practice do exist (e.g. de Graaff et al. 2007), their vantage point has usually been that of language pedagogy. A future task is to explore approaches that effectively combine language and content pedagogies, most likely by drawing on an integrated approach which entails "a language-based theory of human knowing" (Byrnes 2005: 281).

Another observation potentially relevant for teacher training and hence for enhancing future practice is that CLIL contexts seem to offer students more, and more varied, opportunities for interaction than do traditional language classrooms (Maillat, Nikula, Smit). Even if the reasons behind this may be varied and partly unintentional, it is possible to use research evidence from authentic classroom interactions to introduce to future CLIL teachers practices that seem to contribute to students' readiness to participate in classroom exchanges. Finally, some papers point to an important area where research results could be used in the future to develop good practice: CLIL teacher strategies at tertiary level. In tertiary institutions, CLIL is quite often considered unproblematic as, in Hellekjær's words, "it is taken for granted that lecturers will have few difficulties teaching in a foreign language". However, as the contributions by Dafouz & Núñez and Hellekjær show, comprehension problems may ensue for various reasons, ranging from teachers' inadequate or even misleading use of discourse organizing devices to problems in pronunciation. This, in turn, suggests that teachers at the tertiary level would benefit from professional guidance and in-service training.

Beyond that, the CLIL landscape also shows noteworthy lacunae. To begin with, the label 'CLIL' itself is not innocent. Its final 'L' points to a potentially ideologically motivated preference for learning over teaching, although naturally both processes are involved. The 'I' points to educational practices that integrate content and language learning in a balanced manner, by far the exception rather than the rule. The initial 'C' hints at just such problematic practices in as much as it hints at the possibility of imagining content as its own entity, separate from language. Finally, the first 'L' seems to imply that this educational approach is applicable to all linguistic codes established and used as foreign languages. None of these assumptions should be accepted at face-value, a conclusion that demands that we critically assess the language policy underlying CLIL use (see 2.2), the reality of English as the overwhelmingly favoured language in educational programmes (see 2.3) and, finally, the juxtaposition of language and content and its theoretical implications (see 2.4).

2.2   Policy and reality: tensions and pretensions

We discussed in the introductory chapter how European-level declarations on multilingual language policy treat CLIL as an integral part of policy measures that are to foster a heightened degree of multilingualism among European citizens. Consequently, CLIL is on this level first and foremost construed as a language teaching and/or learning strategy that has the advantage of delivering 'two' (foreign language and subject content) for the price of 'one' (teaching units). Given this orientation of CLIL, one would expect it to have been provided with the appropriate language learning goals on its way to implementation. A series of European expert groups and think-tanks has worked on this task with arguably ambivalent results: on the one hand the set of goals for CLIL was considerably and justifiably widened beyond mere 'better language competence'. Starting from Coyle's conceptualisation of the 4C's (communication, cognition, content, culture; e.g. Coyle 1999, 2007) the multidimensionality of CLIL as an educational concept has been considerably elaborated (www.ecml.at). On the other hand, the formulations of specific language goals have remained rather general. The version which emerged from the CLIL Compendium project (www.clilcompendium.com), for instance, mentions improving general language competence, oral communication skills and language awareness as CLIL language foci. It is evident, however, that language goals have to be much better elaborated if they are to be as fine-grained as those pertaining to overall content-learning goals or those put forth for foreign languages taught as school subjects. In the end, the formulation of such curricula is of course the responsibility of the respective national agencies but more elaborate conceptual guidelines and structured input would be highly desirable in order to bolster the claims associated with content-and-language integration in the classroom (more on the integration issue below).

Not surprisingly, actual implementation of CLIL has in most contexts proceeded without much attention to grand pronouncements. While its underlying motivation, deep down, will probably always involve aspects of language learning, realities of school life show CLIL to be very much a content-driven affair (cf. Stoller 2004). Rather than being based on integrated content and language curricula, CLIL lessons, almost without exception (but see the Andalusian *currículo integrado*; Lorenzo 2007; Lorenzo et al. 2009), proceed on the basis of the respective, already existing national curricula for the individual content subjects that 'happen' to be taught in the medium of the CLIL language (usually English, see below). Typically, CLIL teachers are subject teachers who have a good command of the target language or hold a dual teaching qualification; in some contexts these teachers are supported by native speaking assistant teachers, but this is by no means the norm. Research has also shown that even if teachers hold a dual-qualification as foreign language and as subject matter teachers they often feel a role-conflict (Dalton-Puffer 2007). A spate of questions arises in this connection: How should appropriate levels of teacher language competence be defined? What further competences are necessary to be a successful CLIL teacher? How should assessment be conceived of? And, linking back to the overall policy goals, exactly what kind of multilingual competence is CLIL supposed to produce and does it do so? Such questions pinpoint some of the faultlines of current CLIL practice; areas, that is, where the contradictions between policy and practice have created tensions that tend to be denied.

Such problems and inconsistencies support Bruthiaux's (2009: 125) statement that "European language education policy reflects not second language acquisition research but highly political horse trading among treaty writers". Yet the intriguing question remains of how to explain the undeniably positive potential of CLIL as an environment for foreign language learning and use, especially when students' level of performance is compared to those involved in regular foreign language instruction only. The advantages that CLIL seems to offer may, in fact, reveal as much about practices and traditions of language teaching as about CLIL *per se*: despite the long existence of calls for more communicative language teaching, the weight put on meaningful functioning with the foreign language may still be relatively low in most foreign language classrooms where, as Hall (2004: 76) suggests, discourse far too often consists of "listing and labelling of concepts" rather than meaningful personal engagement in talk. Content-based situations help steer learners' attention from language forms to things accomplished and meanings conveyed through language, and it may well be that herein lies the success of CLIL as a language learning environment. In other words, many CLIL contexts seem to bring to life and lend support to socially and functionally oriented views of language learning that emphasize the role of social interaction and joint meaning-construction, such as those drawing on sociocultural theory or dialogic inquiry, for example (Lantolf & Thorne 2006; Linell 1998). There is certainly room for more research in this area and for more thorough theoretical considerations of what using a foreign language for the purpose of content learning suggests about processes and practices of learning. While the contributions in this volume provide important indicators for the need of a redefinition of the whole language construct in CLIL, it remains a task for further research to explore more comprehensively how the CLIL enterprise can contribute to the formation of new theoretical insights about language and language learning and to find out whether, as Lorenzo et al. (2009: 18–19) argue, CLIL indeed "implies a new language model".

2.3   CLIL or CEIL (Content and English Integrated Learning)?

Experience tells us that there is a major difference between the potentially unspecific 'language' selected for the intended fused practice of teaching and learning and actual practices regarding the specific language/s being taught within European CLIL settings. In theory, most European systems allow CLIL in a variety of (inter)national and minority languages (cf. e.g. Eurydice 2008: 117–118). Outside the Anglophone countries, however, present CLIL practices seem to favour the use of English over other languages. In Austria, for instance, English is by far the most popular choice at all educational levels (Nezbeda 2005), as is the case in Spain or Finland (Lehti et al. 2006). This overwhelming preference for English is reflected in the research scene as well: most CLIL studies deal with English-based CLIL, as do all contributions in the present volume (but see Haataja 2009; van de Craen et al. 2007; Wiesemes 2007). To put it less gingerly, while the political and applied linguistic talk is about CLIL, what is actually at stake in the majority of cases is CEIL, Content and English Integrated Learning.

This overpowering dominance of English has numerous non-trivial consequences. There is firstly the language policy issue. While the explicit top-down statements underline the relevance of this teaching approach to turning Europeans into multilingual citizens competent in two additional languages, the actual bottom-up practices support bilingualism in the respective L1 and English. The long-term outcome of CLIL in Europe is thus unequivocally directed toward increasing the English language abilities throughout the continent. True multilingualism will remain a characteristic of minority and migrant groups as well as of socio-economic elites (generally involving economically more advantageous languages).

Secondly, and more centrally relevant to our discussion, we need to critically evaluate the generally attested success-story of CLIL. Given that most of the research findings are based on the use of English only, what generalized conclusions on the learning potential of this teaching approach for all foreign languages are justified? Granted, the extant literature on CLIL in languages other than English offers positive learning outcomes as well (e.g. Serra 2007). At the same time, most of these studies draw on learners who, for various reasons, have chosen to follow an unusual educational route. Such select learner groups are by definition poor models for mainstream learners. In sum, on the one hand, CLIL in multiple languages is unrepresentative of the European student population and their language learning success; on the other hand, CLIL in English has too narrow a language base from which to extrapolate findings to languages more generally.

The latter argument gains even more in weight when drawing attention to the unique status of English vis-à-vis all other languages. The extensive recent literature on English as a global language or English as a lingua franca (e.g. Mauranen & Ranta 2009; Seidlhofer 2010; Smit 2010), shows it to be the domineering language in international politics, commerce, as well as academia and many domains of the arts (Graddol 2006). These multi-layered functions for English are also reflected in its popularity as a foreign language: according to the *Special Eurobarometer* (2006) English is the most widely known and used additional language (by 38% of EU citizens), followed by German and French (each at 14%). Language practices favouring English over other additional languages seem to go hand in hand with learning motivation and attitudes, which are overwhelmingly positive in the case of English. While proficiency in other foreign languages is often considered an asset or maybe even an (unnecessary) 'luxury', English has attained such a high level of generally accepted instrumental relevance that the vast majority of Europeans have readily embraced it as a central aspect of general education. As Grin (2001: 75) pointed out at the beginning of the millennium, proficiency in English has become a *conditio sine qua non* for socio-economic success in the 21st century. This also explains why learning English is considered to be one of the present-day basic skills of literacy (Graddol 2006: 118).

Given this unparalleled situation of English in the foreign language learning landscape, one might argue that CLIL has been so successful throughout Europe simply because it has mainly been done in English, in the one language where the average European learner has the required levels of language proficiency and the necessary learning motivation. True or not, all research into CLIL should become more aware of its strong focus on CEIL and the resultantly narrow, if not biased data-base; in turn CLIL in languages other than English should focus more explicitly on potential contrasts with CEIL. Additionally, comparative research across additional languages of teaching and learning would allow insights into the strengths and weaknesses of CLIL language-independently.

2.4   Integrating language and content – from duality to fusion?

Throughout this volume we have argued that the central idea of CLIL lies in its nature as a dual-focused educational approach that seeks to fuse goals of content and language learning (Coyle, Hood & Marsh 2010). While this two-pronged educational goal for CLIL is widely acknowledged, theorizing in CLIL has treated it like a hot potato: much of the existing CLIL research has tended to focus on either its language or its content aspects, with much less attention being devoted to their interface, that is, the integration of language and content. Several reasons for this state of affairs can be adduced. Firstly, the rapid spread of CLIL has given rise to concerns about its viability as a language learning environment in particular, which has resulted in lively research activities especially in the area of SLA-based applied linguistics. Secondly, studies on content mastery in CLIL have tended to conceptualize content learning as learning of core concepts or conceptual structures (e.g. Jäppinen 2005) and content as "a fixed body of knowledge to be (re)constructed by learners" (Barwell 2005: 2005), with little attention to what role language and interaction play in this (re)construction (for an exception, see Alanen et al. (2006) who combine sociocultural, socio-cognitive, and discourse-pragmatic insights when exploring concept formation in a content-based context). Thirdly, given the long tradition of treating language and content learning as separate processes, we even lack proper terminology and vocabulary that would make it easier to address their simultaneity (Barwell 2010).

Therefore, it is imperative for the field to explore what content and language integration entails both at theoretical and empirical levels, in order to steer away from what Byrnes (2005: 280) calls "illusions of the existence and stability of content separate from language". As Gajo (2007: 564) puts it, we still lack "a firm basis of reflection on the very concept of integration". While a comprehensive CLIL theory might be premature, there can be little doubt about the need to begin developing one. Initial considerations are around and worth picking up: Gajo's (2007) sketch of discourse as functioning as intermediary between 'language' and 'content' resonates well with the recent calls for recasting the integrative process as originally postulated for this teaching approach as a more synthetic one – a *fusion* of content and language (e.g. Coyle, Hood & Marsh 2010: 41–45) rather than a simple combination of the two elements. This fusional perspective that would not entail strict divisions between language and content finds fitting theoretical bases for example in sociocultural approaches to learning that highlight language use and learning as mediated activities (e.g. Lantolf & Thorne 2006) or in approaches that emphasize the social, discursive and contextually situated nature of learning (e.g. Block 2003; Firth & Wagner 2007). Consequently, also conceptualizations of language and content and their fusion in CLIL need to be firmly rooted in empirical explorations of classroom practice in order to do full justice to the socially embedded nature of learning, teaching and language use.

Beyond the admittedly demanding task of developing a substantial CLIL theory, 'fusion' as a central notion has important implications for undertaking CLIL research. In contrast to the widespread practice of investigating such educational settings from a clearly identifiable disciplinary vantage point – either applied linguistic or content pedagogy – a fusional understanding would require a similarly 'fused' investigative take. In other words, research based on CLIL as 'fusion' presupposes an inter-, perhaps even transdisciplinary research construct. Instead of the unifocal perspective characteristic for CLIL studies, such as the applied linguistic perspective dominant in this volume, an understanding of CLIL as 'fusion' implies a multiperspectival view on both on language and content, which, taken together, should help us understand the fusion of language-and-content. There would seem to be little doubt that this can succeed only as an interdisciplinary project, both theoretically and empirically. We look forward to such a future for CLIL.

References

Alanen, R., Jäppinen, A.-K. & Nikula, T. 2006. "But big is a funny word": A multiple perspective on concept formation in a foreign-language-mediated classroom. *Journal of Applied Linguistics* 3(1): 69–90.

Barwell, R. 2005. Integrating language and content: Issues from the mathematics classroom. *Linguistics and Education* 16(2): 205–218.

Barwell, R. 2010. Second language learning in the mathematics classroom. A paper given in an invited colloquium 'Research perspectives on content-based second language instruction' at AAAL Conference, Atlanta, Georgia, 6–9 March 2010.

Block, D. 2003. *The Social Turn in Second Language Acquisition*. Edinburgh: EUP.

Bruthiaux, P. 2009. Multilingual Asia. Looking back, looking across, looking forward. In *AILA Review 22, Multilingual Globalizing Asia. Implications for Policy and Education*, L. Lim & E.-L. Low (eds), 120–130. Amsterdam: John Benjamins.

Byrnes, H. 2005. Reconsidering the nexus of content and language: A mandate of the NCLB legislation. *Modern Language Journal* 89(2): 277–282.

Coyle, D. 1999. Theory and planning for effective classrooms: Supporting students in Content and Language Integrated Learning contexts. In *Learning through a Foreign Language*, J. Mashid (ed.), 46–61. London: CILT.

Coyle, D. 2007. Content and language integrated learning: Towards a connected research agenda for CLIL pedagogies. *The International Journal of Bilingual Education and Bilingualism* 10(5): 543–562.

Coyle, D., Hood, P. & Marsh, D. 2010. *CLIL. Content and Language Integrated Learning.* Cambridge: CUP.

Dalton-Puffer, C., Hüttner, J., Jexenflicker, S., Schindelegger, V., Smit, U. 2008. Content and Language Integrated Learning an Österreichs Höheren Technischen Lehranstalten. Final Report. Bundesministerium für Unterricht, Kultur und Kunst.

Dalton-Puffer, C. 2007. *Language Use in Content and Language Integrated Learning (CLIL) Classrooms* [Language Learning & Language Teaching 20]. Amsterdam: John Benjamins.

de Graaff, R., Koopman, G.J., Anikina, Y. & Westhoff, G. 2007. An observation tool for effective L2 pedagogy in Content and Language Integrated Learning (CLIL). *The International Journal of Bilingual Education and Bilingualism* 10(5): 603–624.

de Mejía, A.M. 2002. *Power, Prestige and Bilingualism. International Perspectives on Elite Bilingual Education.* Clevedon: Multilingual Matters.

Eurydice. 2008. *Key Data on Teaching Languages at School in Europe.* European Commission.

Firth, A. & Wagner, J. 2007. Second/foreign language learning as a social accomplishment: Elaborations on a reconceptualized SLA. *The Modern Language Journal* 91(5): 800–819.

Gajo, L. 2007. Linguistic knowledge and subject knowledge: How does bilingualism contribute to subject development? *The International Journal of Bilingual Education and Bilingualism* 10(5): 563–579.

Graddol, D. 2006. *English Next. Why Global English Might Mean the End of 'English as a Foreign Language'.* London: The British Council.

Grin, F. 2001. English as economic value: Facts and fallacies. *World Englishes* 20(1): 65–78.

Haataja, K. 2009. CLIL – Sprache als Vehikel oder "Zweiklang im Einklang"? *Fremdsprache Deutsch. Zeitschrift für die Praxis des Deutschunterrichts* 40.

Hall, J.K. 2004. "Practising speaking" in Spanish: Lessons from high school foreign language classroom. In *Studying Speaking to Inform Second Language Learning,* D. Boxer & A. Cohen (eds), 68–87. Clevedon: Multilingual Matters.

Hall, J.K. 1993. The role of oral practices in the accomplishment of our everyday lives: The sociocultural dimension of interaction with implications for the learning of another language. *Applied Linguistics* 14: 145–166.

Jäppinen, A.-K. 2005. Cognitional development of mathematics and science in the Finnish mainstream education in Content and Language Integrated Learning (CLIL) – teaching through a foreign language. *Language and Education* 19(2): 148–169.

Jenkins, J. 2000. *The Phonology of English as an International Language: New Models, New Norms, New Goals.* Oxford: OUP.

Jiménez Catalán, R.M. & Ruiz de Zarobe, Y. 2007. Does the type of instruction have any bearing on EFL learners' receptive vocabulary? Paper presented at the ELIA 10 Conference. University of Seville, Spain.

Lantolf, J.P. & Thorne, S.L. 2006. *Sociocultural Theory and the Genesis of Second Language Development.* Oxford: OUP.

Lehti, L., Järvinen, H.-M. & Suomela-Salmi, E. 2006. Kartoitus vieraskielisen opetuksen tarjonnasta peruskouluissa ja lukioissa (A survey of content and language integrated teaching in general education). In *Kielenoppija tänään* (Language learner of today) [AFinLAn Yearbook 64], P. Pietilä, P. Lintunen & H.-M. Järvinen (eds), 293–313. Jyväskylä: The Finnish Association of Applied Linguistics.

Linell, P. 1998. *Approaching Dialogue: Talk, Interaction and Contexts in Dialogical Perspectives* [IMPACT: Studies in Language & Society 3]. Amsterdam: John Benjamins.

Lorenzo, F. 2007. An analytical framework of language integration in L2 content-based courses: The European dimension. *Language and Education* 21(6): 502–514.

Lorenzo, F., Casal, S. & Moore, P. 2009. The effects of Content and Language Integrated Learning in European education: Key findings from the Andalusian bilingual sections evaluation project. *Applied Linguistics Advance Access.* <http://applij.oxfordjournals.org/cgi/content/abstract/amp041v1>.

Mauranen, A. & Ranta, E. (eds). 2009. *English as a Lingua Franca. Studies and Findings.* Cambridge: Cambridge Scholars Publishing.

Nezbeda, M. 2005. *EAA Serviceheft 6. Überblicksdaten und Wissenswertes zu Fremdsprache als Arbeitssprache.* Graz: ÖSZ.

Nikula, T. 2008. Learning pragmatics in content-based classrooms. In *Investigating Pragmatics in Foreign Language Learning, Teaching, and Testing,* E. Alcón & A. Martínez-Flor (eds), 94–113. Clevedon: Multilingual Matters.

Prinsloo, M. & Baynham, M. (eds). 2008. *Literacies, Global and Local* [AILA Applied Linguistics Series 2]. Amsterdam: John Benjamins.

Ruiz de Zarobe, Y. 2007. CLIL in a bilingual community: Similarities and differences with the learning of English as a foreign language. In *VIEWS. Vienna English Working Papers* 16(3): 47–53. (Special Issue: *Current Research on CLIL* 2).

Ruiz de Zarobe, Y. 2008. CLIL and foreign language learning: A longitudinal study in the Basque Country. *International CLIL Research Journal* 1(1): 60–73.

Seidlhofer, B. 2010. *Understanding English as a Lingua Franca.* Oxford: OUP.

Serra, C. 2007. Assessing CLIL at primary school: A longitudinal study. *The International Journal of Bilingual Education and Bilingualism* 10(5): 582–601.

Smit, U. 2007. ELF (English as a Lingua Franca) as medium of instruction – interactional repair in international hotel management education. In *Empirical Perspectives on CLIL Classrooms,* C. Dalton-Puffer & U. Smit (eds), 227–252. Frankfurt: Peter Lang.

Smit, U. 2010. *English as a Lingua Franca in Higher Education. A Longitudinal Study of Classroom Discourse.* Berlin: Mouton de Gruyter.

Special Eurobarometer. 2006. *Europeans and Their Languages.* European Commission.

Stoller, F.L. 2004. Content-based instruction: Perspectives on curriculum planning. *Annual Review of Applied Linguistics* 24: 261–283.

Van de Craen, P., Ceuleers, P.E., Lochtman, K., Allain, L. & Mondt, K. 2007. An interdisciplinary research approach to CLIL learning in primary schools in Brussels. In *Empirical Perspectives on CLIL Classroom Discourse,* C. Dalton-Puffer & U. Smit (eds), 253–274. Frankfurt: Peter Lang.

Vollmer, H.J., Heine, L., Troschke, R., Coetzee, D. & Küttel, V. 2006. Subject-specific competence and language use of CLIL learners: The case of geography in grade 10 of secondary schools in Germany. Paper presented at the ESSE8 Conference in London, 29 August 2006.

Wiesemes, R. 2007. Developing a methodology for CLIL classroom research: a case study of a CLIL classroom where the Holocaust is taught. In *Empirical Perspectives on CLIL Classroom Discourse,* C. Dalton-Puffer & U. Smit (eds), 275–290. Frankfurt: Peter Lang.

Subject index

A

academic
  English 235, 246
  language functions 26, 81
  literacy 147, 172, 173
accuracy 31–2, 74, 172,
  175–180, 182
anxiety 50–53, 55
appropriateness
  appropriate genre/register/
    format 91–2, 174–6, 198
  appropriate lexis/term 68,
    165, 175, 181, 269–72
appropriation 170, 280
argumentative texts,
    writing 81, 172, 183
assessment
  of writing 166, 174–5,
  of listening 236–8
  self-assessment of
    comprehension
    237–9, 247
attention
  to form 24, 92, 286
  to social dimension of
    language 105
attitudes
  and motivation 50, 287
  to English 244–5
Austria 13, 66, 169, 170–3, 181,
    183, 261, 273, 281, 286
authentic
  language use 24, 34, 283
  task 173
awareness 165
  of genres/registers
    182, 281
  of mother tongue and
    target language
    192, 203
  pragmatic 182, 281

B

Basque Country 13, 194–6, 206
bilingualism 55, 194, 286

C

classroom
  discourse 8, 89, 98, 106, 115,
    119–20, 260, 264–5,
  discourse analysis 108, 264
  language 261–3, 274–5
clause
  complexes 125, 134–5, 137
  subordinate clauses 29, 136,
    153–4, 161, 180
CLIL
  and language learning 1–2,
    6–8, 10–12
  definition 1–3
  didactics 2, 8, 183
  historical development 3–5
  implementation 1, 3, 5, 9,
    23, 29, 34, 146, 191, 215, 285
  in Europe 1–7, 106, 191, 286
  language goals 2, 10, 284–5
  research 8–12, 105–6, 169,
    279–89
cognition 4, 6, 24, 49, 44–5,
    54–5
coherence 178, 281
  and connectives 175, 178, 182
  thematic 63, 68
communicative
  competence 6, 24, 41, 169,
    171, 203
  strategies 61–2, 64–5, 74–7
community of practice 259,
    263, 267, 270, 272, 274
content-based instruction
    1, 83, 85, 196, 203–4
content, communication,
    coherence and culture
    (4 Cs) 82, 97, 99, 141, 284
contrastive analysis 213–4,
    221, 229

D

discourse
  analysis 11–12, 107–8,
    261, 273

markers 118, 216–17
  pragmatics 11, 107, 110,
    259, 261
discourse pragmatic
    ethnography 261, 273

E

ELF 259, 262–263
  principle of joint forces 259,
    272–4
expertise
  in content/subject 114,
    259, 262
  in language 114, 259,
    274–5, 280
explaining 87–8, 259–261,
    264–5, 267–8, 270–5
  genres 87–88
exposure to foreign/target
    language 2, 24, 46, 151,
    195, 204–7, 244–6

F

field knowledge 85, 89–91, 93
Finland 105, 108, 115,
    151–2, 286
foreign language
  exposure 2, 12, 24, 46,
    66, 151, 195, 204–6,
    244–6
  learning 6, 12, 119, 196, 207,
    285
fossilization 32–3
fusion: content and language
    integration 2, 283, 285,
    288–9

G

general language ability/
    competence 10, 173, 175,
    181–2, 284
genre 62–4, 82
  arguing genres 87–8
  awareness 68, 72, 84, 98,
    100, 144, 165, 213–16

explaining 87–8
exposition genres 93–4, 157
genre-based pedagogy 81–2,
    84–5, 97–101
historical account/
    recount 86, 96, 99,
    127, 129
narrative 62–9, 72–4, 150,
    157, 160, 162
oral narrative 62–3, 67–8,
    72, 76
recording genres 86–8
report 83, 88–9, 95–7
grammar 171, 174–5, 179–182
grammatical intricacy
    154, 157
grammatical metaphor
    87, 93, 145–155, 158, 160,
    163–6

I
ideational function 125, 127,
    130, 149, 216
immersion 1, 7, 24, 33, 45–7,
    52–4, 202
interaction 8, 218, 221,
    268–70
in classrooms 39, 45–8,
    85, 105–7, 126, 141, 261,
    279–80
markers 225–7
patterns of 109, 112,
    114–15, 119,
    phase 127–8
interlanguage
    development 27, 32–4, 43
    pragmatics 41
    system 42–3
interpersonal function 85, 105,
    107–9, 125, 127, 130, 137,
    158–9, 218–19
IRF exchange 266

K
knowledge
    co-construction 264, 271

L
language learning
    goals 5, 146, 249, 284
    naturalistic 6
language (education)
    policy 3–6, 260,
    284–6

lecture
    comprehension 216–17, 225,
        233–5, 238–246
    phase of 216–9, 220,
        221–5, 230
lexical density 149, 152–7,
    164–5
lingua franca 53–4, 120, 227,
    259, 262, 274, 280, 287
listening comprehension/
    proficiency 235–6,
    238–9, 246–7
literacy 1, 10–11, 88, 100,
    148, 182
longitudinal progression/
    evaluation 191, 196, 205–7

M
mask effect 39–40, 50–5
metadiscourse/metadiscursive
    categories 220
    devices 213–14, 220
    phases 216–17
    taxonomy 218
mode 85, 92, 98
    continuum 83, 85, 92–3
Monitor Model: Krashen 6
motivation 24, 50, 52, 77, 245,
    282, 287
multilingualism 263, 284, 287

N
narrative 62–9, 72–4, 150, 157,
    160, 162
    competence 61, 63, 65,
        68–70, 72
    perspective 64, 68, 70–2, 77
neo-Gricean heuristics 42–3
Netherlands 5, 9, 234, 248
nominalisation 32, 87, 94, 96,
    139, 145, 148–9, 151, 155–6,
    160, 163, 166
Norway 235, 237, 240,
    245–6, 248
note taking 182, 232, 234, 238,
    241, 246, 249

O
optimality theory 41
oral
    competence 203, 206
    production 171, 196,
        201–3, 280
    skills 45, 203

P
paragraphing 174–5, 178, 182
plot (elements) 68–9, 72–3, 155
pragmatic
    competence 4, 44, 174
    inhibitor 55
    principles 39, 41–4, 51
pragmatics 12, 39–44, 49–54,
    107
productive skills 46, 170, 193,
    202–3
pronunciation 202, 238, 241,
    246, 248, 280, 284

Q
questionnaires 45, 52, 236–9

R
rapport 174, 176–7, 220, 227
receptive skills 170, 193,
    202–3
recount
    historical 86, 96, 139–40
    narrative 89
    personal/biographical
        86, 91, 95–6
    procedural 83–4
register 85–6, 92–3, 97–8, 115,
    117, 125–7, 134–5, 139–41,
    174, 176–7
relevance theory 43
rheme 149, 159–160
role-play 48–52

S
scaffolding 82, 84, 88, 92, 100,
    129
scientific writing/discourse 145,
    147, 149, 163
second language
    acquisition 39, 42,
        44, 54–5
    SLA research 7, 11, 31, 40, 42
self-assessment 232, 237–9, 247
sociocultural theory 8, 107,
    286, 288
Spain 5, 9, 13, 82, 87, 125, 129,
    183, 194, 214, 281, 286
speaking/oral
    production 171, 196, 201–2,
        279–80
    spoken production
        39, 45–54
    skills 10, 45, 203

student
    questions 234, 242,
        246-7, 249
    workload 242-3, 245-6
style
    informal/ colloquial vs.
        formal/careful 115-17
    monologic vs. dialogic 110,
        112, 114-5
    oral 139
subject-specific
    competence/skills 10, 126,
        148, 170, 172, 182-3
    lexis/terminology 87,
        191, 259, 268-70,
        272-4
    literacy 82, 100
subordination/subordinate
    clause 33, 128, 151,
        153-4, 161
Sweden 171
syllabus
    construction 34
    formal structural 25,
        32, 34
    notional 30
syntactic
    complexity 152-4, 157,
        164, 180
    intricacy 153-4

Systemic Functional
    Linguistics (SFL) 10,
        12-14, 25, 81, 83-4, 127,
        130, 145-7, 163-6, 213-16

T
task fulfilment 174-6, 182
teacher
    education 100, 213-14,
        229-230, 283
    language competence/
        knowledge 146, 165, 285
    teacher talk 106, 109-10,
        114, 118-119
    teachers' language use
        105-9, 119-21
tenor 85, 90
tense
    anchor tense 72-3
    forms 61, 68, 72, 74
tertiary level 213-15, 259,
        260-1, 274, 283-4
text/textual
    competence 171, 174,
        177-8, 182
    construction and
        deconstruction 84, 98
    organisation 169
    types 81, 84-8, 93, 98-100,
        150, 174

thematic
    development 151
    organization 145, 149-51,
        158, 162-4
    progression 150, 160
theme 149-52, 158-66
transfer 26, 31-4, 74, 172, 180,
        192, 224, 229
truncated repertoire 120
T-unit 15-4, 157, 164

U
undergraduate level 234-7,
        248

V
verb forms 72, 74, 175, 179-80
visual aids 243, 248-9
vocabulary
    range 169, 171-2, 175, 180-2
    size 171
    unfamiliar words 230,
        235-6, 241-2, 246
writing/written
    competence, skills,
        proficiency 172-3,
        181-3, 193, 198-9, 201, 203,
        205-6, 234
    prompts/tasks 25, 129, 154,
        169, 173, 175, 203

In the *AILA Applied Linguistics Series* the following titles have been published thus far or are scheduled for publication:

8   **DE HOUWER, Annick and Antje WILTON (eds.):** English in Europe Today. Sociocultural and educational perspectives. ix, 166 pp. + index. *Expected February 2011*

7   **DALTON-PUFFER, Christiane, Tarja NIKULA and Ute SMIT (eds.):** Language Use and Language Learning in CLIL Classrooms. 2010. x, 295 pp.

6   **ARONIN, Larissa and Britta HUFEISEN (eds.):** The Exploration of Multilingualism. Development of research on L3, multilingualism and multiple language acquisition. 2009. vii, 167 pp.

5   **GIBBONS, John and M. Teresa TURELL (eds.):** Dimensions of Forensic Linguistics. 2008. vi, 316 pp.

4   **FORTANET-GÓMEZ, Inmaculada and Christine A. RÄISÄNEN (eds.):** ESP in European Higher Education. Integrating language and content. 2008. vi, 285 pp.

3   **MAGNAN, Sally Sieloff (ed.):** Mediating Discourse Online. 2008. vii, 364 pp.

2   **PRINSLOO, Mastin and Mike BAYNHAM (eds.):** Literacies, Global and Local. 2008. vii, 218 pp.

1   **LAMB, Terry and Hayo REINDERS (eds.):** Learner and Teacher Autonomy. Concepts, realities, and response. 2008. vii, 286 pp.